NATIONAL DIRECTORY OF
Editors & Writers

NATIONAL DIRECTORY OF
Editors & *Writers*

FREELANCE EDITORS, COPYEDITORS, GHOSTWRITERS AND TECHNICAL WRITERS

AND

Proofreaders for individuals, Businesses, Nonprofits, and Government Agencies

Elizabeth Lyon

M. EVANS AND COMPANY, INC.
New York

for my extraordinary daughter
Elaine Lyon

M. Evans and Company, Inc.
216 East 49th Street
New York, NY 10017

Library of Congress Cataloging-in-Publication Data

Lyon, Elizabeth
  National directory of editors & writers for hire : freelance business, proofreading,
copy, technical, literary editors and writers plus book doctors, ghostwriters,
consultants & writing coaches / Elizabeth Lyon.
          p. cm.
      Summary: "This is a Directory with the names and contact information for
      freelance editors and writers from across the country"—Provided by publisher.
      Includes index.
      ISBN 1-59077-069-2 (pbk.)
      1. Editors—United States--Directories. 2. Authors, American—21st century—
      Directories. I. Title: National directory of editors and writers for hire. II. Title.
PN149.8.L96 2005
808'.02'02573—dc22

                                                                        2004022098

Book design and composition by John Reinhardt Book Design

Printed in the United States of America

0 9 8 7 6 5 4 3 2 1

Contents

Acknowledgments

A PROJECT OF THIS COMPLEXITY and picayune detail might have been a snap for a reference publisher with the latest database software, at-the-ready consultants, and a small army of data entry workers, proofreaders, file clerks, and gofers. For a solo writer, editor, and compiler, I did not realize how daunting a task this would be. I sent out an SOS, and friends responded.

I am especially indebted to Stew Meyers, not only for his years of friendship but also for IMPACT, the Access-based database he created for nonprofits but willingly adapted with hundreds of lines of code to accommodate this directory. Few people, friends or not, would walk the extra mile, and he walked on water.

Meta Maxwell was there at the beginning, the first answer to my cry for help. Suse Altengarten's sense of timing was impeccable; her good cheer as sustaining as a hearty stew on a cold night. For stepping in later in the project, she mastered the details and needs almost instantly.

From before the beginning to after the end, my Rock of Gibraltar was Skye Blaine. Her keen sense of discrimination, detail, and formatting, based on talent as well as years of work with Berkana Publishing, her desktop publishing business, kept me on track. She sacrificed on multiple levels, and I am grateful.

Many others supplied the right help at the right time: Marvin Finger, the best masseur in the country; Steve Clark, my computer gearhead and pleasant distracter; Jerrald "Jerry" James, my strength during adversity; and my many loyal friends and family near and far, who stand by me no matter what—and at times, this was a no matter what.

Special thanks to my amazing daughter, Elaine Lyon, who worked tirelessly over the weeks and months and supplied creative solutions to vexing problems at the eleventh hour.

To each and every contributor to this book and to others who spread the word of this first edition, you made this possible, and I appreciate your patience with the process. Likewise, the patience and diligent attention to detail by Mary Dorian, this book's copyeditor, won my admiration.

Last of all, I must acknowledge two people, both of whom had faith in me: PJ Dempsey, my understanding and compassionate editor, and Meredith Bernstein, my literary agent extraordinaire and my friend.

About This Directory

WELCOME TO THE FIRST EDITION of the *National Directory of Editors & Writers*. The 530 contributors are wordsmiths and literary artists. They work with and for individuals, groups, teams, and companies. Representing nearly every state, they are the invisible "pens" and proofreaders behind much of corporate, institutional, and business writing, and they are the developmental editors and ghostwriters behind a substantial number of books.

In this age of specialization, outsourcing, and competition, you or your company will find a match for your specific job or need with an appropriately qualified freelancer in this directory. Nearly every company, from the one-person entrepreneur to the multinational corporation, will benefit from using the sophisticated skills of business or tech writers, editors, public relations experts, and ad copywriters. Publishers, too, from large New York houses to small presses and web-based publishers, often—or sometimes exclusively—utilize freelancers for copyediting and proofreading. Increasingly, nonprofit organizations are also discovering the value of professional presentation by hiring seasoned writers and editors.

Individual writers aspiring to publication will find in this book a first resource for comparison of the skills, specialties, and fees of editors. Rarely, for instance, will a literary agent or in-house editor work with a writer on a promising but unpolished book. You may shorten your journey from novice writer to professional author by gaining the help of an independent editor or book doctor.

If you are a speaker or an expert in your field with no time or no experience in writing, a ghostwriter may enhance your reputation and, in turn, allow you to fill your pocketbook. Or perhaps a writing coach or literary consultant will help you develop your own writing potential and keep you on track toward your goals.

The indexes in this directory will be invaluable if you are looking for an individual with a specific set of skills, whether you seek someone to write jingles, translate a document, or develop content for a website. Although the Internet can sometimes facilitate your search for a writer or editor no matter where you live, it is my hope that the geographic index and address listings in this volume will help you to identify and easily find the right freelancer in your area.

Criteria for Inclusion in This Directory

First, this is a *national* directory of editors, writers, and consultants— freelancers who are citizens of the United States even if they live abroad part or all of the year.

Many if not most of the contributors in this directory have published their own writing, worked at prior jobs related to the written word, earned degrees in various language arts, and received awards or acclaim for their writing. Although laudable accomplishments, the contributors to this book share one condition for inclusion above all others: they work as freelancers *for you.*

Several groups of professionals are excluded from this directory. Many freelance journalists, essayists, and feature writers work for themselves but do not regularly help others with their own writing. The same is true for authors. Many authors write and sell their own books but may not ghostwrite or edit other writers' manuscripts. The contributors to this directory may also write and sell their own works to book publishers or serial publications. The difference is that they solicit, work offering writing, editing, or consulting services.

Also excluded from this directory are professionals who earn money as literary agents or publishers—even if they additionally offer editing or writing services. A number of literary agent and publisher directories already serve their need to find clients and vice versa.

Additionally, those individuals who are only consultants and coaches and do not work for others as editors or writers (except minimally) are excluded due to space constraints. The screenwriting industry has hundreds, if not thousands, of writers and editors serving it. Many contributors to this directory offer to write or edit scripts or screen-plays, but they were accepted for inclusion only if they additionally work on other types of client writing or editing (such as novels, short stories, articles, or business writing).

The information in the profiles was supplied by the contributors and accepted as accurate. Evaluation of their skills and representation of information is left to the discernment of the reader. The author of this book did not evaluate the skills, business practices, or integrity of any contributor. Should you find any misrepresentation, please notify the author. As in any profession, skills run the gamut and are not equal from one freelancer to another. However, most contributors maintain high ethical and financial standards and do the best job they can on behalf of their clients. In the end, it is up to you to ask questions prior to hiring anyone.

Choosing a Freelancer for Your Needs

In a directory of this size, you are bound to find many freelancers who can do a superior job, but how do you decide? If only it were simple! The number of years in business often corresponds with high skill, but those with fewer years may do as well or even better. Or they may not. Bestsellerdom and awards seem to guarantee writing expertise, but can an acclaimed writer produce that same success on your project? Maybe—or maybe not.

Education and other life or work experience usually supply valuable information about qualifications. Yet some of the contributors in this book have little formal education but decades of experience based on learning by doing, and what can substitute for breadth and depth of experience?

In the end, if you consider all of the background information in the profiles, you can make an educated guess, probably right, but one that bears checking out. Many if not most of the contributors have a website where you can gain subjective impressions as well as objective facts.

What about checking references? Some people find it difficult to ask anyone in business for references. Yet this is a reasonable request. If the person you're considering hiring tells you that all clients are kept confidential, that is understandable but not sufficient. Request that the freelancer gain permission from two or three clients so that you may interview them about the service they received.

Naturally, there are different ways to learn about someone you may hire. You may not need to interview former clients. A list of former customers—individuals or companies—or their published works may be sufficient. In other cases, for your personal satisfaction, you may need to get acquainted with the editor, writer, coach, or consultant and possibly meet in person.

What about fees? For many people, higher fees usually go hand in hand with experience, expertise, and a developed reputation, right? Yet most of us who provide literary services know colleagues who charge more than we do and deliver less. Lower fees may indicate people with less skill, but they may be highly skilled professionals who don't believe in charging a lot or who live in regions of the country where fees are lower than in the big cities.

After you select someone, make sure you understand all services, fees, and terms, and articulate any changes you need. Whether your agreements are oral or written, your full satisfaction will be greatest with a full understanding of all details.

Understanding the Editor and Writer Profiles

EVERY PROFILE MAY INCLUDE up to fourteen categories of information, explained as follows:

IDENTIFICATION NUMBER: Contributors are listed in alphabetical order, and each one has an identification number. These numbers, *not page numbers*, are used in the indexes.

HEADING ABBREVIATIONS AND DESCRIPTIONS: For quick reference, the heading tells you what basic service is being offered. F refers to fiction and *NF* refers to nonfiction.

CONTACT INFORMATION: name, company name, address, phone/fax/cell number(s), e-mail address(es), website address(es).

While most of this contact information is self-explanatory, P1/ refers to phone #1, P2/ refers to phone #2, and so forth. In the same manner, F1/ refers to fax #1 and C1 refers to cell phone #1. Because e-mail and website addresses have become nearly universal—and recognizable—they are listed without a heading. E-mail addresses always have the @ symbol in the middle of them. Website addresses generally have www or http preceding them and end with the letters *com* or *net* or another three-letter designation.

Established: The year the freelancer began his or her business or company. However, this date may be deceptive if recent, and it may be followed by an explanation of experience and skill developed prior to establishing the current business.

SKILLS: This category lists the roles and activities the freelancer offers in the broad categories of writing, editing, consulting, and "other," and does not usually list preferred subjects or types of writing, which are detailed in other categories.

Some of the listed skills may seem redundant, or you may not fully understand the difference between one term and another. The labels that describe the editors and writers were selected by the contributors themselves to describe their skills. See page xviii for the definitions of the different types of editors and writers.

MARKETS SERVED: This category lists or profiles the most common or desired customers served by the contributor. You may read broad and general descriptions such as "individuals, businesses, publishers, nonprofits" or highly specific descriptions such as "Fortune 500 companies" or "literary and mainstream novelists."

SPECIALTIES AND PREFERENCES: Each freelancer conveys his or her personality, approach to work, and favorite or successful specialties. Even though the entire profile is half a page, this section more than any other allows contributors to make their pitch to you, a potential customer.

FICTION—ACCEPTS: NONFICTION—ACCEPTS: From a stock list of common types of fiction and nonfiction, including young adult ("y/a") and juvenile, contributors were asked to choose what kinds of work they accept or consider. Some subtypes or specialties are more often found in the prior section, "Specialties and preferences." For instance, Regency romances are a specialty genre. White papers are a specialty form of informational or technical writing. Further, you'll find most types of fiction or nonfiction, including specialties, indexed separately.

TYPICAL EVALUATION/REPORT: Ghostwriting memoirs and proof-reading newsletters don't require evaluations or reports. If you plan to hire a freelance editor for your short story or article, for instance, corrections and comments on the manuscript may be fully sufficient. But a comprehensive evaluation may help a novelist, nonfiction book writer, or proposal writer with revisions. Make sure to ask if the evaluation or report is custom written, which may be more valuable than a stock explanation or template.

FEES/TERMS/CONTRACTS: The many ways of charging for editing, writing, and consulting services include the following: by the hour, page, and job, or negotiated. The range in fees among contributors, no matter how they are figured, is amazingly large. A few individuals did not list their fees, preferring that you contact them. Because freelancers change their fees periodically, you should always ask for current rates.

"Terms" refers to how business is initiated and paid for and includes prequalifying readings and estimates, retainers, invoicing and collections, and acceptance of credit cards or online payment services like PayPal. "Contracts" refers to the use of a contract or agreement provided by the freelancer, or the absence of one. You should know that the wording in a contract is negotiable, as may be the fees and terms, and you should suggest changes that will make you comfortable. Perhaps you need a six-month payment plan, for instance. And, if the freelancer does not use a contract and you prefer one, supply one.

ACCOMPLISHMENTS: Contributors listed whatever information they wanted you to know about them, within the small number of available lines. Typically, you'll find publishing successes and awards of the contributors or of their clients. Because of limited space, titles of published books or magazine articles were omitted, *unless* they garnered an award, honor, or other distinction. Go to contributor websites, when available, to gain full background information, or ask for more details by e-mail.

EDUCATION: In addition to formal education, contributors also indicated coursework or experience related to editing and writing, and in some cases, they included names of notable teachers. In lieu of formal education, some contributors listed relevant educational or life experiences.

MEMBERSHIPS: Although acronyms may, in some cases, be more recognizable than an organization's name, the latter was used for complete clarity to readers.

CLIENTS WITHIN PRIOR YEAR: The last category in the profiles shows the number of clients in a most recent or typical year. In many cases, this figure offers an accurate picture of the scale or development of a business. In others, the number range may be deceptive. Some freelancers work on a few giant projects annually or may be highly selective, so this statistic is but one fact to consider among many others.

The Indexes

The indexes for this directory are different from those of most books, because they list the *identification numbers* of the contributors rather than the page numbers where they appear.

Changes in Contact Information

In our fast-changing technological and mobile society, contact information may change in the blink of an eye. If you have tried unsuccessfully to contact one of the contributors through e-mail addresses, phone(s) and/or fax numbers, and websites, then mail an old-fashioned letter; or last of all, contact the author of this book.

Future Editions of the Directory

Because the directory will be updated and published every two years, freelancers who would like to be considered as contributors to future directories should contact the author, Elizabeth Lyon, at elyon123@comcast.net, or through www.editorsandwritersforhire.com.

DISCLAIMER: All errors are strictly the fault of the database and in no way involve any human intention.

Types of Editors and Writers

Every contributor in this directory is a freelancer rather than an employee working for someone else. Below is a description of the type of services these freelancers offer:

EDITORS: freelance editor: edits writings of any length.

INDEPENDENT BOOK EDITOR: edits book-length material. Prefers the word independent to freelance as a way to describe working for oneself rather than for an employer.

BOOK DOCTOR: the colloquial term for a freelance or independent book editor. The use of "doctor" usually means that the editor seeks to fix all that "ails" a book. Book doctors offer substantive or developmental editing—editing that addresses the elements of craft and style.

COPYEDITOR: edits manuscripts for mistakes in grammar, punctuation, and spelling; polishes style; ensures parallelism of development (nonfiction); and checks facts. Some copyeditors also check format and design. Outside of publishing houses, copyeditors may *not* check facts, formats, and page design. Some freelancers use the terms copyediting and line editing interchangeably, as if they are identical services.

LINE EDITOR: edits manuscripts for mistakes in grammar, punctuation, and spelling but does not typically address problems of development, organization, or style.

PROOFREADER: edits for final mistakes, checking against the typeset, copyedited revision. Corrects mistaken letters, words, format anomalies, symbols, or any misplaced "scratch."

NOTE: Most people outside the writing and publishing industry don't make such fine distinctions between copyeditors, line editors, and proofreaders. Tell the freelancer what you think you need and ask if he or she can provide it.

Writers

FREELANCE WRITER: writes for oneself, or is hired to write for others.

GHOSTWRITER: writes manuscripts for which someone else claims authorship or credit, whether that work is a book, article, report, or other form. Occasionally, ghostwriters may be acknowledged, although most of the time another person or organization pays the ghostwriter and claims, through agreement and purchase, the copyright and authorship.

BUSINESS WRITER: writes marketing, public relations, or in-house communications for business or industry, either as a ghostwriter or for byline credit.

COPYWRITER: writes copy, as in content for advertisements, websites, or businesses. Usually a copywriter is a ghost and a business writer, although the term carries a narrower meaning.

TECHNICAL WRITER: writes material of a specialized, technical content, usually as a ghostwriter.

NATIONAL DIRECTORY OF
Editors & Writers

1	EDITOR	WRITER	CONSULTANT	F	NF

Abrahms, Judith. Editcetera. 2500 Durant, #304, Berkeley, CA 94704.
P1/ 510-644-3766. F1/ 510-548-4686. abrahms@pacbell.net. Established: 1984.

SKILLS: freelance editor, copyeditor or line editor, proofreader. MARKETS SERVED: computer software and hardware corporations; publishers of textbooks, nonfiction, technical books; individual writers of works on technology and scientific subjects.

SPECIALTIES AND PREFERENCES: edits computer software/hardware manuals, social sciences and business documents, technical, and engineering books. I take on only as much work as is consistent with doing a thorough job, because every client deserves my best work. Prefers working at home.

FICTION—ACCEPTS: short stories, novels (literary, contemporary), poetry. NONFICTION—ACCEPTS: y/a or juvenile, articles/features, creative or narrative, biography/autobiography, self-help, how-to/instruction, technical, text or reference, business, humor, inspirational/religious, spiritual. TYPICAL EVALUATION/REPORT: 750 words.

FEES/TERMS/CONTRACTS: $35–$50/hour for all services. No credit cards.

ACCOMPLISHMENTS: judged over twenty documents and edited eleven that won awards for the Society for Technical Communications' Touchstone competition. Led technical editing seminars. Edited more than 200 books for corporations, textbook houses, university, academics.

EDUCATION: BA English, Mathematics, with honors and distinction, Phi Beta Kappa, Cornell University, Ithaca, NY. MEMBERSHIPS: Media Alliance. Bay Area Editors' Forum.

CLIENTS WITHIN PRIOR YEAR: 5–10.

2	EDITOR	WRITER	CONSULTANT	F	NF

Acheson, Carolyn. 20714 76th Ave. W., Unit, Edmonds, WA 98026.
P1/ 425-771-8933. carolyn.acheson@verizon.net. Established: 1989.

SKILLS: freelance editor, independent book editor, copyeditor or line editor, indexing. MARKETS SERVED: prefers authors and small firms over large companies because of the personal interaction with the former. Contracts primarily with publishers.

SPECIALTIES AND PREFERENCES: I enjoy the variety of topics and pride myself on time sensitivity, and good communication, with the aim of producing the best possible book.

NONFICTION–ACCEPTS: memoirs, creative or narrative, biography/autobiography, self-help, how-to/instruction, technical, text or reference, inspirational/religious. TYPICAL EVALUATION/REPORT: several pages.

FEES/TERMS/CONTRACTS: Fee structure varies; usually hourly; some smaller projects–flat fee. Some textbook publishers–per-page rate. Small projects— invoiced upon completion, discounted if paid within a month; or a fixed fee–half retainer. Large projects–invoiced monthly, discounted if paid within a month. No credit cards. No contracts.

ACCOMPLISHMENTS: experience as a technical editor/writer for an engineering firm plus thirteen years with a book publishing firm prior to becoming a freelance editor/indexer. Two decades of experience with a wide variety of topics and authors.

EDUCATION: BS Technical Journalism, Iowa State University, Ames. **MEMBERSHIPS:** Northwest Independent Editors Guild. American Society of Indexers.

CLIENTS WITHIN PRIOR YEAR: 6–10.

3	EDITOR	WRITER	CONSULTANT	F	NF

Adams, Ariana. 900 Bascom St., Charlotte, NC 28205. P1/ 704-965-4447. P2/ 704-370-0404. F1/ 704-370-0401. aadams@carolina.rr.com. Established: 2002.

SKILLS: freelance editor, copyeditor or line editor, proofreader, ghostwriter, business writer or copywriter, technical writer, writing coach. **MARKETS SERVED:** small to medium businesses in services, consulting, and financial services industries.

SPECIALTIES AND PREFERENCES: I provide services in project management, proposal writing/management, resume writing, marketing brochures, advertising copy, newsletters, and various other marketing/communications collateral. I have an auditing background, so I specialize in writing/editing audit reports, audit committee materials, and other financial documents.

FICTION—ACCEPTS: all. **NONFICTION—ACCEPTS:** all.

FEES/TERMS/CONTRACTS: hourly; half up front, half upon completion. No credit cards.

ACCOMPLISHMENTS: published in *Chicken Soup for the Bride's Soul* (2004). Having worked in the Big 4 for nine years, I am well versed in the world of public accounting.

EDUCATION: BBA, accounting concentration, James Madison University, Harrisonburg, VA. **MEMBERSHIPS:** Association for Women in Communications.

CLIENTS WITHIN PRIOR YEAR: 1–5.

4	EDITOR	WRITER	CONSULTANT	F	NF

Adams, Michelle. 8916 Crest Ridge Dr., Fort Worth, TX 76179. P1/ 817-236-8740. F1/ 817-236-8740. iufan@michellemedlockadams.com. goiu@earthlink.net. www.michellemedlockadams.com. Established: 2000.

SKILLS: freelance editor, ghostwriter, business writer or copywriter, writing coach, children's author, newspaper journalist, health and fitness writer, devotional writer, nonfiction book writer, travel book editor, writing contest judge, writers' conference speaker, magazine journalist, advertising writer. **MARKETS SERVED:** independent clients, magazines, book publishers, writers' conferences, and worldwide ministries.

SPECIALTIES AND PREFERENCES: ministries, nonprofits, travel-book companies. Brochures, children's picture books, 'tween devotionals, women's nonfiction, and Christian living.

FICTION—ACCEPTS: picture books, poetry. **NONFICTION—ACCEPTS:** y/a or juvenile, articles/features, biography/autobiography, how-to/instruction, business, humor, inspirational/religious, spiritual, book proposals, queries.

FEES/TERMS/CONTRACTS: maintains price sheet. No credit cards. May use contracts.

ACCOMPLISHMENTS: sold more than 3,000 articles over the last ten years, mostly to Christian, women's, and health magazines. Numerous writing awards 1992–2003.

EDUCATION: BS Journalism, Indiana University, Bloomington. **MEMBERSHIPS:** Society of Children's Book Writers & Illustrators. Society of Professional Journalists.

CLIENTS WITHIN PRIOR YEAR: 11–20.

5	EDITOR	WRITER	CONSULTANT	F	NF

Adelman, Beth. 69 Poplar St. 2C, Brooklyn, NY 11201. P1/ 718-488-0749. cbhbklyn@earthlink.net. Established: 1994.

SKILLS: freelance editor, independent book editor, book doctor, copyeditor or line editor, proofreader, ghostwriter, business writer or copywriter, project editor. **MARKETS SERVED:** writers, publishers, book packagers, magazines, corporate clients.

SPECIALTIES AND PREFERENCES: provides writing, editing, and project management services. Current projects include editing books about ancient history, various faiths, cookbooks, and art. As a writer, I specialize in cats, dogs, companion animals, and music.

FICTION—ACCEPTS: short stories, novels (mainstream, literary, contemporary, historical). **NONFICTION—ACCEPTS:** articles/features, essays, creative or narrative, how-to/instruction, text or reference, business, humor, book proposals, queries. **TYPICAL EVALUATION/REPORT:** 2–10 pages.

FEES/TERMS/CONTRACTS: vary by project. Prefers a flat fee based on time required. Hourly rates negotiable. Check or cash 30 days after completion. No credit cards. Agreements.

ACCOMPLISHMENTS: editor of two award-winning magazines and an award-winning online magazine; about a dozen award-winning books. Author of one non-fiction book and dozens of magazine articles.

EDUCATION: MS Journalism, Northwestern University, Chicago, IL. MEMBERSHIPS: Cat Writers Association. American Book Producers Association. CLIENTS WITHIN PRIOR YEAR: 6–10.

6	EDITOR	WRITER	CONSULTANT	F	NF

Adin, Richard. Freelance Editorial Services. 52 Oakwood Blvd., Poughkeepsie, NY 12603-4112. P1/ 845-471-3566. P2/ 845-483-0327. rhadin@text2cover.com. Established: 1984.

SKILLS: freelance editor, copyeditor or line editor, proofreader, illustration, desktop publishing. MARKETS SERVED: book publishers only. Our fields are medical, education, business, and computer.

SPECIALTIES AND PREFERENCES: We provide online copyediting to publishers and do not accept work outside our areas of expertise or from individuals. No writing services provided.

NONFICTION—ACCEPTS: self-help, how-to/instruction, technical, text or reference, business. TYPICAL EVALUATION/REPORT: line or copyediting, camera-ready proofreading, desktop publishing/formatting, track changes, editing and comment.

FEES/TERMS/CONTRACTS: per-page or project fee basis only. No credit cards. Invoices need to be paid within 15 days. No contracts.

ACCOMPLISHMENTS: began company as a one-person business; now includes six people. Average-size project is 3,000 manuscript pages. Able to handle multiple projects simultaneously. Former attorney; in-house editor; banker. Retired from law practice and began working for a book publisher.

EDUCATION: JD University of San Fernando Valley College of Law, Sepulveda, CA. BA Political Science, State University College of New York, Fredonia. MEMBERSHIPS: Editorial Freelancers Association. Mid-Hudson Freelancers Association.

CLIENTS WITHIN PRIOR YEAR: 6–10.

7	EDITOR	WRITER	CONSULTANT	F	NF

Albrecht, Donna. Concord, CA. P1/ 925-825-6861. F1/ on request. donna@albrechts.com. www.albrechts.com/donna. Established: 1985.

SKILLS: independent book editor, book doctor, ghostwriter, business writer or copywriter, writing coach, writing instructor, conference and workshop presenter. MARKETS SERVED: corporations, individuals, conference managers.

SPECIALTIES AND PREFERENCES: helps individuals and corporations meet personal and professional goals through writing for publication. Crafts successful articles for your industry publications. Prepares book proposals. Organizes materials to create a coherent presentation. Researches for specific information and resources to support your work.

NONFICTION—ACCEPTS: articles/features, creative or narrative, biography/auto-biography, self-help, how-to/instruction, business, inspirational/religious, spiritual, book proposals.
FEES/TERMS/CONTRACTS: Fees vary. No credit cards. Typically uses contract.
ACCOMPLISHMENTS: seven books published. Hundreds of articles in national magazines. Angel Award for Excellence in Media 2000. Organized/chaired multiple writing conferences including American Society of Journalists & Authors 2002 Conference that exceeded all previous records.
EDUCATION: MA (in progress) California State University, Dominguez Hills. **MEMBERSHIPS:** American Society of Journalists & Authors. The Authors Guild.
CLIENTS WITHIN PRIOR YEAR: information kept confidential.

8	EDITOR	WRITER	CONSULTANT	F	NF

Alic, Margaret. 122 Raccoon Point Rd., Eastsound, WA 98245. P1/ 360-376-6504. maranjam@rockisland.com. www.rockisland.com/~maranjam. Established: 1997.

SKILLS: freelance editor, independent book editor, book doctor, ghostwriter, literary consultant, writing coach, writing instructor, freelance scientific writer/editor, reference book writer. **MARKETS SERVED:** scientists around the world, including non-native English speakers.
SPECIALTIES AND PREFERENCES: science, social science, history books, and articles. Edits/rewrites research papers, other scientific writings for peer-reviewed publications. Specialties—molecular biology, biochemistry, genetics, biotechnology, etc., and the history of science. Also researches and writes entire books and entries for reference books.
NONFICTION—ACCEPTS: articles/features, essays, memoirs, biography/autobiography, technical, text or reference, business. **TYPICAL EVALUATION/REPORT:** 1–2 pages.
FEES/TERMS/CONTRACTS: editing $35/hour, due on completion, free estimates. Writing fees negotiable. Uses contract. Accepts checks, money orders, electronic fund transfers.
ACCOMPLISHMENTS: dozens of published reference books, especially Gale publications, such as biographies of blacks and Hispanics and encyclopedias on medical topics, plus scientific articles in publications such as Journal of Biotechnology, Journal of Insect Physiology.
EDUCATION: PhD Molecular Biology, Dept. of Biochemistry and Molecular Biology, Oregon Graduate Institute (now: Dept. of Environmental and Biomolecular Systems, OGI School of Science & Engineering, Oregon Health & Science University), Portland.
CLIENTS WITHIN PRIOR YEAR: 6–10.

9	EDITOR	WRITER	CONSULTANT	F	NF

Alperin, Michele. 56 Robert Rd., Princeton, NJ 08540. P1/ 609-924-6944. F1/ 609-924-6944. alperinma@aol.com. Established: 2000.

SKILLS: freelance editor, independent book editor, copyeditor or line editor, proofreader, ghostwriter, business writer or copywriter, technical writer. MARKETS SERVED: Jewish educational and communal organizations, business newspapers, businesses, online.

SPECIALTIES AND PREFERENCES: newsletters, business and personal profiles, program pamphlets, feature articles, educational pieces, web content. I am interested in writing that is lively, yet has depth and perspective.

NONFICTION—ACCEPTS: all.

FEES/TERMS/CONTRACTS: $40/hour.

ACCOMPLISHMENTS: published articles on business, technology, health care, language, and Judaism in *U.S. 1*, business weekly; in *Language*, a journal for language professionals; and in *Agenda*, a research organization for Jewish Education Service of North America (JESNA). Created newsletters or other marketing materials for Drisha, JESNA, the United Synagogue, and YIVO. Edited Bible curriculum for Melton Center.

EDUCATION: MBA, University of Maryland, College Park. MA Jewish Education, Jewish Theological Seminary, New York, NY. BA General Studies, Univeristy of Michigan. MEMBERSHIPS: Princeton Writers Alliance.

CLIENTS WITHIN PRIOR YEAR: 5–10.

10	EDITOR	WRITER	CONSULTANT	F	NF

Alpine, Lisa. Fairfax, CA. P1/ 415-454-1754. writing@lisaalpine.com. www.lisaalpine.com. Established: 1983.

SKILLS: freelance editor, independent book editor, book doctor, copyeditor or line editor, ghostwriter, business writer or copywriter, literary consultant, writing instructor, writing coach. MARKETS SERVED: authors and writers who want to get their stories published.

SPECIALTIES AND PREFERENCES: working one-on-one with authors on their book projects from editing to flow consultation, designing book proposals start to finish, guidance on finding a publisher or agent. Also writes website text, brochures, or press releases. Lisa has twenty years of experience as a professional writer and is adept in all these areas.

FICTION—ACCEPTS: y/a or juvenile, short stories, novels (genre, mainstream, romance, literary, contemporary, historical), synopses, queries. NONFICTION—ACCEPTS: y/a or juvenile, articles/features, essays, memoirs, creative or narrative, biography/autobiography, family history, how to, self-help, spiritual.

Fees/terms/contracts: $75/hour. No credit cards.

Accomplishments: articles and short stories in numerous national periodicals and anthologies. Book midwife and writing coach for many successful authors. Twelve years as a travel columnist. Free marketing consulting for several environmental groups.

Education: lived and worked in Europe and South America. Speaks three languages. Published a newspaper. **Memberships:** Wild Writing Women, LLC.

Clients within prior year: 20–25 book authors, about 550 writing students.

11	EDITOR	WRITER	CONSULTANT	F	NF

Amadio, Jill. PO Box 519, Dana Point, CA 92629. P1/ 949-240-8237. jill.amadio@Juno.com. www.ghostwritingpro.com. www.jillamadio.com. Established: 1985.

Skills: freelance editor, copyeditor or line editor, proofreader, ghostwriter, literary consultant, publicist, collaborator, journalist, screenwriter, adaptations, novelizations. **Markets served:** writers, publishers, corporations, periodicals, websites, auto industry, private clients.

Specialties and preferences: biographies, memoirs, true crime, corporate histories, proposals, queries, treatments, motor sports, self-help, lifestyles, travel, profiles.

Fiction—accepts: novels, queries, synopses. **Nonfiction—accepts:** features, memoirs, biography/autobiography, family history, selfhelp, business, proposals, queries. **Typical evaluation/report:** 3–8 pages.

Fees/terms/contracts: copyediting $40/hour. Evaluating book-length manuscripts $2,500. Rewriting manuscripts $75/hour. Proposals $5,000. Queries $350. Writing books $25,000 and up. Negotiable retainers and fees. Uses contracts.

Accomplishments: ghostwriter/collaborator of five books; author of a published biography. Dozens of book proposals. Hundreds of articles. International Automotive Media Award.

Education: courses at universities in the US/abroad–English literature, creative writing, journalism, art history, Thai culture. **Memberships:** Authors Guild. American Society of Journalists and Authors. Motor Press Guild. Mystery Writers of America.

Clients within prior year: 6–10.

12	EDITOR	WRITER	CONSULTANT	F	NF

Amador, Allison. Austin, TX. P1/ 512-565-9308. allisonamador@austin.rr.com. Established: 2003.

Skills: freelance editor, independent book editor, copyeditor, proofreader, business writer, copywriter, feature writer. **Markets served:** businesses, magazines.

Specialties and preferences: high tech, arts and entertainment, sports and fitness. Writes snappy copy, corporate news, magazine feature stories, web content, case studies. Also editor and proofreader.

Nonfiction—accepts: articles/features, narrative, technical, text or reference, business.

Fees/terms/contracts: invoices fixed hourly rate for all clients, accepts checks, uses contract.

Accomplishments: articles published in *Texas Music; Austin Fit;* and *Dialog.*

Education: Dual BAs Art History and Plan II Liberal Arts, University of Texas, Austin. **Memberships:** Freelance Austin.

Clients within prior year: 1–5.

13	EDITOR	WRITER	CONSULTANT	F	NF

Amour, Melissa. Melissa Morley Amour Editorial Services. Levittown, PA. P1/ 267-218-0312. F1/ 267-218-0312. melissa.amour@verizon.net. www.mma-editorial-services.com. Established: 1995.

Skills: freelance editor, independent book editor, book doctor, copyeditor or line editor, proofreader, business writer or copywriter, research, content development, production management, website management. **Markets served:** businesses, individuals, fiction/nonfiction writers.

Specialties and preferences: freelance, home-based writer and editor with more than ten years of experience. Specializes in educational materials development and new media. No project too small or too big. Provides quality editorial services to large corporations, small firms, and individuals with the same level of professionalism and attention to detail.

Fiction—accepts: y/a or juvenile. **Nonfiction—accepts:** articles/features. **Typical evaluation/report:** 2–5 pages.

Fees/terms/contracts: $40/hour or $10/page. Willing to negotiate. Uses contract only if client provides it. Invoices due by check within 30 days. No credit cards.

Accomplishments: My work is on behalf of my clients, and many publications have received honors by educational organizations and press associations. I myself received the Employee Award of Excellence in 1997 from Media Management Services.

Education: BA English, Trenton State College (now The College of New Jersey). **Clients within prior year:** 1–5.

14	EDITOR	WRITER	CONSULTANT	F	NF

Anderson, Gary. Elgin, IA. P1/ 563-426-5222. abciowa@alpinecom.net. www.abciowa.com. Established: 1996.

SKILLS: freelance editor, independent book editor, book doctor, copyeditor, line editor, ghostwriter, business writer, copywriter, technical writer, writing instructor, manuscript analyst. MARKETS SERVED: publishers—all sizes and types; individuals, companies, magazines, newspapers, businesses, nonprofit organizations, newsletter publishers, website owners.

SPECIALTIES AND PREFERENCES: I specialize in taking a writer's words and making them shine, while preserving the author's voice. I have edited seven newsletters, edited and ghosted fiction and nonfiction, and my award-winning writing is wide-ranging.

FICTION—ACCEPTS: y/a or juvenile, novels (genre, mainstream, literary, contemporary, historical). NONFICTION—ACCEPTS: all. TYPICAL EVALUATION/REPORT: 5+ pages.

FEES/TERMS/CONTRACTS: $3/page or $40/hour line editing; ghosting $2,500 and up; manuscript analysis $150; other fees on project-by project basis. Uses contract.

ACCOMPLISHMENTS: edited 2004 Best Business Book IPPY winner. Won Best Personality Feature of 1999 award, Iowa Newspaper Association. Published more than 500 articles, author of four books, ghosted six more, supplied more than 800 manuscript analyses, taught online writing classes, produced three national newsletters, four others.

EDUCATION: BS Communications, Oregon State University. AA English, Clackamas Community College, OR. Certified Technical Writer.

CLIENTS WITHIN PRIOR YEAR: variable, typically 3–5 clients; one large corporate client.

15	EDITOR	WRITER	CONSULTANT	F	NF

Aratyr, Risa. 899 Escondido Court, Sonoma, CA 95476. P1/ 707-935-5917. F1/ 707-935-5917. aratyr@hotmail.com. aratyr2@yahoo.com. Established: 1981.

SKILLS: freelance editor, independent book editor, book doctor, copyeditor or line editor, proofreader, ghostwriter, business writer or copywriter, technical writer, literary consultant, writing coach, writing instructor. MARKETS SERVED: academics, graduate students, and doctoral candidates. Fiction writers and journalists. Lawyers.

SPECIALTIES AND PREFERENCES: I work with academic professionals for whom English is a second language. I'm particularly strong with academic articles, papers, dissertations, theses. I've done extensive work with mainstream and genre fiction writers, and journalists. I work as a consultant for trial lawyers. **FICTION—ACCEPTS:** all. **NONFICTION—ACCEPTS:** all.

FEES/TERMS/CONTRACTS: proofing $25/hour. Editing/research $35/hour. Writing, ghostwriting, consulting $50/hour. Will negotiate set fee for long-term work.

ACCOMPLISHMENTS: published novelist. Written for the *San Francisco Chronicle*, the *Sonoma Index Tribune*. My byline will appear on an upcoming *New York Times* supplement. I have edited manuscripts that were published by St. Martin's Press, Baen, and other houses.

EDUCATION: BA Dramatic Arts, cum laude, University of California, Berkeley. Postgraduate work in Deaf Studies and Sign Language Interpretation, University of California, Northridge. **MEMBERSHIPS:** Science Fiction and Fantasy Writers of America.

CLIENTS WITHIN PRIOR YEAR: 1–5.

16	EDITOR	WRITER	CONSULTANT	F	NF

Ardinger, Barbara. 1037 E. 4th St., #2, Long Beach, CA 90802. P1/ 562-628-9688. bawriting@earthlink.net. www.barbaraardinger.com. Established: 1989.

SKILLS: freelance editor, copyeditor or line editor. **MARKETS SERVED:** traditional and on-demand publishers, authors.

SPECIALTIES AND PREFERENCES: I help authors not embarrass themselves in print. I can't "just edit." I also call the writer's attention to changed or missing details, to leaps of logic, to overblown figurative language, to things that just don't make sense. This is in addition to repairing punctuation, grammar, and syntax.

FICTION—ACCEPTS: y/a or juvenile, novels (genre, mainstream, literary, contemporary, historical), poetry. **NONFICTION—ACCEPTS:** y/a or juvenile, essays, memoirs, creative or narrative, biography/autobiography, family history, self-help, how-to/instruction, technical, humor, inspirational/religious, spiritual.

FEES/TERMS/CONTRACTS: $20/hour with a $100 nonrefundable deposit. Accepts PayPal or personal checks. No credit cards.

ACCOMPLISHMENTS: six published books, dozens of articles and book reviews in national magazines. Reviews and poetry in magazines and on websites.

EDUCATION: PhD English Renaissance Literature, Southern Illinois University at Carbondale, IL. MA English, and BS Secondary Education, Southeast Missouri State University, Cape Girardeau. French. Coursework and reading in spirituality and history.

CLIENTS WITHIN PRIOR YEAR: 20–25.

17	EDITOR	WRITER	CONSULTANT	F	NF

AuCoin, William. AuCoin and Associates, Inc. 5253 Dover St. NE, St Petersburg, FL 33703. P1/ 727-522-2371. F1/ 727-521-2035. wmaucoin@tampabay.rr.com. Established: 1985.

SKILLS: ghostwriter, business writer or copywriter, publicist. MARKETS SERVED: corporations, nonprofits, advertising and public relations agencies.

SPECIALTIES AND PREFERENCES: I specialize in communications for the Great Outdoors, helping brands and causes reach into the hearts and pocketbooks of fifty million anglers, boaters, hunters, hikers, birders, kayakers, and adventure travelers.

NONFICTION—ACCEPTS: y/a or juvenile, articles/features, essays, memoirs, creative or narrative, biography/autobiography, family history, self-help, how-to/instruction, technical, text or reference, business, humor, inspirational/religious, spiritual, book proposals, queries.

FEES/TERMS/CONTRACTS: negotiable. Uses contract.

ACCOMPLISHMENTS: dozens of articles published in national magazines. One published nonfiction book title. Catalogs, newsletters, annual reports, web content, ads, editorials.

EDUCATION: BA English, Spring Hill College, Mobile, AL. MBA courses, Keller Graduate School of Management, Chicago, IL. MEMBERSHIPS: Outdoor Writers Association of America. Boating Writers International. Florida Outdoor Writers Association.

CLIENTS WITHIN PRIOR YEAR: 6–10.

18	EDITOR	WRITER	CONSULTANT	F	NF

Avasthi, Smita. Portland, OR. P1/ 503-288-6959. P2/ 503-490-7960. smitaa@earthlink.net. savasthi@earthlink.net. Established: 2000.

SKILLS: freelance editor, independent book editor, book doctor, copyeditor or line editor, proofreader, business writer or copywriter, literary consultant, writing instructor, indexer, researcher. MARKETS SERVED: educational presses, web page designers, nonprofits, corporations, self-publishing companies, writers.

SPECIALTIES AND PREFERENCES: textbooks, reference materials, biography, novels, women's issues, history, literature, politics, and pop culture.

FICTION—ACCEPTS: y/a or juvenile, novels (genre, mainstream, literary, contemporary, historical), queries. NONFICTION—ACCEPTS: y/a or juvenile, articles/features, essays, narrative, biography/autobiography, how-to/instruction, text or reference, business, queries.

FEES/TERMS/CONTRACTS: $20–$50/hour. No credit cards. Typically uses contract.

ACCOMPLISHMENTS: two published reference volumes. Hundreds of online articles.

EDUCATION: PhD English Literature, University of Oregon, Eugene. MA English

Literature, University of Oregon, Eugene. BA English Literature, Lewis and Clark College, Portland, OR. **MEMBERSHIPS:** Northwest Independent Editors Guild. Willamette Writers. Modern Language Association. **CLIENTS WITHIN PRIOR YEAR:** 1–5.

19	EDITOR	WRITER	CONSULTANT	F	NF

Babcock, Karen. Practical Solutions for Business. P1/ 425-603-9285. karen@karenbabcock.com. karen@psfb.com. www.karenbabcock.com. www.psfb.com. Established: 1995.

SKILLS: book doctor, copyeditor or line editor, proofreader, business writer or copywriter, technical writer, grant writing, web page design, fact checking, marketing. **MARKETS SERVED:** publishers, nonprofits, businesses, individual writers.

SPECIALTIES AND PREFERENCES: fiction—science fiction, fantasy, suspense, mainstream. Nonfiction—all. Comfortable with various flavors of English.

FICTION—ACCEPTS: y/a or juvenile, short stories, novels. **NONFICTION—ACCEPTS:** all.

FEES/TERMS/CONTRACTS: $6/page book editing/substantive editing. $3/page proofreading. $40-$80/hour other writing, editing, depending on type of work, client. Discounts offered to nonprofits. One-half payment due at signing contract, balance at delivery. Accepts all forms of payment.

ACCOMPLISHMENTS: Left successful career as software product manager in 1999 to work as a freelance technical and marketing consultant; began working as a freelance fiction editor in 2002. Taught online grammar workshops, moderated a critique group, published essays in print and online, and served as senior editor for an e-book and print publisher.

EDUCATION: certificate in Software Product Management, University of Washington Extension, Seattle. Honors Program, Japanese Languages and Literature, University of Washington, Seattle.

CLIENTS WITHIN PRIOR YEAR: 6–10.

20	EDITOR	WRITER	CONSULTANT	F	NF

Bachel, Bev. Idea Girls. Minneapolis, MN. P1/ 612-379-7166. F1/ 612-379-0805. Bev.Bachel@ideagirls.com. www.ideagirls.com. Established: 1997.

SKILLS: business writer or copywriter. **MARKETS SERVED:** Fortune 500 companies.

SPECIALTIES AND PREFERENCES: We specialize in employee and marketing communications' material for Fortune 500 clients with whom we can develop long-term relationships. Our work includes benefits communication, employee newsletters, company brochures, websites, and video scripts.

NONFICTION—ACCEPTS: business.

Fees/terms/contracts: $125–$150/hour.

Accomplishments: author of three how-to books for children and young adults published with Free Spirit Press. Cochair of the National Writers Union Book Division.

Education: BA English, Drake University, Des Moines, IA. **Memberships:** National Writers Union.

Clients within prior year: 11–20.

21	EDITOR	WRITER	CONSULTANT	F	NF

Baer, Kathryn. 925 G St. SE, Washington, DC 20003. P1/ 202-547-4287. kbaer@tidalwave.net. kbaer@tidalwave.net. Established: 1996.

Skills: business writer or copywriter. **Markets served:** private-sector organizations.

Specialties and preferences: policy-related and management communications for business, not-for-profit, and government organizations. Special expertise in government relations and corporate social responsibility issues. Services tend to involve substantive editing and/or original writing, including grant proposals, strategic plans, reports, memoranda, talking points, issue papers, fact sheets, lobbying correspondence, development of website structures and content. Also advises on strategy, conducts research, and handles project management.

Nonfiction—accepts: business.

Fees/terms/contracts: Fees vary widely according to nature of service(s) and type of client. For short-term projects, requires payment upon delivery of product. For long-term projects, payment made in portions linked to key deliverables. Also provides services on retainer. No credit cards.

Accomplishments: member of English Department faculty at Washington University in St. Louis. Policy analyst for U.S. Commission on Civil Rights. Staff to U.S. Congress member Government Relations staff, McDonald's Corporation.

Education: PhD English, University of California, Berkeley. **Memberships:** International Association of Business Communicators. Washington Independent Writers.

Clients within prior year: 1–5.

22	EDITOR	WRITER	CONSULTANT	F	NF

Balan, Bruce. PO Box 64455, Los Angeles, CA 90064. P1/ 562-810-5297. F1/ 208-485-1658. author@brucebalan.com. www.brucebalan.com. Established: 1988.

Skills: freelance editor, ghostwriter, business writer or copywriter, technical writer. **Markets served:** children's book publishers, technical publishers.

Specialties and preferences: I provide work-for-hire writing services. My experience spans children's book, technical, and business writing. My strengths lie in writing for young people as well as making technology understandable for non-technical readers.

FICTION—ACCEPTS: y/a or juvenile, picture books, poetry, synopses or treatments. **NONFICTION—ACCEPTS:** y/a or juvenile, picture books, articles/features.

FEES/TERMS/CONTRACTS: Fees are negotiated per job. Uses a contract. Accepts cash or check.

ACCOMPLISHMENTS: I have a broad base of experience. I've authored fourteen published books for children with major New York houses (including the 1998 Parent's Choice Best Book). I've taught writing and provided paid professional manuscript critiques. I've published technical articles as well as chapters for technical books on computer software. I've also authored CD-ROM titles, monthly magazine columns, business brochures, and software and programming manuals.

EDUCATION: BA Radio and Television Production, summa cum laude, San Francisco State University. **MEMBERSHIPS:** The Authors Guild. Society of Children's Book Writers and Illustrators (member of Board of Advisors).

CLIENTS WITHIN PRIOR YEAR: 1–5.

23	EDITOR	WRITER	CONSULTANT	F	NF

Bales, Jefferson. Creative Novel Campaigns. Mocksville, NC.
P1/ 336-751-7125. P2/ 336-751-3688. tutorjb@nuvox.net.
groups.yahoo.com/group/bookdoctorsandeditors. Established: 1980.

SKILLS: freelance editor, independent book editor, book doctor, copyeditor or line editor, proofreader, copywriter, literary consultant, writing coach, writing instructor, publicist. **MARKETS SERVED:** authors, publishers, advertisers.

SPECIALTIES AND PREFERENCES: humor, including all forms of slipstream (from the slightly twisted to the completely bizarre).

FICTION—ACCEPTS: short stories, novels (genre, mainstream, literary, contemporary), poetry, scripts/screenplays, queries, synopses, treatments.

FEES/TERMS/CONTRACTS: fee negotiated based upon fees published online by *Writer's Digest*. Reduction considered for a percentage of advance or royalties. A retainer gets a complimentary line edit or synopsis critique.

ACCOMPLISHMENTS: assisted University of North Carolina, Chapel Hill professor in publishing the first approved edition of a classic novel. Coached and taught writing techniques to a crime novelist and renegotiated his contract with his publisher. Assisted a poet in becoming a prolific science fiction/fantasy novelist.

EDUCATION: BA English, University of North Carolina, Chapel Hill. Graduate advertising and journalism and architectural design studies at Chapel Hill

and Charlotte campuses.
CLIENTS WITHIN PRIOR YEAR: 1–5.

24	EDITOR	WRITER	CONSULTANT	F	NF

Barker, Sandra. Editcetera. 1073 Ave. C, Bayonne, NJ 07002. P1/ 201-436-0604. F1/ 201-436-0604. slbarkersf@verizon.net. Established: 1992.

SKILLS: freelance editor, independent book editor, book doctor, copyeditor or line editor, proofreader, business writer or copywriter, technical writer, literary consultant, writing coach, writing instructor, publicist, desktop publishing, translations. **MARKETS SERVED:** publishers, corporations, nonprofit organizations.

SPECIALTIES AND PREFERENCES: I specialize in copyediting, proofreading, and public relations. I have an expertise in many areas, from fashion to art to science. My writing experience includes writing press releases and newsletters.

FICTION—ACCEPTS: all. **NONFICTION—ACCEPTS:** all.

FEES/TERMS/CONTRACTS: $45/hour copyediting; $30/hour proofreading. No credit cards or PayPal. Uses contract or agreement.

ACCOMPLISHMENTS: production editor, Rockefeller University Press; senior editor, Office of University Publications, Columbia University; production editor, *Mademoiselle* magazine; copyeditor, *The Press Democrat* newspaper; freelance editor, consumer, computer magazines; promotions consultant, Healthcare Foundation Northern Sonoma County.

EDUCATION: BA Biology and BA Russian Studies, Brown University, Providence, RI. **MEMBERSHIPS:** Editcetera.

CLIENTS WITHIN PRIOR YEAR: 1–5.

25	EDITOR	WRITER	CONSULTANT	F	NF

Barnett, Robert. Portland, OR. accurate_editor@yahoo.com. Established: 2002.

SKILLS: freelance editor, independent book editor, book doctor, copyeditor or line editor, proofreader, ghostwriter, business writer or copywriter, literary consultant, writing coach, writing instructor. **MARKETS SERVED:** any and all.

SPECIALTIES AND PREFERENCES: all types of editing, nonfiction preferred, fiction considered. Writing tutor, free advice to a point. E-mail me and let's talk about your project.

FICTION—ACCEPTS: y/a or juvenile, short stories, novels, queries, synopses, treatments. **NONFICTION—ACCEPTS:** all. **TYPICAL EVALUATION/REPORT:** depends on project.

FEES/TERMS/CONTRACTS: depends on project. No credit cards. Uses contracts for larger projects.

ACCOMPLISHMENTS: editorial experience in books and magazines. Writing experience in magazines and newspapers. Experience tutoring writing and teaching ESL.

EDUCATION: MA Writing/Publishing, Portland State University, OR. BA History, BA Sociology, Humboldt State University, Arcata, CA.

CLIENTS WITHIN PRIOR YEAR: 1–5.

26	EDITOR	WRITER	CONSULTANT	F	NF

Baron, Maureen. 150 W. 87th St., #6C, New York, NY 10024. P1/ 212-787-6260. Established: 1991 after more than twenty years of in-house publishing experience.

SKILLS: freelance editor, independent book editor, book doctor, copyeditor or line editor, literary consultant. **MARKETS SERVED:** individual writers.

SPECIALTIES AND PREFERENCES: I provide a complete spectrum of professional advice to make manuscripts publishable. Emphasis on problem solving. Expert line editing, cutting, structuring, perspective analysis. The editor's job is to offer solutions to problems the author doesn't see and/or motivate the writer to create viable solutions aimed at producing a more publishable product.

FICTION—ACCEPTS: novels (genre, mainstream, literary, contemporary. **NON-FICTION—ACCEPTS:** memoirs, creative or narrative, biography/autobiography, family history, book proposals. **TYPICAL EVALUATION/REPORT:** 4–6 pages for overall manuscript; evaluation letter plus 5–8 pages of specific notes.

FEES/TERMS/CONTRACTS: Fee arrangements are discussed in phone interviews. Sometimes uses a contract.

ACCOMPLISHMENTS: editorial posts from 1970-1991 including senior editor, Warner Books; executive editor, Fawcett; editor-in-chief/vice president NAL-Signet (now Penguin). Book club consultant.

EDUCATION: BA Literature, Gonzaga University, Spokane, WA. **MEMBERSHIPS:** Women's Media Group. Independent Editors Group.

CLIENTS WITHIN PRIOR YEAR: 11–20.

27	EDITOR	WRITER	CONSULTANT	F	NF

Barrett, Elizabeth. Newmarket, NH. P1/ 603-659-2292. e.barrett@rcn.com. Established: 2003.

SKILLS: freelance editor, independent book editor, copyeditor or line editor, literary consultant. **MARKETS SERVED:** individual writers and authors.

SPECIALTIES AND PREFERENCES: women's fiction and self-help books.

FICTION—ACCEPTS: novels (genre, mainstream), queries, synopses. **NONFICTION—ACCEPTS:** self-help, book proposals. **TYPICAL EVALUATION/REPORT:** 1–2 pages for a proposal; 2–4 pages for a complete novel, usually with comments written directly on the manuscript.

FEES/TERMS/CONTRACTS: $30/hour for critique, $35/hour for line editing. Bills by the hour. E-mails bill to client. Returns work to client after payment. No credit cards.

ACCOMPLISHMENTS: editorial assistant with Berkeley/Jove in 1981, became an editor with Bantam Books in 1983. I left New York in 1987 and worked under contract as a consulting editor for Bantam until 1998. Author of six novels published with Bantam Books, Harlequin, Dell, Crown (two), and HarperCollins.

EDUCATION: BA English, Carleton College, Northfield, MN.

CLIENTS WITHIN PRIOR YEAR: 11–15.

28	EDITOR	WRITER	CONSULTANT	F	NF

Batcheller, Lori. PO Box 3623, Boulder, CO 80307. P1/ 303-494-6062. C1/ 303-818-7366. lbatcheller@earthlink.net. www.lbcreative.com. Established: 1998.

SKILLS: freelance editor, copyeditor, proofreader, ghostwriter, business writer or copywriter, writing coach, publicist, newsletter design/layout/publication, annual reports. **MARKETS SERVED:** publishers, corporations, nonprofit organizations, magazines, websites.

SPECIALTIES AND PREFERENCES: specialize in personal and company profiles, health, medicine, inspiration, spirituality, psychology, sports, and disability issues.

NONFICTION—ACCEPTS: articles/features, essays, memoirs, creative or narrative, biography/autobiography, self-help, how-to/instruction, text or reference, business, inspirational/religious, spiritual, book proposals, queries.

FEES/TERMS/CONTRACTS: writing $45–$75/hour, editing/proofreading $3–$4/page. Accepts credit cards, PayPal, certified check. Typically uses contract.

ACCOMPLISHMENTS: two self-published nonfiction books, dozens of articles published in national magazines, newspapers, and trade journals.

EDUCATION: MA Journalism and Mass Communication, University of Colorado, Boulder. MPT Physical Therapy, Hahnemann University, Philadelphia, PA. BA Biology, Colby College, Waterville, ME. **MEMBERSHIPS:** International Women's Writing Guild. Boulder Media Women. Rocky Mountain Publishing Professionals Guild.

CLIENTS WITHIN PRIOR YEAR: 5–10.

29	EDITOR	WRITER	CONSULTANT	F	NF

Bauer, Erin. Omaha, NE. P1/ 402-493-1695. hermione9342001@yahoo.com. Established: 2003.

SKILLS: freelance editor, proofreader, ghostwriter, reviewer. **MARKETS SERVED:** fiction and nonfiction writers, writing coaches.

SPECIALTIES AND PREFERENCES: I have experience proofing/editing both fiction and nonfiction, and also do fiction/playwriting. One area of particular interest is children's/juvenile fiction. As a librarian, I am familiar with a multitude of genres, but have discovered that young adult fiction is my favorite because of its appeal to both children and adults.

FICTION—ACCEPTS: y/a or juvenile, picture books, short stories, novels (genre, mainstream, literary, contemporary, historical), scripts/screenplays. **NONFICTION—ACCEPTS:** all.

FEES/TERMS/CONTRACTS: $12+/hour or $30–$50/article. Accepts checks and PayPal.

EDUCATION: MLIS Library and Information Science, Rosary College (now Dominican University), River Forest, IL. BEd Library Science (minor, Psychology), University of Nebraska, Omaha.

CLIENTS WITHIN PRIOR YEAR: 1–5.

30	EDITOR	WRITER	CONSULTANT	F	NF

Baylor, Wendy. PO Box 493, Wilson, WY 83014. P1/ 307-733-5841. wendybaylor@earthlink.net. Established: 1990.

SKILLS: freelance editor, copyeditor or line editor, technical writer, PowerPoint presentations for medical professionals. I do some writing, but mostly editing of content and construction of PowerPoint slides for lectures.

MARKETS SERVED: medical—human and veterinary.

SPECIALTIES AND PREFERENCES: I've been copyediting medical and veterinary books for four years, with the occasional foray into medical writing and PowerPoint presentation for the American Association of Geriatric Psychiatrists. Am interested in copyediting fiction and cookbooks.

FICTION—ACCEPTS: all. **NONFICTION—ACCEPTS:** how-to/instruction, technical.

FEES/TERMS/CONTRACTS: negotiated per project. I work only for companies that have accepted manuscripts or are creating a product. No spec.

ACCOMPLISHMENTS: I wrote and produced an instruction manual about the Bad Ragaz water rehabilitation method. I'm a partner in a small publishing company that produced guidebooks to the national parks, FreeWheeling Guides. Some of our titles were recently purchased by National Geographic Books.

EDUCATION: BSN Nursing, University of Wisconsin, Madison.

CLIENTS WITHIN PRIOR YEAR: 1–5.

31	EDITOR	WRITER	CONSULTANT	F	NF

Bechko, Peggy "P.A." Santa Fe, NM. P1/ 505-983-4159. pbechko@peoplepc.com www.PeggyBechko.50megs.com. Established: business and ghostwriter since 2001; published author since 1974.

SKILLS: ghostwriter, business writer or copywriter, writing instructor, freelance fiction writer in genres of western, romance, and fantasy. **MARKETS SERVED:** businesses, individuals searching for jobs—resumes. Writing instructor for romance writing through UCLA Extension online and instructor of children "on the ground."

NONFICTION—ACCEPTS: articles/features, business.

SPECIALTIES AND PREFERENCES: I write creatively for business, producing resumes, business proposals, and more.

ACCOMPLISHMENTS: I've written extensively in the genre fiction arena, having novels published by Doubleday, Harlequin, Pinnacle, and others. I've had short stories published, and I've optioned several screenplays, written an episode for an animated series, and written proposals for TV. **MEMBERSHIPS:** Author's Guild. Romance Writers of America.

CLIENTS WITHIN PRIOR YEAR: 1–5.

32	EDITOR	**WRITER**	CONSULTANT	F	**NF**

Belfiglio, Genevieve. 7 Tindall Trail, Princeton Jct., NJ 08550. P1/ 609-936-9097. getitwrite@genb.net. Established: 1995.

SKILLS: ghostwriter, business writer or copywriter, technical writer. **MARKETS SERVED:** pharmaceutical, managed care, communications agencies.

SPECIALTIES AND PREFERENCES: freelance medical writing, continuing medical education, clinical articles and reports, consumer health, pharmaceutical, managed care, health-care delivery. As a strong writer, I can capably use medical information to tell a clinical story as opposed to simply slapping together facts and data.

NONFICTION—ACCEPTS: articles/features, technical, text or reference, business.

FEES/TERMS/CONTRACTS: $70/hour, but prefer project-based contracts; contracts required for all projects.

ACCOMPLISHMENTS: more than 100 published articles in prominent clinical journals, as well as a variety of other projects, including slide shows, sales training modules, monographs, newsletters, etc. Recipient, The American Society for Aesthetic Plastic Surgery, Journalistic Achievement Award, 2001.

EDUCATION: MA English, San Francisco State University, CA. BA Creative Writing and the English Honors Program, Pennsylvania State University, State College. **MEMBERSHIPS:** American Medical Writers Association.

CLIENTS WITHIN PRIOR YEAR: 15–18.

33	**EDITOR**	**WRITER**	**CONSULTANT**	F	**NF**

Bellotti, Laura. Los Angeles, CA. P1/ 310-858-2949. lgbellotti@hotmail.com. www.publishersmarketplace.com. Established: 1986.

SKILLS: freelance editor, independent book editor, book doctor, line editor or copyeditor, ghostwriter, literary consultant, collaborator. **MARKETS SERVED:** writers, publishers.

SPECIALTIES AND PREFERENCES: adult nonfiction primarily in the areas of psychology, relationships, women's issues, spirituality, parenting, health, and creativity. I also assist clients in developing their book proposals.

NONFICTION—ACCEPTS: family history, self-help, inspirational/religious, spiritual, book proposals. **TYPICAL EVALUATION/REPORT:** 2–10 pages.

FEES/TERMS/CONTRACTS: hourly rate or flat fee to be discussed with client. No credit cards.

ACCOMPLISHMENTS: I was the developmental editor of *Women Who Love Too Much* and have over twenty years of experience as a developmental/conceptual editor. Five published nonfiction books. Nationally published magazine articles on parenting.

EDUCATION: BA English, University of California, Berkeley. Graduate studies in Film, California State University, San Francisco. **MEMBERSHIPS:** Los Angeles People in Publishing–Editors and Writers.

CLIENTS WITHIN PRIOR YEAR: 11–20.

34	EDITOR	WRITER	CONSULTANT	F	NF

Benesh, Patricia, AuthorAssist. 1109 Oliver Ave., #1, San Diego, CA 92109. P1/ 858-483-7900. pbenesh@authorassist.com. Established: 1999.

SKILLS: freelance editor, independent book editor, book doctor, copyeditor or line editor, proofreader, ghostwriter, business writer or copywriter, technical writer, literary consultant, writing coach, writing instructor. **MARKETS SERVED:** writers, publishers, corporations, professionals, consultants.

SPECIALTIES AND PREFERENCES: We help writers from around the world with manuscript reviews, nonfiction proposal development, query material development, agent search, and memoir writing. We specialize in substantive editing, ensuring consistency, logic, content, tone, and fact. All work is done via the Internet according to the client's needs and schedule.

FICTION—ACCEPTS: all. **NONFICTION—ACCEPTS:** all. **TYPICAL EVALUATION/REPORT:** 5–15 pages.

FEES/TERMS/CONTRACTS: Fees are determined on an individual basis after discussions with the client about the services required and status/length of material. Accepts personal checks and wire transfers, among other payment options.

ACCOMPLISHMENTS: dozens of articles; chapters in books.

EDUCATION: EdD Communications, MS Business Administration, Johns Hopkins University, Baltimore, MD.

CLIENTS WITHIN PRIOR YEAR: 40–60.

35	EDITOR	WRITER	CONSULTANT	F	NF

Bennett, Hal. Hal Zina Bennett & Associates. 9827 Irvine Ave., Upper Lake, CA 95485. P1/ 707-275-9011. F1/ 707-275-9011. halbooks@halzinabennett.com. www.halzinabennett.com. Established: 1971.

SKILLS: freelance editor, independent book editor, book doctor, ghostwriter, writing coach, writing instructor, author/collaborator, developmental editor, writing seminars, project evaluations. MARKETS SERVED: authors, publishers, and literary agents.

SPECIALTIES AND PREFERENCES: personal growth, spiritual development, business, health, popular human consciousness research.

NONFICTION—ACCEPTS: y/a, memoirs, creative or narrative, biography/auto biography, self-help, how-to/instruction, technical, text or reference, business, inspirational/religious, spiritual, book proposals, queries. TYPICAL EVALUATION/REPORT: 8–12 pages. Includes focus of manuscript, appropriateness of writing style, knowledge of market, overall concept, organization, level of excitement or passion for subject.

FEES/TERMS/CONTRACTS: by contract, agreement, or hourly. Accepts all credit cards and PayPal.

ACCOMPLISHMENTS: assisted in the development of over 200 published books, including several *New York Times* bestsellers. Has written over 30 successful books of his own.

EDUCATION: PhD Psychology and MS Holistic Health Sciences, Columbia Pacific University, San Rafael, CA. BA Language Arts/Creative Writing, San Francisco State University, CA. MEMBERSHIPS: Authors Guild.

CLIENTS WITHIN PRIOR YEAR: 20–25.

36	EDITOR	WRITER	CONSULTANT	F	NF

Bennett, Janey. 1225 E. Sunset Dr., Ste. 145, #644, Bellingham, WA 98226. P1/ 250-335-0535. janeybennett@yahoo.com. Established: 1994.

SKILLS: proofreader. MARKETS SERVED: publishers of textbooks and educational aids.

SPECIALTIES AND PREFERENCES: academic texts and educational aids. Architecture, anthropology, archaeology, art history, psychology, other sciences, literary criticism, translations.

NONFICTION—ACCEPTS: articles/features, essays, technical, text or reference, book proposals, queries. TYPICAL EVALUATION/REPORT: 2–10 pages.

FEES/TERMS/CONTRACTS: $25/hour. Retainer with balance due on receipt. No credit cards.

ACCOMPLISHMENTS: have written one philosophy of architecture book and one novel, both (so far) unpublished. Novel was finalist in 2003 Dana Literary Contest. Two long essays, dozens of articles, and half a dozen smaller academic essays on architecture published in US and Finland. Edited a tourist magazine and was music and theatre critic in California.

EDUCATION: MA Architecture History, Southern California Institute of Architecture, Los Angeles. BA Theatre Arts, University of California LA. Fulbright Fellow, Finland. Graham Fellow, Finland. Copyediting and Proofreading training, EditCetera, Berkeley, CA. **MEMBERSHIPS:** Northwest Independent Editors Guild. National Coalition of Independent Scholars. Pacific NW Writers Association. Whatcom Communications Association.

37	EDITOR	WRITER	CONSULTANT	F	NF

Bentley, Tom. The Write Word. Watsonville, CA. P1/ 831-768-7706. bentguy1@yahoo.com. www.tombentley.com. Established: 1996.

SKILLS: freelance editor, independent book editor, copyeditor or line editor, proofreader, business writer or copywriter, technical writer, essayist. **MARKETS SERVED:** corporations, graphic designers, new media companies, nonprofits, small business owners.

SPECIALTIES AND PREFERENCES: book editing, including how-to works and coffee-table photography books. Years of experience writing and editing marketing and technical material, including web content, user documentation, brochures, white papers, direct response, case studies, press releases, and other types of marketing collateral.

FICTION—ACCEPTS: y/a or juvenile, short stories, novels (genre, mainstream, literary, contemporary, historical). **NONFICTION—ACCEPTS:** all.

FEES/TERMS/CONTRACTS: $40–$75/hour, or bid. Accepts PayPal.

ACCOMPLISHMENTS: author of consumer-level computer book and many user documentation software manuals. Winner, National Steinbeck Center's Short Story Contest, 1999. Finalist, Spring 2000 *Glimmer Train* Short Story Award for New Writers. Third Place, Chiaroscuro Short Story Contest, 2000. Honorable Mention, *Writer's Digest* 2001 Personal Essay Contest. 25+ articles published in newspapers and magazines.

EDUCATION: MA Creative Writing, San Francisco State University, CA. BA English, Sonoma State University, Rohnert Park, CA. **MEMBERSHIPS:** National Writers Union.

CLIENTS WITHIN PRIOR YEAR: 6–10.

38	EDITOR	WRITER	CONSULTANT	F	NF

Berger, Aliza. editing-proofreading.com. Jerusalem, Israel. info@editing-proofreading.com. www.editing-proofreading.com. Established: 2003.

SKILLS: copyeditor or line editor, proofreader. **MARKETS SERVED:** academics—

professors and graduate students.

SPECIALTIES AND PREFERENCES: Attention academics and students! I copyedit dissertations, theses, and journal submissions in the following fields: social science, especially education and psychology statistics; research involving statistics; physical science; biology; mathematics; computer science and engineering; and Judaic studies. Is English your second language? I'll make you sound like a well-educated native speaker!

NONFICTION—ACCEPTS: technical.

FEES/TERMS/CONTRACTS: $30/hour. Uses contract.

ACCOMPLISHMENTS: I have been a technical writer at software companies, a researcher and editor at the Educational Testing Service and its Israeli equivalent, the National Institute for Testing and Evaluation.

EDUCATION: PhD Measurement, Evaluation, and Statistics, Columbia University, NY. MS Judaic Studies, Bernard Revel Graduate School of Yeshiva University, NY. BS Engineering Science, Cooper Union for the Advancement of Science and Art, NY.

CLIENTS WITHIN PRIOR YEAR: 1–5.

39	EDITOR	WRITER	CONSULTANT	F	NF

Berger, Deborah. Deborah Berger Writer & Editor. Seattle, WA. P1/ 206-282-1422, F1/ 206-283-0870. dxberger@aol.com. www.dearmomletters.com. Established: 1980.

SKILLS: freelance editor, independent book editor, ghostwriter, business writer or copywriter. **MARKETS SERVED:** nonfiction authors of all types; professionals who are writing books for mainstream audiences as well as for others in their fields.

SPECIALTIES AND PREFERENCES: comfortable working on a wide range of topics, but especially experienced and interested in health, lifestyle, family/parenting issues, self-help, business, coaching/personal development, and memoir/biography/autobiography.

NONFICTION—ACCEPTS: articles/features, essays, memoirs, creative or narrative, biography/autobiography, self-help, business.

FEES/TERMS/CONTRACTS: $60/hour; discount to struggling authors and nonprofits. Retainer required. Has standard letter of agreement. Bills by the hour, all hours credited against retainer. No credit cards.

ACCOMPLISHMENTS: author/coauthor of two books (one health, one women/memoir). Edited three books (one personal development, two business).

EDUCATION: MSW, Graduate School of Social Work, University of Denver, CO, BA University of Chicago, Nondegree study, Dept. of Communications, University of Washington. **MEMBERSHIPS:** Women in Digital Journalism.

CLIENTS WITHIN PRIOR YEAR: 1–5.

40	EDITOR	WRITER	CONSULTANT	F	NF

Bertini, Meg. All Writing Services. Tampa, FL. P1/ 813-833-9717. info@allwritingservices.com. www.allwritingservices.com. Established: 1995.

SKILLS: freelance editor, independent book editor, book doctor, copyeditor or line editor, proofreader, ghostwriter, business writer or copywriter, technical writer, literary consultant, writing coach, writing instructor, publicist, translation, speeches, press releases, seminar materials. MARKETS SERVED: all.

SPECIALTIES AND PREFERENCES: works with a full range of written work.

FICTION—ACCEPTS: all. NONFICTION—ACCEPTS: all. TYPICAL EVALUATION/REPORT: depends on client's needs.

FEES/TERMS/CONTRACTS: Fees vary per project. Accepts MasterCard and Visa.

ACCOMPLISHMENTS: Our editing team's accomplishments include published novels, produced screenplays, published articles, published children's/young adult books, and published nonfiction books. Our translator has lived and studied abroad extensively.

EDUCATION: JD Emory Law School, Atlanta, GA.

CLIENTS WITHIN PRIOR YEAR: 25–30.

41	EDITOR	WRITER	CONSULTANT	F	NF

Biegert, Melissa. Writewell Editing and Writing Service. 14601 Gold Fish Pond Ave. Austin, TX 78728. P1/ 512-989-0386, F1/ 512-989-0387 writewell@sbcglobal.net. Established: 2003.

SKILLS: freelance editor, independent book editor, book doctor, ghostwriter, writing coach. MARKETS SERVED: educational publishers, development houses.

SPECIALTIES AND PREFERENCES: writing and editing Student Education, Teacher Education, print ancillary, and multimedia for all levels of social studies, and for other disciplines including language arts and lower-level science.

FICTION—ACCEPTS: y/a or juvenile. NONFICTION—ACCEPTS: y/a or juvenile.

FEES/TERMS/CONTRACTS: fees depend on level and activity. Business checks. Balance due within 30 days of receipt of acceptable materials, unless other arrangements are made with the client. No credit cards. Typically use contracts.

ACCOMPLISHMENTS: I have overseen production of several social studies projects. Developed model chapter for one company's bestselling history textbook. Winner of two regional awards for historical writing. Five book reviews published in history journals. One historical dictionary entry published. One major historical journal article published.

EDUCATION: PhD American History, University of Texas, Austin. MA Ethics and History, Vanderbilt University, Nashville, TN. BA Government, Harvard

University, Cambridge, MA. **MEMBERSHIPS:** Writers' League of Texas. **CLIENTS WITHIN PRIOR YEAR:** 6–10.

42	EDITOR	**WRITER**	CONSULTANT	F	**NF**

Black, Angela. Technical Communication Solutions. PO Box 46914, Cincinnati, OH 45246. P1/ 513-671-1774. F1/ 413-793-0505. thescribe@juno.com. tcsbymail@aol.com. www.angelablack.com. Established: 1997.

SKILLS: technical writer. **MARKETS SERVED:** publishers, small businesses, and nonprofits. Software and hardware industries or companies that have a need for standard operating procedures (SOPs), user manuals, and tutorials. I have also done work for book, consumer, and trade publishers.

SPECIALTIES AND PREFERENCES: technical writing, consumer and trade writing. More than fifteen years of editorial experience. More than twelve years of library reference and information research experience using published reference sources, databases, and Internet resources. Excellent project management skills with strict adherence to deadlines.

NONFICTION—ACCEPTS: y/a or juvenile, features/articles, creative and narrative, biography/autobiography, how-to/instruction, technical, business.

FEES/TERMS/CONTRACTS: $50/hour unless a project rate is requested, then I negotiate based on project requirements. Accepts checks and PayPal.

ACCOMPLISHMENTS: coauthor of two nonfiction, juvenile books in the Cultures of the World series: Jamaica and Russia.

EDUCATION: BA Communications, University of Cincinnati, OH. **MEMBERSHIPS:** American Library Association. American Society of Business Publication Editors. Editorial Freelancers Association. Society of Writing Consultants. **CLIENTS WITHIN PRIOR YEAR:** 6–10.

43	**EDITOR**	**WRITER**	CONSULTANT	**F**	**NF**

Blackerby, Jerry. PO Box 1496, Quitman, TX 75783. P1/ 903-763-0654. jerryblackerby@cox-internet.com. Established: 2002.

SKILLS: freelance editor, proofreader, ghostwriter, technical writer. **MARKETS SERVED:** telecommunications, electronics, aerospace.

SPECIALTIES AND PREFERENCES: technical writing at all levels of expertise. Also short humorous stories and inspirational stories/articles.

FICTION—ACCEPTS: short stories. **NONFICTION—ACCEPTS:** essays, memoirs, family history, self-help, how-to/instruction, technical, business, humor, inspirational/religious.

FEES/TERMS/CONTRACTS: negotiable.

ACCOMPLISHMENTS: over forty-five years of technical writing. Currently, semi–retired and working from home via telecommuting. **EDUCATION:** some college. **MEMBERSHIPS:** Society for Technical Communications. **CLIENTS WITHIN PRIOR YEAR:** 1–5.

44	EDITOR	WRITER	CONSULTANT	F	NF

Blake, Corey. Elevation 9000 Films, LLC. 2042 N. Beachwood Dr., Ste. 17, Los Angeles, CA 90068. P1/ 213-716-563. cblake@elevation9000films.com. www.elevation9000films.com. Established: 2000.

SKILLS: independent book editor, literary consultant, writing coach. Other business strategist. **MARKETS SERVED:** screenwriters, novelists, businesses, filmmakers.

SPECIALTIES AND PREFERENCES: works creatively with writers in the development phase of their books, assisting as a writing coach. Once the book is in sellable form, he and his partners assist with author branding via marketing and public relations strategies.

FICTION—ACCEPTS: novels (mainstream, historical), scripts/screenplays. **TYPICAL EVALUATION/REPORT:** up to 200 pages depending on budget and depth that writer wants.

FEES/TERMS/CONTRACTS: $125/hour one-on-one services. Projects on retainer $500–$5,000/month. Uses contract only when necessary. Accepts cash, check, or credit.

ACCOMPLISHMENTS: Corey has worked with nearly two hundred writers over the past three years on novels, historical fiction, and screenplays. He is a founding member of the LA Film Lab that develops approximately fifty film projects per year. He directed the San Diego Film Festival winner *Gretchen Brettschneider Skirts Thirty* and produced another award-winner, *The Boy Scout*. Corey speaks around the country at film festivals and seminars on the business of branding an artist.

EDUCATION: BFA Theater, Millikin University, Decatur, IL. Additional acting at Playhouse West School and Repertory Theater. **MEMBERSHIPS:** Screen Actors Guild.

CLIENTS WITHIN PRIOR YEAR: 80–100.

45	EDITOR	WRITER	CONSULTANT	F	NF

Blank, Christine. Orlando, FL. P1/ 407-297-7600. cblankwriter@yahoo.com. www.christineblank.com. Established: 1992.

SKILLS: freelance editor, proofreader, ghostwriter, business writer or copywriter. **MARKETS SERVED:** nonfiction writers, businesses, trade magazines and national newspapers/news services.

SPECIALTIES AND PREFERENCES: I have been a freelance business and news writer for trade magazines and newspapers as well as wire services for about twelve years. My business has expanded to include writing and editing business literature, technical papers, and nonfiction books and query letters. Book ghostwriting and editing is the area I would like to focus on most in the future.

NONFICTION—ACCEPTS: technical, business, inspirational/religious, queries.

FEES/TERMS/CONTRACTS: available upon request.

ACCOMPLISHMENTS: freelance works sold to Archer-Ellison Publishing, Cameo Publications, *The New York Times*, Associated Press.

EDUCATION: AA degree, internships at a business newsletter publisher and at a television news department. **MEMBERSHIPS:** Cassell Network of Writers.

CLIENTS WITHIN PRIOR YEAR: 1–5.

46	EDITOR	WRITER	CONSULTANT	F	NF

Bloomquist, Michele. Bloomquist Publishing. PO Box 259, Heisson, WA 98622. P1/ 360-666-0903. F1/ 360-666-0890. micheleb2@netzero.com. m_Bloomquist@hotmail.com. www.michelebloomquist.com. Established: 1997.

SKILLS: freelance editor, independent book editor, book doctor, copyeditor or line editor, ghostwriter, business writer or copywriter, technical writer, literary consultant, writing coach, writing instructor, feature writer. **MARKETS SERVED:** health and medical, diet and fitness, home and garden, pregnancy, parenting.

SPECIALTIES AND PREFERENCES: I work as a freelance writer and editor in the health, medical, and garden fields for print and online media outlets. I ghostwrite medical Q & As for experts, and edit feature, marketing, and how-to copy.

FICTION—ACCEPTS: y/a or juvenile, short stories, novels (genre, mainstream, literary, contemporary, historical), poetry, scripts/screenplays, queries, synopses, treatments. **NONFICTION—ACCEPTS:** all.

FEES/TERMS/CONTRACTS: writing $1/word. Editing $40–$60/hour, depending on project.

ACCOMPLISHMENTS: I worked for WebMD and other online health and medical websites as an in-house editor before going out on my own.

EDUCATION: BA English and Professional Writing, Portland State University, OR. **MEMBERSHIPS:** National Writer's Union. Society for Self-Employed Creative Professionals.

CLIENTS WITHIN PRIOR YEAR: 5–10.

47	EDITOR	WRITER	CONSULTANT	F	NF

Bolden, Caressa A. Caress-a-Writer Publishing. District Heights, MD. P1/ 301-728-8212. P2/ 301-735-5848. caressa_bolden@yahoo.com. www.caressawriter.com. Established: 2001.

SKILLS: freelance editor, copyeditor or line editor, proofreader, ghostwriter, technical writer, publicist, web copywriter and editor, website and brochure designer. **MARKETS SERVED:** writers, editors, small business owners, nonprofits, associations, and newspapers.

SPECIALTIES AND PREFERENCES: desktop publishing, newsletters, writing and research related to health-related issues, disabilities, home-based businesses, disabled workers, photography, press/news releases. We offer elegant, no-fuss copywriting that addresses your needs and speaks to your audience. Whether print or electronic media, producing clear, effective, attention-grabbing documents is the primary focus.

FICTION—ACCEPTS: short stories, novels (genre, mainstream, literary, contemporary), poetry, queries, synopses, treatments. **NONFICTION—ACCEPTS:** all.

FEES/TERMS/CONTRACTS: copyediting, proofreading, rewriting $25–$40/hour. Writing 50 cents/word. Research $30/hour. Press/news releases $30/hour.

EDUCATION: AA Communicative Arts, University of District of Columbia, Washington, DC. AA Electronics and Computer Technology, TESST College of Technology, Beltsville, MD. Graduate of Defense Information School, Journalist and Editors courses, Fort Meade, MD. **MEMBERSHIPS:** Washington Association of Black Journalists.

CLIENTS WITHIN PRIOR YEAR: 5–10.

48	EDITOR	WRITER	CONSULTANT	F	NF

Borich, Barrie Jean. LeopardLibrary. Minneapolis, MN. P1/ 612-722-8858. C1/ 612-396-5607. leopardlibrary@earthlink.net. www.barriejeanborich.net. Established: 2001, with private consulting for many years prior.

SKILLS: freelance editor, book doctor, copyeditor or line editor, proofreader, literary consultant, writing coach. **MARKETS SERVED:** writers seeking literary critique and mentorship.

SPECIALTIES AND PREFERENCES: Creative Writing Mentorship and Critique Services. Community, academic, and online. My specialty is creative nonfiction. I am a thorough and insightful critic with a craft-focused approach, helping writers create their best work.

FICTION—ACCEPTS: short stories, novels (literary). **NONFICTION—ACCEPTS:** memoirs, creative or narrative, family history, how-to/instruction, text or reference. **TYPICAL EVALUATION/REPORT:** 2–3 pages, more for book length.

FEES/TERMS/CONTRACTS: $50/hour base fee. Accepts checks; accepts credit cards via PayPal. Uses letter of agreement.

ACCOMPLISHMENTS: I've published two literary memoirs, the latest with Graywolf Press, and my literary work has received many kudos including an American Library Association book award and a Bush Artist Fellowship.

EDUCATION: self-designed BA Creative Writing and Poetics, which included graduate-level creative writing workshops, both in and out of the academy. **MEMBERSHIP:** National Writers Union. The Loft. **CLIENTS WITHIN PRIOR YEAR:** 50–60.

49	EDITOR	WRITER	CONSULTANT	F	NF

Bortnem, Brad. Fargo Writers. 620 Main Ave., Apt. 709, Fargo, ND 58103. P1/ 701-293-0313. Brad@fargowriters.com. www.fargowriters.com. Established: 2002.

SKILLS: freelance editor, independent book editor, copyeditor or line editor, proofreader, ghostwriter, literary consultant, writing coach. **MARKETS SERVED:** new writers and first-time authors.

SPECIALTIES AND PREFERENCES: fiction (all genres), some nonfiction.

FICTION—ACCEPTS: short stories, novels (genre, mainstream, literary, contemporary), poetry, queries, synopses, treatments. **NONFICTION—ACCEPTS:** memoirs, creative or narrative, biography/autobiography, family history, humor. **TYPICAL EVALUATION/REPORT:** 2–5 pages. Each evaluation I do is unique to the work—I don't use a "set" template. I listen to each writer, and based on their goals, I offer commentary and criticism that will be relevant to achieving those goals.

FEES/TERMS/CONTRACTS: $2.50/page. No credit cards, but I accept personal and company checks (allow ten days to clear), money orders, cash, and PayPal. Standard contract. No multiwork obligations.

ACCOMPLISHMENTS: content/line editor for two novels to be published spring, 2005. Content/line editor for a novel to be published fall, 2005.

EDUCATION: BA English (Creative Writing) and Philosophy, Moorhead State University, MN.

CLIENTS WITHIN PRIOR YEAR: 1–5.

50	EDITOR	WRITER	CONSULTANT	F	NF

Bourne, Allana. I Love to Edit. 1540 NE 95th St., Seattle, WA 98115. P1/ 206-226-2916. go4joy2@aol.com. Established: 2002.

SKILLS: freelance editor, independent book editor, book doctor, copyeditor or line editor, proofreader, ghostwriter, business writer or copywriter, technical writer, literary consultant, writing coach, screenwriter, news editor. **MARKETS SERVED:** writers, publishers.

SPECIALTIES AND PREFERENCES: I have edited and written book proposals, books, newsletters, short articles for academic quarterlies, and news articles for national print publications.

FICTION—ACCEPTS: novels (contemporary), poetry, scripts/screenplays. **NONFICTION—ACCEPTS:** memoirs, creative nonfiction, biography/autobiography, creative or narrative, book proposals, queries. **Typical evaluation/report:** 1 page for less than 3-page article; up to 30 pages for 300–400-page book.

Fees/terms/contracts: reading $20/hour. Line-by-line nontechnical copyediting $25/hour. Developmental editing/ghostwriting $50/hour. Nontechnical editing $10/page. Nontechnical writing $25/page. Uses contract. Requires one-third down, one-third at first draft or edit, one-third at completion. No credit cards.

Accomplishments: winner of the Newspaper Association of America (NAA) Innovators in Education Award, Washington, DC, 2001, and Best in Print First Place Award, 1990.

Education: MA Education, Seattle University, WA. BA English, University of Massachusetts, Amherst.

Clients within prior year: 21–30.

51	EDITOR	WRITER	CONSULTANT	F	NF

Bouvier, Marie. WordSculpture. PO Box 837, Ridgefield, WA 98642. P1/ 360-607-4334. F1/ 413-669-5781. mariebouvier@wordsculpture.net. www.wordsculpture.net. Established: 2002.

Skills: freelance editor, independent book editor, book doctor, copyeditor or line editor, proofreader, ghostwriter, business writer or copywriter, technical writer. **Markets served:** corporations, nonprofits, writers.

Specialties and preferences: WordSculpture offers writing and editing services. Articles on business practices, education, nonprofits, and family are available for national and regional publication. Original corporate publications and editing services are provided on a consulting basis. CEO/VP-level resumes and cover letters available to individuals.

Fiction—accepts: y/a or juvenile, short stories, novels (genre, mainstream, literary, contemporary, historical). **Nonfiction—accepts:** y/a or juvenile, articles/features, essays, memoirs, creative or narrative, biography/autobiography, business. **Typical evaluation/report:** 1 page, executive summary format.

Fees/terms/contracts: writing and editing $25+/hour. Bids available on a per- project basis. PayPal accepted. No credit cards. Typically uses contract.

Accomplishments: two published nonfiction books, dozens of national magazine articles, numerous corporate publications.

Education: MA International Business Relations, University of Kentucky, Lexington. BA Political Science/English, University of Louisville, KY.

Clients within prior year: 11–20.

52	EDITOR	WRITER	CONSULTANT	F	NF

Boyce, Jim. Jim Boyce, Inc. 225 1st St. SE, Rothsay, MN 56579. P1/ 218-867-2155. jim@boyce.us. www.boyce.us. Established: 1988.

SKILLS: freelance editor, independent book editor, book doctor, ghostwriter, business writer or copywriter, technical writer, writing coach, writing instructor. **MARKETS SERVED:** writers, publishers, nonprofits, corporations, individuals, especially technology end users, technology administrators, and IT professionals, CIOs, CTOs, CEOs.

SPECIALTIES AND PREFERENCES: all how-to subjects; computers, software, and technology subjects; will consider all nonfiction topics.

FICTION—ACCEPTS: y/a or juvenile, picture books, short stories, novels, poetry, scripts/screenplays, queries, synopses, treatments. **NONFICTION—ACCEPTS:** all. **TYPICAL EVALUATION/REPORT:** varies by project.

FEES/TERMS/CONTRACTS: negotiable. Varies by project. Uses contracts.

ACCOMPLISHMENTS: authored and coauthored approximately fifty nonfiction books and hundreds of articles in national magazines and online sites.

EDUCATION: AAS Drafting and Design Technology, Texas State Technical College, Harlingen.

CLIENTS WITHIN PRIOR YEAR: 6–10.

53	EDITOR	WRITER	CONSULTANT	F	NF

Bracken, Michael. 1120 N. 45th St., Waco, TX 76710. P1/ 254-752-0839. F1/ 254-752-0839. Michael@CrimeFictionWriter.com. www.CrimeFictionWriter.com. Established: part-time since 1976; full-time since 2003.

SKILLS: freelance editor, independent book editor, book doctor, copyeditor or line editor, proofreader, ghostwriter, business writer or copywriter, technical writer, literary consultant, writing coach, writing instructor. **MARKETS SERVED:** nonfiction periodical publishers, fiction writers.

SPECIALTIES AND PREFERENCES: I work on manuscripts accepted for publication with nonfiction periodical publishers. Most direct work with individuals involves short manuscripts. I specialize in crime fiction. When I work directly with writers, my goal is to help my writer clients improve their writing so that it is publishable and to teach them how to get their writing published.

FICTION—ACCEPTS: y/a or juvenile, short stories, novels (genre). **NONFICTION—ACCEPTS:** articles/features, essays, memoirs, creative or narrative, business. **TYPICAL EVALUATION/REPORT:** under 50 pages. Primarily works with magazine articles, short stories.

FEES/TERMS/CONTRACTS: negotiable, based on client requirements and budgets. Willing to bill on a per-project basis. No credit cards. Use of contract depends upon client.

Accomplishments: See www.CrimeFictionWriter.com/bracken/bibliog.htm
Memberships: Advertising Club of Waco, local chapter of the American
Advertising Federation. Horror Writers Association. Mystery Writers
of America. Private Eye Writers of America. Science Fiction and Fantasy
Writers of America.
Clients within prior year: 1–5.

54	EDITOR	WRITER	CONSULTANT	F	NF

Brackett, Josh. 17 Rowe Ave., PO Box 706, Rockport, MA 01966. P1/ 978-546-
7498. josh_brackett@post.harvard.edu. www.joshbrackett.com.
Established: over 20 years of experience.

Skills: freelance editor, copyeditor and line editor, ghostwriter, technical writer,
writing coach, freelance supplementary textbooks for secondary English
and mathematics. **Markets served:** nonfiction and educational publishers.

Specialties and preferences: twelve years of English and math teaching
experience, twenty-three years as a writer and editor in the computer and
communications industry. I'm passionate about the written word. Well trained
in the science and art of the English language, I bring years of successful
experience to every project.

Nonfiction—accepts: all.

Fees/terms/contracts: negotiable.

Accomplishments: 7 published books; 180 critical thinking exercises for
middle school students based on English, math, science, social studies, and
life skills content; and many published articles. See my website.

Education: MAT Secondary English, AB Economics, Harvard University,
Cambridge, MA; ABD Language and Communications, New York
University, NY. **Memberships:** Editorial Freelancers Association. Bookbuilders
of Boston.

Clients within prior year: 6–10.

55	EDITOR	WRITER	CONSULTANT	F	NF

Brady, Deanna. words. PO Box 251471, Los Angeles, CA 90025. P1/ 310-
826-2770. P2/ 310-281-7911. F1/ 310-866-748-3348 (ritedit). F2/ 310-826-0212.
getwords@writedit.com. words@getwords.net. www.writedit.com.
www.getwords.net. Established: 1982.

Skills: freelance editor, independent book editor, book doctor, copyeditor
or line editor, proofreader, ghostwriter, business writer or copywriter,
technical writer, literary consultant, author, rewrite specialist, substantive and
stylistic editor, content editor, researcher, critic/reviewer. **Markets served:**
authors, writers, publishers, agents, nonprofit organizations, corporations,

small businesses, advertising agencies, design firms, journals.

Specialties and preferences: literary, children's, self-help, how-to, advertising/marketing/web copy writing/editing, dialects and ESL editing, health, alternative/complementary medicine, ecology, spirituality, American Indian subjects.

Fiction—accepts: all. **Nonfiction—accepts:** all. **Typical evaluation/report:** 2–10 pages.

Fees/terms/contracts: editing, $25–$50/hour by installments or on retainer. Writing fees vary. PayPal. Money orders. Typically uses agreement.

Accomplishments: author of published nonfiction books. Many articles. Major corporate clients. Former editor of international magazines. Successful grants. Fiction and poetry awards. Taught at university.

Education: Theater Arts, California State University, Los Angeles. Writing courses, University of California, Los Angeles.

Clients within prior year: 11-20.

56	EDITOR	WRITER	CONSULTANT	F	NF

Brandstater, Chuck. Accentuated Brandname Creativity, Inc. PO Box 426067, Cambridge, MA 02142. P1/ 617-492-5650. acreatyv1@earthlink.net. Established: 1996.

Skills: freelance editor, independent book editor, copyeditor or line editor, proofreader, translator. **Markets served:** publishers, packagers, businesses.

Specialties and preferences: copyediting and proofreading of technical and business-related materials, book length and shorter.

Nonfiction—accepts: all.

Fees/terms/contracts: page rate calculated after seeing a representative page or two. Accepts PayPal, bank wire, check, or money order. Typically uses agreements.

Education: MBA, Syracuse University, NY. **Memberships:** Editorial Freelancers Association (NYC). Bookbuilders of Boston. Society for Editors and Proofreaders (London).

Clients within prior year: 11–20.

57	EDITOR	WRITER	CONSULTANT	F	NF

Brendel, Scott. Westminster, CO. P1/ 303-460-8152. gideon_scott@yahoo.com. Established: 2000.

Skills: freelance editor, copyeditor or line editor, business writer or copywriter, technical writer, writing coach, product documentation consultant, pre-editing and post-editing consultation. **Markets served:** corporations, consultants, small businesses, and nonprofits.

Specialties and preferences: technical and marketing information, including reports, manuals, brochure copy, sales and marketing information, process descriptions, and web content.

NONFICTION—ACCEPTS: how-to/instruction, technical, text or reference, business. TYPICAL EVALUATION/REPORT: depends on project.

FEES/TERMS/CONTRACTS: per-project or hourly basis. No credit cards. Uses agreement.

ACCOMPLISHMENTS: over twenty years as a writer, editor, and publications manager serving the telecommunications and chemical industries. Received an Award of Excellence from the Society for Technical Communication for a marketing brochure.

EDUCATION: MS Communications, Rensselaer Polytechnic Institute, Troy, NY. BS Interdisciplinary Sciences, Rensselaer Polytechnic Institute, Troy, NY. MEMBERSHIPS: Rocky Mountain Fiction Writers. Pikes Peak Writers.

CLIENTS WITHIN PRIOR YEAR: 1–5.

58	EDITOR	WRITER	CONSULTANT	F	NF

Brenneman, Judy. Greenfire Creative, LLC. 2160 Ryeland Lane, Fort Collins, CO 80526. P1/ 970-416-6353. judyb@greenfire-creative.com. www.greenfirecreative.com. Established: 2001.

SKILLS: freelance editor, copyeditor or line editor, ghostwriter, business writer or copywriter, writing coach, writing instructor, interpretive writer. MARKETS SERVED: interpretive sites; government agencies; businesses; authors in science, mental health, neurology, psychology, medicine, special needs education, and marketing.

SPECIALTIES AND PREFERENCES: helping you tell the story. Provides training, strategic and creative planning, consulting, writing, and editing.

NONFICTION—ACCEPTS: articles/features, essays, memoirs, creative or narrative nonfiction, biography/autobiography, family history, self-help, how-to/instruction, business humor, book proposals, queries.

FEES/TERMS/CONTRACTS: $75/hour. Advance required. Retainer possible. Balance due ten days after completion. PayPal accepted. Typically uses contracts.

ACCOMPLISHMENTS: many publications in national and literary magazines. Over forty awards, including seven literary awards and three international awards.

EDUCATION: BA Biology and Psychology, Case Western Reserve University, Cleveland, OH. Certified Interpretive Trainer, National Association for Interpretation, Fort Collins, CO. MEMBERSHIPS: National Association for Interpretation. Business Marketing Association.

CLIENTS WITHIN PRIOR YEAR: 6–10.

59	EDITOR	WRITER	CONSULTANT	F	NF

Brian, Cynthia. Starstyle® Productions, LLC. PO Box 422, Moraga, CA 94556. P1/ 925-377-STAR (7827). cynthia@starstyle.com. www.star-style.com.

www.bethestaryouare.org. Established: 1984.

Skills: freelance editor, ghostwriter, literary consultant, writing coach, writing instructor, media/speaking coach. **Markets served:** authors, writers, actors, speakers, and other professionals.

Specialties and preferences: coaching writers to success with their manuscripts, media, and presentations. Ghostwrites nonfiction. Writes resumes, press kits, ads, newsletters, letters, queries.

Nonfiction—accepts: all.

Fees/terms/contracts: uses retainers and letters of agreement. Hourly fees, check, credit card, or PayPal.

Accomplishments: author of *New York Times* bestseller, *Chicken Soup for the Gardener's Soul*, and three other motivational titles. Award-winning writer, syndicated columnist, radio/TV host, national speaking, coaching, consulting credits.

Education: BA History, University of California, Berkeley (also studied at UCLA, University of Hawaii, Universite de Bordeaux, France). National and California design certification. **Memberships:** Garden Writers Association. Publisher's Marketing Association. Author's Guild. Screen Actors Guild. American Federation of Television and Radio Artists. National Academy of Television Arts and Sciences. Others.

Clients within prior year: 11–20.

60	EDITOR	WRITER	CONSULTANT	F	NF

Brinton, Elizabeth. 1310 Ash Ave., Coeur d' Alene, ID 83814. Lizzieb@adelphia.net. www.elizabethbrinton.com. Established: 2003.

Skills: freelance editor, independent book editor, book doctor, proofreader, business writer or copywriter, assists with college essays. **Markets served:** anyone who is trying to express their ideas on paper. I have written extensively for Coldwater Creek.

Specialties and preferences: My editing experience comes from years of practice perfecting my own technique. While studying creative writing at Mills College, part of our grade came from editing and critiquing other works. My contribution can best be described in terms of figuring out how to help people express what they are trying to say.

Fiction—accepts: novels (historical). **Nonfiction—accepts:** business, humor.

Fees/terms/contracts: 50 cents/page, payment due on acceptance. Accepts PayPal. No credit cards.

Accomplishments: I created two book clubs and a critique group to further this end. In business, I have helped word e-mails, policies, newsletters, and product description for Coldwater Creek. College essays have been a particular field of interest for me with 100 percent success so far.

EDUCATION: BA English, Mills College, Oakland, CA. Studied Creative Writing at Humber College, Toronto, University of California at San Diego, and University of California at Davis. MEMBERSHIPS: Idaho Writer's League. CLIENTS WITHIN PRIOR YEAR: 1–5.

61	EDITOR	WRITER	CONSULTANT	F	NF

Brodsky, Beverly. All One Light. 12031 Via Felicia, El Cajon, CA 92019. P1/ 619-660-5106. F1/ 619-244-8495. Bevbrodsky@aol.com. www.allonelight. com. Estaablished: 2003

SKILLS: freelance editor, independent book editor, book doctor, copyeditor or line editor, proofreader, business writer or copywriter, technical writer, writing coach, business copyediting and graphic design.

SPECIALTIES AND PREFERENCES: My business, All One Light, develops my clients' potential by connecting to their unlimited potential. I believe writing is the language of the soul. I am most interested in and specialize in inspirational and spiritual writing, but I also have twenty years of experience with business and technical writing. I also offer book coaching and line editing for the adult nonfiction markets.

FICTION—ACCEPTS: scripts/screenplays, queries, synopses, treatments. NONFICTION— ACCEPTS: articles/features, essays, memoirs, creative or narrative, technical, business, humor, inspirational/religious, spiritual, book proposals, queries. TYPICAL EVALUATION/REPORT: 3–5 pages for books or comments with a brief summary online.

FEES/TERMS/CONTRACTS: $30–$40/hour. Accepts cash or check.

ACCOMPLISHMENTS: editor, columnist, researcher, and business writer. Featured in *Lessons from the Light*, Dr. Kenneth Ring, New York (Moment Point Press), 1998. *Seattle IANDS* newsletter, editor, writer, and publisher, 2002 to the present.

EDUCATION: BA Psychology, Vassar College, Poughkeepsie, New York. 654 hours of computer science, 296 hours of logistics analysis, and 279 hours of management classes.

CLIENTS WITHIN PRIOR YEAR: 1–5.

62	EDITOR	WRITER	CONSULTANT	F	NF

Brody, Dylan. 14380 Foothill Blvd., #12, Sylmar, CA 91342. P1/ 818-362-2550. speedwrite@aol.com. www.dylanbrody.com. Established: 1989.

SKILLS: ghostwriter, business writer or copywriter, screenwriter, joke writer, speechwriter, literary consultant. MARKETS SERVED: stand-up comics, anyone needing ad copy and humor/jokes, trailer copy for films, screen, stage, fiction markets.

SPECIALTIES AND PREFERENCES: Mr. Brody writes advertising copy for use in movie trailers, jokes, full-length screenplays, and novels. Clients call on him to meet deadlines with literary style and humor.

FICTION—ACCEPTS: y/a or juvenile, short stories, novels (genre), scripts/screenplays, synopses, treatments. **NONFICTION—ACCEPTS:** articles/features, essays, memoirs, creative or narrative, biography/autobiography, how-to/instructional.

FEES/TERMS/CONTRACTS: vary greatly; general rates posted at website; everything is negotiable. Uses contracts if desired by client.

ACCOMPLISHMENTS: Work performed as a ghostwriter cannot be listed under the terms of the contracts. Mr. Brody's novels have been published by Royal Fireworks Press and Silk Label. Articles have been published in *NMH* magazine (several), *Dragon* magazine, *The Intermountain Jewish News,* and *The Annals of Improbable Research.* Jay Leno's *Tonight Show* monologues have included Dylan Brody's jokes.

EDUCATION: BA Theater, Sarah Lawrence College, Bronxville, NY.

CLIENTS WITHIN PRIOR YEAR: 6–10.

63	EDITOR	WRITER	CONSULTANT	F	NF

Brooks, Marnie. Marnie, Ink. Cary, NC. P1/ 919-387-8904. Marnieink@earthlink.net. Established: 1985.

SKILLS: freelance editor, independent book editor, book doctor, copyeditor or line editor, proofreader, ghostwriter, business writer or copywriter, writing coach, writing instructor, manuscript analysis. **MARKETS SERVED:** academic, professional/business.

SPECIALTIES AND PREFERENCES: fiction, science fiction, fantasy, mystery, adventure, thriller, children's writers. Works with all skill levels from first draft to final along with market research and queries. Everyone deserves respect and individual consideration—from the beginner to the multipublished.

FICTION—ACCEPTS: y/a or juvenile, picture books, short stories, novels (genre, historical), queries, synopses. **NONFICTION—ACCEPTS:** all. **TYPICAL EVALUATION/ REPORT:** 2–20 pages, depending on size/type of project.

FEES/TERMS/CONTRACTS: write/edit $40/hour, or $3–$5/page. No credit cards. Uses agreement.

ACCOMPLISHMENTS: two nonfiction books. Three novels. Dozens of short stories, essays, articles, in national publications. Book review columnist. Several awards/contest winner.

EDUCATION: BS Journalism/PR and Advertising, Northern Arizona University, Flagstaff. **MEMBERSHIPS:** Society of Children's Book Writers and Illustrators.

CLIENTS WITHIN PRIOR YEAR: 11–20.

64	EDITOR	WRITER	CONSULTANT	F	NF

Brown, Beth. 219 Lexington St., Lancaster, KY 40444. P1/ 859-792-6272. beth@kih.net. Established: 1991.

Skills: freelance editor, independent book editor, book doctor, copyeditor or line editor, proofreader, ghostwriter, business writer or copywriter, technical writer, literary consultant, writing coach, writing instructor. **Markets served:** Catholic Campus Ministry Association, Catholic Diocese of Lexington, Christian Appalachian Project, Cliffview Retreat and Conference Center, First Southern National Bank, Forward in the Fifth, Lusk McFarland Funeral Home.

Specialties and preferences: I greatly enjoy helping nonprofit organizations tell their stories through newsletters and other publications. I also enjoy helping novice fiction writers discover how to tell their story.

Fiction—accepts: all. **Nonfiction—accepts:** all. **Typical evaluation/report:** depends on project.

Fees/terms/contracts: $35/hour. Half of estimated charge up front, half upon completion.

Accomplishments: I have received awards from the Catholic Press Association and International Network of Young Journalists for my nonfiction and fiction work. My work has been published locally, nationally, and internationally.

Education: BS Journalism, Ball State University, Muncie, IN. **Memberships:** Catholic Press Association. International Women's Writing Guild. International Union of the Catholic Press.

Clients within prior year: 6–10.

65	EDITOR	WRITER	CONSULTANT	F	NF

Brown, Linda. Multi-Dimensional Solutions. 8805 Coastal Dr., Austin, TX 78749-4922. P1/ 512-282-6079. C1/ 512-659-5704. lbrown56@austin.rr.com. Established: 2001.

Skills: freelance editor, independent book editor, proofreader, writing coach, project management. **Markets served:** independent and grant writing, nonprofit business.

Specialties and preferences: punctual and precise with vision for the written word. Expertise includes technical, scientific, education, and administrative. Author can provide rough information and use Linda's help to refine words. Interest areas are educational research and policy, science education, women studies, and legal issues in education.

Nonfiction—accepts: articles/features, self-help, how-to/instruction, business, book proposals.

Fees/terms/contracts: editor $30–$45/hour. Coach $75–$85/hour. No credit cards. Uses contract.

Accomplishments: ten college- and private-contract-published science education curricula. Four private contract middle school science books. Government training manual for nuclear energy human factors engineer guidelines. Dozens of published articles.

Education: pursuing PhD in Curriculum Studies, MA Middle School Education, University of Northern Colorado, Greeley. BS Clinical Psychology, Colorado State University, Fort Collins. **Memberships:** Association of Supervision and Curriculum Development. Project Management Institute. American Society for Training and Development.

Clients within prior year: 1–5.

66	EDITOR	WRITER	CONSULTANT	F	NF

Bruno, Beth. Wordcaster. Danbury, CT. P1/ 203-790-1114. F1/ 203-790-1115. bethbruno@comcast.net. Established: 1995.

Skills: freelance editor, independent book editor, book doctor, copyeditor or line editor, proofreader, business writer or copywriter, technical writer, literary consultant, publicist, writes features, workshop leader. **Markets served:** writers, publishers, universities, nonprofits, corporations, literary conferences.

Specialties and preferences: book editing, features writing, and conference/library workshops.

Fiction—accepts: all. **Nonfiction—accepts:** all. **Typical evaluation/report:** 1–3 pages.

Fees/terms/contracts: editing $45/hour, proofreading $35/hour, workshops $100/hour, writing $50/hour. Uses agreement.

Accomplishments: self-published book; more than 600 articles published in newspapers, magazines, and online; editor of dozens of book manuscripts; leader of workshops at literary conferences and libraries.

Education: sixth year School Psychology, Alfred University, NY. MA Clinical Psychology, Yeshiva University, NY. EdM Education, Harvard University, Cambridge, MA. BA Psychology, University of California, Berkeley. **Memberships:** Connecticut Authors. Publishers Association.

Clients within prior year: 31–40.

67	EDITOR	WRITER	CONSULTANT	F	NF

Brunson, Karen. 705 Lavaca St., #205, Yoakum, TX 77995. P1/ 361-293-5500. karenbrunson@msn.com. karenlbrunson@yahoo.com. Established: 1995.

Skills: freelance editor, independent book editor, book doctor, copyeditor or line editor, proofreader. **Markets served:** academic and trade publishers;

fiction and nonfiction authors.

SPECIALTIES AND PREFERENCES: copyediting nonfiction books and journals in psychology, psychiatry, and the social sciences; copyediting encyclopedic reference books on many subjects; developmental editing and copyediting religious nonfiction; developmental editing and copyediting fiction.

FICTION—ACCEPTS: novels (genre, mainstream, contemporary, historical). **NONFICTION—ACCEPTS:** self-help, how-to/instruction, technical, text or reference, business, humor, inspirational/religious, spiritual. **TYPICAL EVALUATION/REPORT:** 10–15 pages.

FEES/TERMS/CONTRACTS: $2.50–$4.00/page or $18–$28/hour. No credit cards.

ACCOMPLISHMENTS: managing editor/contributing author, best-selling reference book on business management. Master's level psychologist experienced in assessment, treatment planning, and therapeutic service delivery.

EDUCATION: MA Psychology, Texas A&M University, Commerce. BA General Studies, Northeast Louisiana University, Monroe.

CLIENTS WITHIN PRIOR YEAR: 6–10.

68	EDITOR	WRITER	CONSULTANT	F	NF

Bryan, Mollie. 224 Stonewall Dr., Waynesboro, VA 22980. P1/ 540-943-2478. C1/ 540-471-0517. molliebryan@adelphia.net. Established: 1999.

SKILLS: freelance editor, independent book editor, book doctor, proofreader, ghostwriter, business writer or copywriter, literary consultant, writing coach, writing instructor, poet, columnist, page layout. **MARKETS SERVED:** newspapers, publishers, magazines, associations, lawyers, restaurants, museums.

SPECIALTIES AND PREFERENCES: food/garden writing, poetry, newsletters (writing, editing and layout), women's spirituality, parenting, memoirs/biographies, personality and corporate profiles, rural issues, education.

FICTION—ACCEPTS: all. **NONFICTION—ACCEPTS:** all. **TYPICAL EVALUATION/REPORT:** 1–4 pages.

FEES/TERMS/CONTRACTS: fees are generally negotiable, start $20–$40/hour. Uses contract.

ACCOMPLISHMENTS: publications, awards, and client successes. APEX award for newsletter writing. Honorable mention for poetry published in *Deus Loci, The Lawrence Durrell Journal*. Published in various regional magazines, newspapers, and some national magazines. Published first book 1997, second book 2005.

EDUCATION: BA Journalism and Communications, Point Park College, Pittsburgh, PA. Completed many classes at Editorial Experts in Alexandria, VA. Was selected as a participant in the Jenny McKean Moore Poetry Workshop at George Washington University. **CLIENTS WITHIN PRIOR YEAR:** 5–10.

69	EDITOR	WRITER	CONSULTANT	F	NF

Burt, Wendy. 9545 Oak Tree Ct., Colorado Springs, CO 80925. P1/ 719-527-8225. WendyBurty@aol.com. www.burtcreations.com. Established: 1994.

SKILLS: freelance editor, independent book editor, book doctor, copyeditor or line editor, proofreader, ghostwriter, business writer or copywriter, technical writer, literary consultant, writing coach, writing instructor. MARKETS SERVED: various national and local magazines, newspapers, and websites.

SPECIALTIES AND PREFERENCES: writing and editing for publishers, magazines, newspapers.

FICTION—ACCEPTS: y/a or juvenile, short stories, novels (genre, mainstream, literary, contemporary), poetry, queries, synopses. NONFICTION—ACCEPTS: all.

FEES/TERMS/CONTRACTS: varies—typically $25/hour for editing. Minimum 30 cents/word for writing.

ACCOMPLISHMENTS: written two books for McGraw-Hill. Edited two award-winning books with third to be published. Editing magazines and newspapers. More than 500 published pieces.

EDUCATION: BA Psychology, University of Vermont, Burlington. Editing class. MEMBERSHIPS: PEN Women. Just C.A.W.S. (Creative Alliance of Women's Support).

CLIENTS WITHIN PRIOR YEAR: various national and regional magazines and newspapers.

70	EDITOR	WRITER	CONSULTANT	F	NF

Buterbaugh, Corinne. Buterbaugh Partners. 9405 Lagovista, Great Falls, VA 22066. P1/ 703-438-1774. F1/ 703-759-2075. Established: 1985.

SKILLS: freelance editor, copyeditor, proofreader, business writer or copywriter, consultant for corporate communications, especially internal communications.

SPECIALTIES AND PREFERENCES: communicating highly complex, technical information in an easily understood, engaging style; extensive experience in telecommunications, information technology, and pharmaceutical industries. Has written and edited magazine and newsletter articles, websites, direct mail, brochures, video scripts, annual reports, press releases, and executive presentations. Never misses a deadline.

FEES/TERMS/CONTRACTS: negotiated based on project scope, deadline, and other factors.

ACCOMPLISHMENTS: have helped clients achieve marketing and communications objectives for twenty-six years, nineteen of them as a freelance writer/consultant. Have increased clients' revenue, generated sales leads, increased membership and donation levels (for nonprofit and charitable organizations), enhanced employee morale, and communicated corporate priorities.

Education: BS Marketing, McIntire School of Commerce, University of Virginia, Charlottesville. **Memberships:** Washington Independent Writers. **Clients within prior year:** 10–15.

71	EDITOR	WRITER	CONSULTANT	F	NF

Butler-Ross, Nancy L. The Book Muse. PO Box 112, Woodstock, Key West, FL 33041. P1/ 845-679-9154. P2/ 305-293-8519. F1/ 270-633-6832. TheBookMuse@aol.com. www.TheBookMuse.com. Established: 1997.

Skills: freelance editor, book doctor, business writer or copywriter, literary consultant, writing coach, manuscript development, marketing consultant. **Markets served:** writers, literary agents, retail establishments.

Specialties and preferences: I support an author by being an objective set of eyes checking for typos, glitches in continuity, and manuscript development. I assist new writers in approaching an agent (queries and proposals), obtaining book endorsements, and creating postpublishing marketing plans.

Fiction—accepts: short stories, novels (genre, mainstream, literary, contemporary), queries. **Nonfiction—accepts:** articles/features, essays, memoirs, creative or narrative, biography/autobiography, family history, self-help, how-to/instruction, business, humor, spiritual, book proposals, queries. **Typical evaluation/report:** 5–10 pages.

Fees/terms/contracts: $60–$150/hour, copy, development, marketing. 50 percent deposit. No credit cards.

Accomplishments: *Miami Herald* columnist. Author, Book of the Month Club selection.

Education: BA Art History/Education, State University of New York, Plattsburgh. **Memberships:** International Women's Writing Guild. **Clients within prior year:** 5–10.

72	EDITOR	WRITER	CONSULTANT	F	NF

Buyer, Laurie. Creative Adventure—A Guide Service for Writers. 125 Rolling Park Dr., Woodland Park, CO 80863. P1/ 719-687-3791. luzdelsol@earthlink.net. Established: 2002.

Skills: freelance editor, independent book editor, ghostwriter, literary consultant, writing coach, writing instructor. **Markets served:** writers of all ages.

Specialties and preferences: poetry, creative nonfiction, nonfiction, fiction. Nurtures writing strengths. Identifies writing weaknesses. Helps discover the authentic voice. Provides the jumpstart needed to get started and stay motivated. Teaches techniques to learn to love the art of revising.

FICTION—ACCEPTS: y/a or juvenile, picture books, short stories, novels (genre, mainstream, literary, contemporary, historical), poetry. NONFICTION—ACCEPTS: y/a or juvenile, articles/features, essays, memoirs, creative or narrative, biography/autobiography, family history. TYPICAL EVALUATION/REPORT: 5–10 pages.

FEES/TERMS/CONTRACTS: $30/hour. Checks acceptable. No credit cards. Up-front consultation and reading fee, then billing at hourly rate. No referral fees paid or received.

ACCOMPLISHMENTS: novel and award-winning memoir under contract. Two collections of poetry, a children's story, 100+ nonfiction articles in national magazines.

EDUCATION: MFA Creative Writing, Goddard College, Plainfield, VT. MEMBERSHIPS: Colorado Council on the Arts Online Poetry Project and Young Audiences Roster. Women Writing the West. Western Writers of America.

CLIENTS WITHIN PRIOR YEAR: 1–5.

73	EDITOR	WRITER	CONSULTANT	F	NF

Byrne, Janet. Words into Print. New York, NY. P1/ 215-579-2499. jbyrne18940@yahoo.com. www.wordsintoprint.org. Established: 1987.

SKILLS: independent book editor, book doctor, copyeditor or line editor, ghostwriter, literary consultant. MARKETS SERVED: publishers, agents, and writers.

SPECIALTIES AND PREFERENCES: development. Bias toward intellectual, literary.

FICTION—ACCEPTS: y/a or juvenile, novels (literary), picture books.

NONFICTION—ACCEPTS: y/a or juvenile, memoirs, creative or narrative, biography/autobiography, text or reference. TYPICAL EVALUATION/REPORT: verbal or 2–4 pages.

FEES/TERMS/CONTRACTS: $100/hour. No credit cards. Uses contract.

ACCOMPLISHMENTS: author of a biography of Frieda Lawrence (HarperCollins, Bloomsbury), a *New York Times* Notable Book of 1995. Edited Winnie Mandela's bestselling autobiography (WW Norton). As an independent magazine publisher and editor, worked with contributors Gay Talese, Norman Mailer, Joyce Carol Oates, William Burroughs, Allen Ginsberg.

EDUCATION: BA English Literature, Montclair State College, Upper Montclair, NJ. Studied Danish Literature at University of Copenhagen. MEMBERSHIPS: Words into Print.

CLIENTS WITHIN PRIOR YEAR: 10–12.

74	EDITOR	WRITER	CONSULTANT	F	NF

Cain, Christopher. Christopher Communications, Inc. 1007 Green Branch Ct., Oviedo, FL 32765. P1/ 407-365-3618. C1/ 407-719-4912. F1/ 407-365-3618. vacvalue@aol.com. www.vacationpropertyowners.com. Established: 1998.

Skills: freelance editor, copyeditor or line editor, ghostwriter, business writer or copywriter, writing coach, speeches, annual reports, business articles, media relations. **Markets served:** consumer and technical.

Specialties and preferences: real estate, especially vacation property and second homes. Assists developers in marketing their vacation homes and condos through a unique Developer/Author Reception program to target highly qualified buyers.

Fees/terms/contracts: normal rate $100/hour. Prefer predetermined price to design and complete project.

Nonfiction—accepts: articles/features.

Accomplishments: owner of a seaside villa at Kiawah Island, SC, for sixteen years. Author of two books and dozens of articles on vacation property featured in *Barron's, Business Week, USA Today, Money* magazine, and SmartMoney. Have helped developers sell millions in vacation property with programs designed to reach baby boomers.

Education: MS Journalism, Medill School of Journalism, Northwestern University, Evanston, IL. BA History and English, Hiram College, OH. **Memberships:** National Association of Real Estate Editors. Public Relations Society of America.

Clients within prior year: 1–5.

75	EDITOR	WRITER	CONSULTANT	F	NF

Calabro, Marian. Hasbrouck Heights, NJ. P1/ 201-288-2036. F1/ call first. calabro@reporters.net. info@mariancalabro.com. www.mariancalabro.com. www.CorporateHistory.net. Established: 1984.

Skills: freelance editor, book doctor, copyeditor or line editor, ghostwriter, business writer or copywriter, writing instructor, writer and project manager of corporate histories. **Markets served:** corporations, organizations, publishers, writers.

Specialties and preferences: "trouble-free freelancer" to business clients, publishers, and individuals who are serious about writing. Specialist in company and organizational histories. Former publishing manager. Can create and/or fine-tune proposals and books involving business, history, law, or the arts. Open to ghostwriting or collaboration.

Nonfiction—accepts: biography/autobiography, business, book proposals, queries. **Typical evaluation/report:** 2–10 pages.

Fees/terms/contracts: hourly or project rate. Retainer required. No credit cards. Uses contract or agreement.

Accomplishments: six published nonfiction history books for y/a and adults. Four commissioned corporate histories. Many corporate projects and trade magazine articles.

EDUCATION: Post-BA Paralegal Diploma, Fairleigh Dickinson University, Teaneck, NJ. BA English, Rutgers College, New Brunswick, NJ. Certified creative writing workshop leader, Amherst Writers & Artists. MEMBERSHIPS: Authors Guild. American Society of Journalists and Authors. CLIENTS WITHIN PRIOR YEAR: typically no more than six.

76	EDITOR	WRITER	CONSULTANT	F	NF

Calhoun, Bob. PO Box 1701, Pacifica, CA 94044. P1/ 650-355-5624. P2/ 415-279-2634. bobbakid@pacbell.net. Established: 1997.

SKILLS: ghostwriter, business writer or copywriter, research, speechwriting. MARKETS SERVED: consumer magazines, trade magazines.

SPECIALTIES AND PREFERENCES: martial arts, music, and professional wrestling biographies/autobiographies; articles and exposes on music, movies and television; speechwriting and letter writing; compiling, writing, and editing research reports.

NONFICTION—ACCEPTS: articles/features, essays, memoirs, creative or narrative, biography/autobiography, family history, business.

FEES/TERMS/CONTRACTS: will send collaboration contract upon request. Will also accept work for hire. Rates determined by size and detail of job.

ACCOMPLISHMENTS: published in *Salon.com, Bass Player, Emmy* magazine, the *San Francisco Examiner, SFGate.com*, and *Inside Kung-Fu*. I am the coauthor of the autobiography of martial arts and Hollywood stunt legend "Judo" Gene LeBell.

EDUCATION: BA Broadcasting and Electronic Communications, *cum laude*, San Francisco State University, CA.

CLIENTS WITHIN PRIOR YEAR: 6–10.

77	EDITOR	WRITER	CONSULTANT	F	NF

Calkhoven, Laurie. 1175 York Ave., New York, NY 10021. P1/ 212-486-3907. lcalkhoven@nyc.rr.com. lauriewriter42@hotmail.com. Established: 2003.

SKILLS: freelance editor, independent book editor, book doctor, copyeditor or line editor, ghostwriter. MARKETS SERVED: publishers, book packagers, writers.

SPECIALTIES AND PREFERENCES: children's fiction and nonfiction. Primarily middle grade and young adult. Works with children's writers to help them polish their work and write series books for publishers/packagers.

FICTION—ACCEPTS: y/a or juvenile, picture books, short stories, novels (genre, mainstream, literary, contemporary, historical), queries, synopses. NONFICTION—ACCEPTS: all. TYPICAL EVALUATION/REPORT: 3–10 pages.

FEES/TERMS/CONTRACTS: hourly or per-project fee negotiated. Half due upon signing agreement. No credit cards.

ACCOMPLISHMENTS: twenty years of experience in book publishing, most recently with the Scholastic Book Clubs. Two published novels. Four published nonfiction books. Articles.

EDUCATION: BA English Literature, Syracuse University, NY. MEMBERSHIPS: Society of Children's Book Writers and Editors. Authors Guild.

CLIENTS WITHIN PRIOR YEAR: 5–10.

78	EDITOR	WRITER	CONSULTANT	F	NF

Camenson, Blythe. Fiction Writer's Connection. 222 Dartmouth Dr. SE, Albuquerque, NM 87106. P1/ 505-352-9490. BCamenson@aol.com. www.fictionwriters.com. Established: 1993.

SKILLS: freelance editor, independent book editor, book doctor, copyeditor or line editor, ghostwriter, business writer or copywriter, literary consultant, writing coach, writing instructor. MARKETS SERVED: new writers.

SPECIALTIES AND PREFERENCES: I work with new writers who want to improve their work to a publishable standard and learn the ropes to getting published. I help with query letters and synopses, nonfiction book proposals, books, plotting, and novel writing. I am director of Fiction Writer's Connection. I work with both fiction and nonfiction writers. I offer critiquing services as well as mentoring, a newsletter, free consultation, and more.

FICTION—ACCEPTS: all. NONFICTION—ACCEPTS: all. TYPICAL EVALUATION/REPORT: critique reports 3–5 pages, single spaced.

FEES/TERMS/CONTRACTS: membership programs vary from $74–$475.

ACCOMPLISHMENTS: I am the author of fifty books, many on the subject of how to write and get published (Writer's Digest Books and McGraw Hill).

EDUCATION: MEd Counseling, Northeastern University, Boston, BA English and Psychology, University of Massachusetts, Boston. MEMBERSHIPS: National Writers Union.

CLIENTS WITHIN PRIOR YEAR: 20–30.

79	EDITOR	WRITER	CONSULTANT	F	NF

Campbell, Andrea. Hot Springs Village, AR. P1/ 501-922-0050. campbell@arkansas.net. www.andreacampbell.com. Established: 2004.

SKILLS: proofreader, ghostwriter, copywriter, writing instructor, indexer. MARKETS SERVED: writers, agents, publishers.

SPECIALTIES AND PREFERENCES: criminal justice, forensic science, entertainment and party books, and interior design.

NONFICTION—ACCEPTS: y/a or juvenile, memoirs, creative or narrative, biography/autobiography, self-help, how-to/instruction, text or reference,

business, inspirational/spiritual, book proposals, queries. TYPICAL EVALUATION/
REPORT: 2–10 pages.

FEES/TERMS/CONTRACTS: negotiable fees. PayPal. Retainer. Agreement and contract.

ACCOMPLISHMENTS: nine nonfiction books published, online teaching, national
magazine articles. Former public relations assistant. Forensic artist with
Arkansas State Crime Lab.

EDUCATION: AA Criminal Justice, Tri-C College, Hot Springs, AR. Diploma,
Fellow, American College of Forensic Examiners. MEMBERSHIPS: The Amer-
ican Society of Journalists and Authors, Inc. Mystery Writers of America.
Sisters in Crime. American College of Forensic Examiners International.
The International Association for Identification. Simian Society.

CLIENTS WITHIN PRIOR YEAR: 1–4.

80	EDITOR	WRITER	CONSULTANT	F	NF

Campbell, Karen. Sacramento, CA. P1/ 916-448-3840. SacWriterEditor@aol.com.
Established: 1980.

SKILLS: freelance editor, book doctor, copyeditor or line editor, proofreader,
business writer or copywriter, nonfiction, humor writer, researcher, paralegal.
MARKETS SERVED: legal field, book authors.

SPECIALTIES AND PREFERENCES: primarily serves those involved in legal work,
though also edits and writes fiction and nonfiction. Twenty years of
experience as litigation paralegal. Reads, writes, and translates German and
French. I specialize in law, politics, women's issues, sports, health, cats,
needlework. I do not accept erotica.

FICTION—ACCEPTS: all. NONFICTION—ACCEPTS: all.

FEES/TERMS/CONTRACTS: general editing/writing $25/hour; legal work $50/hour.

ACCOMPLISHMENTS: publications, awards, client successes—too many to list.
Writing since 1974 when I started with *The Amityville Record*. Have won
awards for both writing and desktop publishing. Currently producing a
monthly column for Embroiderers Guild newsletters throughout the US and
Canada.

EDUCATION: BA German and Political Science, Muhlenberg College, Allentown,
PA. Coursework at University of San Diego School of Law, CA.

CLIENTS WITHIN PRIOR YEAR: 10–20.

81	EDITOR	WRITER	CONSULTANT	F	NF

Carder, Carol. 1035 S. Josephine St., Denver, CO 80209. P1/ 303-777-9194.
F1/ 303-777-3261. carolcarder@msn.com. Established: 1985.

SKILLS: freelance editor, ghostwriter, business writer or copywriter, technical
writer. MARKETS SERVED: construction, architectural, engineering, landscaping,

historical, general consumer, nonprofits.

Specialties and preferences: researches and writes trade magazine articles mainly in construction-related fields; also places articles for clients. Writes text for brochures, ads, marketing materials.

Nonfiction—accepts: articles/features, creative or narrative, how-to/instruction, technical, text or reference, business, inspirational/religious, queries.

Fees/terms/contracts: writing 50 cents–$1/word. Editing or public relations $55/hour. 50 percent retainer on large projects. Contract. No credit cards.

Accomplishments: have written ten years (104 features) for regional construction publication; have written six award-winners in American Council of Engineering Companies. Received the Minnie award from Denver Woman's Press Club.

Education: BA English and French, Western Michigan University, Kalamazoo. Graduate studies in journalism/advertising at University of Colorado, Boulder. Technical writing, Arapahoe Community College, Littleton, CO.

Memberships: Denver Woman's Press Club. Roadrunners Toastmasters.

Clients within prior year: 6–10.

82	EDITOR	WRITER	CONSULTANT	F	NF

Carrel, Dorene. Seattle, WA. P1/ 206-242-5956. Dorenea5@yahoo.com. Established: 1985.

Skills: freelance editor, book doctor, copyeditor or line editor, proofreader. **Markets served:** nonprofit agencies, publishers, schools, individual authors, companies.

Specialties and preferences: I offer copyediting and proofreading for books, newsletters, websites, magazines, manuals, and brochures. Specialties include self-help/spirituality, social sciences, psychology, education, environment, and the outdoors. Extensive experience with nonnative authors.

Nonfiction—accepts: y/a, articles/features, essays, memoirs, creative or narrative, biography/autobiography, family history, self-help, how-to/instruction, technical, text or reference, business, humor, inspirational/spiritual.

Fees/terms/contracts: $30/hour for most copyediting and proofreading. $30–$50/hour for technical and developmental editing. Uses contract. No credit cards.

Accomplishments: several articles in national newspapers and magazines.

Education: MS Psychology, Columbia Pacific University, San Rafael, CA. BA Journalism, Michigan State University, Lansing. Studied web design and development in Seattle, WA. **Memberships:** NW Independent Editors Guild.

83	EDITOR	WRITER	CONSULTANT	F	NF

Carsen, Jennifer. Between the Covers. 433 Burton Ave., Highland Park, IL 60035-4940. P1/ 847-681-1339. F1/ 208-955-2220. jennifercarsen@yahoo.com. www.jennifercarsen.com. Established: 2002.

SKILLS: freelance editor, independent book editor, book doctor, copyeditor or line editor, ghostwriter. **MARKETS SERVED:** authors, writers.

SPECIALTIES AND PREFERENCES: books—writing, ghostwriting, and editing. My specialties are law, food, fitness, and self-help. I'm a former employment law attorney. I also edit dissertations and application essays for college and law school.

FICTION—ACCEPTS: novels (genre, mainstream). **NONFICTION—ACCEPTS:** articles and features, self-help, how-to/instruction, humor. **TYPICAL EVALUATION/REPORT:** a few paragraphs, comments throughout the work.

FEES/TERMS/CONTRACTS: vary by project. Prefers fixed rate. Accepts credit cards via PayPal. Accepts money orders, personal checks. 50 percent up front. Uses contract.

ACCOMPLISHMENTS: regular newsletter contributor. Copy- and line-edited two novels. Edited and contributed to nonfiction fitness and nutrition book. Consultant, writer, and legal content provider for leaplaw.com. Ghostwriter and editor of a novel. Author of a divorce guide.

EDUCATION: JD New York University School of Law, New York. BA Political Science, Williams College, Williamstown, MA. **MEMBERSHIPS:** Chicago Women in Publishing. American Society of Indexers. Editorial Freelancers Association.

CLIENTS WITHIN PRIOR YEAR: 6–10.

84	EDITOR	WRITER	CONSULTANT	F	NF

Carson, Mary. 3916 Tappan Ave., Cincinnati, OH 45223. P1/ 513-542-7922. C1/ 513-405-5602. mkc@fuse.net. mkcarson@nasw.org. www.marykaycarson.com. Established: 1994.

SKILLS: freelance editor, ghostwriter, presenter at schools. **MARKETS SERVED:** educational publishers, magazines, organizations.

SPECIALTIES AND PREFERENCES: author of books for young people and teachers for trade publishers, educational publishers, and packagers. Writer of teaching materials and student educational materials for educational publishers, packagers, and organizations. Freelance magazine writer for adult magazines and kids' magazines. Presenter at schools for "author visits."

NONFICTION—ACCEPTS: y/a or juvenile, articles/features, essays, creative or narrative, biography, how-to/instruction, text or reference.

FEES/TERMS/CONTRACTS: invoice by the project or by the hour at $40–$50/hour.

ACCOMPLISHMENTS: six published children's trade titles, fourteen published student educational publishing titles, seven published professional titles for teachers, dozens of articles published in national magazines for adults and kids, dozens of teaching guides and supplemental education materials titles published.

EDUCATION: fall semester of the Science and Environmental Reporting Program, New York University, BS Biology, University of Kansas, Lawrence. MEMBERSHIPS: National Association of Science Writers. Society of Children's Book Writers and Illustrators.

CLIENTS WITHIN PRIOR YEAR: 6–10.

85	EDITOR	WRITER	CONSULTANT	F	NF

Cartaino, Carol. White Oak Editions. 2000 Flat Run Rd., Seaman, OH 45679. P1/ 937-764-1303. P2/ 937-764-1551. cartaino@aol.com. Established: 1986.

SKILLS: freelance editor, independent book editor, book doctor, copyeditor or line editor, proofreader, ghostwriter, business writer or copywriter, technical writer, literary consultant, writing coach, writing instructor. MARKETS SERVED: writers, aspiring writers, book publishers, literary agents, custom book producers.

SPECIALTIES AND PREFERENCES: helps writers and publishers create the book they have in mind. Fixes problem manuscripts, especially how to, self-help, household subjects, personal organization, gardening, nature, animals, Americana.

NONFICTION—ACCEPTS: all. TYPICAL EVALUATION/REPORT: 3–10 pages.

FEES/TERMS/CONTRACTS: $35/hour for content/line editing or collaboration. Bills monthly after work is done. Might require advance for new clients. Does not usually use contract.

ACCOMPLISHMENTS: more than thirty years of experience helping writers and publishers produce quality, satisfying books. Twenty years of staff experience with large national publishers, including nine as editor-in-chief. Coauthor of *Get Organized, Get Published!* and *Keeping Work Simple* with Don Aslett. Editor/collaborator on all of his books, which have sold over three million copies.

EDUCATION: BA English, Rutgers University, NJ, plus some postgraduate courses at New York University.

CLIENTS WITHIN PRIOR YEAR: 6–8.

86	EDITOR	WRITER	CONSULTANT	F	NF

Carter, Cheryl. Carter Writing Consultants. PO Box 5642, Santa Barbara, CA 93150. P1/ 805-969-5314. F1/ 805-565-5700. info@carterwriting.com. www.carterwriting.com. Established: 1998.

SKILLS: freelance editor, independent book editor, copyeditor or line editor, business writer or copywriter, technical writer, literary consultant, writing coach, writing instructor. **MARKETS SERVED:** writers, nonprofit organizations, universities, businesses and corporations, nonprofessional writers.

SPECIALTIES AND PREFERENCES: excellent writing and editing services in a timely and cost-effective manner respecting and maintaining the original and unique voice of the writer. We understand not only the mechanics but the psychology of language.

FICTION—ACCEPTS: y/a or juvenile, picture books, short stories, poetry. **NON-FICTION—ACCEPTS:** all.

FEES/TERMS/CONTRACTS: $75/hour. 50 percent deposit. 50 percent upon completion. PayPal. Typically uses contracts.

ACCOMPLISHMENTS: published nonfiction, journal articles, poetry.

EDUCATION: ME Educational Psychology, University of California, Santa Barbara. BA Monterey Institute of International Studies, CA.

CLIENTS WITHIN PRIOR YEAR: 1–5

87	EDITOR	WRITER	CONSULTANT	F	NF

Carter, Sandy. WordsCount. PO Box 311, Marylhurst, OR 97036. P1/ 503-655-0649. sandycarter@gbronline.com. www.wordscount.biz. Established: 2003.

SKILLS: freelance editor, independent book editor, book doctor, copyeditor or line editor, proofreader, ghostwriter, business writer or copywriter, grant doctor. **MARKETS SERVED:** writers, publishers, nonprofits, corporations.

SPECIALTIES AND PREFERENCES: WordsCount provides high technical skills, edits, proofs, constructive feedback on content, layout, flow, style, and tone of business and personal writing. Language is nuance, accessible through structure. Each word counts with persnickety editing, clean copy.

FICTION—ACCEPTS: all. **NONFICTION—ACCEPTS:** all.

FEES/TERMS/CONTRACTS: $50/hour, minimum increment $50. Free first meeting. Books, annual reports, corporate history fees are negotiable. Agreements based on estimates. No credit cards.

ACCOMPLISHMENTS: newspaper writer, published six nonfiction magazine pieces. Have written grants and proposals since 1989, winning $6 million. Newsletter editor and writer. Outstanding Graduate.

EDUCATION: BS Journalism (News-Editorial and Magazine), University of Oregon, Eugene. **MEMBERSHIPS:** Northwest Independent Editors Guild. Willamette Valley Development Officers. Northwest Association of Book Publishers.

CLIENTS WITHIN PRIOR YEAR: 1–5.

88	EDITOR	WRITER	CONSULTANT	F	NF

Caruba, Alan. The Caruba Organization. 28 W. Third St., Suite 1321, South Orange, NJ 07079. P1/ 973-763-6392. acaruba@aol.com. www.caruba.com. www.bookviews.com. Established: 1975.

SKILLS: freelance editor, ghostwriter, business writer or copywriter, literary consultant, writing coach, writing instructor, public relations, editorials, news releases. MARKETS SERVED: corporations, trade associations, think tanks, public relations firms, entrepreneurs, educational institutions, and individuals.

SPECIALTIES AND PREFERENCES: particularly skilled at the rapid "packaging of information" for dissemination via the Internet, print, or broadcast media. Extensive background in public affairs issues. Writes newsletters, articles, commentaries, op-eds. My work for my clients reaches a potential Internet audience of 30 million or more.

NONFICTION—ACCEPTS: all.

FEES/TERMS/CONTRACTS: varies by project. Longer projects—advance partial payment. Book-length projects require a contract.

ACCOMPLISHMENTS: author of three books. Writer of a weekly commentary, "Warning Signs," widely syndicated on the Internet and excerpted in publications. Numerous published articles and commentaries, and recipient of many awards. Profiled by *Insight on the News* magazine in April 2003. Founder of The National Anxiety Center, a clearinghouse for info on media-driven "scare campaigns." Visit caruba.com website.

CLIENTS WITHIN PRIOR YEAR: 11–20.

89	EDITOR	WRITER	CONSULTANT	F	NF

Caruso, Iyna. Long Island, NY. P1/ 516-594-8578. iyna@optonline.net. www.iynacaruso.com. Established: 1998.

SKILLS: copyeditor or line editor, ghostwriter, business writer or copywriter, freelance writer, scriptwriter. MARKETS SERVED: corporations, small-to-midsized businesses, nonprofit organizations, magazines, newspapers, writers.

SPECIALTIES AND PREFERENCES: I have wide-ranging editorial experience—from marketing, public relations, and advertising to business communications and features. I can assess, strategize, and satisfy clients' overall editorial needs.

NONFICTION—ACCEPTS: all.

FEES/TERMS/CONTRACTS: vary based on complexity/term of project and deadline. No credit cards. PayPal accepted. Uses contract.

ACCOMPLISHMENTS: more than 150 articles published in regional and national publications. Award winner for marketing and promotional campaigns. Winner, Cable ACE, on-air promotion series; Winner, Cable Television

Advertising & Marketing MARK, on-air promotion series; Finalist, Promax Medallion Finalist, on-air promotion spot; Winner, Long Island Coalition for Fair Broadcasting FOLIO, documentary; Finalist, International Film & TV Festival Finalist, television spot.

EDUCATION: BA Journalism, Hofstra University, Hempstead, NY.
CLIENTS WITHIN PRIOR YEAR: 11–20.

90	EDITOR	WRITER	CONSULTANT	F	NF

Cashdan, Linda. The Word Process. PO Box 9407, Washington, DC 20016. P1/ 202-234-7116. Wordpro@verizon.net. www.TheWordProcess.com. Established: 1997.

SKILLS: freelance editor, independent book editor, book doctor, copyeditor or line editor, proofreader, ghostwriter, business writer or copywriter, literary consultant, writing coach, writing instructor, book proposal writer. **MARKETS SERVED:** authors.

SPECIALTIES AND PREFERENCES: memoirs, how-to books, biographies, adult mainstream novels, business books, self-help books. We help clients write book proposals to attract agents and/or publishers, prepare query letters, do both line and developmental editing of fiction and nonfiction, critique manuscripts, and ghostwrite memoirs and other nonfiction books.

FICTION—ACCEPTS: short stories, novels (genre, mainstream, literary, contemporary, historical), queries, synopses, treatments. **NONFICTION—ACCEPTS:** all. **TYPICAL EVALUATION/REPORT:** several pages single spaced, offering both criticisms and suggestions for ways to strengthen manuscript.

FEES/TERMS/CONTRACTS: $50/hour. Works on a percentage basis for some projects.

ACCOMPLISHMENTS: My partner, Molly McKitterick, and I are veteran journalists (radio and television), freelance magazine writers, and published novelists.

EDUCATION: BA English, Vassar College, Poughkeepsie, NY. **MEMBERSHIPS:** Washington Independent Writers. Authors Guild. Bethesda Writers' Center.
CLIENTS WITHIN PRIOR YEAR: 21–30.

91	EDITOR	WRITER	CONSULTANT	F	NF

Catalano, Robin. 83 Partridge Lane, Stephentown, NY 12168. P1/ 518-733-9681. F1/ 518-733-9681. RGWorld@aol.com. Established: 1996.

SKILLS: freelance editor, copyeditor or line editor, proofreader, ghostwriter, business writer or copywriter, literary consultant, writing coach, writing instructor, writer magazine feature. **MARKETS SERVED:** writers, book and magazine publishers, packaging companies, commercial businesses.

SPECIALTIES AND PREFERENCES: developmental writing and editing, especially health, wellness, food, and women's sports topics. Fiction writing, editing, and consulting.

Fiction—accepts: y/a or juvenile, novels (genre, mainstream, literary, contemporary). **Nonfiction—accepts:** articles/features, essays, memoirs, humor.

Fees/terms/contracts: $35–$50/hour, more for work-for-hire writing. Invoices upon completion. Net 30 days. No credit cards. Uses contract if client desires.

Accomplishments: features in many magazines, e.g., *HomeStyle, Dance Spirit, Culinary Trends,* and *Gourmet.* Editorial clients include Penguin Putnam, Inner Traditions, Storey Books, Chelsea Green, Simon & Schuster. Copywriting for Comfortex, International Masters Publishers, USA Gymnastics, more. Published, award-winning fiction writer.

Education: MA English, BA English/Anthropology, University of Rhode Island, Kingston. **Memberships:** The Berkshire Writers Room. USA Gymnastics. Honor societies.

Clients within prior year: 10–15.

92	EDITOR	WRITER	CONSULTANT	F	NF

Cattani, Pat. Pat Cattani Editorial Services. 2806 N. Tucson Blvd. #2, Tucson, AZ 85716. P1/ 520-318-9117. cattani@wvcnet.com. Established: 2001.

Skills: freelance editor, copyeditor or line editor, proofreader, indexer. **Markets served:** educational, reference, academic, trade book publishers.

Specialties and preferences: provides copyediting and proofreading services for educational, reference, academic, and trade book publishers.

Nonfiction—accepts: y/a or juvenile, articles/features, essays, memoirs, creative or narrative, biography/autobiography, technical, text or reference, business, humor.

Fees/terms/contracts: per-project fee basis. Varies, depending on state of manuscript or page proofs and what client wishes to have done. Clients pay by company check.

Education: BA English, Ithaca College, NY. **Memberships:** Editorial Freelancers Association.

Clients within prior year: 6–10.

93	EDITOR	WRITER	CONSULTANT	F	NF

Cavelos, Jeanne. Jeanne Cavelos Editorial Services. PO Box 75, Mont Vernon, NH 03057. P1/ 603-673-6234. jcavelos@sff.net. www.sff.net/people/jcavelos. Established: 1994.

Skills: freelance editor, copyeditor or line editor, ghostwriter, technical writer, literary consultant, writing instructor. **Markets served:** publishers, book packagers, agents, and authors.

SPECIALTIES AND PREFERENCES: Jeanne Cavelos, formerly a senior editor at Bantam Doubleday Dell, provides services ranging from light edit to heavy edit to major rewrite to ghostwriting. A bestselling author and award-winning editor, she handles all types of adult fiction and nonfiction, and specializes in thrillers, literary fiction, fantasy, science fiction, horror, popular culture, self-help, and health.

FICTION—ACCEPTS: short stories, novels (genre, mainstream, literary), queries, synopses, treatments. **NONFICTION—ACCEPTS:** all. **TYPICAL EVALUATION/REPORT:** 35 pages.

FEES/TERMS/CONTRACTS: fees confidential. Most new clients must pay in advance. No credit cards. Uses contract only if client requests it.

ACCOMPLISHMENTS: In her eight years in New York publishing, Jeanne edited numerous award-winning and bestselling authors and won the World Fantasy Award.

EDUCATION: MFA Creative Writing, American University, Washington, DC. Graduate study astronomy, Cornell University, Ithaca, NY. BS Astrophysics/ Mathematics, Michigan State University, East Lansing. **MEMBERSHIPS:** Horror Writers Association. Science Fiction and Fantasy Writers of America.

CLIENTS WITHIN PRIOR YEAR: 6–10.

94	EDITOR	WRITER	CONSULTANT	F	NF

Celeste, Carol. Orange, CA. P1/ 714-283-3552. P1/ 714-283-3552. F1/ 714-283-3552. celestewrites@juno.com. Established: 1992.

SKILLS: freelance editor, copyeditor or line editor, proofreader, ghostwriter, business writer or copywriter, technical writer, writing instructor, research, fact checking. **MARKETS SERVED:** corporations, writers, publishers, nonprofits.

SPECIALTIES AND PREFERENCES: feature articles, reports, newsletters, press releases, personal and company profiles, general nonfiction, web content.

NONFICTION—ACCEPTS: articles/features, essays, memoirs, creative, biography/ autobiography, family history, self-help, how-to/instruction, technical, reference, business, humor, book proposals, and queries.

FEES/TERMS/CONTRACTS: most writing $75/hour. Proofreading $1/page. Editing $2/page. Variable minimums. Three payments on large projects. No credit cards. Uses contracts.

ACCOMPLISHMENTS: dozens of articles in national publications/websites. Author of one business book. Contributor to one history book, one how-to, and two anthologies. Dozens of writing columns. Hundreds of corporate projects. Awards.

EDUCATION: MBA Marketing/Finance, West Coast University, Orange, CA. MA Latin American Studies, University of Arizona, Tucson. BA Latin American Studies, University of the Americas, Mexico City. **MEMBERSHIPS:** California

Writers Club. General Society Mayflower Descendants.
CLIENTS WITHIN PRIOR YEAR: 1–5.

95	EDITOR	WRITER	CONSULTANT	F	NF

Chamberlain, Lyn. Arcadian House. Columbus, OH. P1/ 614-451-5479. C1/ 614-537-3229. lyn@arcadianhouse.com. Established: 1998.

SKILLS: freelance editor, independent book editor, copyeditor or line editor, proofreader, ghostwriter, business writer or copywriter, technical writer, electronic edit and proof, desktop publishing, prepress, Spanish translation. **MARKETS SERVED:** business, publishing, independent authors.

SPECIALTIES AND PREFERENCES: prepress solutions for independent authors—folktales, storytelling, cultural stories, personal histories. Full range of writing and editing services.

FICTION—ACCEPTS: y/a or juvenile, short stories, novels, scripts/screenplays, queries, synopses. **NONFICTION—ACCEPTS:** all. **TYPICAL EVALUATION/REPORT:** 2–10 pages.

FEES/TERMS/CONTRACTS: $40+/hour. Proofing $2.00–$3.50/page. Job prices available. Hourly payable biweekly. Per job in 2–4 installments. Agreement or contract. No credit cards.

ACCOMPLISHMENTS: two self-published novels. Many articles in regional and national magazines.

EDUCATION: BA English Education, Heidelberg College, Tiffin OH. **MEMBERSHIPS:** American Business Women's Association. The Writer Online Community. AmSpirit Business Connections. Storytellers of Central Ohio. Novels in Progress.

CLIENTS WITHIN PRIOR YEAR: 6–12.

96	EDITOR	WRITER	CONSULTANT	F	NF

Chance, Lori. Destination—Words. Portland, OR. P1/ 503-866-9509. LoriChance@TeleStream.com. Established: 2004.

SKILLS: ghostwriter, business writer or copywriter, literary consultant, writing coach. **MARKETS SERVED:** coaches, speakers, trainers, consultants, as well as individuals creating memoirs.

SPECIALTIES AND PREFERENCES: I help people put words to stories that have helped shape their lives so that they can share the lessons learned with others.

FICTION—ACCEPTS: y/a or juvenile, short stories, novels (genre, mainstream, literary, contemporary, historical). **NONFICTION—ACCEPTS:** y/a or juvenile, articles/features, essays, memoirs, creative or narrative, biography/autobiography, family history, self-help, how-to/instruction, business, humor, inspirational/religious, spiritual. **TYPICAL EVALUATION/REPORT:** depends on length of piece being evaluated. The longer the piece, the longer the report, typically.

Fees/terms/contracts: per contract, retainer required to start. Payment accepted by check, money order, Visa or MasterCard.

Education: BA English Literature, Certificate in Women's Studies, Portland State University, OR. Two years of Psychology and Criminology at Southern Oregon State University, Ashland. Continuous classes and self-study of business, marketing, writing, coaching, and teaching of adults. **Memberships:** Business Network International.

Clients within prior year: 15–20.

97	EDITOR	WRITER	CONSULTANT	F	NF

Chapman, Vicky. Victoria Chapman & Associates, Inc. Brooklyn, NY. P1/ 718-499-1445. vlchapman@nyc.rr.com. Established: 1992.

Skills: freelance editor, ghostwriter; develop and package books and magazines. **Markets served:** copywriter for trade and text publishers, nonprofits, educational institutions.

Specialties and preferences: book packaging and magazine development focused on nonfiction for ages 8–18. We write, edit, and package products for library, trade, or classroom use.

Nonfiction—accepts: y/a or juvenile, articles/features, essays, how-to/instruction, text or reference. **Typical evaluation/report:** When consulting for a client, report depends on nature of assignment and need.

Fees/terms/contracts: uses contract. Material in works we develop for publishers and nonprofit groups is prepared by assignment only (no blind submissions).

Accomplishments: twenty-five years at Scholastic. Author of hundreds—even thousands—of magazine articles for youngsters. Editor, editorial director, editor-in-chief producing children's materials in social studies, math, science, reading, health, career and college education, more. Principal investigator for Natural Science Fondation science magazine project. Packager of reference books (Latin American history, science, health). Research markets, develop and launch children's magazines.

Education: BA English Literature, Hamline University, St. Paul, MN.

Clients within prior year: 1–5.

98	EDITOR	WRITER	CONSULTANT	F	NF

Chapple, Beth. Lake Forest Park, WA. P1/ 206-417-2861. F1/ 206-417-2861. bchapple@dellby.com. www.dellby.com/chapple.htm. Established: 1990.

Skills: freelance editor, copyeditor or line editor, proofreader, web designer. **Markets served:** writers, publishers, book packagers, software companies.

Specialties and preferences: academic writing, including scientific and business journal articles, theses, scholarly books, textbooks, travel, web writing. Specializes in editing works by non-native speakers of English and translated works. Attentive to the writer's voice. Proofreads thoroughly in German and Spanish as well as English.

FICTION—ACCEPTS: y/a or juvenile, short stories. **NONFICTION—ACCEPTS:** articles/ features, memoirs, creative or narrative, how-to/instruction, technical, text or reference, business, book proposals. **TYPICAL EVALUATION/REPORT:** 2 pages.

FEES/TERMS/CONTRACTS: $25–$45/hour, with substantive editing at the high end. Accepts credit cards, checks, ProPay. Typically uses agreement.

ACCOMPLISHMENTS: *ForeWord Magazine*'s 2002 Book of the Year Gold Award for self-published book I edited. Brown University Book Award for superior English expression.

EDUCATION: MS Technical Communication, University of Washington, Seattle. BA German Studies, Stanford University, CA. Senior year abroad in Berlin. Media Alliance (San Francisco) course in copyediting. **MEMBERSHIPS:** Northwest Independent Editors Guild.

CLIENTS WITHIN PRIOR YEAR: 11–20.

99	EDITOR	WRITER	CONSULTANT	F	NF

Chase, Lisa. The Editor's Room, LLC. 46 Stuyvesant Ave., Larchmont, NY 10538. lisa@editorsroom.net. www.booknoise.net. Established: 2000.

SKILLS: freelance editor, book doctor, ghostwriter. **MARKETS SERVED:** publishers and individuals.

SPECIALTIES AND PREFERENCES: I run an editorial consulting and editing service with my partner, Laura Hohnhold. We also created Booknoise.net (www. booknoise.net), which builds websites for good books.

NONFICTION—ACCEPTS: articles/features, essays, memoirs, creative or narrative, biography/autobiography, family history, how-to/instruction, book proposals, queries.

FEES/TERMS/CONTRACTS: varies by project. Requires half up front, half upon project completion. Does not use contract.

ACCOMPLISHMENTS: many clients' published books. Former senior editor for *Outside* magazine, senior editor for *Premiere* magazine, deputy editor for *The New York Observer*, features editor for *Talk* magazine.

EDUCATION: BS Journalism, Northwestern University, Evanston, IL.

CLIENTS WITHIN PRIOR YEAR: 6–10.

100	EDITOR	WRITER	CONSULTANT	F	NF

Cheatham, Karyn. Helena, MT. P1/ 406-458-0131. aqk@kaios.com.

www.kaios.com/karyn/litserv.htm. **Established: 1994.**

SKILLS: freelance editor, independent book editor, proofreader, business writer or copywriter, literary consultant, writing instructor, web design and copy. MARKETS SERVED: writers, publishers.

SPECIALTIES AND PREFERENCES: I offer candid input to improve a final product for authors and publishers. During twenty-five years in writing, editing, and critiquing, I have developed a good eye and ear, no matter the subject. My background and interests are eclectic, but very strong in 19th-century history.

FICTION—ACCEPTS: y/a or juvenile, novels (genre, mainstream, historical), queries, synopses. NONFICTION—ACCEPTS: all. TYPICAL EVALUATION/REPORT: 5–20 pages.

FEES/TERMS/CONTRACTS: manuscript evaluation $75–$200. Editing $15/hour. Advance $45. Rewrites $450–$600, half up front. PayPal. Uses agreement.

ACCOMPLISHMENTS: five y/a fiction and nonfiction books, three historical fiction, one science fiction. Numerous articles in newspapers and national magazines, poems in national publications and anthologies. Finalist for a 1998 SPUR Award.

EDUCATION: English, History, Spanish, Ohio State University, Columbus. MEMBERSHIPS: Western Writers of America. Broad Universe.

CLIENTS WITHIN PRIOR YEAR: 6–10.

101	EDITOR	WRITER	CONSULTANT	F	NF

Chernauskas, Susan. Susan's Homeworks. 111 E. 14th St., Georgetown, IL 61846. P1/ 217-662-2743. jvcskc@yahoo.com. **Established: 1999.**

SKILLS: freelance editor, independent book editor, copyeditor or line editor, proofreader. MARKETS SERVED: publishing companies of both fiction and nonfiction.

SPECIALTIES AND PREFERENCES: I take written text either from books, articles, or short stories and put them on disk or CD. No project is too big or too small. I love horror and science fiction but would work on anything. I love to read and so I love to type and enjoy working with many different publishers, both large and small.

FICTION—ACCEPTS: including short stories, novels (genre, mainstream, literary, contemporary, historical), poetry, scripts/screenplays, queries, synopses, treatments. NONFICTION—ACCEPTS: all.

FEES/TERMS/CONTRACTS: I usually charge $2/page. Will work with client if it is a big project. I am very flexible. No credit cards. I do accept personal, company checks, money orders, and PayPal.

ACCOMPLISHMENTS: I have typed data from many venues and publishers and put the manuscripts on disk or CD.

EDUCATION: two years of college—secretarial classes and basic computer classes. CLIENTS WITHIN PRIOR YEAR: 1–5.

102	EDITOR	WRITER	CONSULTANT	F	NF

Childs, Marti. EditPros. 423 F St., Ste. 206, Davis, CA 95616-4144. P1/ 530-759-2000. www.editpros.com. (E-mail contact through website.) Established: 1993.

SKILLS: freelance editor, copyeditor or line editor, proofreader, ghostwriter. MARKETS SERVED: EditPros clientele includes government agencies, trade associations, academic institutions, financial institutions, research agencies, and publishers.

SPECIALTIES AND PREFERENCES: newsletters, brochures, annual reports, trade articles, academic books, website content. We correct errors in grammar or syntax, develop a consistent editorial voice, and crystallize and clarify our clients' messages. We're proficient in distilling complex material into more accessible form.

FICTION—ACCEPTS: all. NONFICTION—ACCEPTS: all.

FEES/TERMS/CONTRACTS: we charge on a per-project basis.

ACCOMPLISHMENTS: coauthor of a nonfiction book on the sixties published by Billboard Books. She has been writing and editing professionally for the past twenty years.

EDUCATION: four years of education in English and graphic design from Sacramento City College and University of California, Davis, Extension.

CLIENTS WITHIN PRIOR YEAR: 11–20.

103	EDITOR	WRITER	CONSULTANT	F	NF

Christmas, Bobbie. Zebra Communications. 230 Deerchase Dr., Suite B, Woodstock, GA 30188-4438. P1/ 770-924-0528. C1/ 404-433-7507. F1/ 770-592-7362. info@zebraeditor.com. www.zebraeditor.com. Established: 1992.

SKILLS: freelance editor, independent book editor, book doctor, copyeditor or line editor, proofreader, ghostwriter, business writer or copywriter, literary consultant, writing coach, writing instructor. MARKETS SERVED: individuals, publishers, and agents.

SPECIALTIES AND PREFERENCES: someone eager to learn and improve. I am a generalist. I act not only as editor, but also as mentor to my clients. No romance novels.

FICTION—ACCEPTS: all. NONFICTION—ACCEPTS: all. TYPICAL EVALUATION/REPORT: 20–60 pages. Electronic transmissions do not include report.

FEES/TERMS/CONTRACTS: editing manuscripts $2.50–$4.15/page. Estimates provided for rewriting, ghosting, organization of manuscript, cover or query letter, submissions.

ACCOMPLISHMENTS: writer and/or editor since 1972. Three books, two on writing with Union Square Publishing, one children's; columns, on creative writing. Ghostwritten large portions of books. Many brochures, commercials,

advertisements, press releases, profiles, and other business items. Expert Editor—FictionAddiction.NET, 2003. Awards for nonfiction 1989–2001.
EDUCATION: Journalism, University of South Carolina, Columbia. Seminars—writing, editing, and communications. **MEMBERSHIPS:** Georgia Writers. The Writers Network. International. Guild of Professional Consultants. The Society for the Preservation of English and Literature. Florida Writers Association. South Carolina Writers Workshop.
CLIENTS WITHIN PRIOR YEAR: over 60.

104	EDITOR	WRITER	CONSULTANT	F	NF

Clarke, Barbara. WindSwept Works. 22085 Mayfield Rd., Sand Springs, OK 74063. P1/ 918-242-3838. C1/ 918-519-7171. F1/ 918-242-3125. windsweptwks@earthlink.net. Established: 1995.

SKILLS: freelance editor, independent book editor, book doctor, copyeditor or line editor, proofreader, ghostwriter, business writer or copywriter, technical writer, literary consult, writing coach, writing instructor. **MARKETS SERVED:** writers, publishers, editors, graphic designers, advertising agencies, corporations.
SPECIALTIES AND PREFERENCES: I enjoy all types of writing and welcome new challenges. I do not enjoy science fiction. My business includes writing, re-writing, proofreading, editing, keying corrections, and consulting with writers.
FICTION—ACCEPTS: all. **NONFICTION—ACCEPTS:** all. **TYPICAL EVALUATION/REPORT:** depends on client's needs and genre.
FEES/TERMS/CONTRACTS: proofreading $2–$4/page. Editing $3–$6/page. Creative copywriting $50–$65/hour. Editing $40/hour. Word processing and keying corrections also available. One-half estimated charge up front. Net ten days. Contracts available.
EDUCATION: MA Journalism/Mass Communications, Oklahoma University, Norman. MA Modern Letters, University of Tulsa, OK. BA English/Journalism, University of Tulsa, OK.
CLIENTS WITHIN PRIOR YEAR: 11–20.

105	EDITOR	WRITER	CONSULTANT	F	NF

Coburn, Broughton. PO Box 1022, Wilson, WY 83014. P1/ 307-733-4124. C1/ 307-690-7574. bcoburn@wyoming.com. www.unusualspeaker.com. Established: 1997.

SKILLS: freelance editor, independent book editor, book doctor, ghostwriter, writing instructor. **MARKETS SERVED:** writers, nonwriters, publishers, celebrities.
SPECIALTIES AND PREFERENCES: Economically, quickly, and on short notice, I edit and help develop nonfiction manuscripts and ideas into salable written

products. One of my collaborations, *Touching My Father's Soul* (Harper-SanFrancisco), a national bestseller, began with a concept.

NONFICTION—ACCEPTS: y/a or juvenile, articles/features, essays, memoirs, creative or narrative, biography/autobiography, humor, inspirational/religious, spiritual, book proposals, queries. **TYPICAL EVALUATION/REPORT:** 2–10 pages.

FEES/TERMS/CONTRACTS: $40/hour or $10/manuscript page. No credit cards.

ACCOMPLISHMENTS: two nonfiction trade books published in multiple editions and languages. One bestselling large-format trade book, a bestselling collaboration, and a y/a photobiography. Several articles published in national magazines. Several national awards.

EDUCATION: BA Social Relations, Harvard University, Cambridge, MA. **MEMBERSHIPS:** faculty, Jackson Hole Writers Conference.

106	EDITOR	**WRITER**	CONSULTANT	F	**NF**

Cochran, Ann. 6718 Tomlinson Terrace, Cabin John, MD 20818. P1/ 301-229-2114. F1/ 301-229-2115. appliedcommunications@comcast.net. Established: 1994.

SKILLS: ghostwriter, business writer. **MARKETS SERVED:** high income, highly educated.

SPECIALTIES AND PREFERENCES: For the National Institutes of Health and for Kaiser Permanente, I do various types of projects including ghostwritten articles, newsletters, speeches, and brochures. I have also prepared congressional testimony.

NONFICTION—ACCEPTS: articles/features, book proposals, queries. Other newsletters, brochures, speeches.

FEES/TERMS/CONTRACTS: $75/hour or an agreed-upon project price based on an estimate of hours. Uses a mutually satisfactory pay schedule with new clients, usually starting with a small part of the job to test the working relationship. No credit cards.

ACCOMPLISHMENTS: many published articles with magazines such as *Washingtonian Magazine, Your Stepfamily, Washington Golf Monthly, TravelAmerica, Virginia Living,* and others. Extensive ghostwriting of company internal communications, including work with the White House as a volunteer in the Social Office during the last two years of the Clinton administration and in Mary Matalin and Vice President Cheney's offices during the beginning of the Bush administration.

EDUCATION: college graduate, paralegal training, writing courses. **MEMBERSHIPS:** Washington Independent Writers.

CLIENTS WITHIN PRIOR YEAR: 6–10.

107	EDITOR	WRITER	CONSULTANT	F	NF

Cohen, Robert. Sterling Media Productions LLC. Fresh Meadows, NY. P1/ 718-595-2082. P2/ 866-EDITING. wordsmith@sterlingmp.com. www.sterlingmp.com. Established: editing since 1978; company founded in 2002.

SKILLS: freelance editor, copyeditor or line editor, book doctor, proofreader, business writer or copywriter, writing coach, writing instructor, speechwriter; lexicographer; radio scriptwriter. MARKETS SERVED: individual authors, academic and trade book publishers, nonprofit organizations, educational institutions, businesses, and corporations.

SPECIALTIES AND PREFERENCES: specializes in books, monographs, and newsletters; academic and trade publishers; authors, especially academics; biographers, memoirists. Subjects include international relations, urban affairs, social sciences, psychology, education, communications, reference books, Judaica, music, media.

NONFICTION—ACCEPTS: biography/autobiography.

FEES/TERMS/CONTRACTS: $25–$50/hour and up, or negotiated project fee.

ACCOMPLISHMENTS: American Jewish Press Association Rockower Award. Thirty articles in newspapers/magazines; documentary on National Public Radio.

EDUCATION: BA Arts & Sciences, Cornell University, Ithaca, NY, and Empire State College, State University of New York, New York City.

CLIENTS WITHIN PRIOR YEAR: 6–10.

108	EDITOR	WRITER	CONSULTANT	F	NF

Cole, Mary. WordQueen. San Antonio, TX. P1/ 210-545-1172. P2/ 800-421-1969, x00. F1/ 210-545-1172. WordQueen@Earthlink.net. www.WordQueen.net/home. Established: 2000.

SKILLS: freelance editor, independent book editor, book doctor, copyeditor or line editor, proofreader, ghostwriter, business writer or copywriter, technical writer, literary consultant, writer instructor, corporate trainer, desktop publisher, advertising copywriter. MARKETS SERVED: corporate, individual, international.

SPECIALTIES AND PREFERENCES: writes and edits for businesses and corporations that need clear, business-like writing with minimal jargon. Highly skilled in writing creative marketing copy.

FICTION—ACCEPTS: all. NONFICTION—ACCEPTS: all. TYPICAL EVALUATION/REPORT: written evaluation/report. I never use stock explanations or templates.

FEES/TERMS/CONTRACTS: $65/hour or 4 cents/word for proofreading, 2–18 cents/word for editing, 40 cents/word for writing. Half on acceptance; half on completion. MasterCard, Visa, personal checks.

ACCOMPLISHMENTS: 200+ articles, reviews, interviews, and character sketches in national publications. Two novels. First screenplay competition awards. Many marketing pieces.

EDUCATION: MBA Marketing, University of Texas, San Antonio. MA English, West Chester University, PA. BA English and History, University of Texas, Austin. **MEMBERSHIPS:** National Writers Association.

CLIENTS WITHIN PRIOR YEAR: 20–25.

109	EDITOR	WRITER	CONSULTANT	F	NF

Collins, Zipporah. Editcetera. 768 Peralta Ave., Berkeley, CA 94707. P1/ 510-527-2140. F1/ 510-527-4155. zipporahcol@aol.com. Established: 1971.

SKILLS: freelance editor, independent book editor, copyeditor or line editor, proofreader, desktop publishing, book designer, book project manager. **MARKETS SERVED:** trade publishers, textbook publishers, individual authors, institutions, businesses.

SPECIALTIES AND PREFERENCES: copyediting and substantive editing of book manuscripts in the fields of art, biography, cookbooks, current affairs/politics, dance, ecology, education, English, law, medicine, music, photography, psychology, women's studies.

FICTION—ACCEPTS: y/a or juvenile, short stories, novels (mainstream, literary, contemporary, historical), poetry. **NONFICTION—ACCEPTS:** y/a or juvenile, essays, creative or narrative, self-help, how-to/instruction, text or reference, business, humor.

FEES/TERMS/CONTRACTS: copyediting $35–$45/hour. Substantive editing $45–$60/hour. Accepts credit cards but prefers checks. Uses contract.

ACCOMPLISHMENTS: Bookbuilders West Book Show, two awards for project management; judge of annual show, 1995. Client publications with Sunset Books, McGraw-Hill, and others. Started in publishing right out of college, at Macmillan Company in New York.

EDUCATION: BA English and French, *magna cum laude*, highest honors, William Smith College, Geneva, NY. **MEMBERSHIPS:** Editcetera. Bookbuilders West. Women's National Book Association. Bay Area Editors' Forum.

CLIENTS WITHIN PRIOR YEAR: 5–10.

110	EDITOR	WRITER	CONSULTANT	F	NF

Conley, Robyn. Robyn Conley Book Doctor and Workshop Leader. PO Box 506, Clyde, TX 79510. P1/ 325-854-1326. bookdoctor@earthlink.net. www.robynconley.com. Established: 1990.

SKILLS: freelance editor, independent book editor, book doctor, copyeditor or line editor, proofreader, ghostwriter, business writer or copywriter, literary consultant, writing coach, writing instructor. **MARKETS SERVED:** agents, publishing houses, independent writers.

SPECIALTIES AND PREFERENCES: nonfiction. Enjoys working with individuals in any capacity.

FICTION—ACCEPTS: all. **NONFICTION—ACCEPTS:** all. **TYPICAL EVALUATION/REPORT:** will receive a critique on all major aspects as well as hands-online editing and revision suggestions.

FEES/TERMS/CONTRACTS: $4/page. $75 for synopses up to ten pages. $25 for query/cover letters.

ACCOMPLISHMENTS: authored ten published books, including a guided journal for Writer's Digest Books, as well as numerous nonfiction informative juvenile books—two for the new invention line for Scholastic's middle school readers. Dozens of published clients who have used my editing/book doctor services. Taught editing/writing workshops around the country for major writing conferences, as well as at Texas Christian University in the continuing education department. Began and led a critique group in Fort Worth for ten years.

MEMBERSHIPS: Society of Southwest Authors. Oklahoma Writers Federation Inc. Freelance Writers Network.

CLIENTS WITHIN PRIOR YEAR: 10–15.

111	EDITOR	WRITER	CONSULTANT	F	NF

Conner, Wendy. Impromptu Creative Services. PO Box 67026, Los Angeles, CA 90067. P1/ 310-247-8154. mpromp2@aol.com. Established: 1984.

SKILLS: freelance editor, independent book editor, book doctor, copyeditor or line editor, proofreader, ghostwriter, business writer or copywriter, technical writer, literary consultant, writing coach, writing instructor, graphic design/ typography consultant. **MARKETS SERVED:** publishers, retail, advertising, film industry, wholesalers, and more.

SPECIALTIES AND PREFERENCES: screenplays, fiction, nonfiction, how-to, arts and crafts, children's books, copywriting, proofreading, press kits, promotional materials, ad campaigns, graphic design, illustration, business plan consulting, trade show consulting, and more. We prefer to work intimately with fewer clients to give the best service.

FICTION—ACCEPTS: all. **NONFICTION—ACCEPTS:** all. **TYPICAL EVALUATION/REPORT:** meets client's needs.

FEES/TERMS/CONTRACTS: hourly, retainer, flat fee; please inquire what will be most cost-effective for your needs.

ACCOMPLISHMENTS: fourteen published books; two award-winning documentaries (one Oscar qualifier); produced playwright; six screenplays; one television show optioned.

EDUCATION: BA Visual Media, California State, Long Beach. **MEMBERSHIPS:**

Association of Los Angeles Playwrights. Women in Film. Screenwriter's Network.

CLIENTS WITHIN PRIOR YEAR: not available.

112	EDITOR	WRITER	CONSULTANT	F	NF

Connor, Charles. Harriette Austin Writers. PMB 570, 2351 College Station Rd., Athens, GA 30605-3664. P1/ 706-743-3810. cconnor@coe.uga.edu. Established: 1994.

SKILLS: freelance editor, writing coach. **MARKETS SERVED:** aspiring and established writers who need a professional editorial eye.

SPECIALTIES AND PREFERENCES: story edits, copyedits, critiques, synopses, query letters, and editorial.

FICTION—ACCEPTS: short stories, novels (genre, mainstream, literary, contemporary, historical), queries, synopses. **NONFICTION—ACCEPTS:** articles/ features, essays, memoirs, creative or narrative, how-to/instruction. **TYPICAL EVALUATION/REPORT:** 5–8 pages.

FEES/TERMS/CONTRACTS: based on the condition of the manuscript. Flat rate for query letters and synopses. Requires prepayment for small jobs. Split payment for large jobs. Permits payment schedules. Accepts PayPal and checks.

ACCOMPLISHMENTS: Director of the Harriette Austin Writing Program at the University of Georgia since 1993. The Harriette Austin Writers Conference and the Elements of Fiction writing workshops on the Internet at http://webhawc.home.att.net/. **EDUCATION:** EdD Instructional Design and Development, University of Georgia, Athens.

CLIENTS WITHIN PRIOR YEAR: 11–20.

113	EDITOR	WRITER	CONSULTANT	F	NF

Cook, Christine M. Write Edit Design. 014 NE 61st St., Seattle, WA 98115. P1/ 206-779-9188. cook@gizzard.org. www.writeeditdesign.com. Established: 1999.

SKILLS: freelance editor, business writer or copywriter, writing coach, writing instructor, project manager, creative director. **MARKETS SERVED:** entrepreneurs, corporations.

SPECIALTIES AND PREFERENCES: develops business/product identity, branding, and messaging that effectively speak to audience/market. Teaches clients to strengthen story writing, business proposals, and public speaking.

NONFICTION—ACCEPTS: articles, essays, spiritual, self-help, how-to, business, marketing, public relations. **TYPICAL EVALUATION/REPORT:** 2–10 pages.

FEES/TERMS/CONTRACTS: $70–$100/hour. PayPal. No credit cards. Contracts.

ACCOMPLISHMENTS: published regional, international. Founder, Northwest Independent Teachers Guild, The Women's Alliance for Entrepreneurs. Dozens of clients who've found their magic and become more successful. EDUCATION: BA English and studied journalism, University of California, Berkeley. Studied with Chief Copy Editor, *San Francisco Examiner*. Studied graphic/web design and programming in Seattle, WA. MEMBERSHIPS: Northwest Independent Editors Guild. Seattle Writers. Women in Digital Journalism. Society of Professional Journalists. Northwest Independent Teachers Guild. Washington Lawyers for the Arts.
CLIENTS WITHIN PRIOR YEAR: 1–5 corporate. 100+ students, coaching clients.

114	EDITOR	WRITER	CONSULTANT	F	NF

Cooper, Kim. Scram. PO Box 461626, Hollywood, CA 90046-1626. P1/ 323-223-2767. scram@scrammagazine.com. Established: 1992.

SKILLS: freelance editor, independent book editor, book doctor, copyeditor or line editor, proofreader, ghostwriter, business writer or copywriter, literary consultant, writing coach, publicist. MARKETS SERVED: writers, someone with an interesting project in the areas of pop culture, music, film, offbeat memoirs, history, true crime, cookbooks.
SPECIALTIES AND PREFERENCES: I specialize in pop culture, music, nonfiction narratives, press releases, and humor.
FICTION—ACCEPTS: picture books. NONFICTION—ACCEPTS: y/a or juvenile, articles/features, essays, memoirs, creative or narrative, biography/autobiography, family history, self-help, how-to/instruction, technical, text or reference, business, humor, book proposals, queries.
FEES/TERMS/CONTRACTS: Fees vary. Uses contract.
ACCOMPLISHMENTS: edited two music history anthologies, one optioned as a VH-1 special. Published and edited magazine named "best of LA" by *LA Weekly*.
EDUCATION: MA Art History, University of California, Santa Barbara. BA Art History/History, University of California, Santa Cruz. MEMBERSHIPS: Los Angeles Cacophony Society.
CLIENTS WITHIN PRIOR YEAR: 11–20.

115	EDITOR	WRITER	CONSULTANT	F	NF

Coster, Barbara. Cross-t.i Copyediting/Proofreading. Santa Barbara, CA 93111. P1/ 805-967-4936. C1/ 805-698-5944. F1/ 805-964-6398. bcoster@silcom.com. Established: 1998.

SKILLS: freelance editor, independent book editor, copyeditor or line editor, proofreader. MARKETS SERVED: writers, publishers, nonprofit organizations, corporations, academic publishers.

SPECIALTIES AND PREFERENCES: copyeditor/proofreader for thirty years of scholarly and nonfiction books in philosophy, religion, social sciences, and self-help, journals, almanacs, catalogues. Also transliterations (with diacritics) from Pali and Sanskrit.

NONFICTION—ACCEPTS: all.

FEES/TERMS/CONTRACTS: $35–$45/hour; 50 percent of estimate up front. Textbook publishers pay by the page; university presses and private clients pay by the hour. Uses contract with self-publishers.

EDUCATION: Zoology, Carnegie Mellon University, Pittsburgh, PA. Zoology, San Francisco State College, CA. Continuing education courses in copyediting, proofreading, law office management, Spanish language, philosophy, business, and political science from the University of California at Berkeley Extension (Center for Media and Independent Learning), University of California at Santa Barbara Extension, Santa Barbara City College Adult Education, and Harvard College Extension. Legal secretary for nineteen years to senior partners in a fast-paced civil litigation law firm. **MEMBERSHIPS:** Media Alliance. Copyediting-L Listserv. National Federation of Press Women.

CLIENTS WITHIN PRIOR YEAR: over 24.

116	EDITOR	WRITER	CONSULTANT	F	NF

Craig, Carol. The Editing Gallery LLC. 2622 Willona Dr., Eugene, OR 97408. P1/ 541-342-7300. carollcraig@cs.com. www.editinggallery.com. Established: 2002.

SKILLS: freelance editor, independent book editor, book doctor, copyeditor or line editor, proofreader, ghostwriter, literary consultant, writing coach. **MARKETS SERVED:** writers, publishers, businesses, agents.

SPECIALTIES AND PREFERENCES: literary and women's fiction. Multicultural fiction, Christian romance, romance, y/a, juvenile, children's fiction, mainstream. Several clients have agents.

FICTION—ACCEPTS: y/a or juvenile, short stories, novels (genre, mainstream, literary, contemporary, historical), queries, synopses. **TYPICAL EVALUATION/ REPORT:** 40–60 pages. I prefer online editing where I insert comments and feedback, ending with an e-mailed evaluation for each chapter. I also edit hard copy.

FEES/TERMS/CONTRACTS: current fees at www.editinggallery.com. Visa. MasterCard. Uses contracts.

ACCOMPLISHMENTS: My accomplishments are my client successes. New author Nikki Arana garnered a three-book deal with Bethany House. Shanna Murchison has an option for a paranormal romance series and several historical romance series under the name Shannon Farrell. Leigh Greenwoods is known for his historical romances.

EDUCATION: English major, University of Oregon, Eugene. MEMBERSHIPS: Women Writing the West. Romance Writers of America. Willamette Writers. Christian Writers of America.

CLIENTS WITHIN PRIOR YEAR: 25–30. For a full listing of my successes, go to www.editinggallery.com.

117	EDITOR	WRITER	CONSULTANT	F	NF

Cron, Lisa. Inside Story Ink. Santa Monica, CA. Lisa@Inside-Story-Ink.com. Established: 1993.

SKILLS: freelance editor, independent book editor, book doctor, ghostwriter, literary consultant, writing coach, writing instructor. MARKETS SERVED: novelists, nonfiction writers, screenwriters, producers, production companies, studios, agents, publishers.

SPECIALTIES AND PREFERENCES: I identify how much of the story you're telling is actually on the page, pinpoint the problems, offer specific story solutions and advice on how to avoid making the same mistakes again. I often work with writers on a continuing basis, brainstorming everything from plot to character arcs to pacing.

FICTION—ACCEPTS: all. NONFICTION—ACCEPTS: all. TYPICAL EVALUATION/REPORT: 4–8 pages, or 15–25 pages, both single spaced.

FEES/TERMS/CONTRACTS: $495 for in-depth, page-by-page analysis; $300 for the short version. Fees are for up to 320 pages, manuscript; 125 pages, screenplay; $1 per page beyond that. Both include a one-hour phone consultation. $65/hour for ongoing consultation. Payment in advance. No credit cards. Accepts PayPal and personal checks.

ACCOMPLISHMENTS: articles in national magazines, three screenplays optioned, two kids raised, passionately love what I do.

EDUCATION: BA Field Studies in Humanities, University of California, Berkeley. MEMBERSHIPS: Women's Entertainment Network. Independent Features Project.

CLIENTS WITHIN PRIOR YEAR: 11–20.

118	EDITOR	WRITER	CONSULTANT	F	NF

Cummens, Linda. Biz Oregon. 3415 Timberline Dr., Eugene, OR 97405. P1/ 541-431-1101. F1/ 541-431-1107. bizoregon@qwest.net. Established: 1998.

SKILLS: ghostwriter, business writer or copywriter, literary consultant, writing coach, writing instructor, lecturer/coach on children's poetry and am a storyteller in schools. MARKETS SERVED: nonprofits, schools.

SPECIALTIES AND PREFERENCES: grant proposal writer for over twenty years earning thousands of dollars for arts organizations and nonprofits. Writer for alternative healing. Lists available. Writes and illustrates comic workbooks for kids; history books, others.

NONFICTION—ACCEPTS: how-to/instruction, business, humor, inspirational/religious, spiritual. Environmental: tree/river preservation. **TYPICAL EVALUATION/REPORT:** 2 pages.

FEES/TERMS/CONTRACTS: negotiable.

ACCOMPLISHMENTS: edited philosophy books by Dr. James A. Diefenbeck. Wrote copy and edited math workbooks for CEMREL. Edited and illustrated a history book, and many brochures and workbooks. Wrote court summaries, news articles, and briefs. Many national awards for illustrations. Several poems published.

EDUCATION: MFA Southern Illinois University, Carbondale. BFA Illinois Wesleyan University, Bloomington. Phi Kappa Phi for both degrees. **MEMBERSHIPS:** Sisters in Crime. Willamette Writers. AAUW Lifetime. Red Moon Writers. Eugene Story Tellers.

CLIENTS WITHIN PRIOR YEAR: 1–5.

119	EDITOR	WRITER	CONSULTANT	F	NF

Cunningham, Dave. Neo Communicating. 17744 Skypark Circle, #290, Irvine, CA 92614. P1/ 949-715-1988. neocommunicating@cox.net. www.neocommunicating.com. Established: 1987.

SKILLS: freelance editor, independent book editor, book doctor, copyeditor, proofreader, ghostwriter, business writer or copywriter, literary consultant, writer coach, speech coach/writer, publicist, PR/media relations specialist. **MARKETS SERVED:** individuals, businesses, executives.

SPECIALTIES AND PREFERENCES: I make you look good, sound good, and feel good about yourself and your business. Writes speeches, provides public relations and media relations services, or writes and edits materials and Internet content.

FICTION—ACCEPTS: novels (genre, mainstream, contemporary), queries, synopses, treatments. **NONFICTION—ACCEPTS:** articles/features, how-to/instruction, text or reference, business, inspirational/religious, spiritual, book proposals, queries. **TYPICAL EVALUATION/REPORT:** as long as is necessary.

FEES/TERMS/CONTRACTS: book projects—negotiated fee. Smaller projects—$40–$100.

ACCOMPLISHMENTS: winner of six national and regional writing awards. Published author—one novel, two anthologies—and longtime newspaper and magazine journalist, published coast to coast in hundreds of large, general circulation publications.

EDUCATION: studied communications, University of California, Los Angeles. Journalism, LA Harbor College. **MEMBERSHIPS:** CA Writers Club. Professional

Communications Exchange. Baseball Writers Association of America. US Ski Writers Association.

CLIENTS WITHIN PRIOR YEAR: 11–20.

120	EDITOR	WRITER	CONSULTANT	F	NF

Curtis, Cathy. textual. Los Angeles, CA. P1/ 323-660-4845. cctextual@earthlink.net. www.textualthelastword.com. Established: 1999.

SKILLS: freelance editor, business writer or copywriter. **MARKETS SERVED:** copywriting for business and nonprofits, midsized or large companies, public utilities.**SPECIALTIES AND PREFERENCES:** vivid, intelligent writing including ads, brochures and collateral, newsletters, press releases, manuals and reports, web content—both consumer oriented and business to business. Also rewriting and structural editing. As a former newspaper staff writer, I'm able to get up to speed quickly in a new subject, and I have years of experience interviewing and writing on tight deadlines. I deliver lively yet focused copy that communicates clearly to today's impatient consumer.

NONFICTION—ACCEPTS: articles/features, how-to/instruction, business.

FEES/TERMS/CONTRACTS: Fees vary. 50 percent up front, remainder on client approval. Uses contract.

ACCOMPLISHMENTS: staff writer for eleven years at *Los Angeles Times*. Editor and publicist, University Art Museum, Berkeley.

EDUCATION: MA Art History, University of California, Berkeley. BA Philosophy, Smith College, Northampton, MA. **MEMBERSHIPS:** Editorial Freelancers Association. American Institute of Graphic Artists.

CLIENTS WITHIN PRIOR YEAR: 6–10.

121	EDITOR	WRITER	CONSULTANT	F	NF

Cypher, Sarah. The Threepenny Editor. 2934 SE Alder St., Apt #17, Portland, OR 97214. P1/ 503-335-1458. sarah@threepennyeditor.com. www.threepennyeditor.com. Established: 2003.

SKILLS: independent book editor, literary consultant, writing coach, cover design, book layout, prepress services. **MARKETS SERVED:** fiction and nonfiction writers. Self-publishing or print on demand (POD) as well as traditional markets.

SPECIALTIES AND PREFERENCES: literary fiction and nonfiction. Helping writers start their careers through intensive, constructive editing that focuses on development of character, structure, theme, plot, and strong prose.

FICTION—ACCEPTS: short stories, novels (genre, mainstream, literary, contemporary, historical), queries, synopses. **NONFICTION—ACCEPTS:** all. **TYPICAL EVALUATION/REPORT:** critiques 2,500–5,000 words.

FEES/TERMS/CONTRACTS: $3–$4/page for substantive editing projects, including critique. $200/month for writing coaching. Cover design quoted on a per-project basis. Accepts checks, money order, PayPal. Uses contract.

ACCOMPLISHMENTS: clients' book successes include consideration for film rights, agent representation, CNN attention.

EDUCATION: BA Creative Writing, Phi Beta Kappa, Carnegie Mellon University, Pittsburgh, PA. Attended the 2001 Irish Writing Program at Trinity College, Dublin, sponsored by Iowa University. **MEMBERSHIPS:** Northwest Independent Editors Guild.

CLIENTS WITHIN PRIOR YEAR: 35–40.

122	EDITOR	WRITER	CONSULTANT	F	NF

DallaCosta, Teri. TechniComm Corp. 2373 NW 185th Ave., PMB 700, Hillsboro, OR 97124. P1/ 503-356-1495. F1/ 503-430-5582. info@technicommnet.com. teri@technicommnet.com. www.technicommnet.com. Established: 1997.

SKILLS: freelance editor, independent book editor, technical editor, copyeditor or line editor, proofreader, business writer or copywriter, technical writer. **MARKETS SERVED:** individual writers, documentation groups, small and medium-sized businesses.

SPECIALTIES AND PREFERENCES: technical editing, copyediting, technical and copywriting.

FICTION—ACCEPTS: y/a or juvenile, short stories. **NONFICTION—ACCEPTS:** articles/ features, self-help, how-to/instruction, technical, text or reference, business, humor, inspirational/spiritual. **TYPICAL EVALUATION/REPORT:** 15 pages.

FEES/TERMS/CONTRACTS: hourly rate or proposal for project. Check or PayPal. Signed statement of work or contract with retainer to begin.

ACCOMPLISHMENTS: more than ten years of copyediting, proofreading, indexing, and style guide development; technical edit in electronic and hard copy, rework nonnative English writing; writes marketing materials, newsletter articles, procedures, hardware and software documentation, and web page content.

EDUCATION: BS Business and Marketing. University of Phoenix (online school). Technical Writing Certificate, Portland Community College, OR. **MEMBERSHIPS:** senior member, Society for Technical Communication. Computer Human Interaction Forum of Oregon. Hillsboro Chamber of Commerce.

CLIENTS WITHIN PRIOR YEAR: 1–5.

123	EDITOR	WRITER	CONSULTANT	F	NF

Davidow, Joie. 6464 Odin St., Los Angeles, CA 90068. joie@joiedavidow.com. www.joiedavidow.com. Established: 1992.

SKILLS: freelance editor, independent book editor, book doctor, copyeditor or line editor, proofreader, ghostwriter, business writer or copywriter, literary consultant, writing coach, writing instructor, contract book writer. **Markets served:** writers, authors, publishers.

Specialties and preferences: I try to help writers express their thoughts in a concise, clear, and organized manner. I encourage them to nourish an individual voice.

Fiction—accepts: y/a or juvenile, short stories, novels (genre, mainstream, literary, contemporary, historical), queries, synopses. **Nonfiction—accepts:** articles/features, essays, memoirs, creative or narrative, family history, how-to/instruction, queries.

Fees/terms/contracts: on request.

Accomplishments: founder, editor-in-chief, and publisher of *L.A. Weekly* and *Sí* magazines. Coeditor of two story anthologies published by A.A. Knopf. Author of a nonfiction book on Mexican-American herbal remedies and a memoir.

Education: MA Music, New England Conservatory of Music, Boston, MA.

Memberships: PEN West. Author's Guild.

Clients within prior year: 1–5.

124	EDITOR	WRITER	CONSULTANT	F	NF

Davis, Candy. Ink Dance. 35226 Perkins Creek Rd., Cottage Grove, OR 97424. P1/ 541-942-8329. cdavis@willamette.net. www.4-edit.com. Established: 2004.

Skills: freelance editor, independent book editor, book doctor, proofreader, ghostwriter, literary consultant, writing instructor, screenplay editor, writer. **Markets served:** novelists, screenwriters, publishers.

Specialties and preferences: sci-fi, fantasy, mystery, police procedural, screenplays.

Fiction—accepts: all. **Nonfiction—accepts:** memoirs, creative or narrative, humor. **Typical evaluation/report:** 30–70 pages, bibliography, resource packet.

Fees/terms/contracts: novel partials, $9/page. Full novel manuscripts, $7/page. Copyediting, $5/page. $75/hour for consults, read-throughs, coaching, or fewer than 100-page manuscripts. $750 for screenplay evaluation. Ghostwriting by special arrangement. One-half due with signed contract; balance at completion.

Accomplishments: award-winning novels, short stories, and screenplays, two of which have been sold and one produced (*Monsoon Wife,* 2003). Best known for edgy fiction dealing with complex and sensitive themes.

Education: BA Anthropology, Sonoma State University, Rohnert Park, CA. Studied medical Qigong in China. Elementary teaching certificate.

Memberships: Willamette Writers.

Clients within prior year: 30–35.

125	EDITOR	WRITER	CONSULTANT	F	NF

De Simone, Joanne. PO Box 107, Riverhead, NY 11901. P1/ 631-848-0719. P2/ 631-574-8994. jdesi12@optonline.net. Established: 1997.

SKILLS: freelance editor, independent book editor, book doctor, copyeditor or line editor, proofreader, ghostwriter, business writer or copywriter, technical writer, literary consultant, writing coach, writing instructor, newspaper movie-review columnist, researcher for novelist/biographer. **MARKETS SERVED:** authors, journalists, filmmakers.

SPECIALTIES AND PREFERENCES: I have extensive film history knowledge and am able to turn mundane facts into "a good read."

FICTION—ACCEPTS: all. **NONFICTION—ACCEPTS:** all.

FEES/TERMS/CONTRACTS: $35/hour for all services. No credit cards or PayPal. Checks or money orders accepted. Standard contract for hourly rate.

ACCOMPLISHMENTS: edited magazine articles for *U.N. Economic Advisor* (retired). Researched and contributed to published novelist/filmmaker. Film columnist. Director for off-Broadway play. Author of play to be produced off-Broadway, fall 2004. Author of children's book—currently working with publisher.

EDUCATION: BA English, Brooklyn College, NY. Film Studies, New York University, New School University, Rutgers University. Paralegal. **MEMBERSHIPS:** International Women's Writers Guild.

CLIENTS WITHIN PRIOR YEAR: 1–5.

126	EDITOR	WRITER	CONSULTANT	F	NF

DeBellotte, Yvonne. DeBak Desktop Publishing and Information Services, Inc. Atlanta, GA. P1/ 404-819-6910. debakdesktop@yahoo.com. Established: 1997.

SKILLS: freelance editor, independent book editor, book doctor, copyeditor or line editor, proofreader, ghostwriter, business writer or copywriter, technical writer, literary consultant, writing coach, writing instructor. **MARKETS SERVED:** all major markets including writers (mostly nonfiction, but have dealt with all genres), production companies, coaches, market research companies, and private industry.

SPECIALTIES AND PREFERENCES: My company will format the finished product to manuscript specifications including but not limited to proofreading, copyediting, and writing for grammatical content. I advise and consult with the author on the content and purpose of the manuscripts. I transcribe from various media products—cassette (standard and micro), VHS, CD, and streaming video.

FICTION—ACCEPTS: all, adult, y/a or juvenile, short stories, novels (genre, mainstream, literary, contemporary, historical), poetry, scripts/screenplays, queries, synopses, treatments. NONFICTION—ACCEPTS: all.

FEES/TERMS/CONTRACTS: terms negotiated.

ACCOMPLISHMENTS: I write short stories, but have not published yet.

EDUCATION: BS Management/Accounting, Webster University, St. Louis, MO. MEMBERSHIPS: The Writers' Bridge.

CLIENTS WITHIN PRIOR YEAR: 21–30.

127	EDITOR	WRITER	CONSULTANT	F	NF

Decker, Kris. The Write Effect. 11563 Washington St. NE, Blaine, MN 55434. P1/ 763-757-4803. F1/ 763-862-1115. WriteEffect@aol.com. Established: 1981.

SKILLS: copyeditor or line editor, proofreader, business writer or copywriter. MARKETS SERVED: businesses of all types and sizes; arts organizations; publishers; catalogs.

SPECIALTIES AND PREFERENCES: delivers consistently superior writing; amazing turnaround times; dedication to deadlines. For more than two decades, clients have turned to me for persuasive copy and interesting features for their print and online needs. Copywriting or editing of ads, brochures, direct mail, articles/features, press releases, web content.

NONFICTION—ACCEPTS: articles/features, humor, business or copy, inspirational/ religious.

FEES/TERMS/CONTRACTS: $40/hour. Written bid submitted based on assessment of client's needs. If client concurs, contract is submitted outlining details. One-third due at contract signing, one-third upon submission of preliminary copy, and final third upon client sign-off. Client only billed for time worked, not bid. No credit cards. Very flexible about tight deadlines; never charges overtime.

ACCOMPLISHMENTS: top revenue-producing direct mail for business clients. Publication in *Angie's List, A Woman's Journey, Toy Directory Monthly Magazine, The First Line E-zine, High Readership Features, My Craft.com*.

EDUCATION: BA Studio Arts, Metropolitan State University, Minneapolis, MN. English literature, journalism, and sociology were major fields of study at University of Minnesota.

CLIENTS WITHIN PRIOR YEAR: 11–20.

128	EDITOR	WRITER	CONSULTANT	F	NF

Deputat, Kathryn. Boston, MA. P1/ 617-522-2737. kathryn@claritywork.com. www.claritywork.com. Established: 1990.

SKILLS: freelance editor, copywriter, writing coach, writing instructor, clarity consultant. MARKETS SERVED: writers, corporations, organizations.

SPECIALTIES AND PREFERENCES: I facilitate direct, authentic expression; focus is on writer development (voice, style)—process not product. A fine product is the result of our work together, not its aim. My methods cultivate originality. Feedback is specific and nonjudgmental.

FICTION—ACCEPTS: y/a or juvenile, short stories, novels (genre, mainstream, literary, contemporary), poetry, queries, synopses. **NONFICTION—ACCEPTS:** all.

FEES/TERMS/CONTRACTS: $80 /hour, individual work. Fees vary for group work. A "Claritywork" process is $450, or $120/hour. No credit cards or PayPal.

ACCOMPLISHMENTS: various essays/poems published in regional publications. Amanda Butler Sternberg Poetry and American Association of University Women awards. Wellesley College Durant Scholar. Member, Phi Beta Kappa.

EDUCATION: BA Psychology, Wellesley College, MA. AA Liberal Arts, Middlesex Community College, Bedford, MA. Classes with Frank Bidart, Kathleen Spivack, Olga Broumas, Eileen Myles, Julia Thacker, Nat Goldberg, Bruce Weigl, Carole Maso, Demetria Martinez, Stratis Haviaras. **MEMBERSHIPS:** Better Business Bureau, Phi Beta Kappa.

CLIENTS WITHIN PRIOR YEAR: variable; currently 6–10.

129	EDITOR	**WRITER**	CONSULTANT	F	**NF**

DeWayne, Shelley. 1209 Constitution Dr., Indianapolis, IN 46234. P1/ 317-508-3709. sdewayne@indy.rr.com. Established: 2003, but have written intermittently since 1997.

SKILLS: business writer or copywriter. **MARKETS SERVED:** businesses, magazines, newspapers—in health or fitness.

SPECIALTIES AND PREFERENCES: Shelley DeWayne has more than nine years in health care. Primary interests—health/fitness, fundraising. Writes ad copy for newspapers and magazines, direct mail, yellow pages, flyers, brochures, and website copy. Also some nonfiction articles.

NONFICTION—ACCEPTS: self-help, how-to/instruction.

FEES/TERMS/CONTRACTS: based on copy requested, deadline, and background documentation available. Rates may be negotiable. Prefers cash/check but also accepts payment and major credit cards through PayPal. Requires half of payment up front for all new clients. Uses a Writer's Service Agreement.

ACCOMPLISHMENTS: Previous articles were for WriteForCash and novel reviews at Suite101. Currently Publicity Chair for Avon Marching Black & Gold.

EDUCATION: Coursework—American Writers & Artists Institute Copywriting. Angela Booth Copywriting.

CLIENTS WITHIN PRIOR YEAR: 1–5.

130	EDITOR	WRITER	CONSULTANT	F	NF

Dibs, John. Dibs Indexing, Editing & Writing. 1930 Rainier Circle, Petaluma, CA 94954. P1/ 707-781-7306. jdibs@earthlink.net. Established: 1995.

SKILLS: freelance editor, copyeditor or line editor, technical writer, writing instructor, indexer. MARKETS SERVED: publishers, corporations.

SPECIALTIES AND PREFERENCES: I am a technical writer and freelance indexer with ten years of experience primarily in the finance and telecommunications industries. Indexing experience includes a variety of nontechnical subjects.

NONFICTION—ACCEPTS: articles/features, essays, creative or narrative, biography/ autobiography, family history, self-help, how-to/instruction, technical, text or reference, inspirational/religious, spiritual. TYPICAL EVALUATION/REPORT: 2–4 pages.

FEES/TERMS/CONTRACTS: technical writing, average $50/hour. Indexing, starting at $3.50/page. Editing, per-project charge. No credit cards.

ACCOMPLISHMENTS: President, North Bay chapter of Society for Technical Communication. Facilitator for indexing workshop at Sonoma State University. Instructional Designer. Product Development Coordinator. Operations Support Supervisor. Ordained deacon in the Eastern Orthodox Christian Church.

EDUCATION: M.Div., St. Vladimir's Orthodox Theological Seminary, Crestwood, NY. BA History, University of California, Berkeley. MEMBERSHIPS: Society for Technical Communication. American Society of Indexing.

CLIENTS WITHIN PRIOR YEAR: 4.

131	EDITOR	WRITER	CONSULTANT	F	NF

Dickel, Michael. 3419 Harriet Ave. S, Minneapolis, MN 55408. P1/ 612-827-4366. C1/ 612-810-7871. mhdpoet@earthlink.net. dickel@macalester.edu. www.macalester.edu/~dickel. Established: 1989.

SKILLS: freelance editor, copyeditor or line editor, proofreader, ghostwriter, literary consultant, writing coach, writing instructor. MARKETS SERVED: education, higher education, political (lobbyists).

SPECIALTIES AND PREFERENCES: poetry, literary writing, book reviews, essays, academic writing. My preference is to encourage writers to make their own revisions in their own voice, by modeling and assisting them to see how to solve particular problems. I will, depending on the job, write, rewrite, edit, copyedit, but the teacher in me wants to help the writer in the client develop and grow.

FICTION—ACCEPTS: all. NONFICTION—ACCEPTS: all.

FEES/TERMS/CONTRACTS: ask.

ACCOMPLISHMENTS: published poet, short story writer, book reviewer, essayist, feature article author. Chair and board member of the Midwest Writing Centers Association. Former faculty of the University of Minnesota and Metropolitan State University. Current director of the Macalester Academic Excellence Center.

EDUCATION: PhD Literature, MA Creative Writing, BA Psychology, University of Minnesota, Minneapolis. **MEMBERSHIPS:** National Council of Teachers of English. Several other educational associations. Midwest Writing Centers Association. The Loft.

CLIENTS WITHIN PRIOR YEAR: 1–5.

132	EDITOR	WRITER	CONSULTANT	F	NF

Dickerson, James. PO Box 4185, Brandon, MS 39047-4185. Jamesldickerson@cs.com. Established: 1986.

SKILLS: freelance editor, independent book editor, book doctor, copyeditor or line editor, proofreader, ghostwriter.

SPECIALTIES AND PREFERENCES: I specialize in entertainment (music and films), self-help (psychology), politics, and biographies. **MARKETS SERVED:** I work primarily for publishers, but I would consider projects from individuals if I thought they were publishable. I primarily do ghostwriting and book "doctoring" for projects that require thorough revision.

FICTION—ACCEPTS: novels (genre, mainstream, contemporary, historical). **NONFICTION—ACCEPTS:** biography/autobiography, narrative nonfiction, self-help, how-to/instruction, book proposals.

FEES/TERMS/CONTRACTS: negotiable fees. No credit cards or PayPal. Uses contract.

ACCOMPLISHMENTS: author of twenty nonfiction books, more than 2,000 magazine and newspaper articles, short stories, and poetry. Former magazine publisher and editor, newspaper reporter and editor, book critic.

EDUCATION: BA Psychology and English, University of Mississippi, University, MS.

CLIENTS WITHIN PRIOR YEAR: 1–5.

133	EDITOR	WRITER	CONSULTANT	F	NF

Dodd, Lisa. Lisa Lehr Dodd Writer. Grass Valley, CA. P1/ 530-274-1727. C1/ 530-277-6437. lisa@whatever-you-say.com. lisaldodd@hotmail.com. www.whatever-you-say.com. Established: 2000.

SKILLS: freelance editor, independent book editor, book doctor, copyeditor or line editor, proofreader, ghostwriter, business writer or copywriter, writing coach, writing instructor, ESL and Basic Literacy tutor. **MARKETS SERVED:** writers and would-be writers, private individuals, nonprofits, small businesses, medium to large businesses.

Specialties and preferences: I am a writer for hire, willing to work with any client interested in forming a good business relationship. My specialties include pets and service and therapy animals; health/diet/fitness; art and science for kids; special needs kids; creation science and Biblical themes; biography/autobiography.

Fiction—accepts: all. **Nonfiction—accepts:** all.

Fees/terms/contracts: $40–$70/hour depending on project; $3–$4/page for copyediting. 50 percent at beginning of project; 50 percent at completion. Personal check or PayPal. No credits cards.

Accomplishments: published articles, essays, stories. Nominated for *Who's Who in America 2005*.

Education: BA Biology, University of Colorado, Boulder. Additional study in art, Bible, foreign language. Certified ESL and Basic Literacy tutor. **Memberships:** Turning Memories into Memoirs.

Clients within prior year: one large contract last year; typically no more than five.

134	EDITOR	WRITER	CONSULTANT	F	NF

Dold, Catherine. PO Box 4424, Boulder, CO 80306. P1/ 303-543-2390. cd@catherinedold.com. www.catherinedold.com. Established: 1991.

Skills: freelance editor, proofreader, business writer or copywriter, technical writer. **Markets served:** consumer magazines, patient education outlets, pharmaceutical companies, medical associations, hospitals, medical websites, etc.

Specialties and preferences: science/medical writing and editing for consumers (via magazines and corporate publications—feature articles, brochures, booklets, websites, etc.) and for science professionals (materials such as educational items for pharmaceutical sales people).

Nonfiction—accepts: articles/features, self-help, how-to/instruction, technical, text or reference, business.

Fees/terms/contracts: upon request.

Accomplishments: published in many consumer outlets—*Cosmopolitan*, *New York Times*, *Audubon*, *Smithsonian*, *Discover*, *Health*, etc. Corporate clients include Memorial Sloan Kettering Cancer Center, NIH, AMA, major medical/pharmaceutical companies.

Education: MA Journalism and Mass Communication, Certificate, Science and Environmental Reporting, New York University, NY. BA Environmental Biology, University of Colorado, Boulder. **Memberships:** American Society of Journalists and Authors. National Association of Science Writers.

Clients within prior year: 10–15.

135	EDITOR	WRITER	CONSULTANT	F	NF

Domingo, Diane. BookShelf Editing Services. Riverside, CA. editing@earthlink.net. www.writersbreak.com/bookshelf editing.htm. Established: 2003.

SKILLS: freelance editor, independent book editor, book doctor, copyeditor or line editor, proofreader, website editor, author interviews. **MARKETS SERVED:** writers, nonprofit organizations, corporations.

SPECIALTIES AND PREFERENCES: fiction novels/short stories, websites. I handle all work personally. Electronic editing from files, but also prefer to have hard copy on hand.

FICTION—ACCEPTS: y/a adult or juvenile, short stories, novels (genre, mainstream, literary, contemporary, historical). **NONFICTION—ACCEPTS:** articles/features, essays, memoirs, creative or narrative, biography/ autobiography, business, humor. **TYPICAL EVALUATION/REPORT:** 1–2 pages plus comments during editing.

FEES/TERMS/CONTRACTS: negotiable; 0.5–3 cents/word. Half upon acceptance, half upon completion for amounts over $300. Free sample edit. PayPal. Uses agreement.

ACCOMPLISHMENTS: I have no publications of my own (though I have five novels and a short story that I've written, I've never tried to publish). Clients have published. I copyedit two newsletters that are published four days a week for retailers and pharmacists, and a website and monthly e-zine for writers.

EDUCATION: AA English Literature, Riverside Community College, CA. CMA Los Angeles College of Medical and Dental Assistants, CA. Instructor yoga course. **MEMBERSHIPS:** Editorial Freelancers Association.

CLIENTS WITHIN PRIOR YEAR: 6–10.

136	EDITOR	WRITER	CONSULTANT	F	NF

Doty, Hope. HOPE PCS—Documentation Consulting. Austin, TX. P1/ 512-751-9107. hopedoty@hopepcs.com. www.hopepcs.com. Established: 2001.

SKILLS: freelance editor, independent book editor, book doctor, copyeditor, proofreader, documentation consultant. **MARKETS SERVED:** technology (hardware and software producers), industry report companies, nonfiction and educational publishers, graphic design firms (production-ready proofing).

SPECIALTIES AND PREFERENCES: copyediting technical documentation. Twelve years of experience in the documentation production process. Editing, documentation conversion (Word to FrameMaker, including template creation and system training), production-ready proofing.

NONFICTION—ACCEPTS: articles/features, self-help, how-to/instruction, technical, text or reference, business, book proposals, queries.

FEES/TERMS/CONTRACTS: per-project basis based on complexity of the work required, size of the project, and estimated time to complete to meet required deadlines.

ACCOMPLISHMENTS: winner of the Society for Technical Communication International Award of Excellence, 2001, for the *Cisco 6100 with NI-2 Hardware Installation Guide.*

EDUCATION: BA English, University of Texas, San Antonio.

CLIENTS WITHIN PRIOR YEAR: 5–10.

137	EDITOR	WRITER	CONSULTANT	F	NF

Drouin, Franzeca. Eugene, OR. P1/ 541-683-5025. chezbuggles@msn.com. franzeca@go.com. Established: 2001.

SKILLS: freelance editor, independent book editor, book doctor, copyeditor or line editor, proofreader, historical researcher. **MARKETS SERVED:** writers of historical romance.

SPECIALTIES AND PREFERENCES: I have worked with romances set in Regency England, to ensure the historical accuracy of their books. I edit for style, continuity, plot, character development, and anachronistic vocabulary. I am eager to expand my fields of expertise, both chronologically and geographically. I love working with enthusiastic writers.

FICTION—ACCEPTS: short stories, novels (genre, mainstream, literary, contemporary, historical), books, queries, synopses, treatments. **NONFICTION—ACCEPTS:** essays, memoirs, creative or narrative, biography/autobiography, family history. **TYPICAL EVALUATION/REPORT:** 30–35 pages. Includes consulting before/after evaluation submitted.

FEES/TERMS/CONTRACTS: research $40/hour. Editing $30/hour. Sample editing for no fee. Fee negotiable for research and editing of entire manuscript. Payment by check only.

ACCOMPLISHMENTS: researched and edited six historical romances, three of which were listed on the *New York Times* bestseller lists.

EDUCATION: MA Medieval History, University of California, Santa Barbara. BA English History, University of California, Santa Cruz. Received instruction and mentoring from Carol Craig, formerly of Editing International, to enhance editing skills.

CLIENTS WITHIN PRIOR YEAR: 1–5.

138	EDITOR	WRITER	CONSULTANT	F	NF

Dumond, Val. PO Box 97124, Tacom, WA 98497. P1/ 253-582-5453. F1/ 253-582-5453. jazzyval@aol.com. Established: 1983.

SKILLS: freelance editor, independent book editor, copyeditor, proofreader, business writer or copywriter, technical writer, literary consultant, self-publishing consultant. **MARKETS SERVED:** authors seeking publication, self-publishing writers, business organizations.

SPECIALTIES AND PREFERENCES: assists writers to prepare manuscripts for publication. Editing, formatting, and rewrite services. Finds best agent, publisher, Internet, or self-publisher.

FICTION—ACCEPTS: short stories, novels (mainstream, contemporary, historical), scripts/screenplays. **NONFICTION—ACCEPTS:** articles/features, memoirs, creative, biography/autobiography, self help, how-to/instruction, technical, business, humor, spiritual, book proposals, treatments, queries. **TYPICAL EVALUATION/ REPORT:** 2–10 pages.

FEES/TERMS/CONTRACTS: $4–$6/page or $40–$60/hour. Half up front, balance when complete.

ACCOMPLISHMENTS: published four nonfiction language and seven history books. Self-published novel. Numerous articles. Writes and publishes monthly newsletter.

EDUCATION: BS Psychology, New York Institute of Technology, NY. BA Education, University of Wisconsin, Madison. Post graduate work in law and special education. **MEMBERSHIPS:** Seattle Free Lances. Tacoma Writers Roundtable. American Association of University Women. Girl Scouts.

CLIENTS WITHIN PRIOR YEAR: 11–20.

139	EDITOR	WRITER	CONSULTANT	F	NF

duPont, M. Kay. The Communication Connection. 2137 Mt. Vernon Rd., Atlanta, GA 30338. P1/ 770-395-7483; F1/ 770-395-1931. Kay@TCC-WSA.com. www.TCC-WSA.com. Established: 1979.

SKILLS: freelance editor, copywriter. **MARKETS SERVED:** speakers, consultants, businesses, ad agencies, publishers, individuals.

SPECIALTIES AND PREFERENCES: training programs/materials, shell letters, marketing materials, newsletters, proposals, nonfiction books/manuals (no medical), articles, websites.

NONFICTION—ACCEPTS: all. **TYPICAL EVALUATION/REPORT:** 2–25 pages.

FEES/TERMS/CONTRACTS: $90–$120/hour. Bills one-third of estimate up front, balance at completion. Accepts credit cards. Does not use contract unless assignments are ongoing.

ACCOMPLISHMENTS: authored four business books, one historical novel, many articles and newsletters. Has won awards in every category of writing. Teaches/coaches on writing skills across the nation, with a twenty-four-year success record of improvement.

EDUCATION: Samford University, Birmingham, AL, prelaw General Studies, CLA designation. Studied/taught Creative Writing, University of Alabama, Birmingham. Ongoing continuing education. **MEMBERSHIPS:** Georgia Writers

Association. Southern Order of Storytellers. National Speakers Association. CLIENTS WITHIN PRIOR YEAR: approximately 15–20.

140	EDITOR	WRITER	CONSULTANT	F	NF

Dupree, Andrea E. Lighthouse Writers Workshop. 817 27th St., Denver, CO 80205. P1/ 303-297-1185. F1/ 303-292-9425. aedupree@lighthousewriters.org. www.lighthousewriters.org. Established: 1997.

SKILLS: freelance editor, independent book editor, copyeditor or line editor, proofreader, business writer or copywriter, literary consultant, writing coach, writing instructor, publicist. MARKETS SERVED: writers.

SPECIALTIES AND PREFERENCES: I teach creative writing at the University of Denver and Lighthouse Writers Workshop. My specialty is literary and mainstream writing, particularly short stories. I work with novelists and essayists.

FICTION—ACCEPTS: short stories, novels (mainstream, literary, contemporary), queries, synopses, treatments. NONFICTION—ACCEPTS: articles/features, essays, memoirs, creative or narrative, biography/autobiography, business, queries. TYPICAL EVALUATION/REPORT: 2–10 pages.

FEES/TERMS/CONTRACTS: $70/hour, provides estimates. Accepts credit cards, PayPal, checks. Frequently uses contract.

ACCOMPLISHMENTS: over a dozen literary fiction publications in journals; nonfiction articles published in papers and journals; Rocky Mountain Women's Institute fellowship for writing; fiction reader for *Ploughshares*. Writing-teaching fellowship at Emerson College; Phi Beta Kappa.

EDUCATION: MFA Writing, Literature and Publishing, Emerson College, Boston, MA. MEMBERSHIPS: Associated Writing Programs.

CLIENTS WITHIN PRIOR YEAR: 10–15.

141	EDITOR	WRITER	CONSULTANT	F	NF

Durio, Sue. Durio PR & Marketing Communications. 17049 Trail of the Woods, Austin, TX 78734. P1/ 512-266-7908; F1/ 512-266-3389. sue@durio.com. www.durio.com. Established: 2000.

SKILLS: freelance editor, copyeditor, ghostwriter, business writer, magazine writer. MARKETS SERVED: businesses and magazines.

SPECIALTIES AND PREFERENCES: award-winning marketing and public relations communicator with more than twenty-two years of experience. Impactful writing and strategies that hit the mark. Services include direct mail, brochures, magazine features, and case studies, web copy, press releases, and strategic plans.

NONFICTION—ACCEPTS: articles/features, biography/autobiography, self-help, how-to/instruction, business.

Fees/terms/contracts: prices based on project. Invoices monthly, due within 30 days.

Accomplishments: see website.

Education: BJ Journalism, University of Texas, Austin. **Memberships:** Freelance Austin.

Clients within prior year: 11–20.

142	EDITOR	WRITER	CONSULTANT	F	NF

Duros, Sally. Sduros Communications—Orenda Communications. 1900 W. Ainslie, Chicago, Il 60640. P1/ 773-769-6070. C1/ 773-744-5770. Sally@Sduros.com. orendalife@mac.com. www.Sduros.com. www.orenda.us. Established: 2000.

Skills: freelance editor, independent book editor, book doctor, copyeditor or line editor, ghostwriter, business writer or copywriter, literary consultant, writing coach, writing instructor, journalist, researcher, web writer, business development from coached content. **Markets served:** new businesses, writers.

Specialties and preferences: nonfiction, feature articles, essays and memoirs, narrative nonfiction, spiritual, business self-help, women, work/life balance, social change, book proposals. Ideal client is aware of unique voice and has idea of the story to be told.

Nonfiction—accepts: all. **Typical evaluation/report:** interviews/conversations.

Fees/terms/contracts: coaching $100/hour. Line editing and rewriting $75/hour. Flexible payment arrangement. Client pays for transcription services. PayPal. Uses simple agreement.

Accomplishments: former managing editor of *Crain's* City & State. Writing and research has been published by *Time* magazine, *The Chicago Sun-Times*, *The Wall St. Journal*, *Chicago* magazine, *The Chicago Reader*, and www.WorldWIT.org.

Education: MS Communication, Northwestern University, Evanston, IL. BA Psychology, University of Illinois, Chicago. **Memberships:** WorldWIT. Independent Feature Project. Chicago Women in Philanthropy.

Clients within prior year: 1–5.

143	EDITOR	WRITER	CONSULTANT	F	NF

Dykewomon, Elana. Changing the World Word by Word. Oakland, CA. P1/ 510-562-2605. dykewomon@yahoo.com. www.dykewomon.org. Established: 2000.

Skills: freelance editor, independent book editor, book doctor, copyeditor or line editor, proofreader, literary consultant, writing coach, writing instructor. **Markets served:** small publishers, individuals.

Specialties and preferences: literary fiction, poetry, and memoir. Particularly interested in works that deal with social change in any form, lesbian and feminist writing.

FICTION—ACCEPTS: short stories, novels (literary, contemporary, historical), poetry. NONFICTION—ACCEPTS: all. TYPICAL EVALUATION/REPORT: 12–30 pages.

FEES/TERMS/CONTRACTS: $3–$5/page for fiction, narrative, essays, nonfiction. $10–$8/page (after 63 pages) poetry. $40/hour consultation, ongoing support. Deposits prior to work.

ACCOMPLISHMENTS: published two novels, two short story collections, two poetry books, including *Beyond the Pale*, Lambda and Ferro-Grumley award winner, Lesbian Fiction. Editor, the feminist literary journal *Sinister Wisdom* 1987–1995. Published essays, stories, and poems. Currently on the board of *The Journal of Lesbian Studies* and teaching at SFSU.

EDUCATION: MFA Creative Writing, San Francisco State University, CA. BFA Creative Writing, California Institute of Art, Valencia, CA. MEMBERSHIPS: PEN West. Modern Language Association. Associated Writing Programs.

CLIENTS WITHIN PRIOR YEAR: 15–20.

144	EDITOR	WRITER	CONSULTANT	F	NF

Eberl, Karuna. Wandering Dog Films. PO Box 2066, Nederland, CO 80466. dognose@prodigy.net. Established: 1996.

SKILLS: freelance editor, independent book editor, copyeditor or line editor, proofreader, ghostwriter, business writer or copywriter, technical writer, literary consultant, writing coach, writing instructor, film/video production, screenwriting, photography, graphic design. MARKETS SERVED: writers, publishers, organizations, corporations, government, filmmakers.

SPECIALTIES AND PREFERENCES: interesting projects from simple copyediting to writing, production, author feedback, sales consultation, etc. Frequent subjects include travel, adventure sports, social justice, dogs, business, health, documentaries, and more.

FICTION—ACCEPTS: short stories, novels, scripts/screenplays, queries, synopses, treatments. NONFICTION—ACCEPTS: all. TYPICAL EVALUATION/REPORT: meets needs.

FEES/TERMS/CONTRACTS: fees vary. No credit cards. Contracts.

ACCOMPLISHMENTS: writing/editing for dozens of magazines/newspapers/websites, editor for tourism guides, contributing writer to coffee-table books, writing/newsletters for businesses, photography awards, one fiction award, one novel, two screenplays, two documentaries with PBS distribution, various film credits.

EDUCATION: BA Journalism, University of Montana, Missoula. Minor in geology. MEMBERSHIPS: Outdoor Writers Association of America. National Snowsports Journalists Association. Rocky Mountain Fiction Writers.

CLIENTS WITHIN PRIOR YEAR: 6–10.

145	EDITOR	WRITER	CONSULTANT	F	NF

Eboch, Chris. PO Box 1084, Socorro, NM 87801. P1/ 505-270-6430. scbwi_nm@blarg.net. www.chriseboch.com. Established: 2003.

SKILLS: freelance editor, independent book editor, book doctor, copyeditor or line editor, proofreader, ghostwriter, business writer or copywriter, literary consultant, writing coach, writing instructor. **MARKETS SERVED:** authors, writers.

SPECIALTIES AND PREFERENCES: children's books, both fiction and nonfiction. Uses experience as a writer, editor, and teacher to help writers find the power in their words.

FICTION—ACCEPTS: y/a or juvenile, short stories, novels (genre, mainstream, contemporary, historical), queries, synopses, treatments. **NONFICTION—ACCEPTS:** all. **TYPICAL EVALUATION/REPORT:** 1–3 pages plus extensive line editing on the manuscript.

FEES/TERMS/CONTRACTS: $1.50/page for general editorial comments. $2.50/page for the above plus detailed line editing. Hourly rates available. Minimum $25 per story. Response time, 1–4 weeks. Contract upon request. No credit cards.

ACCOMPLISHMENTS: books include a middle-grade historical drama, three nonfiction books for junior high students, and over 100 articles for children and adults.

EDUCATION: MA Professional Writing and Publishing, Emerson College, Boston, MA. BFA Photography, Rhode Island School of Design, Providence. **MEMBERSHIPS:** Society of Children's Book Writers & Illustrators. International Women's Writing Guild.

CLIENTS WITHIN PRIOR YEAR: 10–15.

146	EDITOR	WRITER	CONSULTANT	F	NF

Edmands, Allan. The Wordsman Editorial Services. 4 Jones Quarry Rd., Woodstock, NY 12498. P1/ 845-679-1065. allan@thewordsman.com. www.thewordsman.com. Established: 1973.

SKILLS: freelance editor, independent book editor, book doctor, copyeditor or line editor, proofreader, website designer and maintainer. **MARKETS SERVED:** publishers.

SPECIALTIES AND PREFERENCES: manuscripts written by people with English as a second language. I sharpen words to the point. I convert opaque, dry, and intimidating text into unambiguous, concise, readable, and interesting prose. Substantial experience with nonnative writers of English. Please see website.

FICTION—ACCEPTS: y/a or juvenile, short stories, novels (mainstream, contemporary, historical), scripts/screenplays. **NONFICTION—ACCEPTS:** all.

FEES/TERMS/CONTRACTS: $3–$7/1,500-character page. Depending on depth of edit needed, free quote. Fifty percent deposit for new clients. Balance due 30 days after completion. Credit cards accepted with PayPal. Uses agreement.

ACCOMPLISHMENTS: thirty years of editing. Two published nonfiction titles, dozens of papers presented and published for technical symposia, numerous technical videos, and web animations.

EDUCATION: BA History, University of Washington, Seattle. **MEMBERSHIPS:** Editorial Freelancers Association.

CLIENTS WITHIN PRIOR YEAR: 1–20.

147	EDITOR	WRITER	CONSULTANT	F	NF

Edrich, Alyice. Knox City, Knoxville, TN. P1/ 865-691-7739. F1/ 865-691-7739. dabblingmum@yahoo.com. Established: 1999.

SKILLS: freelance editor, proofreader, literary consultant. **MARKETS SERVED:** entrepreneurs, small businesses, consumers, writers.

SPECIALTIES AND PREFERENCES: small business copy, how-to books, newsletters, articles, and brochures. Preferred subject areas: parenting, home business, writing, Christian materials.

NONFICTION—ACCEPTS: how-to/instruction, business, inspirational/religious, e-book proposals, complete article manuscripts, queries.

FEES/TERMS/CONTRACTS: Flat fee services found on site. Rates for writing assignments (articles, features, columns, etc.) are negotiated according to the publication's guidelines. Accepts business checks, credit cards, and PayPal.

ACCOMPLISHMENTS: won APEX 2004 Award of Excellence in the websites' category. Client's poetry accepted in Hallmark card line. Have stories in two anthologies. Have self-published several e-books. Two books to be published by Obadiah Press. Have articles published in *Merrill Courier* newspaper, *Faithful Times* newspaper, *Venice Gulf Coast Living*, *Families First Parenting* magazine, *Kaiser Permanente Hospital*, and many others.

EDUCATION: AA Business Administration. Certificates in Paralegal Studies and Mediation Skills. Certificates in Exceptional Customer Service and The Exceptional Assistant.

CLIENTS WITHIN PRIOR YEAR: 21–30.

148	EDITOR	WRITER	CONSULTANT	F	NF

Edwards, Jill. Milwaukee, WI. P1/ 414-975-8569. editor_edwards@juno.com. indexer@blazemail.com. Established: 2000.

SKILLS: freelance editor, book doctor, copyeditor or line editor, proofreader, ghostwriter, business writer or copywriter, technical writer, literary consultant, writing coach, writing instructor, indexer. **MARKETS SERVED:** authors, publishers, book packagers, grant writers, businesses.

SPECIALTIES AND PREFERENCES: help writers effectively convey their message in a manner that is interesting, informative, accessible, and entertaining. Find solutions to issues that may diminish the quality, logic, or believability of the writer's plot, characters, or argument. Help authors produce their best possible manuscript.

FICTION—ACCEPTS: short stories, novels (genre, mainstream, contemporary, historical). **NONFICTION—ACCEPTS:** articles/features, essays, memoirs, creative or narrative, biography/autobiography, family history, self-help, how-to/instruction, technical, text or reference, business, book proposals, queries. Typical evaluation/ report: 8–30 pages plus style sheet.

FEES/TERMS/CONTRACTS: $2–$10/page. PayPal, money order, certified check. Written contract or agreement.

ACCOMPLISHMENTS: author of medical materials.

EDUCATION: BS Medical Technology, University of Wisconsin, Milwaukee.

MEMBERSHIPS: American Society of Indexers.

CLIENTS WITHIN PRIOR YEAR: 6–10.

149	EDITOR	WRITER	CONSULTANT	F	NF

Elam, Glenda. Intersos Consultant. via Cesare Pavese 45 Int. C 13, Roma, IT 00144. P1/ 0039(06). C1/ 348-857-4621. glendajohnsonelam@hotmail.com. Established: 1980.

SKILLS: freelance editor, proofreader, ghostwriter, business writer or copywriter, technical writer, writing coach, writing instructor, bilingual texts. **MARKETS SERVED:** agencies, corporations, independent technical writers.

SPECIALTIES AND PREFERENCES: cleans up text and makes information more incisive. Proofreads for publications that are difficult to edit, usually translated from a foreign language into English. Expanding into more net publications.

FICTION—ACCEPTS: all. **NONFICTION—ACCEPTS:** all. **TYPICAL EVALUATION/REPORT:** 0–2 pages.

FEES/TERMS/CONTRACTS: rates are international depending upon country source. Usually my rates are similar to the United Nations' fee scale—deposit, and payment upon consignment.

ACCOMPLISHMENTS: referrals by satisfied clients. UN, General Electric, film producers, and screenwriters.

EDUCATION: Master's in Peacekeeping, Rome University 3, Italy. Certificate from TNU-Ultrecht University, Amsterdam, online, in Transforming Civil Conflicts in Rome. John Cabot University Certificate in Development Management for UN Managers at Rome Campus. BA Latin American Studies/History,

Hartwick College, Oneonta, NY. **MEMBERSHIPS:** International Women's Writing Guild.
CLIENTS WITHIN PRIOR YEAR: 1–5.

150	EDITOR	WRITER	CONSULTANT	F	NF

Elcano, Jennifer. Elcano Communications. 13529 Wood St., Woodbridge, VA 22191. P1/ 703-491-8489. C1/ 703-608-5918. F1/ 703-490-5427. elcanocomm@aol.com. 7-Steps@comcast.net. Established: 1994.

SKILLS: freelance editor, ghostwriter, business writer or copywriter, technical writer, writing coach, writing instructor, teach original curriculum called "7 Steps to Better Writing." **MARKETS SERVED:** federal government, private industry, nonprofits, small businesses.

SPECIALTIES AND PREFERENCES: I am a good reader of others' writing and have a gift for homing in on the best way of saying a thing. My career as a technical writer, while not always brimming with fascinating subject matter, has nonetheless done something important, immersed me in other people's writing—most of it bad. Fifteen year in this business has taught me how writing works mainly by seeing how it doesn't. It has also given me a reverence for the written word and for the power embedded in the code.

NONFICTION—ACCEPTS: articles/features, essays, memoirs, creative or narrative, biography/autobiography, family history, self-help, how-to/instruction, technical, text or reference, business, humor, inspirational/religious, spiritual, queries.

FEES/TERMS/CONTRACTS: $65/hour. Works on contract, pre-agreed limits.

ACCOMPLISHMENTS: too many to list.

EDUCATION: MA English, George Mason University, Arlington, VA. **MEMBERSHIPS:** Society of Technical Communicators.

CLIENTS WITHIN PRIOR YEAR: 1–5.

151	EDITOR	WRITER	CONSULTANT	F	NF

Ellison, James. 92 Christopher St., 2nd Floor, New York, NY 10014. P1/ 212-366-5106. editorjwe@aol.com. Established: not available.

SKILLS: freelance editor, independent book editor, book doctor, line editor. Writer ghost. Consultant literary. **MARKETS SERVED:** writers.

SPECIALTIES AND PREFERENCES: As the author of seven novels published by major houses, I specialize in fiction. I also book doctor and/or collaborate on adult nonfiction (most recently wrote a narrative on the Mexican War based on the author's extensive research).

FICTION—ACCEPTS: novels (genre, mainstream, literary, contemporary, historical).

NONFICTION—ACCEPTS: essays, memoirs, creative or narrative, biography/

autobiography, family history, self-help, humor, book proposals. **Typical evaluation/report:** 2–5 pages.

Fees/terms/contracts: fee varies, but never charges by the hour. Accepts credit cards. Uses contract unless he enters into an agreement to share in the publishing contract.

Accomplishments: I have ghostwritten nonfiction and novels published by WW Norton, HarperCollins, and others. Also have collaborated on five works of nonfiction, and have written ten novelizations of major motion pictures, including *Finding Forrester*, which won a NYC Library YA award. I hold a lifetime fellowship in the Novel at the Bread Loaf Writers' Conference, and my papers are in the Boston University collection.

Education: BA Michigan State University, East Lansing. **Memberships:** Consulting Editors Alliance. Author's Guild.

Clients within prior year: 6–10.

152	EDITOR	WRITER	CONSULTANT	F	NF

Elmore, Barbara. WordScene. 4201 Morrow Ave., Waco, TX 76710. P1/ 254-753-2300. belmore1@hot.rr.com. www.wordscene.com. Established: 2002.

Skills: freelance editor, independent book editor, copyeditor or line editor, proofreader, ghostwriter, business writer or technical writer. **Markets served:** individuals and businesses throughout the United States.

Specialties and preferences: anything with words; writing website content, newsletters, magazines, books, and workbooks. One of my strengths in nonfiction writing is asking the right questions. When editing books, I prefer fiction.

Fiction—accepts: y/a or juvenile, short stories, novels (genre, mainstream, literary, contemporary, historical). **Nonfiction—accepts:** y/a or juvenile, articles/features, creative or narrative, biography/autobiography, self-help, how-to/instruction, business, humor, inspirational/religious, spiritual.

Fees/terms/contracts: Writing $50/hour; editing $15–$30/hour. Uses contract.

Accomplishments: one traditionally published and two self-published young adult novels. Two Texas Institute of Letters awards. Dozens of periodical articles.

Education: BA Journalism, Texas State University, San Marcos. **Memberships:** Society of Children's Book Writers and Illustrators. Publishers Marketing Association. Small Publishers Association of North America.

Clients within prior year: 11–20.

153	EDITOR	WRITER	CONSULTANT	F	NF

Engelsen, Karen. Champlin, MN. P1/ 651-308-0083. F1/ 651-308-0083. siribear@earthlink.net. Established: 1995.

SKILLS: freelance editor, book doctor, copyeditor or line editor, ghostwriter, business writer or copywriter, technical writer, literary consultant, writing coach. MARKETS SERVED: writers, business, nonprofits.

SPECIALTIES AND PREFERENCES: research to ghostwriting, developmental, substantive, and line editing, query letters and proposals. Fantasy/science fiction and romance, self-help, spirituality, psychology, and business. Goal: enable successful navigation through the publishing pipeline.

FICTION—ACCEPTS: novels (genre). NONFICTION—ACCEPTS: articles/features, self-help, business, inspirational/religious, spiritual, book proposals, queries. TYPICAL EVALUATION/REPORT: 5–15 single-spaced pages.

FEES/TERMS/CONTRACTS: averages $50/hour for writing and $60/hour for editing. Cash on delivery, no credit cards. Is considering use of contracts in future.

ACCOMPLISHMENTS: developed *The Self Defeating Habits of Otherwise Successful People*, by Anna Maravelas, now under purchase discussions by three major houses! Comments by New York acquisitions editors include "Unique and powerful material …will generate media and articles."

EDUCATION: editing and publication, University of Minnesota. MEMBERSHIPS: Association for Women in Communications. Professional Editors Network. National Writers Union.

CLIENTS WITHIN PRIOR YEAR: 6–10.

154	EDITOR	WRITER	CONSULTANT	F	NF

Engelson, Joyce. 1160 Fifth Ave., New York, NY 10029. P1/ 212-369-6604. www.bookdocs.com. Established: 1992.

SKILLS: freelance editor, independent book editor, book doctor, literary consultant, writing coach, writing instructor, publicist. MARKETS SERVED: writers, publishers, agents.

SPECIALTIES AND PREFERENCES: sympathetic hands-on editing style, the distillation of half a century of editing major and minor writers with the goal of commercial publication. Method—full blueprint for revision or shorter overview of strengths/challenges. Best sense of humor in the biz!

FICTION—ACCEPTS: y/a or juvenile, short stories, novels (mainstream, literary, contemporary, historical), queries, synopses, treatments. NONFICTION—ACCEPTS: y/a or juvenile, articles/features, essays, memoirs, creative or narrative, biography/autobiography, family history, self-help, humor, book proposals, queries.

FEES/TERMS/CONTRACTS: negotiable.

ACCOMPLISHMENTS: forty years in mainstream publishing at key editorial and management positions. Prodigious list of famous writers available by personal contact or via www.bookdocs.com. Published two novels and prize-winning short stories.

EDUCATION: BA History, Barnard College, New York.

CLIENTS WITHIN PRIOR YEAR: 20–25.

155	EDITOR	WRITER	CONSULTANT	F	NF

Esposito, Anne. Cranford, NJ. P1/ 908-272-8395. Anne@expert-edit.com. www.expert-edit.com. Established: 1996.

SKILLS: freelance editor, copyeditor or line editor. **MARKETS SERVED:** trade publishers, newsletter publishers, public relations firms, websites.

SPECIALTIES AND PREFERENCES: highly experienced. Comfortable editing with Microsoft Word (using track changes) or on hard copy. Edits all types of fiction, as well as nonfiction (health, medical, parenting, relationships, pets, education). Respects the author's voice; good at incorporating the publisher's style. Reads music. Knows HTML.

FICTION—ACCEPTS: y/a or juvenile, short stories, novels (genre, mainstream, literary, contemporary, historical). **NONFICTION—ACCEPTS:** all.

FEES/TERMS/CONTRACTS: paid per hour or per page. No credit cards. Usually paid by check. Use agreement or contract.

ACCOMPLISHMENTS: Many years of in-house editorial experience. Dozens of copyedited books published. Long relationships with satisfied publishing clients.

EDUCATION: BA Psychology, cum laude, St. John's University, Queens, NY. Continuing education courses in persuasive writing, line editing, and copyediting. **MEMBERSHIPS:** Editorial Freelancers Association.

CLIENTS WITHIN PRIOR YEAR: 6–10.

156	EDITOR	WRITER	CONSULTANT	F	NF

Faass, Nancy. WordWorks and The Writers' Group. 1550 California St., PMB #407, San Francisco, CA 94109. P1/ 415-922-6234. WordWorks@sbcglobal.net. Established: 1995.

SKILLS: freelance editor, book doctor, ghostwriter, literary consultant, writing coach, especially development editing, coauthoring, project development, web content, research, ghostwriting by phone. **MARKETS SERVED:** publishers, nonprofits, professionals, and businesses; consumer books and websites, professional books, and journal articles.

SPECIALTIES AND PREFERENCES: medicine and science, including complementary and integrative medicine, the social sciences, and other areas of nonfiction, including work for authors for whom English is a second language.

NONFICTION—ACCEPTS: articles/features, essays, self-help, how-to/instruction, technical, text or reference, spiritual, book proposals, queries.

FEES/TERMS/CONTRACTS: hourly rate—volume discounts (large projects); retainers; contracts.

ACCOMPLISHMENTS: 2001 Book of the Year, Doody's Publishing, review service. Has developed or coauthored seven books published with major publishing houses such as McGraw-Hill, New World Library, HarperCollins, Celestial Arts, Jones & Bartlett, others.

EDUCATION: Master of Public Health, University of California, Berkeley. Master of Social Work, Catholic University, Washington, DC. BA with honors, English literature, University of Maryland, College Park.

CLIENTS WITHIN PRIOR YEAR: 5–10 clients annually, primarily books and large websites.

157	EDITOR	WRITER	CONSULTANT	F	NF

Faintich, Alice S. The Word Doctor, LLC. 10509 Brevity Dr., Great Falls, VA 22066. P1/ 703-759-6434. C1/ 703-868-2373. F1/ 703-759-6434. Asfaintich@aol.com. www.theworddoctor.com. Established: 1984.

SKILLS: freelance editor, independent book editor, copyeditor or line editor, project management services. **MARKETS SERVED:** international organizations, consulting companies working on international development contracts, universities, associations, corporations, authors.

SPECIALTIES AND PREFERENCES: I provide the full spectrum of editing services for a range of nonfiction publications, specializing in international development issues and in working with non-native English speakers. Topics and types of publications vary widely, but tend to be technical (economics, education, agriculture, population, environment, health, public policy).

NONFICTION—ACCEPTS: text or reference.

FEES/TERMS/CONTRACTS: editing $60/hour, project management $80/hour. Terms negotiable. Uses contract. No credit cards or PayPal.

ACCOMPLISHMENTS: clients have had nine book-length manuscripts accepted for publication, mostly by the World Bank's own imprint or Oxford University Press.

EDUCATION: Postgraduate Certificate of Education, Nottingham University, UK. BSc (with Honors) Psychology, Nottingham University, UK. Publication specialist courses, George Washington University, Washington, DC.

CLIENTS WITHIN PRIOR YEAR: 6–10.

158	EDITOR	WRITER	CONSULTANT	F	NF

Fandrich, Barbara. Fandrich Publishing Arts. 512 Hanna Ave., Aberdeen, WA 98520. P1/ 360-532-2563. C1/ 206-498-0566. F1/ 360-537-1262. bjfandrich@hotmail.com. bjfandrich@yahoo.com. Established: 1998.

SKILLS: book doctor, copyeditor, proofreader, copywriter, technical writer, writing coach, writing instructor, publicist, technical editor, project editor, page designer. **MARKETS SERVED:** new and previously published authors; printing companies; fiction, nonfiction, and technical publishers; and nonprofits, including churches.

SPECIALTIES AND PREFERENCES: I apply skillful copy and project editing as needed; design and format text; and assist through self-publishing and marketing process from A to Z.

FICTION—ACCEPTS: y/a or juvenile, short stories, novels, picture books, poetry, scripts/screenplays, queries, synopses, treatments. **NONFICTION—ACCEPTS:** all. **TYPICAL EVALUATION/REPORT:** 2 pages.

FEES/TERMS/CONTRACTS: $25/hour; invoice monthly; typically use letter of agreement.

ACCOMPLISHMENTS: edited eighty-five books of every genre; trained by McGraw-Hill and Microsoft. I average one self-published project a month while working with two to three clients at a time.

EDUCATION: BS Business Administration, California Coast University, Santa Ana. **MEMBERSHIPS:** CTM, Toastmasters International.

CLIENTS WITHIN PRIOR YEAR: 10–15.

159	EDITOR	WRITER	CONSULTANT	F	NF

Farrar, Amy. Farrar Writing & Editing. 4638 Manchester Rd., Mound, MN 55364. P1/ 952-472-6884. writeandedit@bitstream.net. www.writeandedit.net. Established: 1999.

SKILLS: freelance editor, independent book editor, book doctor, copyeditor or line editor, proofreader, business writer or copywriter, writing coach, writing instructor. **MARKETS SERVED:** nonprofits, individuals, public speakers, publishers, marketing and public relations firms, general businesses.

SPECIALTIES AND PREFERENCES: high-quality writing and editing services for nonprofits, public speakers, and other individuals; marketing and public relations firms; and publishers, with a concentration in philanthropic, health/medical, travel, and journalistic subject material. Solid background backed by more than fifteen years of professional experience.

FICTION—ACCEPTS: y/a or juvenile, picture books, short stories, novels (genre, mainstream, literary, contemporary, historical), scripts/screenplays, queries, synopses, treatments. **NONFICTION—ACCEPTS:** all.

FEES/TERMS/CONTRACTS: $40–$60/hour. Uses contract.

ACCOMPLISHMENTS: hundreds of articles published in local and national magazines, newspapers, and other venues. Has edited book-length manuscripts and wide variety of print and electronic materials. Delivered speeches on writing and freelancing.

EDUCATION: BA English, Rutgers University, New Brunswick, NJ. MEMBERSHIPS: Professional Editors Network (PEN) of Minnesota. CLIENTS WITHIN PRIOR YEAR: 3–9.

160	EDITOR	WRITER	CONSULTANT	F	NF

Fasulo, Jim. 3150 SW Bertha Blvd., #3, Portland, OR 97239. P1/ 503-244-3961. jafasulo@juno.com. www.jimfasulo.net. Established: 2002.

SKILLS: freelance editor, copyeditor or line editor, proofreader, ghostwriter, business writer or copywriter, writing instructor. MARKETS SERVED: business professionals, college students.

SPECIALTIES AND PREFERENCES: I edit and write business documents including press releases, e-mails, letters, and cover letters for professionals. I help college students with a full range of writing projects, including essays, reports, and any academic writing. I provide teaching strategies for them to become better writers, and edit their work as well. Another area of expertise is helping students write or edit admission essays for professional/graduate schools.

NONFICTION—ACCEPTS: articles/features, essays, memoirs, creative or narrative, self-help, how-to/instruction, business, humor, inspirational/religious, spiritual, book proposals, queries.

FEES/TERMS/CONTRACTS: $25/hour for small projects; for longer projects the fee is negotiable.

ACCOMPLISHMENTS: Community college English tutor. Published freelance writer.

EDUCATION: BA English Literature, Villanova University, PA.

CLIENTS WITHIN PRIOR YEAR: 10–15.

161	EDITOR	WRITER	CONSULTANT	F	NF

Ferlazzo, Ellen. Sprezzatura Systems. Pleasanton, CA. P1/ 925-461-2303. F1/ 925-461-2303. ellen@ellenferlazzo.com. www.ellenferlazzo.com. Established: 1991.

SKILLS: freelance editor, copyeditor, business writer or copywriter. MARKETS SERVED: primarily high tech, but not exclusively.

SPECIALTIES AND PREFERENCES: e-mail newsletters, white papers, web content, user documentation/online help, white papers, press kit information, and website content.

NONFICTION—ACCEPTS: articles/features, technical, text or reference.

FEES/TERMS/CONTRACTS: Fees are typically project based or on monthly retainer. Uses a contract.

ACCOMPLISHMENTS: on time and under budget is the norm.

EDUCATION: BS Information Systems Management, University of San Francisco,

CA. AAS Electronics Engineering, Heald College, CA. **Memberships:** Software Developer's Forum. San Francisco Women on the Web. Pleasanton Chamber of Commerce.

Clients within prior year: 11–20.

162	EDITOR	WRITER	CONSULTANT	F	NF

Fifield, Anne. All That's Published. PO Box 116954, Carrollton, TX 75011. P1/ 972-395-0012. P2/ 972-395-0803. annef@allthatspublished.com. www.allthatspublished.com. Established: 2001.

Skills: freelance editor, independent book editor, book doctor, copyeditor or line editor, proofreader, ghostwriter, business writer or copywriter, technical writer, desktop publishing; translations, indexing, typing/formatting. **Markets served:** writers, academics, businesses, publishers.

Specialties and preferences: life stories, self-help, motivational, how-to, health/fitness/environment, finance, real estate, food, academic, technical, business, website content, book proposals, novels—mainstream, mystery/suspense/thriller, romance.

Fiction—accepts: short stories, novels (genre, mainstream), short stories, queries, synopses. **Nonfiction—accepts:** all. **Typical evaluation/report:** 5–25 pages.

Fees/terms/contracts: writing and editing services, $45–$85/hour. Proofreading, indexing, and typing, $30–$50/hour. Internet research, fact verification, finding quotes, formatting, and desktop publishing, $45–$75/hour. Cash, credit cards, PayPal. Contract.

Accomplishments: two decades as an executive administrative assistant. Project manager, production manager, copyeditor, and proofreader. Editing, proofreading, and manuscript preparation of academic books, e-books, e-zines, and narrative nonfiction.

Education: studied deaf education and business administration, University of Science and Arts of Oklahoma, Chickasha. Level V American Sign Language certification, OK. **Memberships:** Editorial Freelancers Association. International Virtual Assistants Association.

Clients within prior year: 120–130.

163	EDITOR	WRITER	CONSULTANT	F	NF

Figler, Stephen. Authorcoach. 1855 Cardiff Dr., Cambria, CA 93428. F1/ 805-924-1233. skfigler@earthlink.net. Established: 1979.

Skills: freelance editor, independent book editor, book doctor, copyeditor or line editor, proofreader, ghostwriter, business writer or copywriter, literary consultant, writing coach, writing instructor. **Markets served:** general trade and fiction, social science/humanities academic, memoir/personal history (for publication).

SPECIALTIES AND PREFERENCES: I have done a considerable amount of trade nonfiction and academic editing over twenty-five years.

FICTION—ACCEPTS: y/a or juvenile, short stories, novels (genre, mainstream, literary, contemporary, historical). **NONFICTION—ACCEPTS:** all. **TYPICAL EVALUATION/REPORT:** several pages plus in-text notes and editing.

FEES/TERMS/CONTRACTS: Fees are arranged with client per page, per total words, or preset figure. Token up front fee is required. Typical per-page fee: $2–$4.

ACCOMPLISHMENTS: sociology textbook in three editions (McGraw-Hill), two self-help books (Peterson's Guides); three years in print journalism (New York City, Philadelphia); academic articles, short story awards, three completed novels.

EDUCATION: PhD Social Science and Education with distinction, Stanford University, CA. MEd, American University, Washington, DC. **MEMBERSHIPS:** Authors Guild. Cambria Writers Workshop. Nightwriters of San Luis Obispo.

CLIENTS WITHIN PRIOR YEAR: 6–10.

164	EDITOR	WRITER	CONSULTANT	F	NF

Fischer, Rusty. A Likely Story—Bringing Out the Best (Seller) in You!.
5934 Bent Pine Dr., #336, Orlando, FL 32822. P1/ 407-888-4816
Freelancer86@aol.com. www.alikelystory.itgo.com. Established: 1999.

SKILLS: freelance editor, independent book editor, book doctor, copyeditor or line editor, proofreader, ghostwriter, business writer or copywriter, technical writer, literary consultant, writing coach, writing instructor. **MARKETS SERVED:** businesspeople who need a book to sell based on a product or service, speakers who want a book in the back of the room, celebrities needing bios, and others.

SPECIALTIES AND PREFERENCES: I specialize in editing/writing book length fiction and nonfiction on a variety of interesting topics. One specialty not listed above is true crime.

FICTION—ACCEPTS: y/a or juvenile, short stories, novels (genre, mainstream, literary, contemporary, historical), poetry, scripts/screenplays, queries, synopses, treatments. **NONFICTION—ACCEPTS:** all. **TYPICAL EVALUATION/REPORT:** 4–5 pages.

FEES/TERMS/CONTRACTS: $1,250/10,000 words, or per client basis. No credit cards. Invoice on the 15th of each month.

ACCOMPLISHMENTS: I have worked for satisfied clients such as McGraw-Hill, HarperCollins, and Harcourt Brace. My work has appeared in popular magazines and has been anthologized in bestsellers.

EDUCATION: BA English/BS English Education, University of Central Florida, Orlando.

CLIENTS WITHIN PRIOR YEAR: 20–30.

165	EDITOR	WRITER	CONSULTANT	F	NF

Fisher, Enicia. Living Education. Lake Elsinore, CA. P1/ 951-245-0234. eniciafisher@yahoo.com. www.livinged.com. Established: 1999.

SKILLS: freelance editor, book doctor, proofreader, ghostwriter, copywriter, technical writer, literary consultant, writing coach, writing instructor. MARKETS SERVED: newspaper and magazine publishers; nonprofit and educational organizations; self-publishing authors.

SPECIALTIES AND PREFERENCES: editing nonfiction; writing/editing educational materials; editing children's and young adult literature.

FICTION—ACCEPTS: y/a or juvenile, picture books, short stories, novels (literary, contemporary), poetry. NONFICTION—ACCEPTS: y/a or juvenile, articles/features, essays, memoirs, creative or narrative nonfiction, biography/autobiography, family history, self-help, how-to/instruction, inspirational/religious, spiritual. TYPICAL EVALUATION/REPORT: 1–2 pages.

FEES/TERMS/CONTRACTS: $40/hour or project fee determined upon assessment of material. No credit cards or PayPal. Uses contract.

ACCOMPLISHMENTS: numerous book reviews published in the Christian Science Monitor (see website—search Enicia Fisher).

EDUCATION: MS Education, University of Kansas, Lawrence. BA English, Principia College, Elsah, IL.

CLIENTS WITHIN PRIOR YEAR: two large contracts; typically 6–10.

166	EDITOR	WRITER	CONSULTANT	F	NF

Fitzgerald, Waverly. Seattle, WA. P1/ 206-325-1452. waverly@waverlyfitzgerald.com. www.waverlyfitzgerald.com. Established: 1982.

SKILLS: freelance editor, writing coach, writing instructor. MARKETS SERVED: individual writers. University of Washington Extension program, Richard Hugo House, continuing education programs.

SPECIALTIES AND PREFERENCES: like to work with writers at a developmental stage in a project, through coaching or evaluation of a first draft. Favorite clients—writers working on genre novels, historical fiction, memoir, family history, nonfiction book proposals, or nonfiction books. I'm especially good at helping writers eliminate jargon to appeal to a general audience. And I have an amazing talent for writing a zippy synopsis of a novel.

FICTION—ACCEPTS: novels (genre, mainstream, contemporary, historical), queries, synopses. NONFICTION—ACCEPTS: articles/features, essays, memoirs, creative or narrative, biography/autobiography, family history, self-help, how-to/instruction, spiritual, book proposals, queries. TYPICAL EVALUATION/

REPORT: 5–10 pages.

FEES/TERMS/CONTRACTS: $70/hour. Manuscript consultation $1/page, includes written critique and one-hour consultation. PayPal accepted. No credit cards.

ACCOMPLISHMENTS: four published historical novels. Many articles in national magazines.

EDUCATION: MA Educational Psychology, California State Northridge. BA English Literature, University of California at Santa Barbara. MEMBERSHIPS: Editors Guild. Sisters in Crime. Historical Novel Society.

CLIENTS WITHIN PRIOR YEAR: 11–20.

167	EDITOR	WRITER	CONSULTANT	F	NF

Flanagan, Brian. Word Association. Iowa City, IA. P1/ 319-338-6250. worda1@wordassociation1.net. wordsmyth1@earthlink.net. Established: 1985.

SKILLS: freelance editor, independent book editor, book doctor, copyeditor or line editor, proofreader, business writer or copywriter, technical writer, literary consultant, writing coach, writing instructor. MARKETS SERVED: writers, publishers, universities, nonprofits, corporations.

SPECIALTIES AND PREFERENCES: prefer projects offering a high degree of intellectual, scientific, artistic, and humanitarian interest. I'm primarily a creative writer, with most of my work divided between literary fiction and nonfiction science. I also enjoy editing; I love to sculpt text into a pleasing form. Often, my clients are so thrilled to see their words gleam on the page, they get the "aha" right away, and go on to be fine writers.

FICTION—ACCEPTS: all. NONFICTION—ACCEPTS: all. TYPICAL EVALUATION/REPORT: varies per project.

FEES/TERMS/CONTRACTS: free initial consultation, bid. Standard contract.

ACCOMPLISHMENTS: critical and popular acclaim for scientific and literary work. In addition to my creative works, I have made numerous pioneering contributions to the nascent field of "quantum mind" studies. Many of these efforts can be found by googling "Flanagan" and "wordsmyth."

EDUCATION: BA Psychology, University of Iowa. Largely self-taught. Background in sciences and humanities.

CLIENTS WITHIN PRIOR YEAR: 1–5.

168	EDITOR	WRITER	CONSULTANT	F	NF

Flynn, Sarah. 3120 Munz Dr., Annapolis, MD 21403. P1/ 410-268-2966. F1/ 410-268-0369. sarahflynn@comcast.net. www.publishersmarketplace.com/members/SarahFlynn/. Established: 1988.

SKILLS: freelance editor, independent book editor, book doctor. MARKETS SERVED: authors of trade books.

SPECIALTIES AND PREFERENCES: veteran of Houghton Mifflin (1980–1988). Most clients are seasoned novelists, journalists, academics writing for the sophisticated general reader. Work on every aspect from structure, tone, and argument/plot/character development to line-by-line, viewing the process as a collaborative enterprise. Interests include political and social history, current affairs, high quality fiction, cookbooks. Will travel.

FICTION—ACCEPTS: novels (mainstream, literary, contemporary, historical). **NONFICTION—ACCEPTS:** memoirs, creative or narrative, biography/autobiography, book proposals. **TYPICAL EVALUATION/REPORT:** by consultation.

FEES/TERMS/CONTRACTS: $100/hour. No credit cards. Uses agreement.

ACCOMPLISHMENTS: coauthor of oral history of the civil rights movement. Editor of dozens of books for the general reader. Possessor (per one client) of "refreshing intelligence, solid grasp of narrative structure, terrific sense of history, wonderful nose for a memorable phrase."

EDUCATION: BA Sociology, Rutgers University, New Brunswick, NJ. **MEMBERSHIPS:** PEN American Center. Washington Independent Writers. National Writers Union.

CLIENTS WITHIN PRIOR YEAR: One lengthy project, plus several smaller ones.

169	EDITOR	WRITER	CONSULTANT	F	NF

Foley, Mike. Writer's Review. PO Box 1441, Big Bear Lake, CA 92315. P1/ 909-585-0059. F1/ 909-266-0710. duffen@aol.com. Established: 1986.

SKILLS: freelance editor, independent book editor, book doctor, copy editor, proofreader, business writer, literary consultant, writing coach, writing instructor, online writing instructor in fiction and nonfiction. **MARKETS SERVED:** aspiring writers and business people.

SPECIALTIES AND PREFERENCES: full editing of fiction and nonfiction; a full report details a work's strengths and weaknesses. Writing services for business; online classes and individual coaching for writers. Request e-mail newsletter, *The Writer's Edge*, via e-mail.

FICTION—ACCEPTS: short stories, novels (contemporary). **NONFICTION—ACCEPTS:** articles/features, memoirs, creative or narrative, self-help, business, spiritual, book proposals, queries. **TYPICAL EVALUATION/REPORT:** 3–5 pages.

FEES/TERMS/CONTRACTS: $3/double-spaced page for shorter works (up to 100 pages). Book length manuscripts—fee reduced to $1.50/page, negotiated for extreme lengths. Coaching—$100–$250/ month. Fees payable in advance. Uses contracts for writing jobs.

ACCOMPLISHMENTS: Have edited a book published by Kallisti Publishing. Writing instructor, University of California, Riverside (Extension). Former newspaper staff writer/reporter. Editor—*Dream Merchant* magazine (1990–present; now part-time).

EDUCATION: BA Creative Writing and BS Business Administration, California State University, Long Beach. **MEMBERSHIPS:** California Writers. Teachers and Writers Collaborative.
CLIENTS WITHIN PRIOR YEAR: more than 60.

170	EDITOR	WRITER	CONSULTANT	F	NF

Ford, Marcia. Ford Editorial Services. PO Box 740184, Orange City, FL 32774-0184. P1/ 386-668-7486. ford2200@bellsouth.net. misfit@marciaford.com. www.marciaford.com. Established: 1999.

SKILLS: freelance editor, independent book editor, book doctor, copyeditor or line editor, proofreader, ghostwriter, literary consultant, writing coach, writing instructor. **MARKETS SERVED:** writers, book and magazine publishers, websites.

SPECIALTIES AND PREFERENCES: helping others become better writers through book doctoring and editing, and writing instruction (through conferences and private manuscript critiquing).

FICTION—ACCEPTS: novels (genre, mainstream, literary, contemporary, historical). **NONFICTION—ACCEPTS:** all. **TYPICAL EVALUATION/REPORT:** varies.

FEES/TERMS/CONTRACTS: project fee based on complexity of manuscript and/or word count. Two-thirds of total fee upon agreement to terms; one-third payable upon completion. PayPal or check. Written agreement.

ACCOMPLISHMENTS: author of fourteen traditionally published books; writer and editor with thirty years of experience in newspaper, magazine, and book publishing. See website for complete résumé.

EDUCATION: Graduate Monmouth University, West Long Branch, NJ. **MEMBERSHIPS:** Florida Writers' Association. National Association of Women Writers. National Writers Union. Toastmasters International. Advanced Writers and Speakers Association.

CLIENTS WITHIN PRIOR YEAR: 12–15.

171	EDITOR	WRITER	CONSULTANT	F	NF

Fox, Anne. Oakland, CA. P1/ 510-482-0265. writefox@aol.com. Established: 1978.

SKILLS: freelance editor, independent book editor, copyeditor or line editor, proofreader, writing coach. **MARKETS SERVED:** writers.

SPECIALTIES AND PREFERENCES: editorial support, manuscript polishing, read-through only. Helps writers to focus, develop, organize, and clarify ideas and presentation, strengthen skills in craft, style, and meaning. Prefers writers accustomed to literary critiquing.

FICTION—ACCEPTS: y/a or juvenile, short stories, novels (genre, mainstream, literary, contemporary, historical), queries. **NONFICTION—ACCEPTS:** y/a or juvenile, articles, essays, memoirs, creative or narrative, biography/ autobiography, queries. **TYPICAL EVALUATION/REPORT:** 1–5 pages.

FEES/TERMS/CONTRACTS: $30/hour. Sample editing. No credit cards.

ACCOMPLISHMENTS: acknowledged in books. Wrote newspaper column for thirteen years and currently as lead copyeditor for neighborhood newspaper (7,000 circ.). Eight years copyeditor for anthology; equally for a seniors' magazine. Copyeditor for food industry newsletters. Coedited brochures for food mail-order business. Copyeditor of California Writers Club newsletter. Many years consultant for writers in general.

EDUCATION: BA Spanish, English, University of California, Los Angeles, Berkeley. Editorial workshops, conferences. **MEMBERSHIPS:** California Writers Club (Berkeley). Museums.

CLIENTS WITHIN PRIOR YEAR: 5–10.

172	EDITOR	WRITER	CONSULTANT	F	NF

Frank, Perry. American Dreams & Associates, Inc. 1401 N St. NW, Apt. 106, Washington, DC 20005. P1/ 202-483-7424. C1/ 202-997-3011. F1/ 202-483-2505. perryf@erols.com. perryf@americandreams.cc. www.americandreams.cc. Established: 1993.

SKILLS: copyeditor or line editor, proofreader, ghostwriter, business writer or copywriter, instructor, curricula developer. Historian—research, synthesis, and analysis. Print and electronic archives and databases; interviews and oral histories. **MARKETS SERVED:** government contractors, businesses, cultural organizations, local and federal government.

SPECIALTIES AND PREFERENCES: original research and writing to a client assignment. Finalize document or manuscript—content, format, and style guidelines; reviewing drafts. Manage publications systems. Small print or electronic publications jobs.

NONFICTION—ACCEPTS: all. **TYPICAL EVALUATION/REPORT:** 2–15 pages.

FEES/TERMS/CONTRACTS: writing $50–$75/hour. Rewriting/heavy substantive editing, $40/hour; copyediting, $35/hour; proofreading, $30/hour. Prefers payment in thirds.

ACCOMPLISHMENTS: collaborating on a book based on oral histories of African-American museum founders and directors. Wrote and edited proposals for numerous clients targeted to government and foundation sources; managed two book projects; wrote articles for scholarly and cultural publications.

EDUCATION: PhD American Studies, George Washington University, DC. MA American Literature, University of Texas, Austin. **MEMBERSHIPS:** American Studies Association. Washington Independent Writers. Fulbright Association. Women's Business Center.

CLIENTS WITHIN PRIOR YEAR: 10–15.

173	EDITOR	WRITER	CONSULTANT		NF

Franklin, Penelope. PenFrank. New York, NY. P1/ 212-242-3724. F1/ 212-675-0575. penfrank@yahoo.com. Established: 1980.

Skills: freelance editor, independent book editor, book doctor, copyeditor or line editor, ghostwriter, business writer or copywriter, literary consultant, writing coach, writing instructor, author, journalist, essayist, food columnist. **Markets served:** writers, publishers, literary agencies.

Specialties and preferences: versatile editor with over twenty-five years of non-fiction publishing experience. Works with authors worldwide, including those using English as second language; many first-time as well as established authors. Focuses on preserving the author's unique voice.

Nonfiction—accepts: articles/features, essays, memoirs, creative or narrative, biography/autobiography, family history, self-help, business, humor, book proposals, queries. **Typical evaluation/report:** 2–6 pages.

Fees/terms/contracts: $100–$125/hour. Uses letter of agreement or contract.

Accomplishments: author, women's diaries anthology. Over 100 published articles and essays.

Education: BA Psychology and Art, Columbia University, NY. Postgraduate work, The Publishing Institute of New York University. **Memberships:** Editorial Freelancers' Association. Words into Print. National Writers Union. Association of Personal Historians. Women Writing Women's Lives.

Clients within prior year: 5–10.

174	EDITOR	WRITER	CONSULTANT	F	NF

Fraser, Joanne. JEFraser Editorial Services. Amherst, MA. P1/ 413-256-5414. jefraser@comcast.net. www.jefraser.com. Established: 1988.

Skills: freelance editor, independent book editor, book doctor, copyeditor or line editor, proofreader, ghostwriter, business writer or copywriter, technical writer, literary consultant, writing coach, writing instructor, professional book indexing, web page development. **Markets served:** textbook and academic publishers, government publishers, trade publishers.

Specialties and preferences: social, life, and biological sciences; history, medical publications, and book-length academic publications. I handle all stages of the editorial process—research, development, substantive writing and editing, copyediting, proofreading, and indexing—and pride myself on having great working relationships with both authors and publishers.

Fiction—accepts: all. **Nonfiction—accepts:** all. **Typical evaluation/report:** depends on project.

Fees/terms/contracts: competitive, please contact.

Accomplishments: I was an in-house editor for W.B. Saunders and Saunders. College publishing before becoming a freelancer.

Education: MBA Marketing, University of Massachusetts, Amherst. MA American History, Johns Hopkins University, Baltimore, MD. BA American Studies, Scripps College, Claremont, CA.

Clients within prior year: 10–15.

175	EDITOR	WRITER	CONSULTANT	F	NF

Friedman, Arnold. 5701 Coach Gate Wynde, Louisville, KY 40207. P1/ 502-896-0008. C1/ 502-314-5658. F1/ 502-896-0008 (call first). arnif@aol.com. Established: 2000.

Skills: freelance editor, independent book editor, book doctor, copyeditor or line editor, proofreader, ghostwriter, business writer or copywriter, literary consultant, writing coach, writing instructor. **Markets served:** all writers, fiction or nonfiction; university presses.

Specialties and preferences: I am a retired newspaper editor who does freelance editing, proofreading, and writing. I can edit anything from a school paper to a full-length fiction or nonfiction book. I am a careful, prompt, nitpicking editor who believes in making your words say what you want to say.

Fiction—accepts: all. **Nonfiction—accepts:** all.

Fees/terms/contracts: preferably by page or job. Copyediting $3.50/page, $30/ hour. Proofreading $2.50/page, $25/hour. All negotiable.

Accomplishments: former newspaper editor for forty-two years, also adjunct college professor. Freelance editor since 2000. Have edited over thirty published books.

Education: BS Journalism/Advertising/English, Syracuse University, NY.

Clients within prior year: 15–20.

176	EDITOR	WRITER	CONSULTANT	F	NF

Gabell, Julia C. CyberPen Editing. Bayonet Point, FL. P1/ 727-869-3069. jcgabell@gte.net. www.cyberpen.e-webtool.com. Established: 1987.

Skills: freelance editor, copyeditor or line editor, proofreader, ghostwriter, business writer or copywriter, technical writer. **Markets served:** writers, publishers, nonprofits.

Specialties and preferences: editor/writer for several large corporations. Online and web editing. A broad range of genres from academic journals to advertising brochures to technical journals. Helps writers to tighten sentence structure and/or storyline.

Fiction—accepts: y/a or juvenile, short stories, novels (genre, mainstream, literary, contemporary, historical), queries, synopses. **Nonfiction—accepts:** all. **Typical evaluation/report:** 2–8 pages.

FEES/TERMS/CONTRACTS: $8–$15/page. Negotiable.

ACCOMPLISHMENTS: biography and two short essays in published anthologies and online. Editor's award for poem "No Poem." Developed comprehensive website published by Gerald F. Steiner, PhD. Edited an all-inclusive website on condominium law that discusses problems that arise from condominium ownership. Most recently organized and wrote a comprehensive author and publisher database that addresses publication issues and the various aspects of getting published.

EDUCATION: MA English Literature, Villanova University, PA. BA English, Chestnut Hill College, Philadelphia, PA. **MEMBERSHIPS:** Florida Writer's Association. **CLIENTS WITHIN PRIOR YEAR:** 6–10.

177	EDITOR	WRITER	CONSULTANT	F	NF

Gagliani, William. Milwaukee, WI. P1/ 414-764-6132. P2/ 414-288-2114. tarkusp@execpc.com. www.williamdgagliani.com. Established: 2004.

SKILLS: freelance editor, independent book editor, book doctor, copyeditor or line editor, proofreader, ghostwriter, business writer or copywriter, technical writer. **MARKETS SERVED:** publishers, anthology publishers, book packagers, magazine publishers, fellow writers.

SPECIALTIES AND PREFERENCES: While I have not yet made a business of editing, I have edited a fiction literary magazine (not for pay) and I have edited and coedited my employer's newsletter. I would like to become involved in editing anthologies and/or collections in the dark fantasy/horror/fantasy/mystery/suspense areas.

FICTION—ACCEPTS: y/a or juvenile, picture books, short stories, novels (genre, mainstream, literary, contemporary, historical). **NONFICTION—ACCEPTS:** essays, memoirs, creative or narrative, family history, self-help, how-to/instruction, text or reference, business, humor.

FEES/TERMS/CONTRACTS: checks only. No credit cards or online payment.

ACCOMPLISHMENTS: published award-nominated novel, e-book story collection, numerous short stories in various print anthologies and e-zines, as well as articles, interviews, and book reviews in a variety of magazines. Winner of several awards.

EDUCATION: MA English (Writing), University of Wisconsin at Milwaukee. BA Geology, University of Wisconsin at Milwaukee. **MEMBERSHIPS:** Horror Writers Association.

CLIENTS WITHIN PRIOR YEAR: Although I have not made a business of editing yet, I have fairly extensive experience with editing my own and others' fiction.

178	EDITOR	WRITER	CONSULTANT	F	NF

Galanter, Lea. Cardiff, Wales, UK, and Seattle, WA. P1/ 011-44-2920-318525. leagal99@yahoo.com. leagal99@hotmail.com. Established: 1985.

SKILLS: freelance editor, copyeditor or line editor, proofreader, technical writer, academic writer. **MARKETS SERVED:** writers, publishers, corporations.

SPECIALTIES AND PREFERENCES: academic articles and books (particularly history, archaeology, and mythology), business and legal documents, software documentation. Plays and screenplays. Can edit to both American and British styles. Spends part of year in Seattle, part in Wales.

FICTION—ACCEPTS: plays/screenplays. **NONFICTION—ACCEPTS:** articles/features, creative or narrative, biography/autobiography, self-help, how-to/instruction, technical.

FEES/TERMS/CONTRACTS: copyediting $30/hour. Substantial editing/rewriting $40/hour. Proofreading $20/hour. UK rates available. Check or PayPal. Contract required.

ACCOMPLISHMENTS: edited and wrote for lifestyle and business publications. Wrote and edited encyclopedia articles. Edited legal documents and software documentation. Edited websites. Wrote screenplays and stage plays, and had a one-act play read publicly.

EDUCATION: MA Early Celtic Studies, University of Cardiff, Wales. BA History, State University of New York, Fredonia. Studied philosophy (two years) at the University of Washington, Seattle, and at St. Thomas University, Houston, TX. Studied Journalism (four years) at the University of Houston, TX.

CLIENTS WITHIN PRIOR YEAR: varies.

179	EDITOR	WRITER	CONSULTANT	F	NF

Galeno, Eda. Fallsington, PA. P1/ 215-428-1330. edagaleno@aol.com. Established: 1984.

SKILLS: freelance editor, copyeditor, ghostwriter, business writer, writing coach. **MARKETS SERVED:** trade, corporate, women's, public relations.

SPECIALTIES AND PREFERENCES: My writing/editorial experience encompasses assignments from newspapers, national magazines, newsletters and trade publications to interactive media and training/feature scripts. A formal writing education, my writing experience, and a background in public relations and business management lend me unique qualifications and strengths.

FICTION—ACCEPTS: scripts/screenplays, synopses, treatments. **NONFICTION—ACCEPTS:** articles/features, how-to/instruction, business.

FEES/TERMS/CONTRACTS: Payment depends on the job and client.

ACCOMPLISHMENTS: I am an editor for a trade publication and a national freelancer. My publications include major market newspapers, national magazines, and trade publications. Additionally, I handled public relations for a Grammy Award-winning artist, I was Artist Relations Manager for a national radio syndication company, and I wrote a training script for a Fortune 500 company.

EDUCATION: MA Journalism, New York University, NY.

CLIENTS WITHIN PRIOR YEAR: 1–5.

180	EDITOR	WRITER	CONSULTANT	F	NF

Gallares-Japzon, Leticia. JAE Design. 20385 Harmony Ct., Ashburn, VA 20147-3300. P1/ 703-729-4538. P2/ 571-332-8338. LJapzon@prodigy.net. www.japzon-author.com. Established: 1992.

SKILLS: freelance editor, independent book editor, copyeditor or line editor, proofreader, technical writing, research, and analysis. **MARKETS SERVED:** consultants (business; training and development), cross-cultural groups.

SPECIALTIES AND PREFERENCES: technical writing and editing.

NONFICTION—ACCEPTS: articles/features, essays, memoirs, creative or narrative, biography/autobiography, family history, self-help, how-to/instruction, technical, text or reference, business, humor, book proposals, queries. **TYPICAL EVALUATION/REPORT:** 10–20 pages.

FEES/TERMS/CONTRACTS: $35–$50/hour depending on complexity; per contract or project.

ACCOMPLISHMENTS: clients—designed and developed training programs (print-based and computer-based) for private and public organizations in diverse topics for broad population. Published two books.

EDUCATION: MA Education (instructional design major), George Washington University, Washington, DC. MA Human Resource Management, Marymount University, Arlington, VA. **MEMBERSHIPS:** International Society for Performance and Instruction. Toastmasters International.

CLIENTS WITHIN PRIOR YEAR: 1–5.

181	EDITOR	WRITER	CONSULTANT	F	NF

Garber, Craig. Words That Sell. 1844 N. Nob Hill Rd., #307, Plantation, FL 33322. P1/ 954-723-0677. craig@kingofcopy.com. www.kingofcopy.com. Established: 1999.

SKILLS: business writer or copywriter, direct-response, direct-marketing consultant. **MARKETS SERVED:** business owners.

SPECIALTIES AND PREFERENCES: direct marketing using direct mail, display ads, and websites. You won't find anyone else better equipped to give you compelling outside-the-box marketing ideas that put your business on auto-pilot than Craig Garber. Craig can provide camera-ready proofreading, word processing, desktop publishing and formatting, instructional material, pre-editing consultation, postediting consultation, and ongoing coaching.

Nonfiction—accepts: articles/features, essays, creative or narrative, biography/autobiography, self-help, how-to/instruction, technical, text or reference, business.

Fees/terms/contracts: usually fixed fee plus royalties.

Accomplishments: Before becoming a direct-response copywriter and direct-marketing consultant, Craig successfully used direct response marketing to turn his own business around. Since then, Craig has helped dozens of clients make their own transition from anxiety and frustration to consistent cash flow.

Education: BBA Public Accounting, City University of New York, NY.

Clients within prior year: 10–12.

182	EDITOR	WRITER	CONSULTANT	F	NF

Garner, Sharon K. James Creek, PA. P1/ 814-658-2119. F1/ 814-658-2119. sharonsbooks@penn.com. www.sharonkgarner.com. Established: 2002.

Skills: proofreader. **Markets served:** writers and businesses.

Specialties and preferences: proofreading/light copyediting for those submitting manuscripts or proposals to agents and editors, or for those desiring a clean manuscript before self-publishing/POD (print on demand).

Fiction—accepts: y/a or juvenile, short stories, novels (genre, contemporary), queries, synopses. **Nonfiction—accepts:** y/a or juvenile, articles/features, memoirs, creative or narrative, biography/autobiography, family history, self-help, business, humor, spiritual, book proposals, queries. **Typical evaluation/report:** 2–3 pages plus comments on project hard copy.

Fees/terms/contracts: $1/page (plus 6 percent sales tax), 250 words; 2 cents/page printing. Fees for priority mail, insurance, and delivery confirmation on return. Half up front, half upon completion. Send printable file in Word or hard copy. Cashiers check or money order.

Accomplishments: four commercially published novels, several novellas, numerous short stories for adults and children; participated in one short story anthology.

Education: Library Assistant certificate, PA. Library Cataloguing course, Pittsburgh, PA. Two years/college. **Memberships:** Romance Writers of America. Pennwriters. Kiss of Death.

Clients within prior year: 6–10.

183	EDITOR	WRITER	CONSULTANT	F	NF

Garrett, Joanne. Seattle, WA. P1/ 206-782-1067. joanneg@mindspring.com. Established: 2001.

SKILLS: freelance editor, independent book editor, copyeditor or line editor, proofreader, ghostwriter. **MARKETS SERVED:** writers, book and magazine publishers, nonprofits, corporations, website content developers.

SPECIALTIES AND PREFERENCES: fiction, creative and narrative nonfiction.

FICTION—ACCEPTS: y/a or juvenile, short stories, novels (mainstream, literary, contemporary). **NONFICTION—ACCEPTS:** y/a or juvenile, articles/features, essays, memoirs, creative or narrative, biography/autobiography, family history, self-help, how-to/instruction, business, humor, inspirational/religious, spiritual.

FEES/TERMS/CONTRACTS: $50–$70/hour; flat fee possible. Generally payment due on delivery. No credit cards. Usually uses agreement.

ACCOMPLISHMENTS: one published nonfiction title. Scores of articles in major newspapers.

EDUCATION: BA English Literature, St. Mary's College, South Bend, IN.

MEMBERSHIPS: Northwest Independent Editors Guild.

CLIENTS WITHIN PRIOR YEAR: 1–5.

184	EDITOR	WRITER	CONSULTANT	F	NF

Garrett, Michael. Creative Inspirations Inc. PO Box 100031, Birmingham, AL 35210. P1/ 205-907-0140. mike@writing2sell.com. BookDoctor@bham.rr.com. www.writing2sell.com. Established: 1986.

SKILLS: freelance editor, independent book editor, book doctor, copyeditor or line editor, proofreader. **MARKETS SERVED:** writers, publishers.

SPECIALTIES AND PREFERENCES: I serve authors seeking professional publication through evaluation of original manuscripts, identifying both minor and major issues, with detailed report explaining problems and appropriate correction. Regularly refuse business when I feel I cannot be of significant help to a potential client. Perform all services myself. My focus is on commercial fiction, and while my opinions are always honest, I strive to offer encouragement.

FICTION—ACCEPTS: short stories, novels (genre, mainstream, literary, contemporary, historical). **TYPICAL EVALUATION/REPORT:** 8–15 pages.

FEES/TERMS/CONTRACTS: $2.50/page, in advance. No credit cards.

ACCOMPLISHMENTS: as editor, twelve volumes of an internationally published award-winning short story anthology. Have been published internationally as an author for over twenty years and have served in a professional editorial capacity for Pocket Books and Kensington Publishing over fifteen years. Teach writing workshops for colleges across the Southeast and for the Writer's Digest School.

EDUCATION: BS Accounting, University of Alabama, Birmingham.

CLIENTS WITHIN PRIOR YEAR: 21–30.

| 185 | EDITOR | WRITER | CONSULTANT | F | NF |

Gaulden-Falstrom, Georgeanne. Irving, TX. P1/ 972-887-0497. gigifal@aol.com. Established: 2003.

Skills: freelance editor, independent book editor, book doctor, copyeditor or line editor, proofreader, ghostwriter, business writer or copywriter, technical writer, literary consultant, writing coach, writing instructor, professional curriculum vitae and resumes. **Markets served:** I am trying to break into the business.

Specialties and preferences: essays on current events or health topics, devotional/inspirational pieces, personal interviews, community or business-related news, and self-help or personal growth topics. I have written procedure manuals, curriculum, proposals, business correspondence, skits, marketing materials, speeches, seminar and workshop material, and newsletter/internal communications.

Fiction—accepts: all. **Nonfiction—accepts:** all.

Fees/terms/contracts: based on amount of research required, number of pages, and time requirement.

Accomplishments: began a writer's group; devotions; contributor to anthology on bereavement; campus newspaper; editor of an inspirational journal.

Education: MA Counseling Psychology, Pepperdine University, Malibu, CA. MS Psychology, East Texas State University, Commerce. BS Nursing, Baylor University, Waco, TX. **Memberships:** Christian Writers Guild.

Clients within prior year: 15–20.

| 186 | EDITOR | WRITER | CONSULTANT | F | NF |

Geldens, Linda. Linda Jay Geldens Editorial Services. 1115 Sir Francis Drake Blvd., #22, Kentfield, CA 94904. P1/ 415-456-4334. F1/ 866-422-2926. LindaJay@aol.com. www.lindajaygeldens.com. Established: 1990.

Skills: freelance editor, independent book editor, book doctor, copyeditor or line editor, proofreader, ghostwriter, business writer or copywriter, technical writer, literary consultant, writing coach, writing instructor, researcher, interviewer. **Markets served:** education, business, multimedia, coaches/therapists, technical.

Specialties and preferences: somewhat "academic" subjects in articles and book manuscripts and individuals' website text, press kits, and promotional material.

Fiction—accepts: short stories, novels (genre, mainstream, literary, contemporary, historical), scripts/screenplays. **Nonfiction—accepts:** all.

Fees/terms/contracts: usually an hourly rate—$50/editing, $60/writing. I am experienced, fast, and thorough. Discusses proposed editing and writing.

If the project involves a great deal of research or interviewing, that will be reflected in the fee.

ACCOMPLISHMENTS: articles in *TV Technology*, *The Artist's Magazine*, *Woman Engineer*, *Business Woman*, *Video Computing*, *U.S. Banker*. University case studies. Wrote story in *From the Heart: Stories of Love and Friendship*. Contributed to a monthly newsletter.

EDUCATION: BA English Literature, George Washington University, Washington, DC. **MEMBERSHIPS:** Bay Area Editors' Forum. Marin Editors' Group. North Bay Multimedia Association.

CLIENTS WITHIN PRIOR YEAR: 6–10.

187	EDITOR	WRITER	CONSULTANT	F	NF

Gelles-Cole, Sandi. Gelles-Cole Literary Enterprises. Box 341, Woodstock, NY 12498. P1/ 845-247-8111. gellescole@yahoo.com. www.consulting-editors.com. Established: 1983.

SKILLS: independent book editor, literary consultant, writing coach, collaborator. **MARKETS SERVED:** first-time authors; bestselling authors who seek perfection.

SPECIALTIES AND PREFERENCES: I work with commercial fiction and nonfiction, offering help with story development, characterization, and structure. For nonfiction, expert in all areas of health; psychology; victims and survivors of trauma; women's issues; general books—from a well-known etiquette expert's reference book, to a senator's memoir, to a celebrity's first novel—these authors all need different help. Also offer development of ideas from conception through the proposal or the entire nonfiction or fiction manuscript.

FICTION—ACCEPTS: short stories, novels (genre, mainstream, literary, contemporary), scripts/screenplays. **NONFICTION—ACCEPTS:** memoirs, creative or narrative, self-help, how-to/instruction, inspirational/religious, spiritual, book proposals. **TYPICAL EVALUATION/REPORT:** 3 pages.

FEES/TERMS/CONTRACTS: from $750 to $1,500. Details available upon request.

ACCOMPLISHMENTS: eleven years in corporate publishing, then established my own editorial consultancy agency in 1983. I have worked with Danielle Steel, Victoria Gotti, Alan Dershowitz, Governor Ann Richards, and many other authors.

EDUCATION: BA English/Journalism, Northeastern University, Boston, MA. **MEMBERSHIPS:** Consulting Editors Alliance.

CLIENTS WITHIN PRIOR YEAR: 6–10.

188	EDITOR	WRITER	CONSULTANT	F	NF

Gellman, Janet. Santa Cruz, CA. P1/ 831-425-7306. C1/ 831-332-2305. janetgel@pacbell.net. Established: 1997.

SKILLS: freelance editor, copyeditor or line editor, proofreader, business writer or copywriter, technical writer. **MARKETS SERVED:** manufacturing, financial and educational institutions, publishers, corporations, nonprofits.

SPECIALTIES AND PREFERENCES: health care, business procedures, software and hardware manuals, online help, feasibility studies, and grant writing. Specialize in writing and editing that enables readers to easily understand concepts. Excellent grammar and proofreading. Fully equipped home office or will work on-site within sixty-mile radius.

NONFICTION—ACCEPTS: all.

FEES/TERMS/CONTRACTS: $35–$70/hour. Invoice every two weeks—payment, by check or PayPal, within 30 days. Uses simple written agreement.

ACCOMPLISHMENTS: wrote numerous user manuals, online help systems, health education pamphlets, articles for parenting publications, feasibility study for multi-million-dollar children's center, and grants for projects ranging from education to health care. Edited monthly 40+ page newspaper, two published books, numerous magazine articles.

EDUCATION: BA Psychology, University of California, Santa Cruz. Certificate in Technical Communication, University of California at Santa Cruz. **MEMBERSHIPS:** Society of Technical Communicators.

CLIENTS WITHIN PRIOR YEAR: 6–10.

189	EDITOR	WRITER	CONSULTANT	F	NF

Germain, Shanna. 5242 SE Hawthorne Blvd., Portland, OR 97215. P1/ 503-281-3555. s.germain@comcast.net. www.shannagermain.com. Established: 1997.

SKILLS: freelance editor, copyeditor or line editor, proofreader, ghostwriter, business writer or copywriter, writing coach, writing instructor. **MARKETS SERVED:** consumer, literary and trade magazines, websites, and newspapers.

SPECIALTIES AND PREFERENCES: business, health and fitness, women's issues, food and coffee.

NONFICTION—ACCEPTS: articles/features, essays, memoirs, creative or narrative, self-help, how-to/instruction, business, humor, queries.

FEES/TERMS/CONTRACTS: editing, research, coaching $30/hour. Writing 50 cents–$2/word.

ACCOMPLISHMENTS: articles have appeared in publications such as *Delicious Living*, *MSNBC.com*, *Pizza Today*, *Portland Tribune*, and *Portrait of Portland*. Creative work has appeared in publications such as *American Journal of Nursing*, *Ink Pot*, *Pre-Hospital Emergency Care*, *Salon.com*, *Zuzu's Petals Quarterly*. I was the editor-in-chief of *Nervy Girl* magazine for three years. During that time, the publication won the Best New Zine award from *Utne Reader*. I am currently the freelance/contract editor of *Roast* magazine, a trade publication for specialty coffee roasters. The publication recently received the

Best New Education Product award from the Specialty Coffee Association of America.

EDUCATION: BA Psychology, Binghamton University, NY.

CLIENTS WITHIN PRIOR YEAR: 55–60.

190	EDITOR	WRITER	CONSULTANT	F	NF

Gettler, Nina. PO Box 60133, Seattle, WA 98160-0133. P1/ 206-368-7355. ninagettler@comcast.net. ninaget@aol.com. www.gettlertranslationediting.com. Established: 1995.

SKILLS: freelance editor, copyeditor or line editor, proofreader, ghostwriter, business writer or copywriter, translator. **MARKETS SERVED:** writers, publishers, corporations.

SPECIALTIES AND PREFERENCES: translation from/into German; editing of translations and client-generated business texts; editing book length fiction, nonfiction; business writing, copywriting.

FICTION—ACCEPTS: novels (genre, mainstream, contemporary, historical). **NONFICTION—ACCEPTS:** all. **TYPICAL EVALUATION/REPORT:** 5–8 pages.

FEES/TERMS/CONTRACTS: translation of German into English 12–16 cents/target word; English into German 14–18 cents/target word. Invoice after project is finished. Editing, writing-for-hire, copywriting $40–$75/hour. For large projects, partial payment as the project proceeds. No credit cards.

ACCOMPLISHMENTS: eight historical romance novels.

EDUCATION: MA German Literature, University of Massachusetts, Amherst. BA French Literature, University of Massachusetts, Amherst. Studied French and Russian literature, philosophy at University of Graz, Austria, for two years. **MEMBERSHIPS:** American Translators Association. Northwest Translators and Interpreters Society. Northwest Independent Editors Guild. Romance Writers of America. Novelists, Inc.

CLIENTS WITHIN PRIOR YEAR: 40–60.

191	EDITOR	WRITER	CONSULTANT	F	NF

Geyer, Bernadette. Arlington, VA. P1/ 703-243-4843. berniegeyer@yahoo.com. Established: 2000.

SKILLS: freelance editor, proofreader, business writer or copywriter, literary consultant, write reviews, poetry. **MARKETS SERVED:** authors, publishers.

SPECIALTIES AND PREFERENCES: newsletters, poetry collections, and business brochures. A poet as well as a writer, with a keen knowledge of energy and environment technologies and issues.

FICTION—ACCEPTS: poetry. **NONFICTION—ACCEPTS:** articles/features, technical, business.

FEES/TERMS/CONTRACTS: proofreading $2.50/page. Technical documents $4/page. $10 minimum.

ACCOMPLISHMENTS: proofreading for seven books. Poetry published in various literary journals. Serves on Editorial Board of The Word Works and codirects the Washington Prize, an annual poetry book competition sponsored by The Word Works.

EDUCATION: BA Communication Arts, Allegheny College, PA. **MEMBERSHIPS:** The Word Works (serves as vice president, and on editorial board). The Writer's Center.

CLIENTS WITHIN PRIOR YEAR: 1–5.

192	EDITOR	WRITER	CONSULTANT	F	NF

Gilbert, Matthew. Eastsound, WA. P1/ 360-376-4351. mgedit@hotmail.com. Established: 1996.

SKILLS: freelance editor, independent book editor, book doctor, copyeditor or line editor, ghost, business writer or copywriter, literary consultant. **MARKETS SERVED:** writers, business professionals, magazines, websites, publishers.

SPECIALTIES AND PREFERENCES: written and edited everything from operations manuals, newsletters, and press releases to feature articles and books. Book specialties include developmental and substantive editing in the areas of health, business, self-help, spiritual, and esoteric. Have worked with ideas-only to finished manuscripts.

NONFICTION—ACCEPTS: articles/features, essays, memoirs, creative or narrative, self-help, how-to/instruction, technical, business, inspiration, spiritual, book proposals, queries. **TYPICAL EVALUATION/REPORT:** 2–10 pages.

FEES/TERMS/CONTRACTS: $35–$60/hour depending on the service. Half up front, half upon delivery unless project is less than $1,000. Typically uses contract.

ACCOMPLISHMENTS: I have written and published three nonfiction books. Numerous articles on the publishing business. Features articles in national and trade magazines.

EDUCATION: Graduate Fellowship, MBA, University of Nevada, Reno. BA Statistics, BA Business Economics, State University College at Oneonta, NY. **MEMBERSHIPS:** Northwest Editors Guild. Northwest Association of Book Publishers. Authors Guild.

CLIENTS WITHIN PRIOR YEAR: 6–10.

193	EDITOR	WRITER	CONSULTANT	F	NF

Glenn, Joanne. EduInk. 6600 Potomac Ave., B2, Alexandria, VA 22307. P1/ 703-721-2088. F1/ 703-721-2089. jmgfete@aol.com. Joanne@mentorme.info. www.mentorme.info. Established: 1997.

SKILLS: editor and writer. **MARKETS SERVED:** education, health, human resources.
SPECIALTIES AND PREFERENCES: writing and editing education-, health-, and work-place-related materials such as books, articles, teaching guides, and newsletters for lay and professional audiences. Repurposing material.
NONFICTION—ACCEPTS: articles/features, how-to, curriculum, adult/online learning, business, book proposals. **TYPICAL EVALUATION/REPORT:** varies by project.
FEES/TERMS/CONTRACTS: Rates vary, depending on project. Structures rates as flat fee or hourly $50–$75/hour work for hire. Invoices clients at intervals described in a mutually approved letter of agreement. Accepts checks.
ACCOMPLISHMENTS: author of a guide for the workplace and coauthor of a business education book on communication strategies. Member/content team for Lab Tests Online, 2003 winner of the ASAE Summit Award. Many published works in education, health, and human resources publications. First-place writing awards and residency.
EDUCATION: Postgraduate, Miami University Ohio Writing Project Fellow. MS and BS Education (English minor), University of Dayton, OH. **MEMBERSHIPS:** American Society for Training and Development. International Women's Writing Guild.
CLIENTS WITHIN PRIOR YEAR: 5–10.

194	EDITOR	WRITER	CONSULTANT	F	NF

Golani, Yocheved. Yocheved Golani INK Writing Services. Teivat Doar 36255, Jerusalem, IS 91361. P1/ 972-2-999-8392. C1/ 067-681-836. F1/ 972-2-999-8392. yocheved@yochevedgolani.com. www.ygolani.com. www.yochevedgolani.com. Established: 1992.

SKILLS: freelance editor, independent book editor, book doctor, copyeditor or line editor, proofreader, ghostwriter, business writer or copywriter, technical writer, literary coach, instructor, speechwriting, feature stories. **MARKETS SERVED:** mainstream and Jewish readerships of above-average intelligence.
SPECIALTIES AND PREFERENCES: feature stories, speechwriting, editing nonfiction. A reputation for accuracy and timeliness.
FICTION—ACCEPTS: all. **NONFICTION—ACCEPTS:** all.
FEES/TERMS/CONTRACTS: hourly or per-project flat fee payable by wire transfer/ electronic deposit.
ACCOMPLISHMENTS: Apex Award for Communication Excellence/Websites from Communication Concepts, 2001. Anthologized in Targum/Feldheim Press, Baltimore Writers Alliance, and Booklocker publications. *Baltimore/Washington Business Journals. Baltimore Jewish Times. Horizons Family* magazine. israel-nationalnews.com. Jewish Law website. jewishworldreview.com. The Jewish Press. *Voices* magazine/website.
EDUCATION: BA English, Oakland University, Rochester, MI. Medical Coder

Certification from SUNY/Downstate. **MEMBERSHIPS:** American Jewish Press Association. National Writers Union. Washington Independent Writers. **CLIENTS WITHIN PRIOR YEAR:** 1–5.

195	EDITOR	WRITER	CONSULTANT	F	NF

Gold, Melanie. 2199 Ackermanville Rd., Bangor, PA 18013-9336. P1/ 610-588-4849. MelanieInPA@aol.com. Established: 1995.

SKILLS: freelance editor, copyeditor or line editor, proofreader. **MARKETS SERVED:** I serve mainly commercial and academic book publishers. I've also done work for individual authors and worked in-house to proof journal articles and promotional copy. Willing to branch out into magazines, book packagers, corporations.

SPECIALTIES AND PREFERENCES: I love the book publishing industry. I tend to enjoy nonfiction the most, especially cookbooks—typically the projects that cause production and managing editorial the most headaches. I prefer proofreading to copyediting. I have a good working knowledge of (but not fluent in) Spanish.

FICTION—ACCEPTS: y/a or juvenile, novels (genre, mainstream, literary, contemporary, historical). **NONFICTION—ACCEPTS:** all.

FEES/TERMS/CONTRACTS: vary by deadline, length and type of work. Typically, for publishers, $16/hour+ proofreading, $18/hour+ copyediting. Contracts with individuals.

ACCOMPLISHMENTS: clients include Ballantine Books, HarperCollins, Henry Holt & Co., Countryman Press, Storey Communications, The Lyons Press, Soho Books, St. Martin's Press, Alfred A. Knopf, Prometheus Books, and others. Ask for book title list.

EDUCATION: BFA Journalism, School of Visual Arts, New York, NY.

CLIENTS WITHIN PRIOR YEAR: dozens of projects.

196	EDITOR	WRITER	CONSULTANT	F	NF

Goldhaber, F.I. Salem, OR. fi@goldhaber.net. www.goldhaber.net. Established: 1984.

SKILLS: freelance editor, independent book editor, copyeditor or line editor, proofreader, ghostwriter, business writer or copywriter, writing instructor, public speaker. **MARKETS SERVED:** all.

SPECIALTIES AND PREFERENCES: no specialties or preferences. I consider all submissions.

FICTION—ACCEPTS: short stories, novels (genre, mainstream, contemporary, historical). **NONFICTION—ACCEPTS:** articles/features, essays, memoirs, creative or narrative, biography/autobiography, family history, self-help, how-to/

instruction, business, humor.

FEES/TERMS/CONTRACTS: $4/page for book/story editing. $50–$75/hour for business writing/editing. $250 minimum for one-time projects. No credit cards. Use agreement.

ACCOMPLISHMENTS: more than twenty-five years as a professional writer, six years as a newspaper reporter/editor; seventeen years as business writer, editor, marketing communications consultant. Writers of the Future Quarterfinalist. Third place in Paul B. Duquette Memorial Short Sci-Fi contest. National Charlotte Danstrom Woman of Achievement Award by Women in Management. Award-winning, internationally published fiction writer. Pacific North Writers Literary Contest judge. Creative writing instructor.

EDUCATION: BA Communications, University of Washington, Seattle. **MEMBERSHIPS:** Willamette Writers. Pacific Northwest Writers Association. Oregon Writers Colony.

CLIENTS WITHIN PRIOR YEAR: 1–5.

197	EDITOR	WRITER	CONSULTANT	F	NF

Gómez, Leticia. Spanish Language Solutions. 7 Bayou Springs Ct., The Woodlands, TX 77382. P1/ 936-273-3443. C1/ 281-682-7508. F1/ 936-273-3443. leticia@flex.net. Established: 2001.

SKILLS: freelance editor, copyeditor or line editor, proofreader, ghostwriter, business writer or copywriter, technical writer, literary consultant, literary translator. **MARKETS SERVED:** writers, book publishers, nonprofit organizations, and corporations.

SPECIALTIES AND PREFERENCES: creative English-Spanish writing services, commercial and literary translations, line and copyediting, proofreading, technical writing, ghostwriting, literary and publishing consultant.

FICTION—ACCEPTS: all. **NONFICTION—ACCEPTS:** all. **TYPICAL EVALUATION/REPORT:** 2–25 pages.

FEES/TERMS/CONTRACTS: creative writing, fee is negotiable. Editing services $20/ hour. Proofreading $18/hour. Translation $125/1,000 words. Uses agreement.

ACCOMPLISHMENTS: one romance novel published, one reference book published, dozens of articles published in national magazines and newspapers, edited two published fiction novels and one nonfiction, translated half a dozen novels.

EDUCATION: BA Journalism, Eastern New Mexico University, Portales. **MEMBERSHIPS:** Romance Writers of America.

CLIENTS WITHIN PRIOR YEAR: 5–10.

198	EDITOR	WRITER	CONSULTANT	F	NF

Goodman, John. Good Code Works. 9472 Central Ave., Garden Grove, CA 92844-1505. P1/ 714-537-6400. F1/ 775-254-3146. john@agoodman.com. Established: 1969.

SKILLS: freelance editor, independent book editor, writing coach, writing instructor, graphic artist, designer. **MARKETS SERVED:** businesses, especially involved with technical material or products.

SPECIALTIES AND PREFERENCES: clear explanations in words/pictures of arcane technical material. Grant proposal writing/editing, Small Business Innovation Research grants.

NONFICTION—ACCEPTS: articles/features, essays, memoirs, biography/autobiography, family history, self-help, how-to/instruction, technical, text or reference, business, book proposals, queries.

FEES/TERMS/CONTRACTS: negotiable by the hour, by the page, or by fixed-price contract.

ACCOMPLISHMENTS: author of seven mass-market books, several bestsellers on how computers work, including a Computer Press Association award winner (*Hard Disk Secrets*). Numerous articles on computer-related topics, awarded grant proposals, etc.

EDUCATION: PhD Physics and History of Science & Technology, Cornell University. Ithaca, NY. BA Physics, Mathematics, & Chemistry, Swarthmore College, PA. **MEMBERSHIPS:** American Association for the Advancement of Science. American Association of Museums. American Association of Physics Teachers. American Physical Society. Computer Press Association. Institute of Electrical and Electronic Engineers. Mensa. Museum Educators of Southern California. Orange County Arts Alliance.

CLIENTS WITHIN PRIOR YEAR: not disclosed.

199	EDITOR	WRITER	CONSULTANT	F	NF

Goodness, Candice. Candice A Goodness Freelance Proofreading. 95006 Spring Valley Lane, Marcola, OR 97454. P1/ 541-933-1207. F1/ 541-933-1207. candyg@holtintl.org. Established: 1987.

SKILLS: copyeditor or line editor, proofreader, transcriber. **MARKETS SERVED:** publishers, nonprofits.

SPECIALTIES AND PREFERENCES: My specialties are varied. I have twenty-eight years of experience word processing, proofreading, transcribing, and editing. This includes financial documents, reports, scientific articles, and manuscripts of all kinds. I have no specific preferences and enjoy a variety of subjects.

FICTION—ACCEPTS: y/a or juvenile, short stories, novels (genre, mainstream, literary, contemporary, historical), poetry, scripts/screenplays, queries, synopses, treatments. NONFICTION—ACCEPTS: all.

FEES/TERMS/CONTRACTS: hourly rate, but this is negotiable.

ACCOMPLISHMENTS: going back to school after thirty years, and being a mom.

EDUCATION: I am currently enrolled full-time at a private college to become a Nationally Certified Medical Assistant and plan to use my medical knowledge to expand my client base.

CLIENTS WITHIN PRIOR YEAR: 1–5.

200	EDITOR	WRITER	CONSULTANT	F	NF

Gottlieb, Sherry. The Novel Doctor. Oxnard, CA. P1/ 805-382-3425. F1/ 805-658-8601. writer@wordservices.com. www.wordservices.com. Established: 1991.

SKILLS: freelance editor, independent book editor, book doctor, copyeditor or line editor, literary consultant, writing coach. MARKETS SERVED: writers.

SPECIALTIES AND PREFERENCES: I specialize in fiction, discerning exactly what an individual manuscript needs, from plot structure and point of view to character development, dialog, pacing, and marketability. I provide detailed notes and intensive, specific line editing throughout the manuscript itself, as well as a detailed 2–4 page single-spaced letter explaining general problems and suggested solutions. Available for postediting consultation and coaching.

FICTION—ACCEPTS: y/a or juvenile, short stories, novels (genre, mainstream, literary, contemporary, historical), scripts/screenplays, treatments. NONFICTION—ACCEPTS: creative or narrative, biography/autobiography.

FEES/TERMS/CONTRACTS: $40/hour, averaging 8–10 pages/hour. $500 deposit, balance upon completion of work. Checks and credit cards (MC/Visa/Amex).

ACCOMPLISHMENTS: one nonfiction book and two novels from major publishers, one filmed as TV movie.

EDUCATION: BA Dramatic Arts (playwriting), University of California, Berkeley.

CLIENTS WITHIN PRIOR YEAR: 5–6.

201	EDITOR	WRITER	CONSULTANT	F	NF

Gould, Gerry. 4 Arlington Pl., Fair Lawn, NJ 07410. P1/ 201-794-1023. ggedit@optonline.net. Established: 20+ years.

SKILLS: freelance editor, independent book editor, book doctor, copyeditor or line editor, rewrite particularly for ESL researchers. MARKETS SERVED: fiction—trade; nonfiction—medical, technical; food technology; young adult.

SPECIALTIES AND PREFERENCES: cookbooks; religion; biography; Continuing Medical Education; HIV, AIDS.

FICTION—ACCEPTS: y/a or juvenile, short stories, novels (mainstream, literary, contemporary, historical), poetry. NONFICTION—ACCEPTS: y/a or juvenile, articles/features, essays, memoirs, creative or narrative, biography/autobiography, how-to/instruction, technical, text or reference, humor, religious.

FEES/TERMS/CONTRACTS: per hour or page depends on length and technicality of report; contracts for longer works; payments due one-third at start, one-third mid-project, final third at completion.

ACCOMPLISHMENTS: Copyeditors don't usually receive awards, but do receive nice mentions in intros. "Published work" doesn't apply here. I'm hired only for committed work. All of my medical/technical and continuing medical education work has been published. Also my edited journal articles (except for two I discovered were plagiarisms).

EDUCATION: BFA, University of New Mexico at Albuquerque. **MEMBERSHIPS:** Copy Editor. Editorial Freelancers Association.

CLIENTS WITHIN PRIOR YEAR: 5–10.

202	EDITOR	WRITER	CONSULTANT	F	NF

Gould, Meredith. Supreme Word Goddess of the Universe. PO Box 63, Rocky Hill, NJ 08553. P1/ 609-924-8664. F1/ 609-924-8664. Meredith@meredithgould.com. www.meredithgould.com. Established: 1989.

SKILLS: freelance editor, book doctor, developmental and line editor, freelance writer, writing coach. **MARKETS SERVED:** writers who want to become authors (traditional or print on demand, i.e., POD).

SPECIALTIES AND PREFERENCES: translating impenetrable prose into reader-friendly copy. Nonfiction business, self-help, literary nonfiction, religion, health, health care, chick lit. Prefers good humored, coachable clients.

NONFICTION—ACCEPTS: creative or narrative, how-to/instruction, business, inspirational/religious.

FEES/TERMS/CONTRACTS: $65–$85/hour. Read-through and evaluation $250 minimum. Coaching $75/hour. Terms negotable.

ACCOMPLISHMENTS: authored four nonfiction books; book reviews for *Times of Trenton*; columnist for *Faith & Family* and *godspy.com*; numerous magazine pieces. Check out: www.meredithgould.com.

EDUCATION: PhD Sociology, New York University; undergraduate work in graphic design and illustration, Rochester Institute of Technology, NY.

CLIENTS WITHIN PRIOR YEAR: 11–20.

203	EDITOR	WRITER	CONSULTANT	F	NF

Gramon, Jim. PO Box 2100, Manchaca, TX 78652-2100. P1/ 512-736-2499. Jim@JimGramon.com. www.JimGramon.com. Established: 1997.

SKILLS: freelance editor, copyeditor, ghostwriter, technical writer, literary consultant, writing coach, writing instructor, freelance photographer, public speaker, instructor on writing and marketing. **MARKETS SERVED:** all businesses and writers.

SPECIALTIES AND PREFERENCES: My specialty is putting complex concepts into people-friendly and humorous terms.

FICTION—ACCEPTS: all. **NONFICTION—ACCEPTS:** all.

FEES/TERMS/CONTRACTS: Fees are always competitive. Rates vary depending on the skills required and the duration of the project.

ACCOMPLISHMENTS: three nonfiction books published with Republic of Texas Press. Hundreds of columns, articles, and numerous screenplays.

EDUCATION: BS Biology, Chemistry, and English, University of Texas at Austin.

MEMBERSHIPS: vice president of The Writers' League of Texas.

CLIENTS WITHIN PRIOR YEAR: 11–20.

204	EDITOR	WRITER	CONSULTANT	F	NF

Gray, Linda. RoadRunner BookWorks. Santa Barbara, CA. P1/ 805-683-7549. F1/ 805-683-7549. rrbw@cox.net. lgraypoet@cox.net. Established: 2002.

SKILLS: freelance editor, independent book editor, book doctor, copyeditor or line editor, proofreader, ghostwriter, writing coach, writing instructor. **MARKETS SERVED:** publishers, writers, graduate students.

SPECIALTIES AND PREFERENCES: developmental editing, copyediting, and proofreading of academic journals, books, textbooks, master's theses, and dissertations. Electronic or hard copy. Some graphics work. Reliable, responsive service at reasonable prices. Ideal project—copyediting academic work, preferably APA style.

NONFICTION—ACCEPTS: y/a, articles/features, essays, memoirs, creative or narrative, biography/autobiography, family history, self-help, how-to/instruction, text or reference, dissertations, theses, inspirational/religious, spiritual.

FEES/TERMS/CONTRACTS: fees start at $25/hour or $4.50/page. Payment due in 14 days.

ACCOMPLISHMENTS: former senior copyeditor at Sage Publications.

EDUCATION: MA English, University of Northern Colorado, Greeley. BA Physical Education, University of Northern Colorado, Greeley.

CLIENTS WITHIN PRIOR YEAR: 11–20.

205	EDITOR	WRITER	CONSULTANT	F	NF

Gray, Stephanie. Portland, OR. P1/ 503-241-0227. stephw11@yahoo.com. Established: 2002.

SKILLS: freelance editor, copyeditor or line editor, proofreader, business writer or copywriter, technical writer, educational books, manuals and all imaginable marketing materials. **MARKETS SERVED:** for-profit, nonprofit, publishers, corporations, writers.

SPECIALTIES AND PREFERENCES: copyediting and all its many layers; marketing materials; educational materials; presentation materials; working with broad and tight deadlines. From simple punctuation to paragraph flow to presentation, I work independently and with teams to produce the tightest and strongest copy. While I prefer more creative writing to technical writing, I put as much energy into editing literature as I do into dessert recipes.

FICTION—ACCEPTS: y/a or juvenile, picture books, short stories, novels (genre, mainstream, literary, contemporary, historical), poetry, scripts/screenplays. **NONFICTION—ACCEPTS:** all.

FEES/TERMS/CONTRACTS: nonprofit $30/hour. Other $50/hour. No credit cards.

ACCOMPLISHMENTS: I began my writing/editing career with news stations, and online and print magazines. Then I was hired to be the sole copyeditor for a tight marketing team.

EDUCATION: BA Journalism, University of Montana, Missoula.

CLIENTS WITHIN PRIOR YEAR: 1–5.

206	EDITOR	WRITER	CONSULTANT	F	NF

Green, Brent. Brent Green & Associates, Inc. 1011 S. Valentia St., Suite #86, Denver, CO 80247. brent@bgassociates.com. www.marketingtoboomers.com. Established: 1986.

SKILLS: freelance editor, business writer or copywriter. **MARKETS SERVED:** health and fitness, high tech, direct mail marketers, and businesses targeting baby boomers.

SPECIALTIES AND PREFERENCES: all aspects of marketing communications with an emphasis on direct-response copywriting, magazine-style business articles, catalogs, brochures, promotional pieces, and essays.

FICTION—ACCEPTS: novels (mainstream). **NONFICTION—ACCEPTS:** articles/features, how-to/instruction, text or reference.

FEES/TERMS/CONTRACTS: $125/hour or negotiated project budget.

ACCOMPLISHMENTS: author of self-published nonfiction books on marketing and public relations, and of a literary novel. Over fifty creative and marketing industry awards, including Direct Marketer of the Year, Rocky Mountain Direct Marketing Association, 2000. Business Marketing Association Gold Key Awards, 2002, 2003, 2004.

EDUCATION: MA Psychology, University of Kansas, Lawrence. BA Psychology, Communications, University of Kansas, Lawrence. **MEMBERSHIPS:** Business Marketing Association. Rocky Mountain Direct Marketing Association. American Society on Aging. Business Forum on Aging. Leadership Council.

CLIENTS WITHIN PRIOR YEAR: 6–10.

207	EDITOR	WRITER	CONSULTANT	F	NF

Green, Cynthia. Thema—Ideas in Print. Santa Fe, NM. P1/ 505-988-5185. C1/ 05-699-5945. F1/ 505-988-5185. edit@thema.us. www.thema.us. Established: 2001.

SKILLS: freelance editor, independent book editor, book doctor, copyeditor or line editor, proofreader, ghostwriter, business writer or copywriter, technical writer, literary consultant, writing coach, writing instructor, book reviewer, researcher, brochure designer, cover designer. MARKETS SERVED: writers, publishers, self publishers, nonprofits, corporations, author service providers.

SPECIALTIES AND PREFERENCES: intensive writing consulting. Book development. Book proposals. Prepress layout and design.

FICTION—ACCEPTS: y/a or juvenile, picture books, short stories, novels (genre, mainstream, literary, contemporary, historical), poetry, queries, synopses, treatments. NONFICTION—ACCEPTS: all. TYPICAL EVALUATION/REPORT: 5–25 pages.

FEES/TERMS/CONTRACTS: editing $40/hour, 5 pages/hour. Ghostwriting/per project. Coaching $50/hour. Payment in advance/arrange. No credit cards. Written agreement.

ACCOMPLISHMENTS: Winner fiction writing award. Ten published clients in four years.

EDUCATION: MS Educational Psychology, University of Wisconsin, Madison. BS Education, University of North Dakota, Grand Forks. BA Anthropology, Lake Forest College, IL. MEMBERSHIPS: New Mexico Book Association. Story Circle Network. National Association of Women Writers.

CLIENTS WITHIN PRIOR YEAR: 20–25.

208	EDITOR	WRITER	CONSULTANT	F	NF

Greenlee, Michelle. Lubbock, TX. P1/ 806-549-5694. P2/ 806-885-5411. michelle@theinfojunkie.com. lrnews@quixnet.net. www.theinfojunkie.com. Established: 2003.

SKILLS: freelance editor, copyeditor or line editor, proofreader, ghostwriter, business writer or copywriter. MARKETS SERVED: nonprofit organizations, private corporations, small businesses, individuals.

SPECIALTIES AND PREFERENCES: web copy/rewrite, copyedit, ghostwriting, business materials. Works with mildly technical material.

FICTION—ACCEPTS: y/a or juvenile, picture books, short stories, novels (genre, mainstream, literary, contemporary), poetry. NONFICTION—ACCEPTS: articles/features, essays, memoirs, creative or narrative, biography/autobiography, family history, self-help, how-to/instruction, business, humor.

FEES/TERMS/CONTRACTS: read-through/evaluation $35 (excludes book length). Content/substantive editing $25/hour. Word processing $22.50/hour. Desktop publishing base $25.50/hour. Sample edit $19/hour (limit 3 pages).

Additional services available. Retainer fees. Invoice, net due 15 days. PayPal. Checks. Contracts.

ACCOMPLISHMENTS: publication in print newspapers/magazines, various websites.

EDUCATION: sales and marketing management course through Virtual University (vu.org). MEMBERSHIPS: Teachers and Writers Collaborative (twc.org). The Writer's Bridge CoOp of Writers and Editors (thewritersbridge.com). Committee for Concerned Journalists (journalism.org). Team Double Click Virtual Staffing Agency (teamdoubleclick.com).

CLIENTS WITHIN PRIOR YEAR: 1–5.

209	EDITOR	WRITER	CONSULTANT	F	NF

Greenstein, Mike. Mike Greenstein Writing and Editing. 3635 43rd Ave. W, Seattle, WA 98199-1805. P1/ 206-282-2791. mikegreenstein@aol.com. Established: 1998.

SKILLS: freelance editor, independent book editor, book doctor, copyeditor or line editor, proofreader, ghostwriter, business writer or copywriter, technical writer, literary consultant, writing coach, writing instructor. MARKETS SERVED: periodicals, advertising, medical-technical editing.

SPECIALTIES AND PREFERENCES: news/feature articles, clinical study reports, and other regulatory submissions; human resources policies; user manuals for hardware and software. Mike Greenstein is an award-winning editor-writer in journalism and advertising, adept with grammar, spelling, and style and able to create and execute multiple projects under deadline. He is also editor of the annual "Washington State Visitors' Guide" and a technical editor for medical and pharmaceutical firms.

NONFICTION—ACCEPTS: all.

FEES/TERMS/CONTRACTS: $60/hour.

ACCOMPLISHMENTS: won Syracuse Press Club Awards for best criticism, best sports story, and best scenic photograph, plus copywriting awards from Syracuse Ad Club and Cable Advertising and Promotion Awards. Coauthored *Syracuse University Basketball Trivia* and *Music Industry and the Media*.

EDUCATION: MS and BA, Syracuse University Newhouse School of Public Communications, NY. MEMBERSHIPS: Northwest Independent Editors Guild.

CLIENTS WITHIN PRIOR YEAR: 11–20.

210	EDITOR	WRITER	CONSULTANT	F	NF

Greenstein, Ruth. Greenline Publishing Consultants. 131 Fifth Ave., Suite 501, New York, NY 10003. P1/ 212-673-8366. rg@greenlinepublishing.com. www.greenlinepublishing.com. Established: 1998.

SKILLS: independent book editor, book doctor, line editor, ghostwriter, copywriter, literary consultant. **MARKETS SERVED:** writers, agents, publishers, and packagers.

SPECIALTIES AND PREFERENCES: especially skilled at working with first-time writers, and helping all writers refine their voice, polish their presentation, and navigate the publishing scene. Prefers literary fiction, illustrated nonfiction, biography/memoir, travel, nature, visual and performing arts, social and cultural issues, health, psychology, religion and spirituality, media tie-ins, anthologies, reference, poetry, and works in translation.

FICTION—ACCEPTS: short stories, novels (literary, contemporary), poetry, queries, synopses. **NONFICTION—ACCEPTS:** all. **TYPICAL EVALUATION/REPORT:** 3–5 pages.

FEES/TERMS/CONTRACTS: offers a confidential rate quote after a free initial consultation.

ACCOMPLISHMENTS: seasoned editor with over fifteen years of book publishing experience. Formerly with Harcourt and Ecco. Has worked with numerous bestselling and award-winning authors, including Alice Walker, Anita Shreve, Erica Jong, Gary Paulsen, John Ashbery, Dennis Lehane, others. Contributing writer to three books.

EDUCATION: Graduate studies, Annenberg School of Communications, University of Pennsylvania, Philadelphia. BA Communications, University of California, Berkeley. **MEMBERSHIPS:** Association of Writers & Writing Programs. Academy of American Poets.

CLIENTS WITHIN PRIOR YEAR: 21–30.

211	EDITOR	WRITER	CONSULTANT	F	NF

Grimes, Gwin, Grogan. Fort Worth, TX. P1/ 817-989-1374. F1/ 817-989-1374. f.g.grimes@tcu.edu. ggrogan@sbcglobal.net. Established: 1986.

SKILLS: freelance editor, independent book editor, copyeditor or line editor, proofreader, ghostwriter, business writer or copywriter, writing coach. **MARKETS SERVED:** cookbook publishers, health care providers, hospitals, newspapers, magazines, newsletters.

SPECIALTIES AND PREFERENCES: As a freelance editor and writer, I consider all types of jobs but specialize in the health care industry and food/nutrition. I was an editor and reporter for seventeen years for daily newspapers, a weekly business magazine, and a monthly parenting magazine.

NONFICTION—ACCEPTS: articles/features, creative or narrative, how-to/instruction, business.

FEES/TERMS/CONTRACTS: $20–$50/hour for various editing services from proofreading to content editing; fee per word for article writing; fee per page for book writing. Monthly billing, no credit cards. Uses a contract.

ACCOMPLISHMENTS: Nestle National Nutrition Writing Award, 1991.

EDUCATION: MLA, Texas Christian University, Fort Worth. BA Journalism, Louisiana State University, Shreveport. MEMBERSHIPS: Association for Women Journalists.
CLIENTS WITHIN PRIOR YEAR: 1–5.

212	EDITOR	WRITER	CONSULTANT	F	NF

Gross, Andrea. Legacy Prose. Denver, CO. P1/ 303-394-9339. andy@legacyprose.com. www.legacyprose.com. Established: 1990.

SKILLS: ghostwriter, writing coach, personal historian. MARKETS SERVED: individuals, families, throughout the United States.

SPECIALTIES AND PREFERENCES: helps people preserve personal and family history. Works as interviewer, coach, or ghost—in person, by phone, by e-mail. The goal is privately printed memoirs for family and friends; clients rarely aim for professional publication.

NONFICTION—ACCEPTS: articles/features, essays, memoirs, creative or narrative, biography/autobiography, family history, self-help.

FEES/TERMS/CONTRACTS: fees vary according to project. No credit cards. Typically uses contract.

ACCOMPLISHMENTS: hundreds of articles published in national magazines and newspapers, four books by major publishing houses, and numerous privately printed memoirs.

EDUCATION: BS Education, Northwestern University, Evanston, IL. MEMBERSHIPS: Association of Personal Historians. American Society of Journalists and Authors. Society of American Travel Writers. Colorado Authors League.
CLIENTS WITHIN PRIOR YEAR: 10–15.

213	EDITOR	WRITER	CONSULTANT	F	NF

Gross, Jerry. Gerald Gross Associates LLC. 63 Grand St., Croton-on-Hudson, NY 10520-2518. P1/ 914-271-8705. GrosAssoc@aol.com. www.bookdocs.com (click on Jerry Gross). Established: 1978.

SKILLS: freelance editor, independent book editor, book doctor. MARKETS SERVED: writers, editors, publishers, literary agents.

SPECIALTIES AND PREFERENCES: I do in-depth critiques of fiction and nonfiction manuscripts and proposals, identifying what works and suggesting specific solutions to any problems I see. May do line editing of a manuscript after the author revises it.

FICTION—ACCEPTS: y/a or juvenile, novels (mainstream, literary, contemporary, historical), queries, synopses. NONFICTION—ACCEPTS: all. TYPICAL EVALUATION/ REPORT: 10–30 pages.

FEES/TERMS/CONTRACTS: fees and references on request. Fee paid half on signing contract and half on completion of project.

ACCOMPLISHMENTS: author of several books including true crime; *Publishers on Publishing, Editors on Editing*, in its third edition; and one on the responsibility of the press. Presents workshops and panels at writers' conferences.

EDUCATION: BA English, *cum laude*, City College of New York. **MEMBERSHIPS:** Independent Editors Group, President and Cofounder. Poets, Essayists, Novelists (PEN). National Writers Union. Author's Guild. City College of New York Communications Alumni Association.

CLIENTS WITHIN PRIOR YEAR: 40–45.

214	EDITOR	WRITER	CONSULTANT	F	NF

Guzmán, Lila. Two Texas Authors. 1715 Pecos Valley Cove, Round Rock, TX 78664. P1/ 512-255-7440. P2/ 512-388-7800. F1/ 512-388-7801. lorenzo1776@yahoo.com. www.talk.to/Lila. Established: 2000.

SKILLS: freelance editor, independent book editor, book doctor, copyeditor or line editor, proofreader, literary consultant, writing coach, writing instructor, translator—Spanish to English/French to English. **MARKETS SERVED:** all fiction writers and publishers.

SPECIALTIES AND PREFERENCES: I work closely with writers in a long-term relationship to shape fiction into the best product possible. Writers must be open-minded and willing to rewrite. Upon publication, we celebrate with a lobster-and-champagne dinner. You buy.

FICTION—ACCEPTS: y/a or juvenile, short stories, novels (genre, mainstream, literary, historical), queries, synopses. **TYPICAL EVALUATION/REPORT:** 1–5 pages.

FEES/TERMS/CONTRACTS: $3/page/Courier 12 only. Translations: $10/page. See website for terms. No credit cards. PayPal. Uses contract.

ACCOMPLISHMENTS: three published novels; two historical, one fantasy. Dozens of short stories and nonfiction articles on writing. Multiple awards for novels and short stories.

EDUCATION: PhD Modern Spanish Literature, University of Kentucky, Lexington. BA Spanish and French, Western Kentucky University, Bowling Green. **MEMBERSHIPS:** Writers' League of Texas. National League of American Pen Women.

CLIENTS WITHIN PRIOR YEAR: 1–5.

215	EDITOR	WRITER	CONSULTANT	F	NF

Gwartney, Debra. 750 Monroe #2, Eugene, OR 97405. P1/ 541-687-8713. debragwartney@att.net. Established: 1994.

SKILLS: freelance editor, independent book editor, book doctor, ghostwriter, business writer or copywriter, literary consultant, writing coach, writing instructor. **MARKETS SERVED:** writers, publishers.

SPECIALTIES AND PREFERENCES: one-on-one mentoring and editing. Workshop instruction in memoir, essay, and literature. Manuscript consultation.

FICTION—ACCEPTS: y/a or juvenile, short stories, novels (mainstream, literary, contemporary, historical), queries, synopses, treatments. **NONFICTION— ACCEPTS:** articles/features, essays, memoirs, creative or narrative, biography/ autobiography, family history, humor, inspirational/religious, spiritual, book proposals, queries. **TYPICAL EVALUATION/REPORT:** 25-30 page report for a 250-300 page manuscript.

FEES/TERMS/CONTRACTS: $5/page.

ACCOMPLISHMENTS: journalist, editor, memoirist, essayist. Many magazine and newspaper publications, plus publications of creative work. Awards include Bread Loaf Scholar, Helene Wurlitzer Foundation Fellowship, Literary Arts Nonfiction Fellow, and others.

EDUCATION: MA Journalism/Nonfiction, University of Arizona, Tucson. BA English, University of Idaho, Moscow. **MEMBERSHIPS:** Phi Beta Kappa.

CLIENTS WITHIN PRIOR YEAR: 4–6 individual editing projects/6–8 workshops.

216	EDITOR	WRITER	CONSULTANT	F	NF

Haggerty, Maureen. 320 Patrick Pl., Chalfont, PA 18914. P1/ 215-822-2229. maureenhaggerty@juno.com. Established: 1980.

SKILLS: freelance editor, independent book editor, book doctor, copyeditor or line editor, proofreader, ghostwriter, business writer or copywriter, writing instructor, publicist. **MARKETS SERVED:** consumer, professional, special interest.

SPECIALTIES AND PREFERENCES: versatile, award-winning writer/editor with special expertise in health and aging. Skilled at presenting complex material in language that empowers consumers to make informed health care and life-style choices. Additional services include books, speeches, ads, advertorials, publication management, ghostwriting.

FICTION—ACCEPTS: y/a or juvenile, short stories, novels, poetry, scripts/screen-plays, queries, synopses, treatments. **NONFICTION—ACCEPTS:** all.

FEES/TERMS/CONTRACTS: to be negotiated.

ACCOMPLISHMENTS: I have won awards from Catholic Press Association of United States and Canada, and Women in Communications. Some publications include *Gray Panthers Network, Dermatology Insights, CGA World, The Match, Panorama.*

EDUCATION: BA English and Russian (dual major), Lycoming College, Williamsport, PA. **MEMBERSHIPS:** Editorial Freelancers Association. Writers-Editors Network.

CLIENTS WITHIN PRIOR YEAR: 15–20.

217	EDITOR	WRITER	CONSULTANT	F	NF

Haggith, David. Signature Communications. Seattle, WA. P1/ 206-281-7133. haggith@earthlink.net. Established: 1992.

SKILLS: freelance editor, independent book editor, ghostwriter, business writer or copywriter, technical writer, screenplays. **MARKETS SERVED:** commissioned by individuals or families of significant public interest to collaborate under a coauthoring agreement, but will consider ghostwriting.

SPECIALTIES AND PREFERENCES: especially good at interviewing and pulling together material for true-life books.

FICTION—ACCEPTS: all. **NONFICTION—ACCEPTS:** all.

FEES/TERMS/CONTRACTS: $55/hour for short pieces. Contract for books—average about $50/page for full-length book manuscripts with share of royalties after commission/advance is paid back from royalties.

ACCOMPLISHMENTS: one nonfiction book published in UK and US. Articles published in various newspapers around the US. Two minor poetry awards. Two marketing awards for college advertising in the form of a college view book and a series of radio spots.

EDUCATION: BA English, minored in Greek, with a writing emphasis at Western Washington University, Bellingham. Graduated cum laude. One-year screenwriting course and certificate, University of Washington, Seattle.

MEMBERSHIPS: National Writers Union.

CLIENTS WITHIN PRIOR YEAR: 1–5.

218	EDITOR	WRITER	CONSULTANT	F	NF

Hahn, Mary. WriteSuccess Enterprises. 273 Shotwell Park, Syracuse, NY 13206. P1/ 315-424-1372. F1/ 315-424-1372. hahnmah@aol.com. Established: 2000.

SKILLS: freelance editor, book doctor, copyeditor, proofreader, business writer. **MARKETS SERVED:** small businesses, independent professionals, medical and health professionals.

SPECIALTIES AND PREFERENCES: business and marketing writing, such as print and e-mail newsletters, brochures, web content, fliers, telephone scripts, and training manuals.

NONFICTION—ACCEPTS: articles/features, self-help, how-to/instruction, business, queries.

FEES/TERMS/CONTRACTS: writing, $85–$125/page for most projects (newsletters, articles, press releases, website content, marketing and business plans, etc.). Editing and rewriting, the flat rate is $30/page. Proofreading $10/page. Provides project quotes in advance. Accepts payment via PayPal or US mail. Uses a contract.

ACCOMPLISHMENTS: author of numerous articles on career and management topics, which appeared in *Women As Managers*, *Office Hours*, *Supervision*, *Next Step*

Magazine, The Home Business Journal, and others.
EDUCATION: BA Communications, Cornell University, Ithaca, NY.
CLIENTS WITHIN PRIOR YEAR: 6–10.

219	EDITOR	WRITER	CONSULTANT	F	NF

Hake, Mary. 13965 SW Cinder Dr., Terrebonne, OR 97760-9305. P1/ 541-504-4535. trmhake@madras.net. Established: 1995.

SKILLS: freelance editor, independent book editor, copyeditor or line editor, proofreader, ghostwriter, business writer or copywriter, writing coach, writing instructor, publicist, research. MARKETS SERVED: writers, nonprofit organizations.

SPECIALTIES AND PREFERENCES: writing for both adults and children, including nonfiction and fiction, poetry, puzzles, and quizzes. Editing and copyediting work for hire—from newsletters and mailings to books. Research. I pay attention to details.

FICTION—ACCEPTS: all. NONFICTION—ACCEPTS: all.

FEES/TERMS/CONTRACTS: simple editing/proofreading $30/hour. No credit cards.

ACCOMPLISHMENTS: writing for over twenty years. Oregon Newspaper Publisher's Association awards for writing feature article and column for college newspaper. Publishing credits include newspaper articles and columns, contribution to book compilations, fiction, poetry, devotions, puzzles, and nonfiction articles.

EDUCATION: AA Journalism and Mass Communications, Linn-Benton Community College, Albany, OR. 4.0 student. MEMBERSHIPS: Oregon Christian Writers (five years as program coordinator for annual conferences and taught at writers' conferences). Phi Theta Kappa (officer for two years).

CLIENTS WITHIN PRIOR YEAR: 1–5.

220	EDITOR	WRITER	CONSULTANT	F	NF

Halpern, Barbara. Marketing Momentum. 4700 Connecticut Ave. NW, Ste. 208, Washington, DC 20008-5611. P1/ 202-244-9925.
bizguru@marketingmomentum.net. barbara@ioncontent.com.
www.marketingmomentum.net. www.ioncontent.com. Established: 1986.

SKILLS: freelance editor, copyeditor or line editor, proofreader, ghostwriter, business writer or copywriter, technical writer. MARKETS SERVED: corporate, health care, small business, nonprofits.

SPECIALTIES AND PREFERENCES: I am a versatile writer, strategist, and implementer. My forté is business communications and marketing, and how to maximize effectiveness to achieve your goals. I can write everything from advertising copy to annual report, brochure to press release. Great on the implementation, so you get maximum mileage!

NONFICTION—ACCEPTS: articles/features, self-help, how-to/instruction, technical, text or reference, business, book proposals, queries.

FEES/TERMS/CONTRACTS: prefers percentage up front, balance on delivery. Other options (hourly, page, project, retainers) can be arranged. Flexible.

ACCOMPLISHMENTS: business and marketing writing that sizzles. Integrated approach to generate sales and visibility. Like a one-woman band. Can do it all! Hands-on and versatile. Association, business, health care clients.

EDUCATION: MBA Marketing/Finance, Boston College, Chestnut Hill, MA. BA History/Psychology, Union College, Schenectady, NY. Certificate in Web Development. **MEMBERSHIPS:** Washington Independent Writers. Institute of Management Consultants. Washington Healthcare Marketing & PR (WMSHMPR), DC Web Women.

CLIENTS WITHIN PRIOR YEAR: 6–10.

221	EDITOR	WRITER	CONSULTANT	F	NF

Hamilton, Terri. PO Box 47013, Wichita, KS 67201. P1/ 316-207-1027. terri_hamilton@juno.com. www.terrihamilton.net. Established: 2003.

SKILLS: ghostwriter, business writer or copywriter, technical writer, freelance commercial writer, direct mail copywriter. **MARKETS SERVED:** businesses, magazines.

SPECIALTIES AND PREFERENCES: I am a freelance commercial writer with in-depth training in direct mail promotion. I write sales copy—brochures, catalogs, etc. My feature-writing experience qualifies me to write trade articles for companies that desire such exposure. My ideal client communicates his/her needs fully and succinctly, provides materials and contacts as needed. They understand and facilitate the creative copywriting process and allow a reasonable time frame and budget.

NONFICTION—ACCEPTS: adult, articles/features, business.

FEES/TERMS/CONTRACTS: vary, negotiable.

ACCOMPLISHMENTS: "Enemy Healer," *Collector's Guide to MageKnight Vol. I*, won Origins Award for Best Game-Related Fiction, Short Form, of 2002. Other articles and short stories publications.

EDUCATION: BA Ambassador University, East TX. Theology with minor in English Literature (most of the English Literature coursework done at the University of Washington). Graduated from the AWAI (American Writers' and Artists' Institute) copywriting course.

CLIENTS WITHIN PRIOR YEAR: 1–5.

222	EDITOR	WRITER	CONSULTANT	F	NF

Hamilton, Tresaca. Black Unicorn Communications Inc. PO Box 50028, Atlanta, GA 30302-0028. P1/ 404-381-3232. F1/ 404-381-3232. info@blackunicorninc.com. www.blackunicorninc.com. Established: 2003.

Skills: business writer or copywriter, marketing writer. Markets served: small businesses.

Specialties and preferences: specializes in helping small businesses create a big impact with effective marketing communications. Services include writing and design of brochures, press releases, newsletters, pamphlets, marketing plans, postcard newsletters, articles, and e-books.

Nonfiction—accepts: articles/features, how-to/instruction, business.

Fees/terms/contracts: Fees are based on the project. Terms: 50 percent of balance required as up front deposit, along with a signed contract. Payments accepted: checks, money orders, and credit card via PayPal.

Accomplishments: Published in *Who's Who in Atlanta*.

Education: American Writers and Artists Institute Freelance Writing Course.
Memberships: Metro Atlanta Chamber of Commerce.
Clients within prior year: 11–20.

223	EDITOR	WRITER	CONSULTANT	F	NF

Hancock, Leigh. PO Box 1303, White Salmon, WA 98672. P1/ 509-493-3031. leighbengt@gorge.net. Established: 2001.

Skills: freelance editor, independent book editor, copyeditor or line editor, proofreader, business writer or copywriter, technical writer, writing instructor.
Markets served: individual writers, nonprofit organizations.

Specialties and preferences: prefers teaching writing: fiction, creative nonfiction, and grant writing, and working with individuals as an editor and consultant for their work.

Fiction—accepts: y/a or juvenile, short stories, novels (genre, mainstream, literary, contemporary), poetry. Nonfiction—accepts: y/a or juvenile, articles/features, essays, memoirs, creative or narrative, biography/autobiography, family history, self-help, how-to/instruction, technical, text or reference, business. Typical evaluation/report: 10–15 pages.

Fees/terms/contracts: $50/hour. I work under contract only. No credit cards or PayPal.

Accomplishments: Henry Hoyns Fellowship, Fishtrap Fellowship, World's Best Short Short Story Winner; National Winner of the National Society of Arts and Letters Fiction contest; other fellowships and residencies; work performed on National Public Radio; published in numerous magazines and anthologies.

Education: MFA Fiction Writing, University of Virginia, Charlottesville. BA

English Literature, Reed College, Portland, OR.
CLIENTS WITHIN PRIOR YEAR: 1–5.

224	EDITOR	WRITER	CONSULTANT	F	NF

Hancock, Sharon. Hancock Publishing Group. 7990 Interlaken Dr., Colorado Springs, CO 80920. P1/ 719-282-8744. yhwhmalak@worldnet.att.net. Established: 1996.

SKILLS: freelance editor, copyeditor or line editor, proofreader, ghostwriter. **MARKETS SERVED:** large publishing companies and individual authors.

SPECIALTIES AND PREFERENCES: provides high-quality work in all areas of editing, copyediting, writing, rewriting, and proofreading of manuscripts, magazines, booklets, and articles, both fiction and nonfiction, youth and adult. Focuses on accuracy in grammar, punctuation, spelling, overall flow, clarity, and conciseness, as well as compliance with *The Chicago Manual of Style* and company manuals.

FICTION—ACCEPTS: y/a or juvenile, short stories, novels (genre, mainstream, literary, contemporary, historical). **NONFICTION—ACCEPTS:** all.

FEES/TERMS/CONTRACTS: all forms of payment accepted. Hourly, contract, and per-page rates available. Please contact for specific rates.

ACCOMPLISHMENTS: Hancock Publishing Group was founded in 1996 with clients ranging from first-time authors to such companies as NavPress and the Association of Christian Schools International. I am published in *New Man* and *Citizen* magazines, am a contributing writer for various books, and was an editorial assistant for a large multimedia CD-ROM project.

EDUCATION: BA Public Relations, University of South Florida, Tampa.

CLIENTS WITHIN PRIOR YEAR: 6–10.

225	EDITOR	WRITER	CONSULTANT	F	NF

Hanson, Nels. Hanson Writing & Editing. 2813 Garbaldi Ave., San Luis Obispo, CA 93401. P1/ 805/542-9474. P2/ 805/546-9009. hanson@fix.net. www.freelancefusion.com/us/nhansonediting. Established: 2000, writing/editing since 1972.

SKILLS: freelance editor, independent book editor, copyeditor or line editor, proofreader, ghostwriter, business writer or copywriter, technical writer, résumé writing, thesis editing, printers' galley proofing. **MARKETS SERVED:** academic, business, journals, publishing.

SPECIALTIES AND PREFERENCES: prefers copy rewrites (small and large jobs).

NONFICTION—ACCEPTS: all. **TYPICAL EVALUATION/REPORT:** 1–2 pages.

FEES/TERMS/CONTRACTS: standard fee of $50/hour. For large jobs, e.g., book manuscripts, we require 50 percent payment up front (based on estimate) with balance due on job completion. Handles most contracts, jobs, and invoicing via e-mail.

Accomplishments: has taught university-level writing. Was awarded the San Francisco Foundation's James D. Phelan Award for fiction, the Foundation's honorable mention for short fiction in its Joseph Henry Jackson competition, and has published 20+ short stories in literary quarterlies. He is currently working with two literary agents to place two novels and is seeking agents for three other books.

Education: MFA Creative Writing, University of Montana, Missoula. BA English (honors), University of California, Santa Cruz.

Clients within prior year: 60–65 (shared with business partner).

226	EDITOR	WRITER	CONSULTANT	F	NF

Hanson, Vicki. Hanson Writing & Editing. 2813 Garbaldi Ave., San Luis Obispo, CA 93401. P1/ 805/546-5009. P2/ 805/542-9474. hanson@fix.net. www.freelancefusion.com/us/vhansonediting. Established: 2000, writing and editing since 1972.

Skills: freelance editor, independent book editor, copyeditor or line editor, proofreader, ghostwriter, business writer or copywriter, technical writer, résumé writing, thesis editing, printers' galley proofing. **Markets served:** academic, business, journals, publishing.

Specialties and preferences: prefers copy rewrites (small and large jobs).

Nonfiction—accepts: articles/features, essays, memoirs, biography/autobiography, family history, self-help, how-to/instruction, technical, text or reference, business, spiritual, book proposals, queries. **Typical evaluation/ report:** 1–2 pages.

Fees/terms/contracts: standard fee of $50/hour. For large jobs, e.g., book manuscripts, we require 50 percent payment up front (based on estimate) with balance due on job completion. Handles most contracts, jobs, and invoicing via e-mail.

Accomplishments: served as a senior writer/editor at the National Center for Atmospheric Research (Boulder, CO), as an op/ed columnist for the *Fresno Bee* newspaper, and as publications editor and *Cal Poly Magazine* editor at California Polytechnic State University, San Luis Obispo, for nearly ten years.

Education: MA English, Colorado State University, Fort Collins. BA English (honors), University of Redlands, CA.

Clients within prior year: 60–65 (shared with business partner).

227	EDITOR	WRITER	CONSULTANT	F	NF

Harler, Curt. Curt Harler, Inc. 12936 Falling Water, Strongsville, OH 44136.
P1/ 440-238-4556. curt@curtharler.com. curtharler@adelphia.net.
www.curtharler.com. Established: 1989.

SKILLS: freelance editor, independent book editor, book doctor, ghost writer, business writer or copywriter, literary consultant, writing coach, writing instructor, media training. **MARKETS SERVED:** corporations and executive clients.

SPECIALTIES AND PREFERENCES: offers skilled reporting in all high-technology areas, including computer networking, telecommunications, chemistry, agriculture, environmental issues, outdoor recreation, and general assignment work. Works with a team of proven editors/writers to assure accurate, timely copy is produced on deadline. Ghostwrites articles and writes technical white papers.

NONFICTION—ACCEPTS: y/a or juvenile, articles/features, essays, technical, text or reference, business, humor, book proposals, queries.

FEES/TERMS/CONTRACTS: $1.00–$1.25/word or by contract. No credit cards or PayPal.

ACCOMPLISHMENTS: winner, International Communications Association's 1996 Industry Achievement Award for communications writing. Curt has bylined literally thousands of articles in magazines and newspapers, and coauthored books. See website.

EDUCATION: MS Economics & Rural Sociology, Ohio State University, Columbus. BA Journalism, BS Agriculture, Pennsylvania State University, University Park. **MEMBERSHIPS:** National Speleological Society. PA Mountaineering Association. National Geographic Society.

CLIENTS WITHIN PRIOR YEAR: 35–40.

228	EDITOR	WRITER	CONSULTANT	F	NF

Harold, Connie. Annapolis, MD. P1/ 410-268-3330.
charoldassociates@peoplepc.com. Established: 2001.

SKILLS: business writer or copywriter, articles, marketing, grants. **MARKETS SERVED:** government, nonprofit organizations, small businesses, periodicals.

SPECIALTIES AND PREFERENCES: My focus is marketing and development for nonprofit organizations—writing grants, brochures, manuals, calendars, press releases, and other collateral materials. My areas of concentration are in affordable housing, disabilities, youth, and the arts. Writing is a path with a heart. Let me tell the story of your company's undaunted road to success.

NONFICTION—ACCEPTS: articles/features, essays, how-to/instruction, business, book proposals, queries.

FEES/TERMS/CONTRACTS: $75/hour. Flat fee negotiable. No credit cards. Uses contract.

ACCOMPLISHMENTS: I have written grants funded for $50,000 to $350,000, written copy for a local radio show, and written two manuals of national significance. Numerous articles published on business, affordable housing, and the arts. Playwriting award. Three plays produced and one monologue published.

EDUCATION: General studies, Columbia University, New York. Communication Design, Pratt Institute, Brooklyn, NY. **MEMBERSHIPS:** Association of Fundraising Professionals. Dramatists Guild. Washington Independent Writers.

CLIENTS WITHIN PRIOR YEAR: 6–10.

229	EDITOR	WRITER	CONSULTANT	F	NF

Harper, Tim. 78 Ridge Rd., Ridgewood, NJ 07450. P1/ 201-444-6866. harpertim@aol.com. www.timharper.com. Established: 1984.

SKILLS: independent book editor, book doctor, ghostwriter, writing coach, writing instructor, collaborator, editorial/publishing consultant. **MARKETS SERVED:** writers, individuals, corporations, academics, associations, foundations.

SPECIALTIES AND PREFERENCES: journalism, magazine stories, white papers, op-ed, individual or corporate biography, helping first-time authors get published.

FICTION—ACCEPTS: all. **NONFICTION—ACCEPTS:** all.

FEES/TERMS/CONTRACTS: high end; depends on assignment/project.

ACCOMPLISHMENTS: eleven books, many articles in major publications, various national awards. Teaches writing at the Columbia University Graduate School of Journalism.

EDUCATION: JD University of Wisconsin Law School, Madison. **MEMBERSHIPS:** American Society of Journalists and Authors. American Bar Association.

CLIENTS WITHIN PRIOR YEAR: 15–20.

230	EDITOR	WRITER	CONSULTANT	F	NF

Harris, Katherine "Erin." Katherine Harris Communications and GlitzQueen Marketing. erinharris@comcast.net. glitzqueen@glitzqueen.com. www. glitzqueen.com. Established: 1977.

SKILLS: freelance editor, independent book editor, book doctor, copyeditor or line editor, ghostwriter, business writer or copywriter, writing coach, publicist, marketing strategist, creative director, securities analyst, website developer, adapter of British books for US market. **MARKETS SERVED:** companies of all types and sizes, advertising and public relations firms, publishers, individuals.

SPECIALTIES AND PREFERENCES: serves commercial clients as strategist, creative director, and writer in all media. Journalist/editor and writer of literary fiction, poetry, plays.

FICTION—ACCEPTS: short stories, novels (genre, mainstream, literary, contemporary, historical), poetry, scripts/screenplays, queries, synopses, treatments. **NONFICTION—ACCEPTS:** y/a or juvenile, articles/features, essays, memoirs, creative or narrative, biography/autobiography, family history, self-help, how-to/instruction, business, humor, book proposals, queries. **TYPICAL EVALUATION/REPORT:** as requested by client.

FEES/TERMS/CONTRACTS: fees based on project. Terms as agreed. Typically uses contract.

ACCOMPLISHMENTS: 50+ awards, hundreds of publication credits, always on time and in budget.

EDUCATION: BA English, Theater Arts and Philosophy, Austin College, Sherman, TX. Graduate study in philosophy and theater.

CLIENTS WITHIN PRIOR YEAR: 11–20.

231	EDITOR	WRITER	CONSULTANT	F	NF

Hart, Joyce. Bainbridge Island, WA. P1/ 206-780-7828. jhart774@earthlink.net. Established: 1999.

SKILLS: freelance editor, independent book editor, copyeditor or line editor, proofreader, ghostwriter. **MARKETS SERVED:** individuals, publishers.

SPECIALTIES AND PREFERENCES: full or line editing—fiction/nonfiction materials, elementary through college, literary and social studies. Writing—children/juvenile/adult.

FICTION—ACCEPTS: y/a or juvenile, picture books, short stories, novels (genre, mainstream, literary, contemporary, historical). **NONFICTION—ACCEPTS:** y/a or juvenile, articles/features, essays, memoirs, creative or narrative, biography/autobiography, family history, self-help, text or reference, business, humor, inspirational/religious, spiritual, book proposals, queries. **TYPICAL EVALUATION/REPORT:** 2–10 pages plus notes on text.

FEES/TERMS/CONTRACTS: $25/hour copyediting, 10–15 pages/hour. Fees for writing depend on research required and type of material covered. Prefer contracts.

ACCOMPLISHMENTS: eight books (biography, ESL workbooks, social studies, reference). Hundreds of biographical sketches of authors and critical analyses of literary works.

EDUCATION: BA English, minor in linguistics/Asian studies, University of Oregon, Eugene. **MEMBERSHIPS:** Society of Children's Book Writers and Illustrators.

CLIENTS WITHIN PRIOR YEAR: 5–10.

232	EDITOR	WRITER	CONSULTANT	F	NF

Hattal, Alvin M. The Hattal Group. Kirkland, WA, and New York, NY. P1/ 425-576-1950. P2/ 212-752-8101. C1/ 425-466-7148. F1/ 425-576-1950. al@hattal.com. www.biz2bizwriter.com. Established: 1985.

SKILLS: freelance editor, business writer or copywriter, literary consultant, writing coach, writing instructor, publicist, public relations consultant. MARKETS SERVED: magazines, newsletters, e-zines, newspapers, advertising and public relations firms, writers.

SPECIALTIES AND PREFERENCES: business journalist, feature writer, columnist, scriptwriter focusing on advertising, marketing, public relations, and related fields. Also accept business articles, news releases, marketing features, columns, profiles (company, individual, and media), speeches, corporate case studies.

FICTION—ACCEPTS: scripts/screenplays, queries, synopses, treatments. NON-FICTION—ACCEPTS: essays, creative or narrative, business, humor.

FEES/TERMS/CONTRACTS: $50/hour, $1/word.

ACCOMPLISHMENTS: Philip M. Stern Award—Washington Independent Writers. Ghosted marketing book. Over 250 published articles and columns. Former magazine editor. Freelancing over fifteen years. Taught graduate-level media and public relations.

EDUCATION: MS Journalism, Washington University, St. Louis, MO. BA English Literature, New York University. Know French, Italian, and Spanish. MEMBERSHIPS: Washington Independent Writers. Seattle Freelance Writers. Society of Professional Journalists. Public Relations Society of America.

CLIENTS WITHIN PRIOR YEAR: 5–10.

233	EDITOR	WRITER	CONSULTANT	F	NF

Hatton, Caroline. PO Box 4795, Culver City, CA 90231-4795. P1/ 310-204-6780. F1/ 310-287-2426. ckhatton@aol.com. Established: 1994.

SKILLS: freelance editor, independent book editor, copyeditor or line editor, proofreader, technical writer, French-English and English-French translator. MARKETS SERVED: publishers, writers, scientific, technical, pharmaceutical companies, academic institutions, universities, government agencies, organizations (sports, drug testing, educational).

SPECIALTIES AND PREFERENCES: analytical organic chemistry, sports doping control, toxicology, pharmacology, medicinal and toxic plants, crop protection, pest control, botany, juvenile literature.

FICTION—ACCEPTS: y/a or juvenile, short stories, novels (mainstream, literary, contemporary, historical), queries, synopses. NONFICTION—ACCEPTS: all. TYPICAL EVALUATION/REPORT: tailored.

FEES/TERMS/CONTRACTS: translation $80/hour. Other, negotiate. No credit cards. Uses contract or agreement.

ACCOMPLISHMENTS: three writing awards. Four technical books translated from French. Twenty-three articles published in international science journals. Four children's books. Five children's magazine stories.

EDUCATION: PhD Chemistry, University of California, Los Angeles. Pharmacist University de Paris, France. **MEMBERSHIPS:** Society of Children's Writers and Illustrators.

CLIENTS WITHIN PRIOR YEAR: 1–5.

234	EDITOR	WRITER	CONSULTANT	F	NF

Hayes, Melissa. Hayes Editorial Services. 1012 Trumbull Hwy., Lebanon, CT 06249. P1/ 860-642-4775. melissa@mugup.com. Established: 1991.

SKILLS: freelance editor, independent book editor, book doctor, copyeditor or line editor, proofreader. **MARKETS SERVED:** writers, publishers.

SPECIALTIES AND PREFERENCES: nonfiction, regional/family history, memoir/biography; fact checking, Americanization, indexing; writing catalog/advertising copy/reading guides.

FICTION—ACCEPTS: all. **NONFICTION—ACCEPTS:** all.

FEES/TERMS/CONTRACTS: $20–$30/hour or by contract (project fee) agreement. No credit cards or PayPal. Payment by check or money order.

ACCOMPLISHMENTS: Clients include a wide range of New England publishers and authors.

EDUCATION: BA English/French, Augustana College, Rock Island, IL.

CLIENTS WITHIN PRIOR YEAR: 12–15.

235	EDITOR	WRITER	CONSULTANT	F	NF

Healy, Erin. WordWright Editorial Services. Colorado Springs, CO. P1/ 719-638-6141. F1/ 719-638-6142. wweditorial@earthlink.net. Established: 2002.

SKILLS: independent book editor, copyeditor or line editor, literary consultant, writing coach, writing instructor. **MARKETS SERVED:** publishers.

SPECIALTIES AND PREFERENCES: manuscript critique, development, and editing, specializing in fiction. My preference is to work directly with the author in conjunction with the publisher from concept through line editing.

FICTION—ACCEPTS: y/a or juvenile, picture books, short stories, novels (genre, mainstream, contemporary, historical). **NONFICTION—ACCEPTS:** y/a or juvenile, articles/features, essays, creative or narrative, self-help, how-to/instruction, humor, inspirational/religious, spiritual. **TYPICAL EVALUATION/REPORT:** 2,500–7,500 words.

FEES/TERMS/CONTRACTS: $40/hour or flat fee. Half on initial critique, half on final delivery. No credit cards. Uses contract.

ACCOMPLISHMENTS: one published nonfiction book. Articles in national magazines.

EDUCATION: BA English, *summa cum laude*, Westmont College, Santa Barbara, CA. **MEMBERSHIPS:** Academy of Christian Editors (ACE).

CLIENTS WITHIN PRIOR YEAR: 15–20.

236	EDITOR	WRITER	CONSULTANT	F	NF

Hedrick, Lucy H. Hedrick Communications. 29 Sound Beach Ave., Old Greenwich, CT 06870. P1/ 203-637-1051. lucy@lucyhedrick.com. www.lucyhedrick.com. Established: 1990.

SKILLS: freelance editor, literary consultant, writing coach. **MARKETS SERVED:** unpublished nonfiction book authors.

SPECIALTIES AND PREFERENCES: I work with first-time adult nonfiction authors who need help preparing their book proposals. My deliverable is an "irresistible" proposal that will be read by agents and publishers.

NONFICTION—ACCEPTS: memoirs, creative or narrative, biography/autobiography, family history, self-help, how-to/instruction, humor, inspirational/religious, spiritual.

FEES/TERMS/CONTRACTS: one-half of fee paid on signing with Hedrick, the balance paid on signing with a publisher. Checks. No credit cards. Uses letter of agreement.

ACCOMPLISHMENTS: five published nonfiction how-to titles. Lecturer on how to get published.

EDUCATION: BA Music, Goucher College, Towson, MD. **MEMBERSHIPS:** Board of Directors, Perrot Memorial Library. Board of Directors, Greenwich Arts Council.

CLIENTS WITHIN PRIOR YEAR: 11–20.

237	EDITOR	WRITER	CONSULTANT	F	NF

Heitner, Keri. All Aspects Research. PO Box 1195, Amherst, MA 01004. P1/ 413-549-0154. F1/ 413-549-0154. kheitner@earthlink.net. Established: 1995.

SKILLS: freelance editor, ghostwriter, business writer or copywriter, technical writer, grant writer, training manuals. **MARKETS SERVED:** newsletters and trade publications, health care and educational institutions, nonprofit sector, banks.

SPECIALTIES AND PREFERENCES: public/private grant proposals, research reports, training manuals, newsletters, trade publications, company literature, brochures, advertising copy, technical materials. Education, health/public health, social services, financial.

NONFICTION—ACCEPTS: articles/features, essays, creative or narrative, proposals, biography/autobiography, how-to/instruction, technical, text or reference, business. **TYPICAL EVALUATION/REPORT:** varies widely by field.

Fees/terms/contracts: usually by the hour, sometimes have a fixed fee. Typically invoices at end of project or monthly. No credit cards. Uses own contract or adapts client's.

Accomplishments: merit award from the Massachusetts Broadcasters Association for radio advertising. Successful grant proposals that raised more than $15 million.

Education: PhD Psychology, Philosophy, City University of New York. MA General/Experimental Psychology, New School for Social Research. BA Psychology, SUNY Stony Brook, MA. **Memberships:** American Psychological Association.

Clients within prior year: 20–25.

238	EDITOR	WRITER	CONSULTANT	F	NF

Henry, Jodi. Writers Welcome. 1320 Evergreen Dr., Eugene, OR 97404. P1/ 541-461-0789. willame1@earthlink.net. juancarr@earthlink.net. www.writerswelcome.com. Established: 2001.

Skills: freelance editor, independent book editor, book doctor, copyeditor or line editor, proofreader, ghostwriter, business writer or copywriter, literary consultant, writing coach. **Markets served:** fiction, nonfiction, magazine, academic.

Specialties and preferences: I enjoy working with fiction and nonfiction writers who want to make their work professional, polished, and publishable.

Fiction—accepts: all. **Nonfiction—accepts:** all. **Typical evaluation/report:** evaluations usually range from 5–10 pages.

Fees/terms/contracts: $35/hour critique and analysis. $4/page comprehensive edit: $3/page line edit. Three-month Mentorship Program $500. One-month Mentorship Program $200. Contracts with Mentorship Programs, PayPal accepted.

Accomplishments: I have an extensive background as a journalist, writer, and publicist in corporate and nonprofit environments. I have written newsletters, proposals, press releases, personal essay, and copy for electronic and print media, as well as edited fiction and nonfiction books.

Education: BA Communications Studies; minor Women's Studies, California State University, Sacramento. AA Journalism, Bakersfield Community College, CA. **Memberships:** Willamette Writers, including Eugene chapter, OR. Oregon Writers Colony, Portland.

Clients within prior year: 6–10.

239	EDITOR	WRITER	CONSULTANT	F	NF

Henshell, John. John Henshell. 4760 SW 6th St., Beaverton, OR 97007.
P1/ 503-646-3397. johnhenshell@comcast.net.
http://home.comcast.net/~johnhenshell. Established: 1995.

SKILLS: freelance editor, independent book editor, book doctor, copyeditor or line editor, ghostwriter, business writer or copywriter, technical writer, business communications, marketing communications, web content. MARKETS SERVED: general business, Internet, individuals.

SPECIALTIES AND PREFERENCES: business communications, marketing communications, web content. I am a freelance writer/editor/communications consultant. Strongest skill area is strategic communication. I add value to my client's words through adept use of diction, syntax, context, and visual images. Expertise in internal/employee communications, editing, and marketing communications. Much of my writing has been about technology.

NONFICTION—ACCEPTS: y/a or juvenile, articles/features, essays, biography/autobiography, self-help, how-to/instruction, technical, text or reference, business, humor, book proposals, queries.

FEES/TERMS/CONTRACTS: payment by the project or $60/hour. Discounts for nonprofits or quantity of work. I do not require contracts or accept credit cards.

ACCOMPLISHMENTS: signed contract with McFarland and Co.; book not yet published.

EDUCATION: BA Communications Arts, Evergreen State College, Olympia, WA. MEMBERSHIPS: vice president of Oregon/Columbia chapter of the International Association of Business Communicators. American Communication Association.

CLIENTS WITHIN PRIOR YEAR: 1–5.

240	EDITOR	WRITER	CONSULTANT	F	NF

Hickman, Bobby. BL Hickman and Associates Inc. bobby@blhickmaninc.com. www.blhickmainc.com. Established: 1995.

SKILLS: freelance editor, ghostwriter, business writer or copywriter, technical writer. MARKETS SERVED: insurance and financial services, general business.

SPECIALTIES AND PREFERENCES: As a former journalist, I focus on newsletters, press releases, articles, and business writing for a variety of firms, mostly in the insurance and financial services sector.

NONFICTION—ACCEPTS: all.

FEES/TERMS/CONTRACTS: writing $80+/hour, editing $55+/hour. Usually bills per project. Half up front. Accepts checks or cash, no credit cards. May use contract for small, quick jobs; always requires it for jobs of $500 or more.

ACCOMPLISHMENTS: editing, layout, and writing of newsletters for corporations and nonprofits, all in Georgia. Articles for *Atlanta Business Chronicle*, *Points North Magazine*, Cumming, GA; *Connect Marketing* lifestyle magazines, Woodstock, GA.

EDUCATION: BS Applied Sciences, University of Alabama, Tuscaloosa. Undergraduate work in English and journalism, University of Tennessee, Nashville.

MEMBERSHIPS: Freelance Forum (Atlanta group for freelance creatives), International Association of Business Communicators. Atlanta Press Club. Association of Business Publication Editors.

CLIENTS WITHIN PRIOR YEAR: 40–45.

241	EDITOR	WRITER	CONSULTANT	F	NF

High, Monique Raphel. WriteHigh. Beverly Hills, CA. P1/ 310-788-8413. chinbee2@yahoo.com. www.writehigh.com. Established: 1997.

SKILLS: freelance editor, book doctor, copyeditor or line editor, proofreader, literary consultant, writing coach, writing instructor, publicist, finds agents and publishers for writers, provides literary lawyer. MARKETS SERVED: writers.

SPECIALTIES AND PREFERENCES: management of writers/authors. Teaches writing skills and edit work. Locates agents and/or publishers and helps with platform/publicity. Prepares coauthor agreements, reviews contracts, and helps with publisher/agent financial problems.

FICTION—ACCEPTS: y/a or juvenile. NONFICTION—ACCEPTS: all. TYPICAL EVALUATION/ REPORT: 2–15 pages.

FEES/TERMS/CONTRACTS: $150/hour for tutorials and editing. No credit cards. Requires retainers and contracts for editing jobs.

ACCOMPLISHMENTS: six published novels, including international bestsellers. One nonfiction title. Dozens of articles published in national magazines.

EDUCATION: BA English and Renaissance Studies, Barnard College, New York. Sarah Lawrence College foreign studies program in Florence, Italy.

CLIENTS WITHIN PRIOR YEAR: 25–35.

242	EDITOR	WRITER	CONSULTANT	F	NF

Hile, Kevin. Kevin Hile Freelance Services. 409 E. Oak St., Mason, MI 48854-1780. P1/ 517-244-9735. kevinhile@voyager.net. www.kevinhile.com. Established: 2001.

SKILLS: freelance editor, copyeditor or line editor, proofreader, business writer or copywriter, desktop publishing, book production management, newsletter design and editing, nonfiction writer, brochure designer, website designer. MARKETS SERVED: publishers, nonprofits, educational institutions, businesses.

SPECIALTIES AND PREFERENCES: nonfiction adult and young adult reference, website design, articles for general audiences and college or high school students, newsletter and brochure design, desktop publishing, project management.

NONFICTION—ACCEPTS: y/a or juvenile, articles/features, essays, self-help, how-to/instruction, text or reference, business, humor.

FEES/TERMS/CONTRACTS: fees negotiable. No credit cards. Work-for-hire contracts.

ACCOMPLISHMENTS: published two nonfiction young adult books, one fantasy novel. Edited dozens of reference publications. Designed and serve as web master for nationally accredited zoo. Awarded 2003 Draco Award for best fantasy novel.

EDUCATION: BA English Literature and German, Adrian College, MI. Certificate, Denver Publishing Institute, CO. **MEMBERSHIPS:** Association of Zoo and Aquarium Docents, Potter Park Zoological Society.

CLIENTS WITHIN PRIOR YEAR: 6–10.

243	EDITOR	WRITER	CONSULTANT	F	NF

Hiller, Herbert. 290 Drayton Island Rd., Georgetown, FL 32139-3112. P1/ 386-467-8223. F1/ 386-467-7040. hiller@funport.net. Established: 1980.

SKILLS: freelance editor, writing coach, marketing consultant. **MARKETS SERVED:** state of Florida.

SPECIALTIES AND PREFERENCES: strategic planning, marketing, partner development.

NONFICTION—ACCEPTS: articles/features, essays, memoirs, creative or narrative, biography/autobiography, family history, self-help, how-to/instruction, book proposals, queries. **TYPICAL EVALUATION/REPORT:** invariably varies.

FEES/TERMS/CONTRACTS: strategic planning $150/hour plus expenses; work on manuscripts $50/hour.

ACCOMPLISHMENTS: three published books (one coauthored), hundreds of articles in American magazines and newspapers, notably in and about Florida. As consultant, work with Florida Humanities Council, 1000 Friends of Florida, Florida Park Service, Visit Florida. Initiatives: initiator of Caribbean Tourism Research Centre (today's Caribbean Tourism Organization), Barbados; Florida bicycling movement; Florida bed-and-breakfast movement. Charter recipient, FL Governor's Physical Fitness Honor Award.

EDUCATION: JD Harvard Law School, Cambridge, MA. BA History, English, Union College, Schenectady, NY. **MEMBERSHIPS:** Florida Humanities Council. Stetson Kennedy Foundation. St. Johns River Alliance. Society of American Travel Writers. Various civic and civil rights organizations.

CLIENTS WITHIN PRIOR YEAR: 1–5.

244	EDITOR	WRITER	CONSULTANT	F	NF

Hiller, Terry. TDH & Co. Boston, MA. P1/ 617-510-3790. terryhiller1@yahoo.com. Established: 1985.

SKILLS: freelance editor, independent book editor, book doctor, copyeditor or line editor, proofreader, ghostwriter, business writer or copywriter, writing coach, writing instructor. **MARKETS SERVED:** self-help, spirituality, nonprofit educational.

SPECIALTIES AND PREFERENCES: writing and editing material that uplifts and educates, and encourages transformation and healing. Specialties include how-to for health and yoga and popularization of Eastern spiritual teachings and practices.

NONFICTION—ACCEPTS: y/a or juvenile, features, essays, self-help, how-to/instruction, text or reference, business, humor, inspirational/spiritual, book proposals, queries. **TYPICAL EVALUATION/REPORT:** 2–10 pages.

FEES/TERMS/CONTRACTS: $1/page or $25+/hour. Fees negotiable. Typically use contract.

ACCOMPLISHMENTS: articles published in national spiritual/yoga magazines; national, large daily newspapers. Editor of two self-help books, copywriter for major publishing house, web writer and developer for nonprofits.

EDUCATION: BA Communications, University of Texas, Arlington. Copywriting, New York University, NY. Business writing, American Institute of Business, NY. Fourteen years of Eastern scriptural study and yoga in India and at Siddha Yoga Foundation.

CLIENTS WITHIN PRIOR YEAR: one large contract, ongoing copywriting work for book publisher.

245	EDITOR	WRITER	CONSULTANT	F	NF

Hines, Kimberly. Pentouch Literary. Washington, DC. P1/ 877-778-5481. F1/ 877-778-5481. help@pentouch.com. www.pentouch.com. Established: 2001.

SKILLS: freelance editor, independent book editor, copyeditor or line editor, proofreader, ghostwriter, business writer or copywriter, literary consultant, public relations consultant. **MARKETS SERVED:** authors (especially of African-American literature) and publishers.

SPECIALTIES AND PREFERENCES: African-American literature. We are dedicated to improving clients' writing beyond their current projects. We offer a wide array of editing, public relations, query letter, and nonfiction book-proposal services.

FICTION—ACCEPTS: all. **NONFICTION—ACCEPTS:** creative or narrative, humor, book proposals, queries. **TYPICAL EVALUATION/REPORT:** from a few paragraphs to several pages.

FEES/TERMS/CONTRACTS: fees vary depending on service. Deposit or monthly retainer fee required up front. Payment plans are available. Payments may be divided over duration of the work. Credit cards accepted. Uses service agreement.

ACCOMPLISHMENTS: award-winning short story author. Published poet.

EDUCATION: BA Psychology, Georgetown University, Washington, DC. Certificate, Editing and Publications, Georgetown University, Washington, DC.
CLIENTS WITHIN PRIOR YEAR: 6–10.

246	EDITOR	WRITER	CONSULTANT	F	NF

Hodges, Susan. Jabberwock Communications. 14363 30th Ave. NE, #3, Seattle, WA 98125. P1/ 206-417-9482. jabberwocker@earthlink.net. Established: 1999.

SKILLS: freelance editor, independent book editor, book doctor, copyeditor or line editor, business writer or copywriter, technical writer. **MARKETS SERVED:** writers, publishers, book packagers, nonprofits, corporations.

SPECIALTIES AND PREFERENCES: innovative and resourceful writer/editor with extensive experience in children's publishing for the trade and K-12 markets. Specialties include reading/language arts, social studies, science, health, art, crafts, and cooking. Exceptional research and project management skills.

FICTION—ACCEPTS: y/a or juvenile, picture books, short stories, novels (genre, mainstream, literary, contemporary, historical), poetry, scripts/screenplays, queries, synopses, treatments. **NONFICTION—ACCEPTS:** all.

FEES/TERMS/CONTRACTS: $25–$45/hour. Typically uses contract.

ACCOMPLISHMENTS: editor of two bimonthly magazines for early childhood educators. Author of sixteen activity books for preschool children and their caregivers. Project director for national pre-K literacy program. Scriptwriter for bestselling children's software programs.

EDUCATION: MEd Educational Communication/Technology, University of Washington, Seattle. BA American Studies (literature concentration), Grinnell College, IA.

CLIENTS WITHIN PRIOR YEAR: 5–10.

247	EDITOR	WRITER	CONSULTANT	F	NF

Horn, Amy. Seattle, WA. P1/ 206-295-0183. amy@nvdv.net. Established: 1998.

SKILLS: copyeditor or line editor, proofreader, freelance writer, business writer or copywriter. **MARKETS SERVED:** journalistic, nonfiction, academic, technical, business, medical.

SPECIALTIES AND PREFERENCES: ace copyeditor/proofreader—organized, efficient, and adept at producing and polishing clear, concise, lively prose for the Internet and print. Comfortable with Chicago, AP, MLA, and APA styles. Clients include amazon.com, Microsoft, TrafficGauge, and The Stranger. Specializing in nonfiction, including articles, essays, technical and reference documents, dissertations and academic papers, website copy, and promotional materials.

NONFICTION—ACCEPTS: articles/features, how-to/instruction, technical, text or reference.

FEES/TERMS/CONTRACTS: $21–$45/hour. No credit cards.

ACCOMPLISHMENTS: Edmonds Arts Commission Literary Arts Award Scholarship Recipient. Projects include software content (Microsoft Encarta Encyclopedia), academic papers and theses, and online technical documentation.

EDUCATION: BA Interdisciplinary Degree in English, Linguistics, and Biology, Fairhaven College at Western Washington University, Bellingham. MEMBERSHIPS: Northwest Independent Editors Guild.

CLIENTS WITHIN PRIOR YEAR: 6–10.

248	EDITOR	WRITER	CONSULTANT	F	NF

Horowitz, Shel. Accurate Writing & More. 16 Barstow Lane, Hadley, MA 01035. P1/ 413/586-2388. P2/ 800-683-WORD. shel@frugalfun.com. shel@principledprofits.com. www.frugalmarketing.com. www.principledprofits.com. Established: 1981.

SKILLS: ghostwriter, business writer or copywriter, technical writer, consultant on marketing, publishing. MARKETS SERVED: authors, publishers, and small business.

SPECIALTIES AND PREFERENCES: affordable, ethical, effective marketing and publishing, copywriting, consulting, strategic planning, and coaching for authors, publishers, and small business. First-pass editing to achieve submission quality.

FICTION—ACCEPTS: all. NONFICTION—ACCEPTS: all.

FEES/TERMS/CONTRACTS: marketing copywriting/consulting other than direct sales $125/hour. Ads, direct-mail letters $145/hour. Editing/manuscript evaluation $75/hour.

ACCOMPLISHMENTS: six books (two award winners). Over 1,000 published articles. Over 1,000 press releases.

EDUCATION: BA Communications/Theater, Antioch College, Yellow Springs, OH (at age twenty). Also extensive professional development, including reading and conferences. MEMBERSHIPS: Publishers Marketing Association. National Writers Union. Western New England Editorial Freelancers Network. Independent Publishers of New England.

CLIENTS WITHIN PRIOR YEAR: 25–30.

249	EDITOR	WRITER	CONSULTANT	F	NF

Howe, Andrea. Blue Falcon Editing. 2100 S Lewis St., #217, Anaheim, CA 92802. P1/ 714-937-1480. andrea@bluefalconediting.com. www.bluefalconediting.com. Established: 2002.

SKILLS: freelance editor, independent book editor, book doctor, copyeditor or line editor, proofreader. MARKETS SERVED: all.

SPECIALTIES AND PREFERENCES: I like to work closely with clients to make sure they get what they want—anything from adding a comma to complete rewriting. No religious texts or erotica accepted.

FICTION—ACCEPTS: y/a or juvenile, picture books, short stories, novels (genre, mainstream, literary, contemporary, historical), poetry, queries, synopses. NONFICTION—ACCEPTS: y/a or juvenile, articles/features, essays, memoirs, creative or narrative, biography/autobiography, family history, self-help, how-to/instruction, text or reference, business, humor, book proposals, queries.

FEES/TERMS/CONTRACTS: proofreading $35–$45/hour, copyediting $40–$55/hour. Accepts cash and credit/debit through PayPal, personal check, money order, or cashier's check. Typically uses contract.

ACCOMPLISHMENTS: article published online. "Edited by" credit on cover of novel. Numerous credits inside books.

EDUCATION: BA Philosophy, University of California, Irvine. Copyediting coursework at University of California, Los Angeles.

CLIENTS WITHIN PRIOR YEAR: 20–25.

250	EDITOR	WRITER	CONSULTANT	F	NF

Hudson, Loretta. 10979 Las Casitas, Atascadero, CA 93422. P1/ 805-464-0886. loretta@lorettahudson.com. Established: 1992.

SKILLS: freelance editor, independent book editor, book doctor, writing coach. MARKETS SERVED: writers, organizations, corporations.

SPECIALTIES AND PREFERENCES: specializes in helping fiction writers develop their writing skills—both published and beginning writers.

FICTION—ACCEPTS: all. NONFICTION—ACCEPTS: all. TYPICAL EVALUATION/REPORT: reports run an average of 14 pages, plus reference materials, reading lists, and other materials as needed.

FEES/TERMS/CONTRACTS: flat-rate fee of $5/page for an average edit. Hourly fee is $60/ hour. Contact me for fee information before sending anything.

ACCOMPLISHMENTS: has successfully edited many clients, including Sol Stein, author of *Stein On Writing*; won award at Santa Barbara Writers' Conference for humor/fiction.

EDUCATION: Associate in Arts, Taft College, CA. Creative Writing Program,

University of California, Irvine. Attends yearly workshops in fiction, nonfiction, humor, poetry, biography at Santa Barbara Writers' Conference. Attends yearly workshops in fiction, nonfiction, at Cuesta Writers' Conference, San Luis Obispo, CA.
CLIENTS WITHIN PRIOR YEAR: 6–10.

251	EDITOR	WRITER	CONSULTANT	F	NF

Hudson, Michel. Gnu Gap Consulting. 1805 Gnu Gap, Round Rock, TX 78664. P1/ 512-565-0142. F1/ 512-990-1607. gnugap@aol.com. www.gnugap.com. Established: 1993.

SKILLS: freelance editor, copyeditor or line editor, proofreader, business writer or copywriter, technical writer, writing instructor, web content development, brochure development. **MARKETS SERVED:** nonprofits, corporations, publishers, professional trade associations.

SPECIALTIES AND PREFERENCES: website design, content development and maintenance, as well as nonprofit guidance, research training, and fundraising program audits. Author of campaign case statements, training documentation, marketing literature, and planned-giving brochures for for-profits and businesses. Has written over 100 articles on variety of fundraising topics in professional journals.

NONFICTION—ACCEPTS: how-to/instruction, technical, text or reference, business. **TYPICAL EVALUATION/REPORT:** 2–10 pages.

FEES/TERMS/CONTRACTS: $50–$150/hour, depending upon project. Checks only. No credit cards. Typically uses contract.

ACCOMPLISHMENTS: one published, business how-to manual; over 100 articles published in regional and international professional journals.

EDUCATION: BA Theater, University of St. Thomas, Houston, TX. Postgraduate study in computer science at University of Missouri, Columbia, and Austin Community College, TX. **MEMBERSHIPS:** Writers League of Texas. Freelance Austin.

CLIENTS WITHIN PRIOR YEAR: 11–20.

252	EDITOR	WRITER	CONSULTANT	F	NF

Huff, Ariele. Seattle, WA. P1/ 206-361-6733. ariele@worldnet.att.net. Established: 1979.

SKILLS: freelance editor, independent book editor, book doctor, copywriter, literary consultant, writing coach, writing instructor. **MARKETS SERVED:** writers, publishers, periodical editors, corporations, nonprofit organizations.

SPECIALTIES AND PREFERENCES: books/articles, genre novels, travel/recreation, cookbooks, sports, gardening, medical/legal, children's books, poetry, family

history, nostalgia, animals, humor, alternative healing, metaphysical, autobiographies, inspirational.

Fiction—accepts: all. **Nonfiction—accepts:** all. **Typical evaluation/report:** 2–3
pages but negotiable.

Fees/terms/contracts: $20–$25/hour. Running "kitty" is replenished as needed.

Accomplishments: editor for ten periodicals—three prize-winning. Columnist
at thirteen publications. Dozens of articles. Self-published how-to book.
Radio scripts.

Education: BA English, University of Washington, Seattle. AA Education,
Shoreline Community College, Seattle, WA.

Clients within prior year: 11–20.

253	EDITOR	WRITER	CONSULTANT	F	NF

Hummel, Andre'lle, "Andi." 59A Strawberry Hill Rd., Hulett, WY 82720. P1/
307-467-5697. hummela@trib.com. Established: 1984.

Skills: freelance editor, copyeditor or line editor, proofreader, ghostwriter.
Markets served: writers, businesses, nonprofits.

Specialties and preferences: Need to cut words, strengthen story? I work with
novices and experienced authors who doubt skills and want to say more in
fewer words.

Fiction—accepts: y/a or juvenile, short stories, novels (genre, historical). **Nonfiction—accepts:** articles/features, essays, memoirs, family history, business,
book proposals, queries. **Typical evaluation/report:** honest evaluation,
market suggestions if requested.

Fees/terms/contracts: fees by page, at current market prices. Check. Money
order. Contract.

Accomplishments: over 2,000 sales in fiction, nonfiction, poetry. Two regional
histories.

Education: Gulf Coast Community College, Panama City, FL. Enrichment
courses, Bloomsburg State University, PA, and The Institute of Children's
Literature. **Memberships:** Wyoming Writers, Inc. Pennwriters. Bear Lodge
Writers. Wyoming State Historical Society.

Clients within prior year: 6–10.

254	EDITOR	WRITER	CONSULTANT	F	NF

Hurrle, Shellie. Flair for Words. 14807 SW Woodard Ct., Beaverton, OR 97007.
P1/ 503-530-8259. shelliehurrle@flairforwords.com. shelliehurrle@comcast.net.
www.flairforwords.com. Established: 1997.

Skills: freelance proofreader, copyeditor, line editor, book doctor, ghostwriter,
consultant. **Markets served:** writers.

SPECIALTIES AND PREFERENCES: published author with more than eight years of professional editing experience. Specialty is writing and editing children's literature. Also consults about marketing, offers substantive editing and critiques, proofreading, word processing.

FICTION—ACCEPTS: y/a or juvenile, short stories, novels (genre: mainstream, contemporary), queries, synopses, treatments. NONFICTION—ACCEPTS: all. TYPICAL EVALUATION/REPORT: provides comprehensive 5–20 page manuscript evaluations.

FEES/TERMS/CONTRACTS: proofreading $20+/hour; copyediting $25+/hour; substantive editing or writing $30+/hour; word processing $15+/hour; marketing and consulting $25+/hour. Typically requires a deposit and contract. Pay via check or PayPal.

ACCOMPLISHMENTS: work has appeared in many traditional trade publications, including the *BNAC Communicator*. Children's stories and articles purchased by Focus on the Family's *Clubhouse Magazine*, etc. Has written for numerous websites, including Wcities, where I was the city editor. Provides high-quality, professional work at a fair cost, which always results in happy clients. Praised in many book acknowledgments.

EDUCATION: Graduate, Institute of Children's Literature, West Redding, CT. Numerous college writing and secretarial courses. MEMBERSHIPS: online writers' lists.

CLIENTS WITHIN PRIOR YEAR: 21–30.

255	EDITOR	WRITER	CONSULTANT	F	NF

Hussein, Janice. Document Driven. 16420 SE McGillivray #103, Vancouver, WA 98683. P1/ 503-789-6245. husseinj@pdx.edu. Established: 1996.

SKILLS: freelance editor, independent book editor, book doctor, copyeditor or line editor, proofreader, ghostwriter, business writer or copywriter, technical writer, literary consultant, writing instructor. MARKETS SERVED: writers, publishers, nonprofits, corporations, students, magazines.

SPECIALTIES AND PREFERENCES: I work with authors of both fiction and nonfiction. The nonfiction category includes articles and books; the fiction includes everything. I emphasize clarity, logic, and flow, as appropriate. I help to tighten and shape the manuscript, for the benefit of both the writer and reader, and for the potential of "the work." When the author succeeds, the editor succeeds.

FICTION—ACCEPTS: short stories, novels (genre, mainstream, literary, contemporary, historical), poetry, scripts/screenplays, queries, synopses, and treatments. NONFICTION—ACCEPTS: all.

FEES/TERMS/CONTRACTS: depends on the service and the work.

ACCOMPLISHMENTS: confidential.

EDUCATION: MBA, Washington State University, Vancouver. **MEMBERSHIPS:** Independent Editors Guild.

CLIENTS WITHIN PRIOR YEAR: currently 1–5, variable depending on workload.

256	EDITOR	WRITER	CONSULTANT	F	NF

Hutchison, Craig E. Wandering Wolverine Publishing Company. 23275 Beech, Dearborn, MI 48124. P1/ 313-277-2256. cehceh@peoplepc.com. www.wanderingwolverine.com. Established: 1999.

SKILLS: freelance editor, independent book editor, book doctor, copyeditor or line editor, proofreader, ghostwriter, business writer or copywriter, technical writer, literary consultant, writing coach, writing instructor, researcher, graphic design, desktop publishing, computer imaging. **MARKETS SERVED:** publishers, published and unpublished writers, nonprofits, corporations.

SPECIALTIES AND PREFERENCES: I typically work on history-related writing as well as editing literary criticism. Opinion/editorial writing is also an area in which I specialize. I welcome work related to religion and Christianity.

FICTION—ACCEPTS: all. **NONFICTION—ACCEPTS:** all.

FEES/TERMS/CONTRACTS: accepts credit cards, checks, and PayPal. Uses contract or agreement.

ACCOMPLISHMENTS: numerous research, editing, proofreading, and writing projects regarding literary criticism for The Gale Group. Inspirations from Michigan. History of Dearborn, Michigan. Commemorative Program of the Ford Festival. Uncommon Friends Musical Featuring Henry Ford and His Uncommon Friends.

EDUCATION: BA History, University of Michigan, Dearborn. **MEMBERSHIPS:** Great Lakes Lighthouse Keepers Assocociation. Dearborn Historical Society. Henry Ford Heritage Association.

CLIENTS WITHIN PRIOR YEAR: 10–15.

257	EDITOR	WRITER	CONSULTANT	F	NF

Ide, Kathy. 203 Panorama Ct., Brea, CA 92821. P1/ 714-529-1212. F1/ 714-529-5267. kathy@kathyide.com. www.KathyIde.com. Established: 1998.

SKILLS: freelance editor, independent book editor, book doctor, copyeditor or line editor, proofreader, ghostwriter, business writer or copywriter, technical writer, literary consultant, writing coach, writing instructor, coauthor, website editor and proofreader. **MARKETS SERVED:** writers, publishers, experts, speakers, writers' conferences, other editors, corporations, screenplay producers.

SPECIALTIES AND PREFERENCES: Christian fiction and nonfiction.

FICTION—ACCEPTS: all. **NONFICTION—ACCEPTS:** all. **TYPICAL EVALUATION/REPORT:** 2–10 pages.

FEES/TERMS/CONTRACTS: $35/hour proofreading. $40/hour editing or coaching. $50/hour copywriting, technical writing, website editing, or coauthoring. $75/hour ghostwriting.

ACCOMPLISHMENTS: books for writers, ghostwritten books, stories, play scripts, articles, and Sunday school curriculum. Screenplay optioned by Hollywood director. Finalist, ACRW's Noble Theme Contest, Women's Fiction and Contemporary. Romance categories. Speaker at writers' conferences. Nominated for Best Editor, Editors/Preditors Poll, 2003.

EDUCATION: courses on writing, web page design, and designing brochures, catalogs, ads, newsletters, and reports. CLASSeminar. L.A. Film School. Certified Medical Transcriptionist. **MEMBERSHIPS:** numerous Christian writers' organizations. Writers Info. Network. The Writer's View.

CLIENTS WITHIN PRIOR YEAR: 95–100.

258	EDITOR	WRITER	CONSULTANT	F	NF

Ingle, Beverly. 434 Devonshire, San Antonio, TX 78209. P1/ 210-828-8218. bingle@satx.rr.com. Established: 1999.

SKILLS: freelance editor, copyeditor or line editor, ghostwriter, business writer or copywriter, technical writer, advertising and public relations, web content developer. **MARKETS SERVED:** advertising and public relations agencies, corporations, web content syndicates, businesses, individuals.

SPECIALTIES AND PREFERENCES: As a freelance writer, my business is two-fold: persuasive copy for businesses that combines creativity and strategy, and creative nonfiction. As a freelance editor, I am a grammar gun-for-hire, polishing and perfecting the work of others in any genre and market.

NONFICTION—ACCEPTS: articles/features, essays, memoirs, creative or narrative, business, humor.

FEES/TERMS/CONTRACTS: 50 percent prepayment in advance. Balance due upon receipt of the completed project. Writing and editing $60/hour. No credit cards. Uses contract.

ACCOMPLISHMENTS: press releases and countless advertisements for which I wrote copy have appeared in local, regional, and national media outlets. I have written persuasive copy for tourism, catering, health care, entertainment, finance, nonprofits, consumer goods, automotive service, and education. Creative nonfiction published in *American Style Magazine, San Antonio Woman, San Antonio Kids, Que Pasa,* and *Virigo Violet.*

EDUCATION: BS Advertising, University of Texas, Austin.

CLIENTS WITHIN PRIOR YEAR: 11–20.

| 259 | EDITOR | WRITER | CONSULTANT | F | NF |

Ireland, Robin. 1200 Sudden Valley, Bellingham, WA 98229. P1/ 360-647-7036. robin@robinireland.com. www.robinireland.com. Established: 1996.

SKILLS: freelance editor, copyeditor or line editor, proofreader, ghostwriter, business writer or copywriter, writing coach. MARKETS SERVED: writers, corporations, publishers.

SPECIALTIES AND PREFERENCES: children's, sci-fi, spiritual, new science, memoir, mind/body connection, self-help, travel, humor. No violence or horror.

FICTION—ACCEPTS: y/a or juvenile, short stories, novels (genre, mainstream, literary, contemporary, historical), synopses, treatments. NONFICTION— ACCEPTS: y/a or juvenile, articles/features, essays, memoirs, creative or narrative, biography/autobiography, self-help, how-to/instruction, technical, text or reference, humor, inspirational/religious, spiritual. TYPICAL EVALUATION/ REPORT: 10–20+ pages.

FEES/TERMS/CONTRACTS: editing/writing $45/hour. Proofreading $25/hour. Retainer $100; balance upon completion. Client pays expenses. Flat fees for revision letters and quick evaluations. Hard copy only. Contract.

ACCOMPLISHMENTS: awards for editing, ad copy, and design. Textbook abstracts. 200+ articles/reviews. Web copy. Speaker for writers' conferences.

EDUCATION: BA International Relations, Oregon State University, Corvallis. MEMBERSHIPS: NW Independent Editors Guild. Pacific NW Writers Association.

CLIENTS WITHIN PRIOR YEAR: 15–20.

| 260 | EDITOR | WRITER | CONSULTANT | F | NF |

Jacobs, Julie. Wynne Communications. Scotch Plains, NJ. P1/ 908-889-6960. F1/ 908-889-6961. wynnecomm@aol.com. Established: 1996.

SKILLS: freelance editor, copyeditor or line editor, proofreader, ghostwriter, business writer or copywriter, feature writer, desktop designer. MARKETS SERVED: magazine publishers, nonprofit organizations, health care institutions.

SPECIALTIES AND PREFERENCES: offers the full range of editorial services, including writing, editing, proofreading, interviewing, and project management, to produce such communications as feature articles, newsletters, brochures, directories, case studies, testimonials, press kits/releases, and web copy.

NONFICTION—ACCEPTS: articles/features, essays, creative or narrative, biography/ autobiography, self-help, how-to/instruction, business.

FEES/TERMS/CONTRACTS: writing, editing, project management $60/hour. Proofreading $35/hour. Can provide flat-fee estimates. No credit cards. Uses agreement.

Accomplishments: dozens of articles on the Internet and in national/local publications.

Education: BA Literature and Rhetoric (Journalism), State University of New York, Binghamton. **Memberships:** National Association of Women Writers.

Clients within prior year: variable depending upon workload; currently 5–10.

261	EDITOR	WRITER	CONSULTANT	F	NF

Jai, Janet. Vision and Values. 842 N. Euclid Ave., Pittsburgh, PA 15206. P1/ 412-362-7607. F1/ 412-362-0812. jai@vision-and-values.com. Established: 1996.

Skills: freelance editor, independent book editor, copyeditor or line editor, proofreader, ghostwriter, business writer or copywriter, technical writer, writing coach, writing instructor, marketing communications consultant, creative project manager, poet, artist, songwriter. **Markets served:** primarily nonprofits. Special expertise in higher education.

Specialties and preferences: I am a communications specialist, highly experienced in marketing, informational, technical, and development communications, especially for nonprofits and higher education.

Fiction—accepts: poetry, scripts/screenplays, queries, synopses, treatments. **Nonfiction—accepts:** all.

Fees/terms/contracts: $40–$80/hour. PayPal and Bidpay accepted. Sometimes uses contract/agreement.

Accomplishments: national and regional bylines. National and regional marketing communication awards.

Education: BA English and Philosophy, Duquesne University, Pittsburgh, PA. **Memberships:** American Marketing Association. Women in Communications. World Business Academy.

Clients within prior year: 6–10.

262	EDITOR	WRITER	CONSULTANT	F	NF

Jay, Mary. Timonium, MD. P1/ 410-252-5183. F1/ 410-560-3584. mljay@comcast.net. Established: 1989.

Skills: freelance editor, business writer or copywriter. **Markets served:** associations (construction, heavy equipment, recreation and parks, gasoline and c-store operations); financial services and insurance companies; health care organizations.

Specialties and preferences: freelance writer with fifteen years of experience. If you need an article written for your business or association—newsletter brief, feature article, mail, brochures, web articles—I can help you with quick turnaround and the ability to grasp the essentials of your operations quickly. Ghostwriting assignments welcomed. I write quickly, effectively, and persuasively; I deliver assignments on time.

NONFICTION—ACCEPTS: articles/features, essays, memoirs, creative or narrative, biography/autobiography, family history, self-help, how-to/instruction, business.

FEES/TERMS/CONTRACTS: $70/hour. Negotiable, per hour or per project. No credit cards.

ACCOMPLISHMENTS: Some of my clients—Washington Contractor (Associated Builders and Contractors of Washington, DC); Naylor Publications (including journals for Alabama Oil Prophets, Florida Recreation and Park Association, Agricultural Aviation, National Asphalt Paving Association, Michigan Associated General Contractors, etc.). T. Rowe Price, numerous newsletters, e-mails, and letters for Retirement Plan Services.

EDUCATION: BA English, University of Delaware, Newark.

CLIENTS WITHIN PRIOR YEAR: 6–10.

263	EDITOR	WRITER	CONSULTANT	F	NF
			CONSULTANT		NF

Johnson, Bill. Bill Johnson Script Consulting. 318 SW Palatine Hill Rd., Portland, OR 97219. P1/ 503-452-4778. bjscript@teleport.com. www.storyispromise.com. Established: 1995.

SKILLS: freelance editor, independent book editor, proofreader, literary consultant, writing coach, writing instructor. **MARKETS SERVED:** writers, literary agents.

SPECIALTIES AND PREFERENCES: teaches the craft of storytelling; helps writers explore the strengths and weaknesses of their writing; explores how popular stories are a promise, and a promise dramatically fulfilled.

FICTION—ACCEPTS: short stories, novels (genre, mainstream, literary, contemporary, historical), scripts/screenplays, queries, synopses, treatments. **NONFICTION—ACCEPTS:** spiritual, book proposals, queries. **TYPICAL EVALUATION/ REPORT:** 8–20 pages.

FEES/TERMS/CONTRACTS: $300–$2,500; $30/hour. E-mail agreement.

ACCOMPLISHMENTS: writing workbook published. Genre novel published. Produced playwright. Film work done for hire. Have worked with clients of literary agents.

EDUCATION: studied with literary agent. **MEMBERSHIPS:** Willamette Writers. Northwest Playwrights Guild.

CLIENTS WITHIN PRIOR YEAR: 10–15.

264	EDITOR	WRITER	CONSULTANT	F	NF
		WRITER			NF

Johnson, Camille. BULLET Pubs, Inc. P1/ 512-826-3776. bulletpubs@yahoo.com. Established: 1988.

SKILLS: technical writer, instructional designer, web content specialist. **MARKETS SERVED:** any business that needs to communicate with its internal or its external customers; typically large software or hardware producers.

SPECIALTIES AND PREFERENCES: I am a professional writer specializing in technical subject matter where engineers and programmers find it difficult to communicate without jargon and tech-speak. I am an advocate for the user. I organize the subject matter in logical, task-based modules based on a user's point of view, not the programmer's point of view. I write the manuals that tell you how to operate the computers and use its features or how to install and use software and its features. I also offer services for websites, training materials, and online training.

NONFICTION—ACCEPTS: how-to/instruction, technical, text or reference, business.

FEES/TERMS/CONTRACTS: $55–$65/hour. Bills monthly or bimonthly. No credit cards, uses a contract.

ACCOMPLISHMENTS: customers include McDonald's (hamburgers), Dell Computers, Lucent, Excite @ Home, VERITAS Software, and many others.

EDUCATION: MA Adult Continuing Education. BA Education. **MEMBERSHIPS:** Society for Technical Communicators. Society for Training and Development.

CLIENTS WITHIN PRIOR YEAR: 1–5.

265	EDITOR	WRITER	CONSULTANT	F	NF

Johnson, Sharon. Wild Rose Communication. P1/ 208-331-2411. F1/ 208-331-2411. awildrosebud@earthlink.net. Established: 2004.

SKILLS: freelance editor, independent book editor, book doctor, copyeditor or line editor, ghostwriter, writing coach. **MARKETS SERVED:** individuals needing guidance or editing services to enhance and improve their written communication.

SPECIALTIES AND PREFERENCES: My business includes editing, writing, design, and consultant on communications. My business specialty is newsletter content, design, and organization. Professional specialties include soft feature writing—human interest. Professional preferences are column writing—real stories/real people; personal notes.

NONFICTION—ACCEPTS: articles/features, memoirs, creative or narrative, self-help, how-to/instruction, business.

FEES/TERMS/CONTRACTS: Rates are hourly or by the assignment, varying with the job.

ACCOMPLISHMENTS: first place winner for writing/photography from Washington State Newspaper Publishers Association, 1987. I left a longtime creative, marketing, and communications position with a large health care system in Portland, Oregon, to relocate to Boise, Idaho, spring 2002.

EDUCATION: BA, Central Washington University, Ellensberg, WA.

CLIENTS WITHIN PRIOR YEAR: 1–5.

266	EDITOR	WRITER	CONSULTANT	F	NF

Jones, Nancy, L. BBCS Publishing (Bits & Bytes). POB 60256, Santa Barbara, CA 93160-0256. P1/ 805-967-1160. P2/ 800-753-4770. C1/ 805-680-6536. F1/ 805-967-1342. bbcspublishing@earthlink.net. Established: 1989.

SKILLS: freelance editor, independent book editor, copyeditor or line editor, proofreader, business writer or copywriter, transcription, nonfiction author. MARKETS SERVED: self-publishing authors. General public. Student dissertations.

SPECIALTIES AND PREFERENCES: copyediting, writing, rewriting, proofreading, transcriptions, book interior design/organization, book covers, printing bids, Internet sales registration, copyright page (ISBN, PCIP, LCCN), project management, press releases, newsletters.

FICTION—ACCEPTS: y/a or juvenile, short stories, novels, poetry. NONFICTION—ACCEPTS: y/a or juvenile, articles/features, essays, memoirs, creative or narrative, biography/autobiography, family history, self-help, how-to/instruction, inspirational/religious, spiritual.

FEES/TERMS/CONTRACTS: per hour, per page, per contract; VISA, MasterCard, contracts.

ACCOMPLISHMENTS: "Nancy at BBCS Publishing was instrumental in helping to prepare a flawless and professionally formatted manuscript for admission to Bread Loaf, the oldest and most prestigious writing conference in the country. Nancy's expertise on presentation and attention to detail is an invaluable asset to any writer's work."—Deborah Donohue.

EDUCATION: MA Music Theory, emphasis in jazz piano, University of Oregon, Eugene. MEMBERSHIPS: Publishers Marketing Association Small Publishers Association of North America.

CLIENTS WITHIN PRIOR YEAR: 1–5.

267	EDITOR	WRITER	CONSULTANT	F	NF

Josey, Charles. Charles Josey, Inc., 4620 Wieuca Rd. NE, #38, Atlanta, GA 30342. P1/ 404-252-8241. cjosey@bellsouth.net. www.charlesjosey.com. Established: 1985.

SKILLS: book doctor, ghostwriter, business writer or copywriter. MARKETS SERVED: individuals, corporations and nonprofit institutions.

SPECIALTIES AND PREFERENCES: ghosting biographies, self-help books, employee relations issues, business-related books, scripts/screenplays (business and industry), and speeches.

NONFICTION—ACCEPTS: biography/autobiography, self help, business.

FEES/TERMS/CONTRACTS: All projects are priced up front and contracted, following free consultation.

ACCOMPLISHMENTS: five years of writing for PBS; additional network credits; seventy-two Fortune 500 clients; one self-help book in print eighteen years and in five languages; scores of script awards. See website for details.

EDUCATION: MA English, BA English, BA Drama,University of Georgia, Athens. MEMBERSHIPS: Georgia Writers, Inc.

CLIENTS WITHIN PRIOR YEAR: sixteen corporations, seventeen schools, two government agencies, two ghosted biographies.

268	EDITOR	WRITER	CONSULTANT	F	NF

Kaplan, Rob. Rob Kaplan Associates. Cortlandt Manor, NY. P1/ 914-736-7182. F1/ 914-736-7182. rkaplan@bestweb.net. www.wordsintoprint.org/Kaplan. www.publishersmarketplace.com/member/RobKaplan. Established: 1998.

SKILLS: freelance editor, independent book editor, book doctor, copyeditor or line editor, ghostwriter, publishing consultant. MARKETS SERVED: book authors.

SPECIALTIES AND PREFERENCES: works with authors of nonfiction books to help them produce proposals and full-length manuscripts on a variety of subjects, including business, history, self-help, popular psychology, parenting, and others.

NONFICTION—ACCEPTS: essays, memoirs, creative or narrative, biography/auto-biography, family history, self-help, how-to/instruction, reference, business, humor, inspirational/religious, spiritual, book proposals, queries. TYPICAL EVALUATION/REPORT: 5–20 pages.

FEES/TERMS/CONTRACTS: fee depends on project, but is figured on the basis of $100/hour. Fee is divided into payments spread out over course of the work. No credit cards. Uses agreement.

ACCOMPLISHMENTS: six published nonfiction titles.

EDUCATION: BA English, City University of New York. MEMBERSHIPS: Words into Print. Publishers Marketplace.

CLIENTS WITHIN PRIOR YEAR: 6–10.

269	EDITOR	WRITER	CONSULTANT	F	NF

Kargel, Iona. 1360 S. Avenida Polar, #108, Tucson, AZ 85710. P1/ 520-514-0583. ikargel@att.net. Established: 2004.

SKILLS: ghostwriter, interviewer, researcher. MARKETS SERVED: writers who need help in organizing and presenting ideas for a nonfiction book, typing manuscript for hard copy, or electronic submission.

SPECIALTIES AND PREFERENCES: anthropology, cross-cultural experience, international travel.

NONFICTION—ACCEPTS: creative or narrative.

FEES/TERMS/CONTRACTS: Because I am new to ghostwriting, I would not expect a contract, and fee would be negotiable with periodic payments upon approval of work.

ACCOMPLISHMENTS: one nonfiction travel book and several travel articles published. One history/anthropology/travel nonfiction manuscript near completion. Volunteer work with International Students and Scholars at Ohio State University for ten years filled our home with international students and brought me to India, Ceylon, and Washington, DC, as a representative of the Central Council for International Visitors. Extensive travel in the South Pacific for a decade makes me particularly familiar with that area.

EDUCATION: the school of life. **MEMBERSHIPS:** Society of Southwestern Authors.

CLIENTS WITHIN PRIOR YEAR: new business.

270	EDITOR	WRITER	CONSULTANT	F	NF

Karr, Susan. WordSuite. 61 Woodland Rd., Chatham, NJ 07928-2008. P1/ 973-701-0229. susankarr@wordsuite.com. www.wordsuite.com. Established: 1989.

SKILLS: freelance editor, independent book editor, copyeditor or line editor, business writer or copywriter, technical writer, literary consultant, writing coach, writing instructor. **MARKETS SERVED:** Fortune 500 companies, start-ups, small companies, financial magazines, children's nonfiction book publishers.

SPECIALTIES AND PREFERENCES: information technology, finance, and marketing communications, children's nonfiction.

NONFICTION—ACCEPTS: y/a or juvenile, articles/features, essays, memoirs, creative or narrative, biography/autobiography, how-to/instruction, technical, text or reference, business.

FEES/TERMS/CONTRACTS: $75/hour or $1.25/word. Typically uses contracts.

ACCOMPLISHMENTS: over a dozen IT C-level executive magazine articles. A dozen corporate/marketing communications documents or web content files. Two economics articles for middle grades. Two nonfiction educational books for middle grades. Under contract for two nonfiction middle-grade books. A dozen articles for a regional NJ magazine.

EDUCATION: MBA General Management/Finance, Golden Gate University, San Francisco, CA. BA Education/English, College of William and Mary, Williamsburg, VA. **MEMBERSHIPS:** Society of Children's Book Writers and Illustrators.

CLIENTS WITHIN PRIOR YEAR: 6–10.

271	EDITOR	WRITER	CONSULTANT	F	NF

Kates, Allen. PO Box 399, Cortaro, AZ 85652. P1/ 520-616-7643. P2/ 888-436-1402. F1/ 520-616-7519. akateswriter@theriver.com. www.writingpublishing.com. Established: 1997.

SKILLS: freelance editor, independent book editor, book doctor, copyeditor or line editor, proofreader, ghostwriter, literary consultant, writing coach, writing instructor. **MARKETS SERVED:** writers, nonprofit organizations, people with a story to tell.

SPECIALTIES AND PREFERENCES: editing and copywriting on all forms of fiction or nonfiction such as books, novels, screenplays, short stories, journalism, memoirs, and biographies.

FICTION—ACCEPTS: all. **NONFICTION—ACCEPTS:** all. **TYPICAL EVALUATION/REPORT:** when applicable, 5–30 pages.

FEES/TERMS/CONTRACTS: $55/hour, 50 percent retainer based on estimate. Contract if requested.

ACCOMPLISHMENTS: two published nonfiction books, over 300 television scripts and screenplays produced, dozens of newspaper and magazine articles published.

EDUCATION: MFA Writing, Goddard College, Vermont. BA English and Drama, University of Windsor, Canada. BA Journalism, Television and Film Production, Ryerson University, Canada. Other courses in psychology, certificates in critical incident stress, traumatology, crisis, and suicide intervention, Board Certified in Emergency Crisis Response, BCECR. **MEMBERSHIPS:** American Academy of Experts in Traumatic Stress. Arizona Authors Association.

CLIENTS WITHIN PRIOR YEAR: 11–20.

272	EDITOR	WRITER	CONSULTANT	F	NF

Kawatski, Jake. Twin Oaks Indexing. 138 Twin Oaks Rd., Louisa, VA 23093. P1/ 540-894-5704. F1/ 540-894-4112. indexing@twinoaks.org. www.twinoaks.org/indexing. Established: 1984.

SKILLS: freelance editor, indexing. **MARKETS SERVED:** scholarly publishers and authors.

SPECIALTIES AND PREFERENCES: We are a collective that has been indexing scholarly manuscripts for over twenty years. We presently have six indexers. We offer dependable, professional indexing at reasonable rates—$3.25–$4.00/page depending on complexity and time frame.

NONFICTION—ACCEPTS: essays, memoirs, biography/autobiography, how-to/instruction, technical, text or reference.

FEES/TERMS/CONTRACTS: $3.25/page of the manuscript for average indexes; $4.00/page for rush jobs. We expect payment by check (net 30 days) when the job is finished. No credit cards.

EDUCATION: Of our six indexers, four have college degrees and two have graduate degrees.
CLIENTS WITHIN PRIOR YEAR: 11–20.

273	EDITOR	WRITER	CONSULTANT	F	NF

Kearns, Gail. To Press and Beyond—GMK Editorial & Writing Services. 825 E. Pedregosa St., Santa Barbara, CA 93103. P1/ 805-898-2263. F1/ 805-898-9460. info@topressandbeyond.com. www.topressandbeyond.com. Established: 1993.

SKILLS: freelance editor, independent book editor, book doctor, copyeditor or line editor, proofreader, ghostwriter, writing coach. MARKETS SERVED: small and independent publishers.

SPECIALTIES AND PREFERENCES: prefers to be hired at the content editing stage and kept through the entire process, shaping books from chapter outlines and then shepherding authors through the publishing process, including production and marketing.

FICTION—ACCEPTS: all. NONFICTION—ACCEPTS: all. TYPICAL EVALUATION/REPORT: 3–4 pages.

FEES/TERMS/CONTRACTS: consulting $75/hour; ghostwriting negotiable; content edit/manuscript review $60/hour; copyediting $50/hour; proofreading $40/hour; production coordination $1,500 flat fee. No credit cards. Uses a deal memo as contract.

ACCOMPLISHMENTS: production coordinator for major motion pictures. Development executive for RKO Pictures in New York City. Editing client William T. Close, M.D., was a finalist in the 2003 Benjamin Franklin Award, popular fiction category, and his book *Ebola—Through the Eyes of the People*, won the *ForeWord Magazine* 2002 Book of the Year gold prize for historical fiction.

EDUCATION: BS Art History, City University of New York. MEMBERSHIPS: Publisher's Marketing Association. Small Publishers Association of North America.

CLIENTS WITHIN PRIOR YEAR: 21–30.

274	EDITOR	WRITER	CONSULTANT	F	NF

Kehrli, Kathy. The Flawless Word. Factoryville, PA. P1/ 570-945-3766. F1/ 305-489-0703. Kathy@TheFlawlessWord.com. www.TheFlawlessWord.com. Established: 1999.

SKILLS: freelance editor, independent book editor, book doctor, copyeditor or line editor, proofreader, ghostwriter, business writer or copywriter, technical writer, literary consultant. MARKETS SERVED: business owners, authors, and website operators.

SPECIALTIES AND PREFERENCES: technical (mathematical, IT, computer technology, etc.); business; self-help; mainstream fiction; educational (mathematics, accounting, business specialties). Whether you need error-free editing of existing material or content written from scratch, The Flawless Word provides perfect copy every time.

FICTION—ACCEPTS: all. NONFICTION—ACCEPTS: all. TYPICAL EVALUATION/REPORT: one to several pages.

FEES/TERMS/CONTRACTS: typically $25/hour, negotiable based on scope of project. Retainer up front; will accept installment payments. No credit cards. Typically uses contracts.

ACCOMPLISHMENTS: A majority of the projects I undertake involve editing of newsletters, articles, web content, promotional/marketing material, etc., for businesses. Three of the past four years I have been a finalist in *Sol Magazine's* annual poet laureate contest. I am the author of a workbook published by Glencoe/McGraw-Hill to accompany *Mathematics with Business Applications*.

EDUCATION: BS/BA Mathematics and French, *magna cum laude*, University of Scranton, NY.

CLIENTS WITHIN PRIOR YEAR: 21–30.

275	EDITOR	WRITER	CONSULTANT	F	NF

Kelly, Kate. Larchmont, NY. P1/ 914-834-0602. C1/ 914-420-6966; kkelly@katekelly.com. F1/ 914-833-2368. kkelly@katekelly.com. www.katekelly.com. Established: 1979.

SKILLS: book doctor, ghostwriter, business writer or copywriter. MARKETS SERVED: business people, medical professionals, corporations, nonprofits, editors.

SPECIALTIES AND PREFERENCES: Kate Kelly is a professional writer and author of twenty-eight books, many of them collaborations. Her proposals frequently receive six-figure advances, and her books are delivered to editors on time and without hassle. She writes in the fields of business, history, medicine, and parenting.

NONFICTION—ACCEPTS: y/a or juvenile, articles/features, essays, memoirs, creative or narrative, biography/autobiography, family history, self-help, how-to/instruction, technical, text or reference, business, book proposals.

FEES/TERMS/CONTRACTS: per project/accepts credit cards and PayPal. Uses agreement.

ACCOMPLISHMENTS: received the National Parenting Publications Gold Award in 2003 and has been published in numerous national magazines including *Woman's Day*, *Redbook*, and *Glamour*.

EDUCATION: BA Theater, Smith College, Northampton, MA. MEMBERSHIPS: American Society of Journalists and Authors. Authors Guild.

CLIENTS WITHIN PRIOR YEAR: 1–5.

276	EDITOR	WRITER	CONSULTANT	F	NF

Kempton, Gloria. Writers Recharge. 3601 Beach Dr. SW, #11, Seattle, WA 98116. P1/ 206-935-3142. glokemp@earthlink.net. www.writersrecharge.com. Established: 1986.

SKILLS: freelance editor, independent book editor, book doctor, literary consultant, writing coach, writing instructor, marketing coach, critique group facilitator. **MARKETS SERVED:** individual writers, critique groups, publishers.

SPECIALTIES AND PREFERENCES: I coach fiction and nonfiction writers who want to perfect their craft in the areas of voice, structure, and form. I help them discover the kind of writing in which they excel and find their authentic voice. I provide marketing guidance when they're searching for a market or an agent. My specialty is fiction and nonfiction storytelling, with an emphasis on theme and structure.

FICTION—ACCEPTS: y/a or juvenile, short stories, novels (genre, mainstream, literary, contemporary, historical), queries, synopses. **NONFICTION—ACCEPTS:** all. **TYPICAL EVALUATION/REPORT:** 2–8 pages.

FEES/TERMS/CONTRACTS: $65/hour for coaching and/or manuscript evaluation. Half up front and half upon completion of evaluation. No credit cards.

ACCOMPLISHMENTS: two novels, eight self-help books, hundreds of short stories and articles in national magazines. Editorial consultant for *Writer's Digest*.

CLIENTS WITHIN PRIOR YEAR: 100–200.

277	EDITOR	WRITER	CONSULTANT	F	NF

Kern, Judith. 460 E. 79th St., New York, NY 10021. P1/ 212-249-5871. kernjt@aol.com. www.consulting-editors.com. Established: 2000.

SKILLS: freelance editor, independent book editor, book doctor, copyeditor or line editor, ghostwriter. **MARKETS SERVED:** writers and authors.

SPECIALTIES AND PREFERENCES: ghostwriter, book doctor, and substantive editor. Areas of expertise include adult fiction, and nonfiction including self-help, spirituality and self-actualization, memoir, and health/diet. I also edit and collaborate on cookbooks.

FICTION—ACCEPTS: novels (genre, mainstream, literary, contemporary, historical). **NONFICTION—ACCEPTS:** memoirs, creative or narrative, biography/autobiography, self-help, how-to/instruction, business, humor, inspirational/religious, spiritual, book proposals, queries. **TYPICAL EVALUATION/REPORT:** varies as required by project.

FEES/TERMS/CONTRACTS: fees determined up front on a book-by-book basis. Prefers flat fee to hourly rate. No credit cards.

ACCOMPLISHMENTS: in-house editor for more than thirty years at Harper's Magazine

Press, Atheneum, and Doubleday. Freelance projects include major nonfiction books published by Gotham, St. Martin's, Rodale, Doubleday, HP, and others.

EDUCATION: BA English, Smith College, Northampton, MA. MEMBERSHIPS: Authors Guild. Consulting Editors Alliance. International Association of Culinary Professionals. James Beard Society.

CLIENTS WITHIN PRIOR YEAR: 11–20.

278	EDITOR	WRITER	CONSULTANT	F	NF

Kindman-Koffler, Bette. Koffler Communications. Monmouth Junction, NJ. P1/ 732-329-6518, P2/ 609-947-0514, F1/ 732-320-3029. BetteK-K@att.net. www.pwawriters.org/pens-for-hire/bkoffler.html. Established: 1987.

SKILLS: freelance editor, book doctor, copyeditor or line editor, business writer or copywriter, report writer. Writer, editor, researcher of marketing communications and public relations materials. MARKETS SERVED: writers, nonprofits, for-profits, government, K–14 schools.

SPECIALTIES AND PREFERENCES: newsletters, brochures, pamphlets, press releases, press kits, technical product descriptions, case histories, catalogs, directories, articles, manuals, reports. Education, business, civil rights, women's issues, manuscript editing.

FICTION—ACCEPTS: short stories, scripts/screenplays. NONFICTION—ACCEPTS: all. TYPICAL EVALUATION/REPORT: 30–50 pages.

FEES/TERMS/CONTRACTS: per-project fee: one-third at start, one-third first draft, one-third completion. Payment due on schedule. Uses contract or agreement.

ACCOMPLISHMENTS: Silver Award, Neographics Association (Direct Mail), published article in *Wm. S. Gray Research Collection in Reading*, dozens of research reports for federal and state agencies. Dozens of federal educational reports, scores of brochures, catalogs, newsletters, press releases, case histories, product descriptions.

EDUCATION: EdD Education, Rutgers University, NJ. MEd Reading, Rutgers University, NJ. BA Literature, SUNY, Plattsburgh. MEMBERSHIPS: Professional Writers Alliance of Central New Jersey.

CLIENTS WITHIN PRIOR YEAR: 11–20.

279	EDITOR	WRITER	CONSULTANT	F	NF

King, Judy. Judy King Editorial Services. PO Box 35038, Houston, TX 77235-5038. P1/ 713-721-3003. judyking@pdq.net. www.judykingedit.com. Established: 1994.

SKILLS: freelance editor, independent book editor, copyeditor or line editor, proofreader, indexer. **MARKETS SERVED:** independent publishers, authors, publishing houses, universities, corporations.

SPECIALTIES AND PREFERENCES: I partner with new and established authors to polish their work for publication. Specialties—humanities, business, genealogy, Christianity, family topics. I respect deadlines and preserve the author's style. Since I've been published (and edited!) myself, I understand what an author needs from an editor.

FICTION—ACCEPTS: y/a or juvenile. **NONFICTION—ACCEPTS:** y/a or juvenile, memoirs, creative or narrative, biography/autobiography, family history, self-help, how-to/instruction, technical, business, humor, inspirational/religious, spiritual. **TYPICAL EVALUATION/REPORT:** 1–3 pages.

FEES/TERMS/CONTRACTS: free estimate. No credit cards. Accepts PayPal. Uses a contract.

ACCOMPLISHMENTS: I am the author of five published books. The Reader's Digest bought 750,000 copies of one, *The Greatest Gift Guide Ever* (Variety Press, Betterway Publishing). I have also had several dozen articles published in periodicals. I am pleased that most of my new clients come from referrals from satisfied clients.

EDUCATION: BA Journalism, University of Texas, Austin, with high honors and special honors in journalism. Graduate course in indexing. Texas teacher's certificate in English and journalism.

CLIENTS WITHIN PRIOR YEAR: 10–20.

280	EDITOR	WRITER	CONSULTANT	F	NF

King, Marlene. PO Box 477, Murphy, OR 97533. P1/ 541-471-9337. marlene@chatlink.com. Established: 1985.

SKILLS: freelance editor, independent book editor, copyeditor or line editor, proofreader, business writer or copywriter, counseling; assist with creative process using expressive therapies/dreamwork. **MARKETS SERVED:** writers, corporations.

SPECIALTIES AND PREFERENCES: line or copyediting and proofing are mainstays, but offer content analysis and counseling to develop new pathways of self-expression that enrich the client's writing and remove writer's block.

FICTION—ACCEPTS: short stories, novels (genre, mainstream, literary, contemporary, historical), scripts/screenplays, queries, synopses, treatments. **NONFICTION—ACCEPTS:** articles/features, biography/autobiography, self-help, how-to/instruction, business, inspirational/religious, spiritual. **TYPICAL EVALUATION/REPORT:** varies.

FEES/TERMS/CONTRACTS: $30/hour, line or copyediting/proofreading/report analysis. $95/hour, counseling services. Payable half down, half on completion based on estimate. Uses agreement.

ACCOMPLISHMENTS: dozens of articles and stories published in national magazines and books. Magazine columnist. Marketing consultant.

EDUCATION: MA Art Therapy, Marylhurst University, Portland, OR. BA Art History, University of California, Santa Barbara. **MEMBERSHIPS:** Willamette Writers.

CLIENTS WITHIN PRIOR YEAR: variable depending upon workload.

281	EDITOR	WRITER	CONSULTANT	F	NF

Kirven, Donna. Pittsburg, CA. P1/ 925-432-1752. F1/ 925-432-1752. donnakirven@yahoo.com. Established: 2000.

SKILLS: technical writer, literary consultant, editorial consultant. **MARKETS SERVED:** health care industry and medical professionals (clinical laboratory science, phlebotomy).

SPECIALTIES AND PREFERENCES: curriculum development for training programs associated with health care or clinical laboratory science. Educator/instructor. Narrative reporting.

FICTION—ACCEPTS: poetry. **NONFICTION—ACCEPTS:** how-to/instruction, technical, text or reference, business. **TYPICAL EVALUATION/REPORT:** varies.

FEES/TERMS/CONTRACTS: Fees are hourly. No credit cards. Contractual agreements acceptable.

ACCOMPLISHMENTS: columnist/editorial consultant. Award-winning poet. Author of poetry book published by Publish America. Currently, an instructor, San Francisco State University. Numerous editorial and focus columns in *Advance Magazine for Medical Laboratory Professional*, 1999 to present. Editor/writer for *The Bleeding Times*, 2003 to present. Editor/writer for California Society for Clinical Laboratory Science, 2001-2003. January 2004 Featured Poet in *Shadow Poetry Quill* (quarterly magazine).

EDUCATION: BA Psychology, Temple University, Philadelphia, PA. **MEMBERSHIPS:** Phlebotomy West, Inc. American Society for Clinical Laboratory Science. California Society for Clinical Laboratory Science. American Society of Clinical Pathologists.

CLIENTS WITHIN PRIOR YEAR: 1–5.

282	EDITOR	WRITER	CONSULTANT	F	NF

Klauser, Lori. Creatively Write. Phoenix, AZ. P1/ 602-595-0075. C1/ 602-334-7811. lakla@netzero.net. www.creativelywrite.com. Established: 2003.

SKILLS: freelance editor, copyeditor or line editor, proofreader, ghostwriter, business writer or copywriter. **MARKETS SERVED:** writers, corporations.

SPECIALTIES AND PREFERENCES: edits newsletters, nonfiction books, articles. Either a full edit or critique depending on how much is needed. Copywrites for businesses, ghostwrites for authors.

Fiction—accepts: y/a or juvenile, short stories. **Nonfiction—accepts:** all. **Typical evaluation/report:** 1–2 pages.

Fees/terms/contracts: editing—$2.50/page. Critique—$1.25/page. Copywriting— $35/hour. No credit cards. Half up front, balance at project end. Uses contract.

Accomplishments: children's story, *The Leader Newspaper*, June 2002. Online article, 2003.

Education: AA Liberal Arts, Rio Salado Community College, Tempe, AZ. Two graduate diplomas, Institute of Children's Literature, Redding, CT. *Writer's Digest* online writing courses. **Memberships:** National Association of Women Writers.

Clients within prior year: 1–5.

283	EDITOR	WRITER	CONSULTANT	F	NF

Kleeberg, Irene. 350 E. 30th St., 4H, New York, NY 10016. P1/ 212-213-6038. F1/ 212-685-2183. ickleeberg@juno.com. Established: 1970.

Skills: freelance editor, independent book editor, copyeditor or line editor, proofreader, business writer or copywriter. **Markets served:** publishers, both US and foreign. Some businesses.

Specialties and preferences: adapting bad foreign English translations into good American English. My eclectic business is based on many years of experience writing and editing for both American and foreign clients. I find my specialties lie in bringing the right tone to each project, and my favorite subjects are always those I am working on at the moment!

Fiction—accepts: novels (genre, mainstream, contemporary, historical). **Nonfiction—accepts:** y/a or juvenile, biography/autobiography, how-to/instruction, text or reference, business, humor, inspirational/religious, spiritual.

Fees/terms/contracts: by arrangement.

Accomplishments: Member of the Year, Romance Writers of America, New York City chapter. Former member of Board of Governors. Editorial Freelancers Association.

Education: BA Wellesley College, MA. **Memberships:** Authors Guild. Romance Writers of America. Editorial Freelancers Association. Sisters in Crime. New York Wellesley Club. Women in Publishing (United Kingdom).

Clients within prior year: 1–5.

284	EDITOR	WRITER	CONSULTANT	F	NF

Klein, Erica. Klein & Kroll, Inc. 444 Washington Blvd., Suite 328, Jersey City, NJ 07310. P1/ 201-876-9067. P2/ 201-876-9366. F1/ 201-876-9368. elk11@aol.com. www.ericaklein.com. Established: 1987.

SKILLS: freelance editor, independent book editor, ghostwriter, business writer or copywriter, technical writer, literary consultant, writing instructor, publicist, speechwriter, brand strategist, business development specialist, public relations consultant. MARKETS SERVED: individuals and businesses. Health care, financial services, and agency communities in NYC and LA metro areas.

SPECIALTIES AND PREFERENCES: solves companies' communications and writing problems to allow them to increase profits from sales. Helps authors to refine salable ideas, prepare proposals and query letters, and market successfully.

NONFICTION—ACCEPTS: all. TYPICAL EVALUATION/REPORT: 1–5 pages.

FEES/TERMS/CONTRACTS: accepts PayPal and personal checks. Uses agreement.

ACCOMPLISHMENTS: seven nonfiction books. Henry Hoke Award—Best Direct Mail Piece in the US. IABC Golden Quill Award—Best Corporate Brochure.

EDUCATION: BA English, Washington University, St. Louis, MO. Teaching Certificate, English. Coursework in direct mail copywriting, online marketing and writing, feature article writing, and executive speechwriting. UCLA-trained screenwriter. MEMBERSHIPS: National Writers Union. Dramatists Guild.

CLIENTS WITHIN PRIOR YEAR: 6–10.

285	EDITOR	WRITER	CONSULTANT	F	NF

Knight, Lynn. 19502 61st Ave. NE, Kenmore, WA 98028. C1/ 206-226-2803. lynxnight@yahoo.com. Established: 2002.

SKILLS: freelance editor, independent book editor, book doctor, copyeditor or line editor, proofreader, ghostwriter, business writer or copywriter, technical writer. MARKETS SERVED: new and intermediate fiction writers; businesses (for newsletters, copywriting).

SPECIALTIES AND PREFERENCES: primarily fiction, especially novels, short stories, plays, and screenplays. Content editing; helping improve a story's impact via structure, scene development, pacing, and character development.

FICTION—ACCEPTS: short stories, novels (mainstream, literary, contemporary, historical), scripts/screenplays. NONFICTION—ACCEPTS: memoirs, creative or narrative, biography/autobiography, family history. TYPICAL EVALUATION/REPORT: 10–30 pages depending on length of manuscript.

FEES/TERMS/CONTRACTS: to be negotiated; credit card and PayPal; contract.

ACCOMPLISHMENTS: I've published short stories, feature articles, book reviews, newsletters, and had seven plays produced.

EDUCATION: BA Creative Writing, Theater, University of New Mexico, Albuquerque. **MEMBERSHIPS:** Seattle Writers Association, Board of Directors. Pacific Northwest Writers Association.
CLIENTS WITHIN PRIOR YEAR: 6–10.

286	EDITOR	WRITER	CONSULTANT	F	NF

Koeppel, Ruth. New York, NY. RAK63@aol.com. Established: 1999.

SKILLS: freelance editor, independent book editor, book doctor, literary consultant, writing coach.

MARKETS SERVED: writers of nearly all types of fiction, for adults and children, including short stories, novels, and screenplays.

SPECIALTIES AND PREFERENCES: commercial and literary young adult and middle-grade fiction and picture books.

FICTION—ACCEPTS: y/a or juvenile picture books, short stories, novels (genre, mainstream, literary, contemporary), scripts/screenplays, queries, synopses, treatments. **TYPICAL EVALUATION/REPORT:** several pages.

FEES/TERMS/CONTRACTS: Fees vary by project. Generally $1,000/young adult or middle-grade novel; $500/picture book. Fee includes written evaluation, marked-up manuscript, sample edit as necessary, evaluation of revised manuscript, coaching regarding writing career. Free consultation, then payment by check before work commences. No contract.

ACCOMPLISHMENTS: worked for twenty years as an editor and writer in publishing, packaging, and licensing at Random House, HarperCollins, Nickelodeon, and Parachute Publishing. Published young adult short fiction, two original novelty picture books, and various titles based on juvenile licenses.

EDUCATION: BA English Literature, Bryn Mawr College, PA. Robert McKee story structure, thriller, and comedy courses. Studied with Madeleine L'Engle.
CLIENTS WITHIN PRIOR YEAR: 11–20.

287	EDITOR	WRITER	CONSULTANT	F	NF

Krawitz, Henry. New York, NY. P1/ 718-846-5118. henry.krawitz@verizon.net. Established: 1996.

SKILLS: copyeditor or line editor. **MARKETS SERVED:** university presses, encyclopedia/reference publishers, art museums.

SPECIALTIES AND PREFERENCES: comparative literary studies (French, German, British, American); world literature; literary criticism; interdisciplinary studies (art/music history; theater; film; dance), especially 19th and early 20th centuries; Judaica/religious studies; bibliographies and notes. I am detail oriented and make every effort to meet deadlines.

NONFICTION—ACCEPTS: y/a or juvenile, essays, memoirs, creative or narrative, biography/autobiography, family history, technical, text or reference, religious.

FEES/TERMS/CONTRACTS: $20–30/hour. Invoice sent after completion. Payment within 30 days. No credit cards.

ACCOMPLISHMENTS: published book-length bibliography.

EDUCATION: PhD Comparative Literature, City University of New York. MA Comparative Literature, City University of New York. BA Comparative Literature, Queens College, City University of New York. **MEMBERSHIPS:** Editorial Freelancers Association.

CLIENTS WITHIN PRIOR YEAR: 6–10.

288	EDITOR	WRITER	CONSULTANT	F	NF

Kreps, Karen. 1741 Spyglass Dr., #229, Austin, TX 78746. P1/ 512-328-4456. KarenKreps@NetIngenuity.com. www.netingenuity.com. Established: 1974.

SKILLS: freelance editor, business writer or copywriter, instructional designer, E-learning, WBT (web-based training) for K-12, college and business training. **MARKETS SERVED:** consumer, business, and technical.

SPECIALTIES AND PREFERENCES: copywriting for consumer, business, and technical markets. Magazine articles, how to books, scripts for rich media productions. I've been creating websites since 1993.

NONFICTION—ACCEPTS: articles/features, how-to/instruction, technical, business.

FEES/TERMS/CONTRACTS: $80/hour, minimum ten hours.

ACCOMPLISHMENTS: I am a nonfiction magazine writer/editor and creative project manager. I am skilled in marketing, search engine optimization, instructional design, and technical writing. Authored *The 60-Day Diet Diary*, a how-to bestseller that had six printings and sold more than 250,000 copies.

EDUCATION: MA Cinema Studies, New York University, New York. BA English and Dramatic Literature, New York University, New York. **MEMBERSHIPS:** American Society for Training & Development. Association of Internet Professionals. International Interactive Communications Society.

CLIENTS WITHIN PRIOR YEAR: 6–10.

289	EDITOR	WRITER	CONSULTANT	F	NF

Krulikowski, Claire. AshootingstarZ Production. PO Box 865, Talent, OR 97540. P1/ 541-535-3390. claire@clairekrulikowski.com. ashootingstar@charter.net. www.clairekrulikowski.com. Established: 2001, freelancing since 1990.

SKILLS: freelance editor, copyeditor, proofreader, business writer or copywriter, literary consultant, writing instructor, website copywriter, researcher of publishers, public relations. **MARKETS SERVED:** individual writers, businesses.

SPECIALTIES AND PREFERENCES: edits/proofs manuscripts, queries, proposals; website analysis; writing seminar instructor.

FICTION—ACCEPTS: short stories, novels (genre, mainstream, literary, contemporary), queries. NONFICTION—ACCEPTS: articles/features, memoirs, creative or narrative, all bios, family history, self-help, how-to/instruction, reference, business, inspirational, spiritual, book proposals, queries. TYPICAL EVALUATION/ REPORT: 3–25 pages.

FEES/TERMS/CONTRACTS: varies by project. Generally $35–$75/hour. Payable by check, money order, or cash. Uses contract in some cases.

ACCOMPLISHMENTS: author of *Moonlight on the Ganga* (Daybue Publishing), third place Best Editing Award by the Northwest Publishers. Self-published poetry book.

EDUCATION: BA Literature, Ramapo College, Mahwah, NJ. CPM in Purchasing; Certification in Procurement from UCLA. MEMBERSHIPS: Authors Guild. National Writers Union. Willamette Writers. PoetsWest.

CLIENTS WITHIN PRIOR YEAR: 25–30.

290	EDITOR	WRITER	CONSULTANT	F	NF

Kutza, Patricia. PO Box 4127, Vallejo, CA 94590. P1/ 707-552-0442. pkutza@pacbell.net. www.mediabistro.com/PatriciaKutza/. Established: 1985.

SKILLS: ghostwriter, business writer or copywriter, technical writer, writing coach, publicist. MARKETS SERVED: custom publishing, corporations, magazines, research firms.

SPECIALTIES AND PREFERENCES: technology, small business, travel niches. White papers, advertorials, trend reports, company profiles, press releases, news and views, features, front of the book, essays, destination pieces, product reviews, interviews, personal histories, online media kits.

NONFICTION—ACCEPTS: all. TYPICAL EVALUATION/REPORT: 2–160 pages.

FEES/TERMS/CONTRACTS: per word, project, or hour. Credit cards, PayPal. Uses contract or agreement.

ACCOMPLISHMENTS: dozens of national and regional magazine articles, two white papers.

EDUCATION: BA, Radio and Television Broadcasting, San Francisco State University, CA. Computer Professional Certification, Institute of Certified Computing Professionals. MEMBERSHIPS: American Society of Journalists and Authors.

CLIENTS WITHIN PRIOR YEAR: 5–8.

291	EDITOR	WRITER	CONSULTANT	F	NF

Kylen, Helene. Little Silver, NJ. P1/ 732-345-7393. hkw33@comcast.net. Established: 1982.

Skills: freelance editor, copyeditor or line editor, proofreader, freelance writer, copywriter or business writer, writing coach, publicist, freelance proposal writer, teacher (college creative writing and editing, private tutor), public speaker, psychotherapy background. **Markets served:** writers, therapists, students, businesses.

Specialties and preferences: biographical, autobiographical, psychological; relationships, character development, societal, cultural. Articles, essays, memoirs, presentations, books, proposals, public relations.

Nonfiction—accepts: all. **Typical evaluation/report:** 1–3 pages.

Fees/terms/contracts: $35/hour, detailed time/work sheet; contract.

Accomplishments: articles in Gannett News chain, *New York Times*, New York *Daily News*, *The Asbury Park Press*, *The Hub*, *Court Review*, *Psychiatric Bulletin*, *NY/Conn/Westchester Family*, *Psychotherapy Networker*. Editor, training manual for NYC Probation Dept. Judge, national essay contest. PR director, radio interviewee, public speaker at Creativity Institute, NY Public Library, City University Graduate Center.

Education: BA Advanced Writing and Psychology, New York University New School for Social Research, NY. Sarah Lawrence College, Bronxville, NY, seminars. **Memberships:** International Women's Writer's Guild. Brookdale Community College.

Clients within prior year: 5–10.

292	EDITOR	WRITER	CONSULTANT	F	NF

Ladd, Louise. 27 Bloomfield Dr., Fairfield, CT 06825. P1/ 203-345-6265. P2/ 203-336-9323. louiseld@optonline.net. www.LouiseLadd.net. Established: 1993.

Skills: freelance editor, book doctor, writing coach, writing instructor. **Markets served:** advanced writers of fiction, nonfiction, adult, y/a, and children's.

Specialties and preferences: advanced only, no beginners. Over ten years of extensive experience. Sample critiques on request. Phone/in-person discussion follow-up if desired. Remarks kind, helpful, and always honest. As a working writer myself, I understand the difficulties and challenges we all face, so I try to be as encouraging as possible while giving a completely honest assessment of the work.

Fiction—accepts: all. **Nonfiction—accepts:** all. **Typical evaluation/report:** line editing, explanatory notes on pages, plus 2–10-page critique.

Fees/terms/contracts: $35–$40/hour, one-half deposit, balance on completion. Uses agreement.

Accomplishments: eighteen novels for kids and y/a, co-editor of one memoir. Nonfiction in *Writer's Digest*. Teacher, Fairfield University, others. Hundreds have studied with me, many now published. Listed in *Who's Who in America*, *Something about the Author*.

EDUCATION: BA History, Wellesley College, MA. Nine years of writing and acting workshops. MEMBERSHIPS: Author's Guild. Women Writing the West. National League of American Pen Women. Society of Children's Book Writers and Illustrators.
CLIENTS WITHIN PRIOR YEAR: 1–5.

293	EDITOR	WRITER	CONSULTANT	F	NF

Lamb, Ellen Clair. PO Box 921, Gardiner, MN 04345. P1/ 310-266-2852. EllenClairLamb@cs.com. www.answergirl.net. Established: 1999.

SKILLS: freelance editor, independent book editor, book doctor, copyeditor or line editor, proofreader, ghostwriter, business writer or copywriter, technical writer, literary consultant, writing coach, writing instructor, publicist. MARKETS SERVED: writers, publishers, associations, government agencies, corporations, nonprofits.

SPECIALTIES AND PREFERENCES: translating complex jargon into plain English; cleaning up timelines and correcting continuity; customizing pieces for specialized audiences.

FICTION—ACCEPTS: short stories, novels (genre, mainstream, literary, contemporary, historical), scripts/screenplays, synopses, treatments. NONFICTION—ACCEPTS: articles/features, essays, memoirs, creative or narrative, biography/autobiography, family history, self-help, how-to/instruction, technical, text or reference, business, humor. TYPICAL EVALUATION/REPORT: 2–5 pages.

FEES/TERMS/CONTRACTS: editing and proofreading $40/hour, per-project terms available. Typically uses contract or agreement.

ACCOMPLISHMENTS: dozens of articles published in banking trade journals. Dozens of association and retail newsletters.

EDUCATION: BS Foreign Service, Georgetown University School of Foreign Service, Washington, DC. MEMBERSHIPS: Women in Housing and Finance.
CLIENTS WITHIN PRIOR YEAR: 10–15.

294	EDITOR	WRITER	CONSULTANT	F	NF

Lance, Kathryn. P1/ 520-326-2555. klance@klance.com. www.klance.com. Established: 1976.

SKILLS: freelance editor, book doctor, copyeditor or line editor, ghostwriter, literary consultant, writing coach, book collaborator—where I write or rewrite the book and get a "with" credit on the cover, proposal writer. MARKETS SERVED: doctors, psychologists, and other health professionals; beginning writers in many fields, including fiction.

SPECIALTIES AND PREFERENCES: I've written or collaborated on more than fifty published books, for adults and young adults, both fiction and nonfiction.

I've edited numerous books, stories, and articles for various clients and served as writing coach for a number of new writers. I also edited a quarterly magazine for seven years..

FICTION—ACCEPTS: y/a or juvenile, novels (genre, mainstream), scripts/screenplays, queries, synopses, treatments. NONFICTION—ACCEPTS: articles/features, biography/autobiography, self-help, book proposals.

FEES/TERMS/CONTRACTS: charges competitively; fees dependent on the project. Requires half on signing a collaboration agreement and half upon completion.

ACCOMPLISHMENTS: have collaborated on five nonfiction titles with major publishers.

EDUCATION: ABD English Education, New York University. MA Russian, BA Russian, University of Arizona, Tucson. Much undergraduate work in science.

MEMBERSHIPS: American Society of Journalists and Authors. Authors Guild. Science Fiction Writers of America.

CLIENTS WITHIN PRIOR YEAR: 6–10.

295	EDITOR	WRITER	CONSULTANT	F	NF

Landalf, Helen. WordPlay Writing and Editing Services. Seattle, WA. P1/ 206-706-1633. rakoova@seanet.com. editors@wordplayink.com. www.wordplayink.com. Established: 2003.

SKILLS: freelance editor, independent book editor, book doctor, copyeditor or line editor, business writer or copywriter, writing coach. MARKETS SERVED: independent authors.

SPECIALTIES AND PREFERENCES: coaching authors through the creation or revision of their work. Specialties include movement/exercise/dance and y/a fiction.

FICTION—ACCEPTS: y/a or juvenile, short stories, novels (genre, mainstream, literary, contemporary, historical), queries, synopses. NONFICTION—ACCEPTS: y/a or juvenile, picture books, articles/features, essays, memoirs, creative or narrative, biography/autobiography, self-help, how-to/instruction, text or reference, business, humor, inspirational/religious, book proposals, queries.

TYPICAL EVALUATION/REPORT: 4–6 pages.

FEES/TERMS/CONTRACTS: manuscript evaluation $1.50/page ($50 minimum). Coaching $25/hour. Copyediting $30/hour. No credit cards.

ACCOMPLISHMENTS: seven published books. National Parent Publishing Honor Award, 1998.

EDUCATION: BA Theater Arts, Certificate in Editing, Extension Program, University of Washington, Seattle. MEMBERSHIPS: Society of Children's Book Writers and Illustrators. Pacific Northwest Writer's Association.

CLIENTS WITHIN PRIOR YEAR: 1–5.

296	EDITOR	WRITER	CONSULTANT	F	NF

Landon, Kristin. 2568 Sharon Way, Eugene, OR 97401-5165. F1/ 541-484-1266. P2/ 541-484-1266. kplandon@comcast.net. Established: 1989.

SKILLS: freelance editor, copyeditor or line editor, technical writer. MARKETS SERVED: scientific and technical publishers, textbook publishers, individuals who need their scientific or technical writing polished, non-native writers (English not a first language).

SPECIALTIES AND PREFERENCES: scientific, technical, and medical fields. Articles for scientific journals, scientific and technical monographs, college and graduate-level textbooks, symposium volumes. I enjoy working with authors who aren't confident about writing in English. I can work with them to produce books and articles in perfect idiomatic English at a level appropriate for their readership.

NONFICTION—ACCEPTS: y/a or juvenile, how-to/instruction, technical, text or reference.

FEES/TERMS/CONTRACTS: copyediting $3–$5/page; writing/ rewriting varies, agreed in advance. Invoices at end of project; terms 30 days. Interim invoices on long projects. No credit cards. Contract for writing and noncorporate clients.

ACCOMPLISHMENTS: I have edited about 300 books since 1989, ~1,000 articles for scientific journals. I have written manuals for industrial software. I won the Pacific Northwest Writers Conference awards for best science fiction/fantasy novel in 1992 and 1995.

EDUCATION: BS Chemistry, Washington State University, Pullman, with coursework in physics and technical writing. MEMBERSHIPS: Willamette Writers. CLIENTS WITHIN PRIOR YEAR: 11–20.

297	EDITOR	WRITER	CONSULTANT	F	NF

Landres, Marcela. Brooklyn, NY. C1/ 718-208-5810. marcelalandres@yahoo.com. www.marcelalandres.com. Established: 2003.

SKILLS: freelance editor, independent book editor, copyeditor or line editor, literary consultant, editorial consultant, and Latino publishing specialist. MARKETS SERVED: writers, and agents who represent writers, of both fiction and nonfiction.

SPECIALTIES AND PREFERENCES: specializes in Latino publishing; offers a website, newsletter, and workshops designed to encourage and enable Latino writers to become successfully published. Especially seeks literary novels, commercial novels, and chick lit; self-help, New Age, spirituality, inspiration, relationships, sexuality, and pop culture.

FICTION—ACCEPTS: novels (genre, mainstream, literary, contemporary, historical), queries. NONFICTION—ACCEPTS: self-help, how-to/instruction, inspirational/

religious, spiritual, book proposals, queries. TYPICAL EVALUATION/REPORT: 6–12 pages.

FEES/TERMS/CONTRACTS: $100/hour. Half due upon signing of contract, the balance upon completion of consultation or editing. No credit cards.

ACCOMPLISHMENTS: editor at Simon & Schuster for seven years.

EDUCATION: BA English Literature, Barnard College, New York City, NY. MEMBERSHIPS: Publishing Latinos Voices for America Committee for the Association of American Publishers. Women in Literature and Letters and New York Women in Communications, Inc. Editorial Freelancers Association.

CLIENTS WITHIN PRIOR YEAR: 1–5.

298	EDITOR	WRITER	CONSULTANT	F	NF

Lanier, Paula. Brooklyn, NY. P1/ 718-398-7085. P2/ 917-847-8896. drugedit@hotmail.com. Established: freelance since 2003.

SKILLS: freelance editor, proofreader, peer-reviewed journals, slide kits, drug launch campaigns, CME instruction manuals; researcher; fact-checker.

SPECIALTIES AND PREFERENCES: pharmaceutical advertising, medical education, publishing, foundations. I freelance on a full-time basis after fifteen years of working in full-time staff positions as a medical editor for pharmaceutical advertising agencies. Most work is on-site; prefer working at home. Most of my night work comes from publishing companies, usually copyediting and coding an author's manuscript or proofreading first galleys against the copyedited manuscript. I also work on-site at night, usually for agencies or foundations related to medicine.

NONFICTION—ACCEPTS: y/a or juvenile, creative or narrative, biography/autobiography, family history, self-help, how-to//instruction, technical, text or reference.

FEES/TERMS/CONTRACTS: $25+/hour (depending on assignment).

EDUCATION: BA English, Brooklyn College, NY. MEMBERSHIPS: Editorial Freelancers Association. American Medical Writers Association. Council of Science Editors.

CLIENTS WITHIN PRIOR YEAR: 10–15.

299	EDITOR	WRITER	CONSULTANT	F	NF

Larson, Anja. Urwald Editorial. PO Box 221, Vancouver, WA 98666. lanja@spiritone.com. Established: 2003.

SKILLS: freelance editor. MARKETS SERVED: individual writers, small businesses.

SPECIALTIES AND PREFERENCES: bringing diplomacy to a given document, learned as an editor of a frequently busy market-research firm over the course of several years. I have become one with the mindset, although I have flown the nest. It is second nature for me to ask the writer to clarify; to boil down the ghee, for to concoct pith.

FICTION—ACCEPTS: short stories, novels (genre, literary, contemporary), poetry, queries, synopses, treatments. NONFICTION—ACCEPTS: articles/features, essays, memoirs, creative or narrative, biography/autobiography, family history, humor. FEES/TERMS/CONTRACTS: sliding scale.

ACCOMPLISHMENTS: editor at a market research firm, editing the results of the surveys for clarity, line by line, year after year (1997-2003). Dramaturg for a Portland Center Stage production, *Measure for Measure*, directed by Ed Call in the mid-nineties. Production assistant for *House of the World*, directed by Esther Podemski—a Holocaust memorial documentary of Polish cemeteries, also mid-nineties.

EDUCATION: BA English, Reed College, Portland, OR. Graduate-level coursework in book editing, Portland State University publishing program. MEMBERSHIPS: Willamette Writers. National Writers Union. CLIENTS WITHIN PRIOR YEAR: 1–5.

300	EDITOR	WRITER	CONSULTANT	F	NF

Larson, Christina. Sacramento, CA. P1/ 916-443-1173. F1/ 916-443-1157. cmlarson@cmlarson.com. www.cmlarson.com. www.the-family-cfo.com. Established: part-time in 1994; full-time since 1998.

SKILLS: freelance editor, book doctor, ghostwriter, business writer or copywriter. MARKETS SERVED: business and personal finance experts, magazines, custom publishers, businesses, anyone seeking collaborations on books.

SPECIALTIES AND PREFERENCES: personal finance, business, and technology. Edits for magazines; ghostwriting or cowriting books/articles for business or personal finance experts. Creates newsletters and custom publications.

NONFICTION—ACCEPTS: articles/features, self-help, business, book proposals, queries.

FEES/TERMS/CONTRACTS: typically $100/hour for writing articles or editing. $15,000– $25,000 for book proposals, depending on scope and scale of project. Percentage of the advance for ghostwriting books. No credit cards.

ACCOMPLISHMENTS: former editor at *Cosmopolitan*, *Glamour*, *Adweek*. Helped launch a custom magazine, *dotCEO*, for Chief Executive Magazine group, which led to writing-for-hire opportunities. Published articles appear in *Wall Street Journal*, *US World Report*, and others. Wrote/sold a book proposal for a personal financial planner; cowrote another published by Rodale.

EDUCATION: BA English, Princeton University, NJ. MEMBERSHIPS: American Society of Journalists and Authors. Authors Guild. CLIENTS WITHIN PRIOR YEAR: 1–5.

301	EDITOR	WRITER	CONSULTANT	F	NF

Larson, Ellen. Typochondria. Boston, MA. F1/ 443-238-0770. enkidu@crosswinds.net. www.enkidu.info. Established: 1993.

SKILLS: freelance editor, business writer or copywriter, technical writer, writing coach. MARKETS SERVED: writers, non-native English writers, publishers, corporations, nonprofit organizations.

SPECIALTIES AND PREFERENCES: mystery, science fiction, adventure, horse, mainstream. Freelance international economic development organizations. Agriculture, conference proceedings, newsletters, annual reports, success stories.

FICTION—ACCEPTS: y/a or juvenile, short stories, novels (genre, mainstream, literary, contemporary, historical), queries, synopses, treatments. NONFICTION—ACCEPTS: all.

FEES/TERMS/CONTRACTS: $50/hour coaching. Will quote on other work. Five cents/word technical editing/copyediting; $5/page text layout. Kicker for tables/figs. Check or PayPal.

ACCOMPLISHMENTS: three published novels, short stories, essays, reviews. Writer, editor, and media consultant for USAID, the World Bank, ICARDA, WARDA. Substantive editor for Poisoned Pen Press.

EDUCATION: MA Humanities, California State University, Dominguez Hills. BA English, Windham College, Putney, VT. MEMBERSHIPS: Mystery Writers of America.

CLIENTS WITHIN PRIOR YEAR: 6–10.

302	EDITOR	WRITER	CONSULTANT	F	NF

Larson, Heather. Write Mix. PO Box 24303, Federal Way, WA 98093. P1/ 253-952-2866. F1/ 253-952-2916. writemix@harbornet.com. writemix@hotmail.com. www.writemix.net. Established: 2001.

SKILLS: copyeditor or line editor, proofreader, ghostwriter, business writer or copywriter, writing instructor. MARKETS SERVED: magazines and small to intermediate-size businesses, mostly in the Seattle-Tacoma area. I teach writers in that same area.

SPECIALTIES AND PREFERENCES: I write feature articles for consumer and trade publications, plus create web content, press releases, newsletters, and brochures for businesses.

NONFICTION—ACCEPTS: all. TYPICAL EVALUATION/REPORT: 3–15 pages depending on length of manuscript.

FEES/TERMS/CONTRACTS: $40/hour. Accepts checks only. Uses a contract.

ACCOMPLISHMENTS: I have been a finalist in the Pacific Northwest Writer's Association contest several times and came in second once. I have been published in *Writer's Digest, Islands, MotorHome, Family Motor Coaching, Master Builders Association magazine, Frontier,* and much more. My clients include Lawyers Title, Dayspring Water Gardens, Stealth Media Solutions, Urban Dog, Master Builders Association, and Federal Way Public Schools. **EDUCATION:** three years of college, and numerous writing courses and writers conferences. **MEMBERSHIPS:** Pacific Northwest Writers Association. **CLIENTS WITHIN PRIOR YEAR:** 6–10.

303	EDITOR	WRITER	CONSULTANT	F	NF

Latimer-Dadzie, Roxann. 3581 Chicago Ave., Suite L, Riverside, CA 92507. P1/ 909-786-0907. F1/ 951-274-0557. wimmedia@yahoo.com. 1997. Established: 1997.

SKILLS: proofreader, ghostwriter, business writer, write grants, proposals, catalogs, annual reports, design brochures. **MARKETS SERVED:** business and writers.

SPECIALTIES AND PREFERENCES: For the past five years I have written articles and edited articles and stories for several newsletters and have designed business plans, marketing plans, and brochures as well as developed annual reports and edited a self-help book.

FICTION—ACCEPTS: novels (genre), poetry, synopses or treatments. **NONFICTION— ACCEPTS:** all.

FEES/TERMS/CONTRACTS: negotiable, but $15/hour for most work. Requires deposit or half down at time of agreement, remainder upon job completion. Accepts credit cards. Sometimes uses contract.

ACCOMPLISHMENTS: published romance novel and self-published poetry and two nonfiction biographies published by African-American publishers. Many articles and essays published in newsletters, newspapers, and magazines. Winner of the San Diego Business Journal Award for Journalism 1999.

EDUCATION: MSW, University of California, Los Angeles. Paralegal diploma, University of San Diego. **MEMBERSHIPS:** Professional Writers Association of California. African Women Writers Association. International Women's Writers Guild.

CLIENTS WITHIN PRIOR YEAR: 11–20.

304	EDITOR	WRITER	CONSULTANT	F	NF

Lawler, Jennifer. Lawler and Daughter. PO Box 4147, Lawrence, KS 66046. P1/ 785-841-0698. C1/ 785-766-5277. jennifer@jenniferlawler.com. www.jenniferlawler.com. Established: 1990.

SKILLS: freelance editor, book doctor, ghostwriter, writing coach. **MARKETS SERVED:** individual writers and book publishers.

SPECIALTIES AND PREFERENCES: coaches a few highly motivated individuals who want to build a platform and become successful book authors. Ghostwrites and coauthors books. Writes book proposals for an up front fee.

NONFICTION—ACCEPTS: articles/features, essays, memoirs, creative or narrative, self-help, how-to/instruction, inspirational/religious, spiritual, book proposals, queries.

FEES/TERMS/CONTRACTS: $150/hour for coaching/retainer discounts apply. Book proposals $5,000 minimum. Accepts all forms of payment. Uses letter of agreement.

ACCOMPLISHMENTS: award-winning (American Society of Journalists and Authors outstanding book award) author of more than twenty books. Freelance writer and editor for book publishers and magazines. Former college English teacher. Book Division co-chair of the National Writers Union.

EDUCATION: PhD English (medieval literature), MA English, BGS (Bachelor of General Studies) English, University of Kansas, Lawrence. **MEMBERSHIPS:** Authors Guild. American Society of Journalists and Authors. National Writers Union. National Writers Association. Society of Children's Book Writers and Illustrators.

CLIENTS WITHIN PRIOR YEAR: 6–10.

305	EDITOR	WRITER	CONSULTANT	F	NF

Lawrence, Tricia. real/**brilliant**, inc. Box 24687, Federal Way, WA 98093.
P1/ 253-661-0371. sensibility@proaxis.com. www.realbrilliant.com.
Established: 1995.

SKILLS: freelance editor, independent book editor, copyeditor or line editor, proofreader, ghostwriter, business writer or copywriter, publicist. **MARKETS SERVED:** book/magazine publishing, businesses, marketing campaigns.

SPECIALTIES AND PREFERENCES: inspirational/religious, fiction, narrative nonfiction. real/**brilliant**, inc. specializes in all sorts of copyediting/proofreading for publication. I strive to make the project look perfect before it's printed. I love helping people with quality projects and I love good writing! I appreciate a good idea and those who dare to dream big and have a vision for their project. If you are committed to doing the work, I'm committed to helping you get where you want to go.

FICTION—ACCEPTS: y/a or juvenile, short stories, novels (genre, mainstream, literary, contemporary, historical), synopses, treatments. **NONFICTION—ACCEPTS:** all.

FEES/TERMS/CONTRACTS: copyediting $7/page and up, 100-page minimum. Ghostwriting $75/hour. 100 percent up front, money order only. No credit cards. Uses contract.

ACCOMPLISHMENTS: author of a library reference book, coauthored seven books sold in specialty gift shops, Target, and COSTCO. Feature articles print/

web magazines. Public relations writing (magazine features). **MEMBERSHIPS:** Editorial Freelancers Association. Freelance Success. Media Bistro. Writers Information Network.

EDUCATION: Accredited classes on editing with American Medical Writers Association.

CLIENTS WITHIN PRIOR YEAR: 40–60.

306	EDITOR	WRITER	CONSULTANT	F	NF

Leese, Jennifer. It's Only Ink! 311 Frederick St., Hagerstown, MD 21740; P1/ 301-797-8312. JenniferLBLeese@msn.com. www.geocities.com/ladyjiraff. Established: 1994.

SKILLS: freelance editor, copyeditor or line editor, proofreader, ghostwriter, book reviewer, book review columnist, freelance writer. **MARKETS SERVED:** Midwest Book Review, Heinemann Library, Foursided-MFNA.

SPECIALTIES AND PREFERENCES: copyediting, reviewing, ghostwriting.

FICTION—ACCEPTS: y/a or juvenile, short stories, novels (genre, mainstream, contemporary). **NONFICTION—ACCEPTS:** y/a or juvenile, family history, self-help, how-to/instruction. **TYPICAL EVALUATION/REPORT:** 1–2 pages.

FEES/TERMS/CONTRACTS: editing fees, $2/page editing of grammar, punctuation, usage; $4–$5/page line-by-line. $50 for resubmitted material. PayPal. No credit cards. Agreement.

ACCOMPLISHMENTS: Freelance—poems, book reviews, articles, children's books, short story anthologies. Author of seven children's books, one y/a, one paranormal fiction. Volunteered as children's book judge for EPIC Eppie Awards and for The Florida Writer's Association. Awarded 2000 RestStop Writer's Literary Award, Children's e-Book Hall of Fame in 2000, James Tiptree Jr. nominee 2002-2003. **MEMBERSHIPS:** Member of World Romance Writersand Potomac Writers Guild.

CLIENTS WITHIN PRIOR YEAR: 6–10.

307	EDITOR	WRITER	CONSULTANT	F	NF

Leffel, Tim. Nashville, TN. P1/ 615-429-2718 . P2/ 615-262-7649. TndLeffel@yahoo.com. www.geocities.com/tndleffel. Established: 1993.

SKILLS: ghostwriter. **MARKETS SERVED:** authors, professional speakers, corporations, small business.

SPECIALTIES AND PREFERENCES: business ghostwriter on three books for McGraw-Hill, one for Wiley and Sons, and one for Thomas Nelson. I have also published more than thirty business articles as ghostwriter, more than fifty travel articles, and one book under own byline.

NONFICTION—ACCEPTS: articles/features, creative or narrative, biography/auto-

biography, how-to/instruction, business, book proposals, and queries.
FEES/TERMS/CONTRACTS: $35/hour. Accepts PayPal and Amex. No minimum requirement.
ACCOMPLISHMENTS: published author, book, articles, and reviews. See author website for long list of publishing credits.
EDUCATION: BA Music, *cum laude*, James Madison University, Harrisonburg, VA.
CLIENTS WITHIN PRIOR YEAR: not available.

308	EDITOR	WRITER	CONSULTANT	F	NF

LeMonds, Jim. WriteTech Northwest. PO Box 651, Castle Rock, WA 98611. P1/ 360-274-7858, P2/ 360-430-4416. seattle0@hotmail.com. Established: 2002.

SKILLS: freelance editor, independent book editor, book doctor, copyeditor or line editor, proofreader, business writer, technical writer, writing coach. **MARKETS SERVED:** writers, corporations, associations, newspapers, magazines.
SPECIALTIES AND PREFERENCES: copy and line editing that produces clear, concise, correct text that flows. I write articles for a wide range of subjects and publications. In a prior year, I edited press releases, newsletters, technical documents for vendors working with a major Northwest software company, two novels, and four nonfiction books. Copyediting and content analysis are part of the service, but line editing is my specialty.
FICTION—ACCEPTS: y/a or juvenile, short stories, novels (genre, mainstream, literary, contemporary, historical), queries, synopses. **NONFICTION—ACCEPTS:** all. **TYPICAL EVALUATION/REPORT:** 2–10 pages.
FEES/TERMS/CONTRACTS: copy/line editing $3+/page. Writing $30+/hour. No credit cards. Payment terms negotiable.
ACCOMPLISHMENTS: author of 2 books and more than 100 newspaper and magazine articles.
EDUCATION: MA Education, Lewis & Clark College, Portland, OR. BA Education, Western Washington University, Bellingham.
CLIENTS WITHIN PRIOR YEAR: 1–5.

309	EDITOR	WRITER	CONSULTANT	F	NF

Lenard-Cook, Lisa. 163 Sol del Oro, Corrale, NM 87048. P1/ 505-898-3816. F1/ 505-898-3816. lisa@lisalenardcook.com. Established: 1993.

SKILLS: freelance editor, independent book editor, book doctor, copyeditor or line editor, proofreader, ghostwriter, business writer or copywriter, technical writer, literary consultant, writing coach, writing instructor, speaks at conferences and seminars. **MARKETS SERVED:** individual writers, publishers.
SPECIALTIES AND PREFERENCES: author/coauthor of ten trade nonfiction books. An

award-winning novelist, and a former editor for major New York publishers and authors. Specializes in big-picture analyses. Detailed ghosts, edits, and rewrites.

FICTION—ACCEPTS: all. **NONFICTION—ACCEPTS:** all. **TYPICAL EVALUATION/REPORT:** 10–20 pages plus recommended reading.

FEES/TERMS/CONTRACTS: $100/hour individual clients; publishers and producers, industry standard. Invoices monthly, net 10 days. No credit cards. Uses contract where applicable.

ACCOMPLISHMENTS: first novel *Dissonance* (UNM Press), winner of Jim Sagel Award; selected as book of the year by libraries in Tucson, Cincinnati, others; selected as summer 2004 Durango-La Plata Reads! book; selected by NPR Performance Today's summer reading series. Second novel published by University of New Mexico Press. Also author/coauthor of ten trade nonfiction books. Contributing editor *authorlink.com*, *Southwest Sage*.

EDUCATION: MFA Writing, Vermont College, Montpelier. BA with honors, University of Buffalo, NY. **MEMBERSHIPS:** Southwest Writers.

CLIENTS WITHIN PRIOR YEAR: 6–10.

310	EDITOR	WRITER	CONSULTANT	F	NF

Lennon, Susan. To the Point. 21 Oak St., Hartford, CT 06106. P1/ 1-860-257-7712. susan@susanlennon.com. STLennon@sbcglobal.net. www.susanlennon.com. Established: 1996.

SKILLS: freelance editor, copyeditor or line editor, proofreader, business writer or copywriter, technical writer, consultant. **MARKETS SERVED:** nonprofit, corporate, individuals.

SPECIALTIES AND PREFERENCES: comprehensive writing/consulting services: managed care, health, mental/behavioral health, addictions, EAPs, HIV/AIDS, pets, and child/adolescent. Preferences include marketing, collaterals, grants, resumes, handbooks, reports, CEO correspondence, newsletters. Favors longer-term, off-site projects. Enjoys building relationship with client to achieve goals.

NONFICTION—ACCEPTS: all. **TYPICAL EVALUATION/REPORT:** 20–40 pages.

FEES/TERMS/CONTRACTS: from $50–$125/hour depending on the nature of the work. Bills monthly. Retainer/project fee for big projects. No credit cards. Uses contract.

ACCOMPLISHMENTS: 1996 Ad Club award, collaterals. 1998 International Association of Business Communicators Bronze QuillAward, brochure. 2003 Literature & Art Open Competition third-place essay, Gutenberg Litegraphic Society. Published in *Washington Post*, *Newsweek*, *AKC Gazette*. Over $6 million in grants; 90 percent success rate.

EDUCATION: MSW, University of Connecticut, West Hartford. Casework/admin. Major. BA Philosophy/Theology, The College of the Holy Cross, Worcester,

MA. Second Degree Black Belt, Tae Kwon Do. **Memberships:** National Association of Social Workers.

Clients within prior year: 1–5.

311	EDITOR	WRITER	CONSULTANT	F	NF

Lerner, Jeanette. PO Box 417, Orinda, CA 94563. P1/ 925-254-2294. F1/ 925-254-6299. wordwizard@sbcglobal.net. Established: 1999.

Skills: freelance editor, copyeditor or line editor, proofreader, writing coach, technical editor. **Markets served:** Most (though not all) of my clients are in the corporate sector.

Specialties and preferences: I specialize in marketing communications, including press releases, advertisements (including job postings), brochures, newsletters, financial reports, biographies, web content. I also do technical editing, for documents such as technical manuals, white papers, specification sheets, FDA collateral. My motto is "Strengthening your words, retaining your voice."

Nonfiction—accepts articles/features, essays, memoirs, creative or narrative, biography/autobiography, how-to/instruction, technical, text or reference, business.

Fees/terms/contracts: $75/hour. Rates for non-corporate entities are lower. Per-page or job rates available after seeing sample text. No credit cards.

Accomplishments: I offer a one-hour seminar, "Tips and Tricks to Improve Your Writing." In this session, I cover the most common mistakes people make, and how to avoid them. The handout provides an easy reference.

Education: MA Linguistics (plus three semesters toward the PhD), University of California, Berkeley. BA English, University of Wisconsin, Madison. **Memberships:** Editors Guild. Bay Area Editors' Forum. California Yoga Teachers Association.

Clients within prior year: 1–5.

312	EDITOR	WRITER	CONSULTANT	F	NF

Leung, Debbie. PO Box 1153, Olympia, WA 98507. P1/ 360-493-1107. dleung2@earthlink.net. Established: 1989.

Skills: freelance editor, copyeditor or line editor, proofreader, ghostwriter, business writer or copywriter, newsletter editor, editor/writer of nonfiction articles and books. **Markets served:** writers, publishers, nonprofit and government agencies, businesses.

Specialties and preferences: With an eye for detail and an ear for voice, I provide editing and writing services to produce nonfiction and promotional materials according to my client's specifications. I bring a wide range of expertise to my projects: health, environment, gardening, agriculture, food, martial arts, and figure skating.

NONFICTION—ACCEPTS: all. **TYPICAL EVALUATION/REPORT:** 5–10 pages (depends on project).

FEES/TERMS/CONTRACTS: $40–$60/hour plus some expenses. No credit cards. Payment due at end of job or monthly. Down payment required for some jobs. Contract usually required.

ACCOMPLISHMENTS: author of book on self-defense for women and articles in national magazines. As editor, clients say: "Debbie finds everything—from consistency to layout to readability." "You are the most patient, diplomatic person I've met in a long time."

EDUCATION: BA Environmental Studies, Evergreen State College, Olympia, WA. Writing skills honed on the job as educator and administrator, and at writing workshops and conferences. **MEMBERSHIPS:** Northwest Independent Editors Guild. Garden Writers Association. Informal writing/editing group of professional writers.

CLIENTS WITHIN PRIOR YEAR: 6–10.

313	EDITOR	WRITER	CONSULTANT	F	NF

Levin, Michael. Writer2Author Inc. 4265 Marina City Dr., Ste. 301, Marina del Rey, CA 90292. P1/ 800-637-6856. P2/ 310-497-8547. Michael@Writer2Author.com. www.Writer2Author.com. www.BusinessGhost.com. Established: 1994.

SKILLS: freelance editor, independent book editor, book doctor, ghostwriter, business writer, literary consultant, writing coach, writing instructor. **MARKETS SERVED:** writers, especially attorneys; ghostwriter for businesses and consultants.

SPECIALTIES AND PREFERENCES: avoids rejection, gains agents and publishers.

FICTION—ACCEPTS: y/a or juvenile, novels (genre, mainstream, literary, contemporary, historical). **NONFICTION—ACCEPTS:** y/a or juvenile, memoirs, creative or narrative, biography/autobiography, family history, self-help, how-to/instruction, technical, business books, humor, inspirational/religious, spiritual. **TYPICAL EVALUATION/REPORT:** summary reports, 10–20 pages. Long reports, 40–60 pages.

FEES/TERMS/CONTRACTS: reads work for free first. Half on agreement; half on client's satisfaction with comment letter. 100% guarantee. Completed within two weeks. Contract: written agreement via email.

ACCOMPLISHMENTS: author, seventeen books. Ghostwriter, fifteen books. Creativity consultant NBC and WB TV. Outstanding reviews, *New York Times, People, New Yorker.*

EDUCATION: JD Columbia Law School, New York; BA Ancient Greek, English, Amherst College, MA. **MEMBERSHIPS:** Authors Guild Council. Writers Guild.

CLIENTS WITHIN PRIOR YEAR: 30–40.

314	EDITOR	WRITER	CONSULTANT	F	NF

Levine, Becky. 19311 Bear Creek Rd., Los Gatos, CA 95033. P1/ 408-354-3492. becky77@gte.net. Established: 1997.

SKILLS: freelance editor, independent book editor, copyeditor or line editor, proofreader, educational writer, book reviews, columns, how-to articles, manuscript consultant. MARKETS SERVED: individual writers, publishers, magazines, educational material developers.

SPECIALTIES AND PREFERENCES: mainstream fiction, mysteries, and young adult fiction.

FICTION—ACCEPTS: y/a or juvenile, short stories, novels (genre, mainstream, literary, contemporary, historical), NONFICTION—ACCEPTS: y/a or juvenile, articles/features, essays, memoirs, creative or narrative, biography/autobiography, family history, self-help, how-to/instruction, humor. TYPICAL EVALUATION/REPORT: 5–10 pages.

FEES/TERMS/CONTRACTS: free sample chapter edit, then $3.50/page. Cash, checks accepted.

ACCOMPLISHMENTS: publications include a "choose your own adventure" guide to money and credit for middle-school students and a literary article about *Wuthering Heights*. I've edited several fiction manuscripts that have been published or accepted by agents. I'm a children's fiction judge for the California Writer's Club's East of Eden conference.

EDUCATION: MA English Literature, University of Virginia, Charlottesville. BA English Literature with concentration in Creative Writing, University of California Irvine. MEMBERSHIPS: Bay Area Editors Forum. California Writer's Club. Sisters in Crime.

CLIENTS WITHIN PRIOR YEAR: 3–5.

315	EDITOR	WRITER	CONSULTANT	F	NF

Levine, Tracy. Tracy Levine-Professional Writing Business. Flower Mound, TX. C1/ 214-415-7866. Tracy.Marie@verzion.net. info@TracyMarieWriter.com. www.TracyMarieWriter.com. Established: 1992.

SKILLS: freelance editor, proofreader, ghostwriter, business writer or copywriter, publicist, feature writer, public relations, marketing plans, book reviews, magazine articles, columns. MARKETS SERVED: all types of businesses, print and electronic media.

SPECIALTIES AND PREFERENCES: freelance journalist/writer for business, health, women's, family, education. Provides marketing plans, branding, creative concepts/campaigns, and copywriting; public relations for firms such as Arnold Palmer Golf Management Company, The Travelers, IBM.

FICTION—ACCEPTS: all. NONFICTION—ACCEPTS: all.

FEES/TERMS/CONTRACTS: $25–$50/hour. 50 percent deposit upon acceptance. Final payment, plus incurred expenses, net 30 days.

ACCOMPLISHMENTS: I worked as health and business editor for a major national magazine and served as columnist specializing in parenting and women's issues. Marketing and communications consultant for sixteen years. Published over eighty articles.

EDUCATION: BA Journalism, University of Central Florida, Orlando. Institute of Children's Literature (writing for children and teens). MEMBERSHIPS: National Association of Women Writers. Society of Children's Book Writers and Illustrators. The Writer's Edge. PenWomen of Faith.

CLIENTS WITHIN PRIOR YEAR: just re-opened writing and marketing services business.

316	EDITOR	WRITER	CONSULTANT	F	NF

Lieberman, Beth. Lieberman Editorial Services. Los Angeles, CA. P1/ 818-610-7492. C1/ 310-403-1602. LiebermanEdit@socal.rr.com. www.publishersmarketplace.com/members/BethLieberman. Established: 2001.

SKILLS: independent book editor, book doctor, copyeditor or line editor, ghost-writer, literary consultant, writing coach, proposal writer. MARKETS SERVED: authors, literary agents, publishers.

SPECIALTIES AND PREFERENCES: I provide coaching and developmental editing services for writers. For nonfiction writers—I develop book proposals and collaborate on manuscripts; for novelists—I provide analysis and guidance on storytelling skills, specifically dialogue mechanics, characterization, plotting, and point of view/narration.

FICTION—ACCEPTS: short stories, novels (genre, mainstream, literary, contemporary, historical), queries, synopses. NONFICTION—ACCEPTS: all. TYPICAL EVALUATION/REPORT: free, by phone.

FEES/TERMS/CONTRACTS: uses agreement.

ACCOMPLISHMENTS: I acquired, edited, and managed more than 500 published books during my tenure in-house at Warner, NAL, and Kensington. Served as speaker, guest instructor, and contest judge at many writing conferences.

EDUCATION: BA English Literature, Barnard College, Columbia University, New York, NY. MEMBERSHIPS: Women's National Book Association. PEN Center West. Editorial Freelancers Association.

CLIENTS WITHIN PRIOR YEAR: 10–15.

317	EDITOR	WRITER	CONSULTANT	F	NF

Lindblom, Christine. To The Letter. PO Box 761, Social Circle, GA 30025. P1/ 770-464-2114. F1/ 770-464-2213. totheletter@totheletter.com. www.totheletter.com. Established: 2000. Professionally editing technical and mainstream since 1996.

SKILLS: freelance editor, independent book editor, book doctor, copyeditor or line editor, proofreader, literary consultant, writing coach, writing instructor, independent literary marketing consultant. MARKETS SERVED: all.

SPECIALTIES AND PREFERENCES: content/line editing, publishing options, marketing.

FICTION—ACCEPTS: all. NONFICTION—ACCEPTS: all. TYPICAL EVALUATION/REPORT: usually a five-page report with suggestions interspersed throughout the manuscript itself. All suggestions are clearly marked in offset color.

FEES/TERMS/CONTRACTS: per-page editing with payments. Monthly payments on all contracts. PayPal with special circumstances.

ACCOMPLISHMENTS: organized the 2002 Florida Writer's Conference in Orlando. Teaching Teams Coordinator, University of Arizona. Sponsored twenty authors to the Book Expo America 2004 in Chicago. Planning on taking thirty authors to Book Expo America 2005 in New York. We also run a Master Mind Writing group that meets monthly and are establishing a program in schools that allow children (grade 5, 8, 11) to experience the publishing business from writing to selling their books. This program includes published authors, motivational speakers, and certified training.

EDUCATION: BA International Politics of Post Soviet Central Asia, University of Arizona.

CLIENTS WITHIN PRIOR YEAR: averages ten new clients/year with all the different services.

318	EDITOR	WRITER	CONSULTANT	F	NF

Little, Portia. Jamestown, RI. P1/ 401-423-0259. panntree@msn.com. www.panntree.com. Established: 1996.

SKILLS: freelance editor, copyeditor or line editor, proofreader, ghostwriter, travel, food writer, book reviewer. MARKETS SERVED: academic, financial, newspaper, magazine, newsletter.

SPECIALTIES AND PREFERENCES: copy/line editing, proofreading. Creating business cards, promotional bookmarks, postcards, brochures. Travel, food writing, news releases.

NONFICTION—ACCEPTS: y/a or juvenile, articles/features, essays, memoirs, creative or narrative, biography/autobiography, family history, self-help, how-to/ instruction, technical, text or reference, business, humor, inspirational/ religious, spiritual, book proposals, queries.

Fees/terms/contracts: $25/hour editing. $20/hour proofreading. $25/hour writing. Credit cards. Typically uses contract.

Accomplishments: five self-published cookbooks. One self-published inspirational book. Food columnist. Travel writer.

Education: MA candidate Liberal Arts, Clark University, Worcester, MA. BA Journalism and Advertising, BA Human Development, Syracuse University, NY. **Memberships:** Theta Sigma Phi Journalism Society. Omicron Nu Home Arts Society. Seacoast Writers' Association. Cassell Network of Writers.

Clients within prior year: 1–5.

319	EDITOR	WRITER	CONSULTANT	F	NF

Loberg, Kristin. KAL Edit., Etc. 11666 Goshen Ave., #114, Los Angeles, CA 90049. P1/ 310-268-1901. F1/ 310-268-1901. pipsterK@msn.com. pipsterK@netscape.net. Established: 1999.

Skills: freelance editor, independent book editor, book doctor, copyeditor or line editor, proofreader, ghostwriter, business writer or copywriter, technical writer, literary consultant, writing coach, publishing consultant, medical editor, newsletter/article/press release writer. **Markets served:** writers, publishing companies, corporations.

Specialties and preferences: health, business, consumer reference. Storytelling and memoirs. Writing and editing for companies, including marketing. Excellent researcher and developmental editor. Medical background. Enjoys first-time authors.

Fiction—accepts: short stories, novels (genre, mainstream, literary, contemporary, historical), queries, synopses, treatments. **Nonfiction—accepts:** all. **Typical evaluation/report:** 2–5 pages.

Fees/terms/contracts: $40–$80/hour. Project rates. No credit cards. Uses contract.

Accomplishments: dozens of articles published in global technical business manual. Coauthor of series (three/year) of how-to consumer reference books. Ghostwriter of personal memoir.

Education: BA Spanish Literature, Cornell University, Ithaca, NY. Completed pre-med requirements. Was active biomedical researcher. **Memberships:** People in Publishing. PEN West.

Clients within prior year: 3–5.

320	EDITOR	WRITER	CONSULTANT	F	NF

LoBrutto, Patrick. Patrick LoBrutto Editorial Services. PO Box 405, Hurley, NY 12443. P1/ 845-339-5499. Pat@PatrickLoBrutto.com. www.PatrickLoBrutto.com. Established: 2000.

SKILLS: freelance editor, independent book editor, book doctor, ghostwriter, literary consultant, writing coach, writing instructor. **MARKETS SERVED:** authors, agents, publishers.

SPECIALTIES AND PREFERENCES: general fiction, science fiction, thrillers, mystery, historical novels, supernatural.

FICTION—ACCEPTS: y/a or juvenile, picture books, novels (genre, mainstream, literary, contemporary, historical). **NONFICTION—ACCEPTS:** y/a or juvenile, creative or narrative, biography/autobiography, family history, self-help.

FEES/TERMS/CONTRACTS: Fees vary. Uses agreement letter.

ACCOMPLISHMENTS: World Fantasy Award Editing. One published novel. Five published short stories. Four published articles.

EDUCATION: MA American History, Hunter College, New York.

CLIENTS WITHIN PRIOR YEAR: 6–10.

321	EDITOR	WRITER	CONSULTANT	F	NF

Long, Julie. 8 Greentree Lane, Cheswick, PA 15024. P1/ 724-444-6466. F1/ 724-444-6460. jlongwrites@mac.com. www.fatplum.com. Established: 1993.

SKILLS: freelance editor, independent book editor, book doctor, copyeditor or line editor, proofreader, ghostwriter, business writer or copywriter, technical writer, literary consultant, writing coach, writing instructor, publicist. **MARKETS SERVED:** writers, corporations, nonprofits, advertising/marketing agencies.

SPECIALTIES AND PREFERENCES: editing/consulting for mainstream fiction and nonfiction. Advertising, marketing, and communications materials—including ads, broadcast, direct mail, brochures, newsletters, articles, websites, and event promotion.

FICTION—ACCEPTS: y/a or juvenile, picture books, novels (mainstream, literary, contemporary) scripts/screenplays, queries, synopses, treatments. **NONFICTION—ACCEPTS:** all.

FEES/TERMS/CONTRACTS: business writing $90/hour. Manuscript consulting $50/hour. Editing $4/page. Manuscript critique $200/100 pages.

ACCOMPLISHMENTS: published nonfiction humor how-to title. Published story in compilation book. Addy Award and Certificates of Merit from the American Advertising Federation. Best in Show, Transportation Communications Award.

EDUCATION: BA Business, Washington & Jefferson College, Washington, PA.

MEMBERSHIPS: Pennwriters. American Advertising Federation.

CLIENTS WITHIN PRIOR YEAR: 6–10.

322	EDITOR	WRITER	CONSULTANT	F	NF

Lotman, Lynda. A+ English/ManuscriptEditing.com. Arlington, TX. P1/ 817-467-7127. editor@manuscriptediting.com. www.manuscriptediting.com. editing.com. Established: 1976.

SKILLS: freelance editor, copyeditor or line editor, proofreader, ghostwriter, business writer or copywriter, technical writer, literary consultant, writing coach, publicist, book design, indexing. MARKETS SERVED: writers, publishers, students, nonprofits, corporations, governments.

SPECIALTIES AND PREFERENCES: science fiction, historical fiction, creative nonfiction, anthropology, sociology, theses, dissertations.

FICTION—ACCEPTS: y/a or juvenile, short stories, novels, picture books, queries, synopses, treatments. NONFICTION—ACCEPTS: all.

FEES/TERMS/CONTRACTS: 2–5 cents/word. Credit cards. PayPal. Uses editorial agreement.

ACCOMPLISHMENTS: 100+ books in publication. Coordinator of international network of editors/writers of legal, medical, scientific, and technical specialists. Also see: www.writingnetwork.com.

EDUCATION: BA Political Science, English, University of Texas, Arlington. MEMBERSHIPS: Science Fiction and Fantasy Writers of America. Horror Writers Association.

CLIENTS WITHIN PRIOR YEAR: 40–45.

323	EDITOR	WRITER	CONSULTANT	F	NF

Love, Tamar. Cranky Editor. Burbank, CA. tamar@crankyeditor.com. www.crankyeditor.com. Established: 2000.

SKILLS: freelance editor, independent book editor, copyeditor or line editor, ghostwriter, business writer or copywriter, developmental editing, manuscript consultation. MARKETS SERVED: anyone who needs a writer or editor.

SPECIALTIES AND PREFERENCES: books, book proposals, feature articles, creative writing, web content, search engine optimization, marketing collateral, direct mail, press releases, newsletters, academic papers, admissions essays, forms, manuals, resumes.

FICTION—ACCEPTS: y/a or juvenile, novels (genre, mainstream, literary, contemporary, historical), poetry. NONFICTION—ACCEPTS: all.

FEES/TERMS/CONTRACTS: net 10 days with 50 percent retainer. PayPal. Uses contract.

ACCOMPLISHMENTS: published party planning book in major market. Edited over thirteen books for top-tier publisher. Written over 200 articles. Ghostwritten three books. Written web copy for several dozen clients. Edited over twenty-five nonfiction and fiction books for smaller publishers and vanity presses.

EDUCATION: MA Creative Writing, San Francisco State University, CA.

Memberships: Bay Area Editor's Forum. National Writer's Union.
Clients within prior year: 71–80.

324	EDITOR	WRITER	CONSULTANT	F	NF

Loveman, Laurie. Chagrin Falls, OH. P1/ 440-543-1640.
lloveman@earthlink.net. www.laurieloveman.com. Established: 1992.

Skills: business writer. **Markets served:** attorneys, physicians, veterinarians, small business owners.

Specialties and preferences: writes or edits letters, reports, legal briefs; types manuscripts.

Nonfiction—accepts: how-to/instruction, technical, text or reference, business.

Fees/terms/contracts: $18/hour word processing with minimal editing, $25/hour word processing with more extensive editing.

Accomplishments: three self-published novels, numerous articles in fire service and equine journals.

Education: BS Fire Engineering and Safety Technology, University of Cincinnati, OH.

Clients within prior year: 5–10.

325	EDITOR	WRITER	CONSULTANT	F	NF

Luger, Diana. US Editors. 1858 Middlebury Dr., Aurora, IL 60504. P1/ 630-978-4126. dlluger@self-serv.net. Established: 1992.

Skills: freelance editor, independent book editor, copyeditor or line editor, proofreader. **Markets served:** ad agencies and businesses.

Specialties and preferences: Diana Luger has been editing books and other published materials for twelve years. She prefers working with nonfiction, genre fiction, and literary fiction. She offers both copyediting and substantive (or line) editing.

Fiction—accepts: all. **Nonfiction—accepts:** all.

Fees/terms/contracts: quote based on job. Requires retainer of one third up front. No credit cards. Accepts PayPal. Uses contract.

Accomplishments: published in *Woman's Day*, *Women's Sports & Fitness*, *Family Fun*, *Flowers&*, *Windy City Woman*, and many others. She has edited a thesis guide, dissertations, white papers, annual reports, newsletters, and magazines. Initially, she edited for a management consultancy and then worked as a financial editor for an investment research company. She has also edited a mystery novel.

Education: English major, University of Arkansas, Fayetteville. **Memberships:** Chicago Women in Publishing.

Clients within prior year: 11–20.

326	EDITOR	WRITER	CONSULTANT	F	NF

Lyndol, Michael. Differentia Inc. Orlando, FL. P1/ 407-380-1812. P2/ 407-384-7172. F1/ 407-384-7172. lyndolmichael@earthlink.net. www.media-theater.com. Established: 1999.

SKILLS: freelance editor, independent book editor, copyeditor or line editor, proofreader, business writer or copywriter, technical writer, writing coach, hosts business theater, live event. MARKETS SERVED: corporations, small to medium businesses.

SPECIALTIES AND PREFERENCES: I write and edit for different literacy levels and different constituencies. My hallmark is the ability to understand and communicate complex projects with proven success.

FICTION—ACCEPTS: scripts, queries, synopses, treatments. NONFICTION—ACCEPTS: articles/features, essays, memoirs, creative or narrative, family history, self-help, how-to/instruction, technical, business, inspirational/religious, spiritual, book proposals. TYPICAL EVALUATION/REPORT: 1–3 pages.

FEES/TERMS/CONTRACTS: $30–$135/hour plus expenses, 50 percent down if project quote. No credit cards. Work-for-hire contract.

ACCOMPLISHMENTS: Quality awards (4); Marketing Communications Awards (2)—Westinghouse; Merit Award—International Association of Business Communicators. Wrote and produced training that effectively doubled the knowledge level of participants.

EDUCATION: MA Radio-TV, Ohio University, Athens. BA Liberal Arts, Florida State University, Tallahassee.

CLIENTS WITHIN PRIOR YEAR: 1–5.

327	EDITOR	WRITER	CONSULTANT	F	NF

Lynn, Joyce. PO Box 682, Mill Valley, CA 94942. P1/ 415-267-7620. joyce@joycelynn.com. www.joycelynn.com. Established: 1995.

SKILLS: freelance editor, independent book editor, book doctor, copyeditor or line editor, proofreader, ghostwriter, writing coach, writing instructor. MARKETS SERVED: independent authors, especially manuscripts with subjects related to the spiritual, political, alternative health, women's.

SPECIALTIES AND PREFERENCES: Most prefer editing, proposals, query letters, brainstorming, manuscript critiques. I consult with writers and authors with work in various stages of creation. Clients are in good hands as I help them focus and clarify their thoughts, story structure, and content. Idea formulation to promotion plan. I also coach you in how to use dreams and inner wisdom to guide your writing and your work.

FICTION—ACCEPTS: short stories, novels (genre, mainstream, literary, contemporary, historical), poetry, queries, synopses. NONFICTION—ACCEPTS: all.

Fees/terms/contracts: individually determined.

Accomplishments: internationally published journalist, political news reporter, Plus Publications, Washington, DC. Assistant Press Secretary, US House of Representatives, Washington, DC. National lecturer: politics, intuition. Screenplay writer.

Education: MA Journalism, American University, Washington, DC. BA Education, University of Michigan, Ann Arbor. **Memberships:** International Women's Writers Guild.

Clients within prior year: 1–5.

328	EDITOR	WRITER	CONSULTANT	F	NF

Lyon, Elizabeth. Editing International, LLC. Eugene, OR. P1/ 541-344-9118. elyon123@comcast.net. www.4-edit.com. www.elizabethlyon.com. Established: 2002; full-time professional editor since 1988.

Skills: freelance editor, independent book editor, book doctor or line editor, ghostwriter, business writer, literary consultant, writing coach, writing instructor, keynote speaker, trainer of editors. **Markets served:** aspiring and published writers of book-length fiction and nonfiction, literary agents, publishers, companies of all sizes.

Specialties and preferences: From concept to completion, I edit novels and nonfiction proposals—my books on these subjects are often considered "the standards." Will consider ghostwriting proposals. I provide the tools of craft and marketing savvy, then support and cajole you, edit and evaluate your writing, strategize and inspire, and finally brag about your success. My strength is explaining the architecture of books, making sure your Taj Majal— or stylish cottage—won't collapse while you're decorating the interior.

Fiction—accepts: all. **Nonfiction—accepts:** all. **Typical evaluation/report:** 15–40 pages (single-spaced), among the most comprehensive, clear, and customized.

Fees/terms/contracts: Fees vary from $5–$9/page; $75/hour consulting on shorter editing; proposals $1,200, ghostwriting proposals $5,000+. Retainer. Accepts credit cards. Uses contract, often sent via e-mail.

Accomplishments: five published nonfiction books on how to write/market (including this one). I have taught thousands of writers. Over fifty of my clients have had their books published, won movie options, received awards.

Education: MA Counseling, Azusa Pacific University, CA. BA Sociology, Whittier College, CA. Former community college writing instructor. **Memberships:** Authors Guild. American Society of Journalists & Authors. Northwest writing organizations.

Clients within prior year: averages 80–100/year.

329	EDITOR	WRITER	CONSULTANT	F	NF

MacBride, Elizabeth. 308 W. Prospect Ave., State College, PA 16801. P1/ 814-861-7609. emacb@earthlink.net. Established: 2004.

SKILLS: freelance editor, ghostwriter, business writer or copywriter, technical writer, literary consultant. MARKETS SERVED: newspapers, magazines, non-profit publications, individuals.

SPECIALTIES AND PREFERENCES: A ten-year business journalism veteran, I specialize in editing and writing complex projects, especially for the NYC market. I also consult for nonprofit publications dealing with international and economic issues, and do some health care writing.

NONFICTION—ACCEPTS: biography/autobiography, how-to/instruction, technical, text or reference, humor, inspirational/religious, spiritual, book proposals, queries. TYPICAL EVALUATION/REPORT: 10–30 pages.

FEES/TERMS/CONTRACTS: $1.50/word writing articles; $50/hour editing services; major projects negotiable. Uses agreement. No credit cards.

ACCOMPLISHMENTS: hundreds of articles and essays written and edited for local and national newspapers and magazines. National awards for business writing and editing.

EDUCATION: BA Journalism, University of Maryland, College Park.

CLIENTS WITHIN PRIOR YEAR: 1 large client, typically no more than 5.

330	EDITOR	WRITER	CONSULTANT	F	NF

Macgirvin, Jackie. Kansas City, MO. P1/ 816-763-1177. C1/ 816-215-5168. F1/ 816-763-5688. Jackiemacgirvin@aol.com. Established: 1977.

SKILLS: freelance editor, book doctor, writing instructor, ghostwriter. MARKETS SERVED: Christian, women, humor.

SPECIALTIES AND PREFERENCES: I ghostwrite Christian books, evangelical to charismatic, adult and children, women's magazine articles, humor. I am a committed Christian and enjoy working with people who want to spread the Good News or encourage others. Everyone has a story, but putting it on paper and getting it published can be intimidating. I like to demystify the writing process by giving people tools. Many students have thanked me, having seen their college essays written or magazine articles published.

FICTION—ACCEPTS: y/a or juvenile. NONFICTION—ACCEPTS: humor, inspirational/religious, spiritual, how-to.

FEES/TERMS/CONTRACTS: articles and editing $25/hour. Ghostwriting nonfiction book $6,000–$8,000. Ghostwriting novel $8,000–$10,000.

ACCOMPLISHMENTS: two humor awards from Evangelical Press Association; one from the Florida Magazine Association. Multiple articles (my own) in *The*

Kansas City Star, The Indianapolis Star, Single-Parent Family, Charisma, Spirit-Led Woman. Humor columnist for *Ministries Today.* **EDUCATION:** MA Counseling, University of Missouri, Kansas City. **CLIENTS WITHIN PRIOR YEAR:** 5–10.

331	EDITOR	WRITER	CONSULTANT	F	NF

Macomber, Carol C. The French Connection. 101 Judith Lane, Media, PA 19063-4924. P1/ 610-891-1983. P2/ 610-891-1887. F1/ 610-891-7870. macuse@ix.netcom.com. macuse@aol.com. www.thefrenchconnection.us. Established: 1985.

SKILLS: freelance editor, copyeditor or line editor, proofreader, ghostwriter, write articles, French translator. **MARKETS SERVED:** French and American authors, US/French publishers, publishing service businesses, corporations, translation agencies, nonprofits.
SPECIALTIES AND PREFERENCES: translation and editing to serve as a cross-cultural liaison.
FICTION—ACCEPTS: y/a or juvenile, short stories, novels (genre, mainstream, literary, contemporary, historical), scripts/screenplays. **NONFICTION—ACCEPTS:** y/a or juvenile, articles/features, essays, memoirs, creative or narrative, biography/autobiography, family history, self-help, business, humor, inspirational/religious, spiritual.
FEES/TERMS/CONTRACTS: editing/writing $25/hour. Translating 11–13 cents/word. Installment invoicing. No credit cards. E-mail contract.
ACCOMPLISHMENTS: twenty published magazine articles. Translated and edited five books (French)—two published. Edited two fiction manuscripts (English), one children's book.
EDUCATION: BA French Literature, Hood College, Frederick, MD. **MEMBERSHIPS:** American Literary Translators Association. Société Française des Traducteurs. **CLIENTS WITHIN PRIOR YEAR:** 15–20.

332	EDITOR	WRITER	CONSULTANT	F	NF

Maiers, Joan. PO Box 33, Marylhurst, OR 97036. P1/ 503-636-8955. jmaiers@yahoo.com. Established: 1995.

SKILLS: freelance editor, independent book editor, business editor, copyeditor or line editor, proofreader, business writer or copywriter, literary consultant, writing coach, writing instructor, publicist. **MARKETS SERVED:** newsletter editors, college students.
SPECIALTIES AND PREFERENCES: My consulting benefits writers who are designing their messages or editing their manuscripts. I prepare copy for brochures and marketing materials. I enjoy developing the verbal-visual aspects of brochures,

marketing materials. I have an emphasis on poetry and freelance prose.

Fiction—accepts: y/a or juvenile, picture books, short stories, novels, poetry. **Nonfiction—accepts:** y/a or juvenile, articles/features, essays, memoirs, biography/autobiography, family history, self-help, how-to/instruction, business, inspirational/religious, spiritual, book proposals, queries.

Fees/terms/contracts: reasonable per-page or per-hour fees.

Accomplishments: dozens of poems, book reviews published in anthologies, books, periodicals.

Education: graduate studies in Education and Poetry Writing; degree in Science, University of Washington, Seattle. **Memberships:** Poets, Editors, Novelists (PEN)—USA. Oregon State Poetry Association.

Clients within prior year: 6–10.

333	EDITOR	WRITER	CONSULTANT	F	NF

Mallett, Kay. Cat's Eye Editing. Columbus, OH. P1/ 614-487-0799. F1/ 614-487-0799. kmallett@columbus.rr.com. Established: 1999.

Skills: freelance editor, business editor, copyeditor or line editor, proofreader, technical writer. **Markets served:** businesses, educational publishers, trade publishers, advertising and marketing agencies, web agencies, graduate students.

Specialties and preferences: My preference is to edit/copyedit/proofread rather than to write. Specialties are advertising/marketing copy, theses and dissertations, web content (including testing for functionality), book reviews, business training documentation.

Nonfiction—accepts: y/a or juvenile, articles/features, essays, memoirs, creative or narrative, biography/autobiography, self-help, how-to/instruction, technical, text or reference, business, humor, spiritual.

Fees/terms/contracts: $35–$50/hour.

Education: attended Ohio State University, Columbus. **Memberships:** Editorial Freelancers Association. Writers' Bloc.

Clients within prior year: 11–20.

334	EDITOR	WRITER	CONSULTANT	F	NF

Malone, Susan. Malone Editorial Services. 280 NW CR 0180, Ennis, TX 75119. P1/ 903-326-4945. Maloneeditorial@hotmail.com. aaasuz@aol.com. www.maloneeditorial.com. Established: 1993.

Skills: freelance editor, independent book editor, book doctor, writing coach, writing instructor. **Markets served:** writers, publishers, some agents.

Specialties and preferences: serious writers. I work best with writers willing to dig in and really learn the craft, whether beginners or established pros.

Fiction—accepts: y/a or juvenile, short stories, novels (genre, mainstream, literary, contemporary, historical). NONFICTION—ACCEPTS: y/a or juvenile, articles/ features, essays, memoirs, creative or narrative, biography/autobiography, family history, self-help, how-to/instruction, humor, inspirational/religious, spiritual, book proposals. TYPICAL EVALUATION/REPORT: 15–30 pages.

FEES/TERMS/CONTRACTS: $6.50/page. One third with submission, balance due before work returned.

ACCOMPLISHMENTS: one published novel; three published nonfiction books. Numerous published short stories. Hundreds of published articles. Ed Mathis Award for Fiction.

EDUCATION: MA hours in English, BS Political Science, minors in English, Journalism, Agriculture, Tarleton State University, Stephenville, TX.

CLIENTS WITHIN PRIOR YEAR: 10–20.

335	EDITOR	WRITER	CONSULTANT	F	NF

Mann, Sue. Working With Words. Beaverton, OR. P1/ 503-644-4317. F1/ 503-644-4317. w3words@zzz.com. Established: 1985.

SKILLS: freelance editor, copyeditor or line editor, proofreader, substantive editor, technical editor. MARKETS SERVED: small presses, self-publishers, small businesses.

SPECIALTIES AND PREFERENCES: works online or on hard copy. Subjects include creativity, memoir, self-help, spirituality, and more. Projects also include cookbooks, training manuals, children's picture books. Turns non-native speakers' manuscripts into American English. Chicago, house styles.

FICTION—ACCEPTS: y/a or juvenile, picture books. NONFICTION—ACCEPTS: all.

FEES/TERMS/CONTRACTS: editing or proofreading $29.50/hour. Due within 30 days of invoice date. No credit card. Typically uses agreement.

EDUCATION: MBA Marketing, Golden Gate University San Francisco, CA. BA Elementary Education, University of Arizona, Tucson. Media Alliance (copyediting, technical editing). Editcetera (copy and substantive editing, proofreading). MEMBERSHIPS: Northwest Independent Editors Guild. Northwest Association of Book Publishers.

CLIENTS WITHIN PRIOR YEAR: 6–10.

336	EDITOR	WRITER	CONSULTANT	F	NF

Mapes, Creston. 2966 Heart Pine Lane, Buford, GA 30519. P1/ 770-932-2606. F1/ 770-932-2659. crestonmapes@mindspring.com. Established: 1990.

SKILLS: freelance editor, independent book editor, book doctor, copyeditor or line editor, proofreader, ghostwriter, business writer, web content, camera-ready proofreading, word processing. MARKETS SERVED: companies, colleges, magazines, and ministries.

SPECIALTIES AND PREFERENCES: freelancing full-time for thirteen years, writing and editing effective communications (ads, brochures, newsletters, magazine stories, books, broadcast ads, web copy, speeches). I find out what my clients want to convey, and I make it happen through creative copywriting. Feel free to call and discuss!

NONFICTION—ACCEPTS: y/a or juvenile, memoirs, creative and narrative, biography/autobiography, self-help, how-to/instruction, business, humor, inspirational/religious, spiritual.

FEES/TERMS/CONTRACTS: Rates vary. Less for ministries. Per-project basis. All fees discussed up front. I bill small jobs once copy has been turned in. On bigger jobs, I break invoicing up into thirds. Editing revisions at no further charge.

ACCOMPLISHMENTS: two novels, three-book contract for three more with Multnomah Publishers. Won a CASE (Council for Advancement and Support of Education) award for marketing copywriting.

EDUCATION: BA Magazine Journalism, Bowling Green State University, OH. MEMBERSHIPS: Writer's View.

CLIENTS WITHIN PRIOR YEAR: 11–20.

337	EDITOR	WRITER	CONSULTANT	F	NF

Marano, Dawn. Dawn Marano & Associates, LLC. PO 58519, Salt Lake City, UT 84158-0519. P1/ 801-466-1323. dawn@dawnmarano.com. www.dawnmarano.com. Established: 2003.

SKILLS: freelance editor, independent book editor, literary consultant, writing coach, writing instructor. MARKETS SERVED: writers, agents, publishers.

SPECIALTIES AND PREFERENCES: development of book-length works or books in progress through intensive, sensitive exploration and instruction.

FICTION—ACCEPTS: novels (mainstream, literary, contemporary). NONFICTION—ACCEPTS: essays, memoirs, creative or narrative, biography/autobiography. TYPICAL EVALUATION/REPORT: editorial review, 5–10 pages; developmental edit, 10–20 pages.

FEES/TERMS/CONTRACTS: editorial review $500. Developmental edit $1,000 retainer, $50/hour. Consulting $50/hour. Coaching $300/120 pages. No credit cards. Uses agreement.

ACCOMPLISHMENTS: published one memoir, several essays in regional and national magazines and journals. Editor at a university press for seven years.

EDUCATION: MFA Creative Writing, University of Utah, Salt Lake City. MEMBERSHIPS: Association of Writers and Writing Programs.

CLIENTS WITHIN PRIOR YEAR: 10–15.

338	EDITOR	WRITER	CONSULTANT	F	NF

March, Jeff. EditPros. 423 F St. Ste. 206, Davis, CA 95616-4144. P1/ 530-759-2000. www.editpros.com. (E-mail contact through website.) Established: 1993.

SKILLS: freelance editor, copyeditor or line editor, proofreader, ghostwriter, business writer or copywriter. MARKETS SERVED: EditPros clientele includes government agencies, trade associations, academic institutions, financial institutions, research agencies, and publishers.

SPECIALTIES AND PREFERENCES: newsletters, brochures, annual reports, trade articles, academic books, website content. We correct errors in grammar or syntax, develop a consistent editorial voice, and crystallize and clarify our clients' messages. We're proficient in distilling complex material into more accessible form.

FICTION—ACCEPTS: y/a or juvenile, short stories, novels (genre, mainstream, literary, contemporary, historical), poetry, scripts/screenplays, queries, synopses, treatments. NONFICTION—ACCEPTS: all.

FEES/TERMS/CONTRACTS: We charge on a per-project basis.

ACCOMPLISHMENTS: coauthor of a nonfiction book about the sixties published by Billboard Books. Thirty years of writing and editing experience.

EDUCATION: BA Journalism, California State University, Northridge.

CLIENTS WITHIN PRIOR YEAR: 11–20.

339	EDITOR	WRITER	CONSULTANT	F	NF

Margulis, Jennifer. Properzio Prose. 350 B St., Ashland, OR 97520. P1/ 541-482-1804. Properzioprose@jeffnet.org. www.toddlertruestories.com. Established: 1999.

SKILLS: freelance editor, independent book editor, business editor, ghostwriter, business writer or copywriter, literary consultant, grant writer, press release writer. MARKETS SERVED: writers, universities, nonprofits, corporations.

SPECIALTIES AND PREFERENCES: nonfiction parenting essays and books. Crafting effective book proposals and query letters, marketing, finding agents.

FICTION—ACCEPTS: y/a or juvenile, picture books, novels (mainstream, literary, contemporary, historical), poetry, queries. NONFICTION—ACCEPTS: y/a or juvenile, articles/features, essays, memoirs, creative or narrative, biography/ autobiography, self-help, humor, book proposals, queries.

FEES/TERMS/CONTRACTS: free initial consult. $55/hour. $150/press release.

ACCOMPLISHMENTS: two nonfiction books, hundreds of articles in national and local magazines and newspapers, winner of Independent Publishers Book Association Award. Honor Society of Phi Kappa Phi. International Fellowship from Tuskegee University. Emory University Women's Club Memorial Award.

EDUCATION: PhD English, Emory University, Atlanta. MA Comparative Literature University of California, Berkeley. BA English/Russian, Cornell University, Ithaca, NY. MEMBERSHIPS: National Writers Union. Society of Children's Book Writers and Illustrators.
CLIENTS WITHIN PRIOR YEAR: 5–10.

340	EDITOR	WRITER	CONSULTANT	F	NF

Mashak, W. Jason. PO Box 80603, Portland, OR 97280. P1/ 503-244-3100. C1/ 503-341-7457. wjm.73@comcast.net. Established: 1973.

SKILLS: copyeditor or line editor, proofreader, literary consultant, "idea guy" with marketing background. MARKETS SERVED: Small or independent 'zines, publishers, writers/poets.

SPECIALTIES AND PREFERENCES: I enjoy copyediting and consulting on poetry, short stories, and academic papers. Less is more; concise, stimulating writing charms readers. Prosaic prose fails. Literary longevity risks being ahead of its time. I prefer nothing stuffy or gruesome. No vanity trips or propaganda. Nothing spewed during overdrunken revelation. No ridiculous deadlines.

FICTION—ACCEPTS: short stories, poetry. NONFICTION—ACCEPTS: essays, memoirs, creative or narrative, biography/autobiography, business.

FEES/TERMS/CONTRACTS: varies by project. Accept check, money order, PayPal. No credit cards.

ACCOMPLISHMENTS: married for a decade. Nominated for 2004 Nina Mae Kellogg writing award. Copyedited for a national feminist magazine. Poems published in various literary journals and anthologies.

EDUCATION: BA English, Portland State University, OR. MEMBERSHIPS: Mountain Writers. Multnomah Village Writers Group.
CLIENTS WITHIN PRIOR YEAR: 1–5.

341	EDITOR	WRITER	CONSULTANT	F	NF

Math, Mara. Ardent Editing. 792 Dartmouth St., San Francisco, CA 94134. P1/ 415-841-1176. mjmath@saber.net. Established: 1992, editing since 1979.

SKILLS: freelance editor, independent book editor, book doctor, copyeditor or line editor, literary consultant, writing coach, writing instructor. MARKETS SERVED: nonprofits, small companies, artists, writers.

SPECIALTIES AND PREFERENCES: I help clients shape, refine, and polish what they need to communicate. I am well versed in the language of progressive political and cultural work. As a former professional art photographer, I also have a strong arts background.

FICTION—ACCEPTS: y/a or juvenile, short stories, novels (genre, mainstream, literary, contemporary, historical), poetry, scripts/screenplays. NONFICTION—

ACCEPTS: articles/features, essays, memoirs, creative or narrative, family history, business, humor. **TYPICAL EVALUATION/REPORT:** varies.

FEES/TERMS/CONTRACTS: $35–$55/hour, on a sliding scale, for editing. Flat fee for book read-throughs, evaluations, and shaping. Accepts checks. No credit cards.

ACCOMPLISHMENTS: short story selected for Intro 14, the Associated Writing Programs annual collection. Journalism, essays, op-eds, and reviews have been appeared in over fifty publications, many in San Francisco. Also online and foreign publication credits.

EDUCATION: BA Liberal Arts, Writing and Anthropology, Sarah Lawrence College, Bronxville, NY. Later studied with Dorothy Allison. **MEMBERSHIPS:** National Gay and Lesbian Journalists Association. Writergrrls, Application into EditCetera.

CLIENTS WITHIN PRIOR YEAR: 11–20.

342	EDITOR	WRITER	CONSULTANT	F	NF

Mattingly, Rosanna. Meta Writing and Education Services, LLC.
PO Box 42363, Portland, OR 97242. P1/ 503-772-3486. metawe@comcast.net.
Established: 1991.

SKILLS: freelance editor, independent book editor, copyeditor or line editor, proofreader, technical writer, writing coach, desktop publishing, research. **MARKETS SERVED:** writers, universities, government agencies, and nonprofit organizations.

SPECIALTIES AND PREFERENCES: provides quality writing, editing, and graphic design of papers, reports, education guides, grants, brochures, and book-length manuscripts, as well as project review and analysis. Expertise in science and technical writing and editing.

NONFICTION—ACCEPTS: all.

FEES/TERMS/CONTRACTS: varies. No credit cards. Typically uses contract.

ACCOMPLISHMENTS: dozens of articles in science/education journals, nine technical reports, six review articles, and five education guides.

EDUCATION: PhD Aquatic Ecology, Oregon State University, Corvallis. MS Limnology, Michigan State University, East Lansing. BA Biology, University of Louisville, KY. Oregon teaching certification in Biology, Mathematics, and Integrated Science. Short courses in graphic design, website development, and writing environmental impact statements. **MEMBERSHIPS:** National Association of Science Writers. National Science Teachers Association. National Writers Union. Oregon Writers Colony. Society of Children's Book Writers and Illustrators. Society for Technical Communication. Willamette Writers.

CLIENTS WITHIN PRIOR YEAR: 5–10.

343	EDITOR	WRITER	CONSULTANT	F	NF

Mayer, Bob. 40 Governors Lane, Hilton Head Island, SC 29928. P1/ 843-338-1623. F1/ 843-671-5118. bob@bobmayer.org. www.bobmayer.org. Established: 1989.

SKILLS: freelance editor, writing coach, public speaker at writing conferences and for business. **MARKETS SERVED:** writers, writing conferences, businesses.

SPECIALTIES AND PREFERENCES: I write fiction full-time with thirty books published, including one on novel writing (*Writer's Digest*) and another title on special operations tactics for success. Eight more books under contract. I run the Writer's Retreat on Hilton Head Island. I am a faculty member of a dozen writer's conferences each year.

FICTION—ACCEPTS: novels (genre, contemporary), queries, synopses, treatments. **NONFICTION—ACCEPTS:** memoirs, creative or narrative. **TYPICAL EVALUATION/ REPORT:** normally 10 pages of evaluation for 20 pages of material.

FEES/TERMS/CONTRACTS: Fees set on a case-by-case basis.

ACCOMPLISHMENTS: *USA Today* bestselling author of Area 51 series at Dell books under Robert Doherty pen name. Two hardcover thrillers coming from Tor under Robert Doherty name. Three thrillers coming from Avon under my own name. Book on novel craft with *Writer's Digest*. Former Special Forces A-Team Leader, Battalion Operations Officer, and Instructor JFK Special Warfare Center & School, Ft. Bragg, NC.

EDUCATION: MA Education, Austin Peay State University, TX. BS United States Military Academy, West Point.

CLIENTS WITHIN PRIOR YEAR: more than 100.

344	EDITOR	WRITER	CONSULTANT	F	NF

McCown, Vicki. 4504 Queen Anne Way, Anacortes, WA 98221. mccown@fidalgo.net. Established: 1988.

SKILLS: freelance editor, independent book editor, book doctor, copyeditor or line editor, proofreader, ghostwriter, business writer or copywriter. **MARKETS SERVED:** authors who self-publish, independent publishing, and public relations companies.

SPECIALTIES AND PREFERENCES: working with authors who want to self-publish but whose manuscript is not reader-ready. Proficient at rewriting or ghostwriting manuscript.

FICTION—ACCEPTS: y/a or juvenile, picture books, short stories, novels. **NONFICTION—ACCEPTS:** y/a or juvenile, articles/features, essays, memoirs, creative or narrative, biography/autobiography, family history, self-help, how-to/instruction, business, humor, inspirational/religious, spiritual.

FEES/TERMS/CONTRACTS: copy $80/hour; ghost $50/hour; rewriting $75/hour. Editing $50–$70/hour either on hard copy or electronic w/tracking. Copyediting

$50/hour hard copy, $60/hour electronic w/tracking. Proofreading $40/hour hard copy, $50/hour electronic w/tracking. Uses agreement. Retainer requested. No credit cards.

EDUCATION: BA Comparative Culture, University of California, Irvine.
CLIENTS WITHIN PRIOR YEAR: 20–25 clients.

345	EDITOR	WRITER	CONSULTANT	F	NF

McDonald, Linda. McD's Creations. Jacksonville, FL. P1/ 904-783-6715. C1/ 904-254-0037. F1/ 904-783-6715. linda@mcdscreations.net. www.mcdscreations.net. Established: 2000.

SKILLS: freelance editor, copyeditor or line editor, proofreader, ghostwriter, business writer or copywriter, writing coach, publicist, event planner.
MARKETS SERVED: corporations, higher education, nonprofits, public relations firms, newspapers, magazines.
SPECIALTIES AND PREFERENCES: business communications, speeches, press releases, news and features, op-eds, web copy, video scripts, advertorials, newsletters, brochures, media relations, publicity, event coordination.
FICTION—ACCEPTS: y/a or juvenile, picture books, short stories, poetry, queries.
NONFICTION—ACCEPTS: y/a or juvenile, articles/features, essays, memoirs, creative or narrative, biography/autobiography, self-help, business, book proposals, queries. **TYPICAL EVALUATION/REPORT:** 2–10 pages.
FEES/TERMS/CONTRACTS: $15–$25/page; advance required. Long projects invoiced monthly, payable/15 days. Credit cards. Typically uses agreement.
ACCOMPLISHMENTS: *Bismarck Tribune, inspire* magazine, *Florida Times-Union, Business Watch, Business Report,* MDU Resources Group, Inc., Women's Giving Alliance.
EDUCATION: BS Business Administration, University of Mary, Bismarck, ND.
MEMBERSHIPS: Florida Writers Association. Florida Freelance Writers Association.
CLIENTS WITHIN PRIOR YEAR: 5–10.

346	EDITOR	WRITER	CONSULTANT	F	NF

McFarlane, Marilyn. 5505 SW 18th Dr., Portland, OR 97239. P1/ 503-245-0243. mmcf@easystreet.com. www.marilynmcfarlane.com. Established: 1979.

SKILLS: freelance editor, independent book editor, copyeditor or line editor.
MARKETS SERVED: writers.
SPECIALTIES AND PREFERENCES: For twenty-three years I have been a freelance writer and editor, working with a variety of projects. I specialize in nonfiction. Travel writing is one of my specialties.
NONFICTION—ACCEPTS: articles/features, memoirs, creative or narrative, biogra-

phy/autobiography, family history, self-help, how-to/instruction, inspirational/ religious, book proposals, queries.

FEES/TERMS/CONTRACTS: free initial half-hour interview. $45/hour reading/copyediting. $60/hour editing/ghostwriting. Usually one-third to start, one-third after first draft, one-third upon completion. Does not accept credit cards. Uses a contract.

ACCOMPLISHMENTS: author of eight nonfiction books, including *Sacred Myths— Stories of World Religions*, which won a Benjamin Franklin Award. Five books are travel directories. Prior work as a newspaper reporter, TV news writer/producer, children's arts specialist in TV, and travel columnist.

EDUCATION: BA English, Portland State University, Portland, OR. **MEMBERSHIPS:** Authors Guild. Oregon Writers Colony.

CLIENTS WITHIN PRIOR YEAR: 1–5.

347	EDITOR	WRITER	CONSULTANT	F	NF

McGinty, Sandra. Master Marketing & PR. 24782 Summerwind Lane, Lake Forest, CA 92630. P1/ 949-699-0115. F1/ 949-699-0116. allme@cox.net. www.mcgintypublishing.net. Established: 1992 but copywriting since 1986.

SKILLS: freelance copywriter, literary and marketing consultant, public relations representative, book editor, copyeditor. **MARKETS SERVED:** individuals and businesses in banking, finance, children's products, health/beauty, automobile, legal, career counseling, medical, and more.

SPECIALTIES AND PREFERENCES: full business-to-business, direct-to-consumer marketing, advertising, and PR (press releases, ads, newsletters, articles, website development, brand building, phone scripts, and more). I enjoy helping people and businesses succeed!

NONFICTION—ACCEPTS: articles/features, how-to/instruction, technical, text or reference, business queries. **TYPICAL EVALUATION/REPORT:** varies.

FEES/TERMS/CONTRACTS: $45/hour editing and administrative services; $60/hour writing; $250 flat fee for press release; $120/hour PR services. Per-project fees available. Invoices with payment due within 30 days of final sign off. Accepts PayPal. No credit cards. Uses contract for larger companies.

ACCOMPLISHMENTS: published trade and consumer publication writer. Marketing copy appears in brochures/websites globally. Produced a children's book; view it: McGintyPublishing.net.

EDUCATION: BA English, California State University, Long Beach. **MEMBERSHIPS:** Saddleback Valley Writers Guild, Lake Forest, CA.

CLIENTS WITHIN PRIOR YEAR: 10–15.

348	EDITOR	WRITER	CONSULTANT	F	NF

McIntosh, Kathy. A Well-Placed Word. Boise, ID. P1/ 208-331-7077. C1/ 208-841-3606. F1/ 208-331-8234. kathy@awellplacedword.com. www.awellplacedword.com. Established: 2003.

SKILLS: freelance editor, copyeditor or line editor, proofreader, ghostwriter, business writer or copywriter, writing coach, publicist, speechwriter. MARKETS SERVED: small businesses, corporations, nonprofit organizations, writers.

SPECIALTIES AND PREFERENCES: Drawing from a dozen years of experience in high-tech marketing, ten in public relations, eight writing fiction, I'll convey your message with power and clarity. Can also help you place and publicize your book. Specialties—high tech, sustainable agriculture, alternative health care, mystery fiction. I love writing about and editing manuscripts about wine, outdoors, travel.

FICTION—ACCEPTS: novels (genre, mainstream, contemporary, historical); queries; synopses. NONFICTION—ACCEPTS: all. TYPICAL EVALUATION/REPORT: 2–12 pages.

FEES/TERMS/CONTRACTS: consulting $50/hour. Editing $40/hour (averages $2/page). Proofreading $30/hour. 50 percent retainer for editing. No credit cards. Uses agreement.

ACCOMPLISHMENTS: one nonfiction book. Articles published regionally. Competent Toastmaster.

EDUCATION: MBA Marketing and Organizational Design, UCLA. BA English Literature, Albertson College, Caldwell, ID. MEMBERSHIPS: Mystery Writers of America. Sisters in Crime. Toastmasters International.

CLIENTS WITHIN PRIOR YEAR: editing 1–5; consulting 10–15.

349	EDITOR	WRITER	CONSULTANT	F	NF

McIrvin, Michael. A-1 Complete Writing and Editing Services. Cheyenne, WY. P1/ 307-637-8657. F1/ 501-325-0305. mcirvinm@earthlink.net. a-1writingandediting.writernetwork.com. Established: 1993.

SKILLS: freelance editor, independent book editor, book doctor, copyeditor or line editor, proofreader, ghostwriter, business writer or copywriter, technical writer, literary consultant, writing coach, writing instructor. MARKETS SERVED: individual authors, publishers, corporations.

SPECIALTIES AND PREFERENCES: book manuscript editor/book doctor (fiction, nonfiction, poetry). Background as a fiction/essay/review/academic writer and poet, university creative writing teacher. Handles dissertations/theses and business/technical materials.

FICTION—ACCEPTS: y/a or juvenile, picture books, short stories, novels (genre, mainstream, literary, contemporary, historical), poetry, scripts/screenplays, queries, synopses, treatments. **NONFICTION—ACCEPTS:** all. **TYPICAL EVALUATION/ REPORT:** 2–10 pages.

FEES/TERMS/CONTRACTS: editing 1.5+ cents/word (academic and technical start higher). Consulting $50/hour. Writing/critiquing fees vary. Half up front, remainder halfway. PayPal. Uses service agreement.

ACCOMPLISHMENTS: one published novel, five poetry collections, and an essay collection. Hundreds of essays, articles, poems, stories, and reviews in a variety of publications.

EDUCATION: MA Literary Criticism, BA English/Anthropology, University of Wyoming, Laramie. **MEMBERSHIPS:** Phi Beta Kappa and Phi Beta Phi Honor Societies. Academy of American Poets.

CLIENTS WITHIN PRIOR YEAR: 40–60.

350	EDITOR	WRITER	CONSULTANT	F	NF

McLennan, Tracy. Shrewsbury, MA. P1/ 617-470-5351. F1/ 508-845-1244. TracyQuinnMcLennan@excite.com. Established: 2000.

SKILLS: editor, book doctor, copyeditor or line editor, proofreader, ghostwriter, literary consultant. **MARKETS SERVED:** traditional and print-on-demand (POD) book publishing.

SPECIALTIES AND PREFERENCES: editing literary and commercial fiction and nonfiction (memoirs/creative nonfiction, biography/autobiography, family history, and narrative nonfiction) and assisting writers through all stages of publication from query letters to proposals to completed manuscripts.

FICTION—ACCEPTS: novels (genre, mainstream, literary, contemporary, historical), queries. **NONFICTION—ACCEPTS:** creative or narrative, biography/autobiography, family history, how-to/instruction, text or reference, humor, book proposals, queries. **TYPICAL EVALUATION/REPORT:** 20 pages.

FEES/TERMS/CONTRACTS: Fees are highly negotiable and based on the project. Payment in agreed-upon installments. Does not accept credit cards. Uses an agreement.

ACCOMPLISHMENTS: clients' work published by Sourcebooks, Ballantine Books, and Hyperion. Authored three nonfiction books published by St. Martin's Press, William Morrow, and Avon Books, and several ghostwritten books for celebrities.

EDUCATION: certification, copyediting and proofreading, New York University. BA English and BS Journalism, Boston University.

CLIENTS WITHIN PRIOR YEAR: 1–5.

351	EDITOR	WRITER	CONSULTANT	F	NF

McNees, Pat. 10643 Weymouth St., Suite 204, Bethesda, MD 20814. P1/ 301-897-8557. pmcnees@nasw.org. www.patmcnees.com. Established: 1971.

SKILLS: freelance editor, book doctor, writing coach, writing instructor, interviewer, collaborator, rewriter, abstract writer. MARKETS SERVED: government, agencies, think tanks, corporations, families.

SPECIALTIES AND PREFERENCES: writing, editing, rewriting, synthesizing—bringing a light touch to heavy subjects, clear language to complex issues, life and storytelling to dry material.

NONFICTION—ACCEPTS: articles, memoirs, creative or narrative, biography/autobiography, family history. TYPICAL EVALUATION/REPORT: 2–10 pages.

FEES/TERMS/CONTRACTS: daily rate. Written agreement.

ACCOMPLISHMENTS: six published nonfiction books. Three anthologies. Countless articles.

EDUCATION: BA English, UCLA. Two years graduate school, teaching at Stanford University. MEMBERSHIPS: Authors Guild. American Society of Journalists & Authors. National Association of Science Writers. PEN.

CLIENTS WITHIN PRIOR YEAR: 1–5.

352	EDITOR	WRITER	CONSULTANT	F	NF

McNichol, Barbara. Barbara McNichol Editorial. Tucso, AZ. P1/ 877-696-4899. P2/ 520-615-7910. editor@barbaramcnichol.com. www.barbaramcnichol.com. Established: 1994.

SKILLS: freelance editor, independent book editor, copyeditor or line editor, proofreader, ghostwriter, business writer or copywriter. MARKETS SERVED: speakers, authors, business, real estate, entrepreneurs.

SPECIALTIES AND PREFERENCES: I write/edit marketing materials (articles, one-sheets, website copy) and edit/ghostwrite manuscripts/proposals (business, real estate, inspirational, self-help). I've created an e-zine and a booklet on words that can trip you up.

NONFICTION—ACCEPTS: articles/features, creative or narrative, self-help, how-to/instruction, business, spiritual, book proposals, queries.

FEES/TERMS/CONTRACTS: $85/hour. For projects over $400, requires half of proposal fee up front. Accepts credit cards through PayPal. Uses contract in the form of a written proposal. Receipt of the initial payment signals the acceptance of my proposal and its terms.

ACCOMPLISHMENTS: Won IABC's Bronze Quill in 1991 for the company magazine I produced. Sept 2003—Conti/Finkel book (I edited) made business bestseller list in *Wall Street Journal*. Have edited several books published by major publishers.

EDUCATION: MA Mass Communications, University of Denver, CO. BA Honors Journalism, University of Western Ontario, Ontario, Canada. MEMBERSHIPS: National Speakers Association. Society of Southwestern Authors. Colorado Independent Publishers Association.
CLIENTS WITHIN PRIOR YEAR: 21–30.

353	EDITOR	WRITER	CONSULTANT	F	NF

Meacham, Jennifer. The Writers' Group. 3527 N.E. 15th Ave., Portland, OR 97212. jd@thewritersgroup.cc. www.thewritersgroup.cc. Established: 1999.

SKILLS: independent book editor, book doctor, freelance editor/reporter, outsourced managing editor (M.E.). MARKETS SERVED: editors for magazines/newspapers and business owners/experts with a story to tell in book form.
SPECIALTIES AND PREFERENCES: general interest, home/lifestyles, business, real estate, finance.
NONFICTION—ACCEPTS: all. TYPICAL EVALUATION/REPORT: mail or e-mail; phone consult.
FEES/TERMS/CONTRACTS: $1,000 monthly retainer for contract M.E. assignments; 50 cents–$2/word for assigned articles; 50 percent on book contracts. All credit cards accepted.
ACCOMPLISHMENTS: 2002 U.S. Small Business Administration "Journalist of the Year" for OR, WA, ID; 2001 Oregon co-winner, TV programming (anchored/coproduced FOX-affiliate business show). Former M.E./current cover story writer, *Revenue* magazine. Co-writer/editor for book on IRA real estate strategies (Square One Publishers). Former contract M.E./reporter for *Executive Vision, Portland UpClose*, and home/garden publication of *The Columbian*. Staff M.E./reporter at *Vancouver Business Journal*; general assignment reporter, *The Seattle Times*; business reporter, *The Columbian*.
EDUCATION: BS Communications, literary law coursework, Washington State University editing certificate. MEMBERSHIPS: American Society of Journalists and Authors, National Writers Union, American Society of Business Publication Editors.
CLIENTS WITHIN PRIOR YEAR: 6–10.

354	EDITOR	WRITER	CONSULTANT	F	NF

Mehling, Randi. 833 E. Palace Ave., Santa Fe, NM 87501. P1/ 505-982-1401. randim11@earthlink.net. Established: 2001.

SKILLS: ghostwriter, business writer and copywriter, technical writer, researcher. MARKETS SERVED: publishers, corporations, nonprofit organizations, writers, government.
SPECIALTIES AND PREFERENCES: fifteen years as communications specialist—

business, public relations, advertising. Niche—bridging medicine and science to lay audience. Health, environment, sustainability, nutrition, alternative medicine, community-supported agriculture, organic food/policy, cross-cultural, travel.
Fiction—accepts: y/a or juvenile. **Nonfiction—accepts:** y/a or juvenile, essays, memoirs, reference, business.
Fees/terms/contracts: $25–$40/hour. Retainer and final payment. Written contract.
Accomplishments: two published young adult nonfiction books. Dozens of published fiction/nonfiction features, articles, poems, short stories.
Education: MPH Environmental Health, Rutgers University, New Brunswick, NJ. BA Journalism, Rutgers University, New Brunswick, NJ. Fluent in Spanish.
Memberships: International Women's Writing Guild.
Clients within prior year: 6–10.

355	EDITOR	WRITER	CONSULTANT	F	NF

Mein, Gardner. Gardner Mein Editing. Vancouver, WA. P1/ 360-699-6311. gardnermein@comcast.net. Established: 1984.

Skills: freelance editor, copyeditor or line editor, book doctor, proofreader, literary consultant, writing instructor. **Markets served:** writers.
Specialties and preferences: I offer mainstream and literary novelists guidance in improving their work's dramatic impact. I focus my recommendations in three broad areas—character development, shape of storyline, and arc of reader involvement. I also take nonfiction projects if I feel I can be useful. My main goal is to be helpful.
Fiction—accepts: novels (mainstream, literary, contemporary). **Nonfiction—accepts:** essays, memoirs, creative or narrative, how-to/instruction. **Typical evaluation/report:** 10–12 pages.
Fees/terms/contracts: $70/hour. Payment in full up front. Checks accepted. No credit cards. Contract if desired.
Education: PhD English Literature, University of Kansas, Lawrence. MFA Fiction, University California at Irvine. BA English, University California at Santa Cruz. **Memberships:** Willamette Writers.
Clients within prior year: 10–15.

356	EDITOR	WRITER	CONSULTANT	F	NF

Melander, Rochelle. LifeRhyme Coaching. Milwaukee, WI. P1/ 414-963-1222. rochelle@LifeRhymeCoaching.com. www.LifeRhymeCoaching.com. Established: 2000.

Skills: freelance editor, proofreader, business writer or copywriter, writing coach, writing instructor. **MARKETS SERVED:** Christian, religious publishers, freelance writers, PhD students, small business owners, professionals.

SPECIALTIES AND PREFERENCES: help develop ideas, sellable manuscript, book proposal. Target the market, create marketing plan. Work for publishers; help writers achieve well-written, organized manuscripts.

FICTION—ACCEPTS: y/a or juvenile, picture books, short stories, novels (genre, mainstream, literary, contemporary). **NONFICTION—ACCEPTS:** all. **TYPICAL EVALUATION/REPORT:** 2–10 pages.

FEES/TERMS/CONTRACTS: $40–$125/hour. Half up front. Uses contract.

ACCOMPLISHMENTS: published six spiritual nonfiction books, 100+ articles. Frequent online columnist. Edited numerous books.

EDUCATION: Master of Sacred Theology, MDiv, Theology, Lutheran Theological Seminary, Philadelphia, PA. Graduate, professional coaching program, Coach University (virtual accredited school), Steamboat Springs, CO. **MEMBERSHIPS:** Society of Children's Book Writers and Illustrators.

CLIENTS WITHIN PRIOR YEAR: 5–10.

357	EDITOR	WRITER	CONSULTANT	F	NF

Melchiorre, Tom. Writing & Editing, Ink. 109 Martin Lane, Norwood, PA 19074. P1/ 610-960-2558. P2/ 610-237-8905. t.melchiorre@rcn.com. Established: 1992.

SKILLS: freelance editor, independent book editor, copyeditor or line editor, proofreader, ghostwriter, business writer or copywriter, technical writer, publicist, grant writer, speechwriter. **MARKETS SERVED:** business, nonprofits, corporations, technical companies, individuals, newspapers/magazines.

SPECIALTIES AND PREFERENCES: translating technical info and jargon to lay language for mass audience for documentation, general reading. Informational news writing articles, biographies/profiles, all types of writing, all fields. Newsletters and brochures (complete design, writing, editing). Public relations materials.

FICTION—ACCEPTS: all. **NONFICTION—ACCEPTS:** all.

FEES/TERMS/CONTRACTS: services by hour or job, fees discussed directly with clients. No credit cards; checks, by term or completion. Will use contract if deemed necessary.

ACCOMPLISHMENTS: First Place Reporting Awards for Continuing Coverage— Pennsylvania Newspaper Association and Journal Register Co. Annual Editorial Awards. Delaware County *Daily Times, Interboro News weekly, Family Values magazine*, internationally published.

EDUCATION: BA English, Minor General Sciences, Pennsylvania State University, University Park. Former EMT. **MEMBERSHIPS:** Delaware County Press Club. Delaware County Chamber of Commerce. Small Publishers, Artists, and Writers Network (SPAWN).

CLIENTS WITHIN PRIOR YEAR: 6–10.

358	EDITOR	WRITER	CONSULTANT	F	NF

Meredith, Fred. The Write Thing. PO Box 100, Manchaca, TX 78652. P1/ 512-282-1987. C1/ 512-636-7480. F1/ 512-282-7413. bikin-fred@macconnect.com. bikin-fred@Austin.rr.com. Established: 1988.

SKILLS: freelance editor, independent book editor, copyeditor or line editor, proofreader, ghostwriter, writing coach. **MARKETS SERVED:** nonwriters who have written something and need to know what to do with it next.

SPECIALTIES AND PREFERENCES: publication concept and design (newsletters, newspapers, magazines) for organizations just entering the publication arena. I am also a consultant on bicycling-related topics. Most normal editing is of writing by bicyclists for cycling or travel-related publication.

NONFICTION—ACCEPTS: articles/features, essays, memoirs, creative or narrative, biography/autobiography, family history, self-help, how-to/instruction, technical, text or reference, business, humor. **TYPICAL EVALUATION/REPORT:** depends on size of job.

FEES/TERMS/CONTRACTS: fees set on a case-by-case basis and depending somewhat on client means and level of interest. No credit cards. Does not use a contract.

ACCOMPLISHMENTS: currently edits Southwest Cycling News—a regional monthly newspaper on bicycling. 1974 Minolta National Photography Competition Grand Prize Winner.

EDUCATION: MA Communications (film), BA Psychology, four years in Fine Arts, University of Texas at Austin. **MEMBERSHIPS:** Writer's League of Texas life member.

CLIENTS WITHIN PRIOR YEAR: 3–5.

359	EDITOR	WRITER	CONSULTANT	F	NF

Middendorf, Bobbye. Independent Writer & Creator. Chicago, IL. P1/ 773-227-4280. jasbjm@earthlink.net. Established: 1999.

SKILLS: ghostwriter, business writer or copywriter, writing instructor, writer of newsletters, profiles, spirituality, reviews, targeted, benefit-focused marketing/PR materials. **MARKETS SERVED:** publishers, entrepreneurs, speakers, coaches, organizations, and independent businesses.

SPECIALTIES AND PREFERENCES: writing for and about publishing, socially responsible business and investing, body-mind-spirit, green building, ecology, environment, community-supported agriculture, natural health, bookstores, libraries/librarians.

NONFICTION—ACCEPTS: articles/features, essays, self-help, how-to/instruction, business, inspirational, spiritual, book proposals, queries.

Fees/terms/contracts: $100/hour copywriting—clients contract for packages of marketing copywriting services, costs dependent on scope of project; discounts for retainer work. Checks only. Deposit of half fee due on signing letter of agreement.

Accomplishments: 2003 Chicago Women in Publishing Excellence Award. Hundreds of articles, features, essays, and profiles in mainstream and progressive publications.

Education: MA Interdisciplinary Arts, Columbia College, Chicago. BA Humanities, University of Chicago. New Dimensions "Deep Listening" graduate. **Memberships:** Sustainable Chicago. The Labyrinth Society. Chicago Company of Friends.

Clients within prior year: 12–16.

360	EDITOR	WRITER	CONSULTANT	F	NF

Milios, Rita. 7150 Cloister Rd., Toledo, OH 43617. P1/ 419-841-4657. rita@milios.net. www.ritamilios.com. Established: 1983.

Skills: freelance editor, independent book editor, writing coach, writing instructor. **Markets served:** writers, publishers.

Specialties and preferences: children's educational, K-8, test assessment materials, questions. Coach for children's and adult nonfiction and children's fiction.

Fiction—accepts: y/a or juvenile, picture books, queries, synopses. **Nonfiction—accepts:** y/a or juvenile, articles/features, essays, memoirs, creative or narrative, self-help, spiritual, book proposals, queries. **Typical evaluation/report:** 30–60 minutes by phone.

Fees/terms/contracts: $55/hour.

Accomplishments: 25 children's books, 5 adult books, 100 + articles. Author, psychotherapist, consultant, and speaker on topics of writing, education, spiritual growth, and personal development.

Education: MSW Social Work, Ohio State University, Columbus. BA Social Work, Lourdes College, Sylvania, OH. **Memberships:** Society of Journalists and Authors. Society of Children's Book Writers & Illustrators.

Clients within prior year: 1–5.

361	EDITOR	WRITER	CONSULTANT	F	NF

Miller, Betsy. 20071 Las Ondas Way, Cupertino, CA 95014. betsy_miller@comcast.net. Established: 1996.

Skills: freelance editor, business writer, technical writer, online help, web content, desktop publisher. **Markets served:** self-published writers, publishers, corporations, health care practitioners.

Specialties and preferences: freelance writer and editor located in the San

Francisco Bay Area. Extensive experience as a technical writer with both print publications and web-based documentation projects. Additional experience editing nonfiction books and publications.

NONFICTION—ACCEPTS: essays, creative or narrative, self-help, how-to/instruction, technical, text or reference, and business.

FEES/TERMS/CONTRACTS: $40-$75/hour; reduced rate for nonprofits. No credit cards. I typically use proposal and agreement.

ACCOMPLISHMENTS: staff technical writer for six years. Freelance and contract writer and editor for eight years. Numerous books, articles, and publications. Can handle Word, HTML, FrameMaker, and Quark files.

EDUCATION: BS Graphic Communication, Graphic Design Option, Cal Poly State University, San Luis Obispo, CA. **MEMBERSHIPS:** Society for Technical Communication, Silicon Valley Chapter.

CLIENTS WITHIN PRIOR YEAR: 6–10.

362	EDITOR	WRITER	CONSULTANT	F	NF

Miller, Maryann. MCM Enterprises. 2552 C.R. 4315 SE, Winnsboro, TX 75494. P1/ 903-365-7585. MCM0704@aol.com. www.maryannwrites.com. Established: 1980.

SKILLS: freelance editor, book doctor, copyeditor or line editor. **MARKETS SERVED:** small presses, production companies, and individuals.

SPECIALTIES AND PREFERENCES: story analysis and detailed editing for novels. Script analysis, editing, doctoring, and rewriting.

FICTION—ACCEPTS: short stories, novels (genre, mainstream), scripts/screenplays, queries, synopses, treatments. **NONFICTION—ACCEPTS:** articles/features, essays, memoirs, creative or narrative, self-help, book proposals, queries. **TYPICAL EVALUATION/REPORT:** 3–5 pages.

FEES/TERMS/CONTRACTS: Novels—story analysis and written report for 300 pages or less $200; detail editing $500–$750; copyediting and proofing: $1.50/page. Scripts—script analysis and written report $200; script editing and doctoring $400–$750. Accepts cash or checks but not credit cards. Sometimes uses a contract.

ACCOMPLISHMENTS: includes editing for a slick quarterly magazine, script editing and doctoring for Stephen Marro Productions, editing for several small presses and individual authors.

EDUCATION: graduate-level creative writing class, University of Texas, Dallas. Numerous writing workshops and seminars. **MEMBERSHIPS:** Sisters In Crime. The Trails Country Center for the Arts. The Greater Dallas Writers' Association.

CLIENTS WITHIN PRIOR YEAR: 1–5.

| 363 | EDITOR | WRITER | CONSULTANT | F | NF |

Miranda, Shari. Seattle, WA. P1/ 206-324-2739. slsmiranda@yahoo.com. Established: 2002.

SKILLS: freelance editor, independent book editor, copyeditor or line editor, proofreader, fact checking, research services. **MARKETS SERVED:** book publishers, magazines, museums, universities, newspapers.

SPECIALTIES AND PREFERENCES: copyediting, proofreading, content editing. I work on hard copy or on-screen and in Chicago style, AP style, and house styles (have written style guides for some clients). My interests are many—art, cooking, history, biography, nature, travel, self-help, health, exercise, instructional, children's, educational, trade.

NONFICTION—ACCEPTS: all.

FEES/TERMS/CONTRACTS: typically uses contract.

ACCOMPLISHMENTS: I have worked as a fundraiser and as a researcher for environmental nonprofit organizations. I worked as a proofreader at an advertising agency, and as an editorial director for a monthly newspaper.

EDUCATION: BA English, University of Dayton, OH. **MEMBERSHIPS:** Northwest Independent Editors Guild. Seattle Writergrrls (that's right, *grrls!*).

CLIENTS WITHIN PRIOR YEAR: 6–10.

| 364 | EDITOR | WRITER | CONSULTANT | F | NF |

Moan, Tamara. 156-B N. Kalaheo Ave., Kailua, HI 96734. P1/ 808-230-8980. tamara.moan@gte.net. Established: 1990.

SKILLS: freelance editor, copyeditor or line editor, proofreader, business writer or copywriter. **MARKETS SERVED:** small publishers, design firms, small business owners who don't feel comfortable with the writing process.

SPECIALTIES AND PREFERENCES: freelance writing, editing, proofing, research on a variety of topics, especially those dealing with Hawaiian cultural or historical subjects. Background and areas of knowledge include the arts, creative writing, travel, Hawai'i and the Pacific.

FICTION—ACCEPTS: poetry. **NONFICTION—ACCEPTS:** articles/features, essays, memoirs, creative or narrative, text or reference, business.

FEES/TERMS/CONTRACTS: $30/hour writing, $20/hour research, $20/hour copyediting, $15/hour proofreading. Payment in thirds within 30 days of invoicing. No credit cards.

ACCOMPLISHMENTS: poems, essays, and book reviews in publications such as *Rainbird, Manoa Journal, Honolulu Advertiser, Honolulu Academy of Arts, 'Ai Pohaku Press*. Former manuscript reader for *Glimmer Train*. Former editor-in-chief of *Hawai'i Review*. Graphic designer, researcher, library assistant (legal and public libraries), legislative aide, art teacher, writing instructor (workshops), painter (interiors), artist, massage therapist.

EDUCATION: MA Literature and Creative Writing, University of Hawai'i, at Manoa, Honolulu. BFA Graphic Design, University of Washington, Seattle.

CLIENTS WITHIN PRIOR YEAR: 1–5.

365	EDITOR	WRITER	CONSULTANT	F	NF

Molino, Paula. 45 Angela Ave., Yardley, PA 19067. P1/ 215-321-7399. F1/ 215-428-2476. pmolino@fashionfix.com. pmolino@comcast.net. www.fashionfix.com. Established: Fashion fix established 2002, freelance writer for years.

SKILLS: freelance editor, independent book editor, proofreader, freelance writer, ghostwriter, business writer or copywriter. **MARKETS SERVED:** fashion, gardening, and lifestyle publications.

SPECIALTIES AND PREFERENCES: consultant and writer on fashion, sewing, home and gardening (roses especially), figure skating, lifestyle.

NONFICTION—ACCEPTS: y/a or juvenile, articles/features, self-help, how-to/instruction, technical, business, humor, queries.

FEES/TERMS/CONTRACTS: to be discussed depending upon assignment.

ACCOMPLISHMENTS: lifestyle and features writer published in NJ and PA newspapers. Twenty-Nine Angels Publishing—editor, proofreader, and writer. The Children's Guild—edited educational books. Writer for Philadelphia Rose Society's newsletter and *American Gardener* magazine. Fashion-related articles in trade/company publications.

EDUCATION: BS Apparel Design, Dean's List, University of Delaware, Newark. Fashion Merchandising Certificate, Salutatorian, Patricia Stevens Institute of Fashion, MD. **MEMBERSHIPS:** Professional Writer's Association of New Jersey. Lower Bucks County, PA, Chamber of Commerce. The American Rose Society & Philadelphia Rose Society United States Figure Skating Association.

CLIENTS WITHIN PRIOR YEAR: 6–10.

366	EDITOR	WRITER	CONSULTANT	F	NF

Mollison, Temah. Word Contractor. Brooklyn, NY. P1/ 718-771-0754. F1/ 718-369-2625. temah@wordcontractor.com. www.wordcontractor.com. Established: 2003.

SKILLS: freelance editor, proofreader, writing coach. **MARKETS SERVED:** writers, educational institutions, students, and professionals from heterogeneous backgrounds.

SPECIALTIES AND PREFERENCES: I assist clients with writing assessments, fresh project perspective developing writing confidence, project outline and development, editing/revision/proofreading. This service is particularly helpful for anyone who has difficulty expressing their written voice. I assist clients to tap into their original voice in order to create outstanding instead of generic copy. I also work on curriculum, dissertations, and academic papers.

NONFICTION—ACCEPTS: articles/features, book proposals, queries. **TYPICAL EVALUATION/REPORT:** 2+ pages.

FEES/TERMS/CONTRACTS: negotiated flat or hourly fee. Cash, check, credit card.

ACCOMPLISHMENTS: dissertation: "Exploring the Effects of Self-Concept, Gender and Race on High Stakes Test Performance—Relationships Between Performance on the Student Self-Concept Scale and the Regents Comprehensive Exam in English."

EDUCATION: PhD English Education, New York University, NY. MS Educational Administration, University of Wisconsin, Madison. BS English Education, New York University, NY. Studied art and philosophy in Greece and France.

CLIENTS WITHIN PRIOR YEAR: 1–5.

367	EDITOR	WRITER	CONSULTANT	F	NF

Monahan, Sherry. PO Box 357, Willow Spring, NC 27592-0357. P1/ 919-577-6399 F1/ 919-577-6399. sherry@wildwestinfo.com. www.wildwestinfo.com. Established: 1998.

SKILLS: freelance editor, copyeditor or line editor, proofreader, ghostwriter, business writer or copywriter, technical writer, literary consultant, writing coach, writing instructor. **MARKETS SERVED:** writers, publishers, nonprofits, and corporations.

SPECIALTIES AND PREFERENCES: creative, concise editing. Award-winning author knowledgeable in many subjects. No erotica.

FICTION—ACCEPTS: all. **NONFICTION—ACCEPTS:** all. **TYPICAL EVALUATION/REPORT:** 2–10 pages.

FEES/TERMS/CONTRACTS: $50–$100/hour depending upon service required. One-half on agreement, balance on completion.

ACCOMPLISHMENTS: three published nonfiction books, several articles in national magazines, procedure manual for Fortune 100 company, newsletters, and brochures. **MEMBERSHIPS:** North Carolina Writer's Network. Women Writing the West. Western Writers of America. Western History Association. Society of Southwest Authors.

CLIENTS WITHIN PRIOR YEAR: 5–10.

368	EDITOR	WRITER	CONSULTANT	F	NF

Monfort, Alison B. Portland, OR. C1/ 971-212-3826. abmonfort@yahoo.com. Established: 1983.

SKILLS: freelance editor, independent book editor, copyeditor or line editor, ghostwriter, business writer and copywriter, literary consultant, script consultant. **MARKETS SERVED:** writers, filmmakers, publishers, literary agents, corporations.

SPECIALTIES AND PREFERENCES: honest, constructive, story analysis with guidance on narrative flow, plot, pacing, character definition, and dialogue for fiction and screenplay. Advertising background for creating queries, proposals, and film prospectus materials with hooks. Turns down unmarketable work. Sends flowers after killing darlings.

FICTION—ACCEPTS: novels (mainstream, literary, contemporary, historical), scripts/screenplays, queries, treatments. **NONFICTION—ACCEPTS:** creative or narrative, self-help, business, humor, spiritual, book proposals, queries. **TYPICAL EVALUATION/REPORT:** 2– 10 pages.

FEES/TERMS/CONTRACTS: $35/hour. Initial meeting free. No credit cards. Uses contracts/agreements.

ACCOMPLISHMENTS: national awards in advertising; public relations, marketing successes.

EDUCATION: "I never let my schooling interfere with my education." —Mark Twain. BA English/Communications, Arizona State University, Tempe. Eternal student. **MEMBERSHIPS:** Willamette Writers. Portland Independent Film Group.

CLIENTS WITHIN PRIOR YEAR: 5–10.

369	EDITOR	WRITER	CONSULTANT	F	NF

Montgomery, Joy. Structural Integrity. PO Box 10956, Pleasanton, CA 94588-0956. P1/ 925-426-1886. joy@structural-integrity.com. integrity.com. Established: 1986.

SKILLS: freelance editor, technical writer, writing coach, writing instructor, speech coach, short story writer. **MARKETS SERVED:** corporations, small companies, start-ups, individuals.

SPECIALTIES AND PREFERENCES: job aids, affordable usability testing, procedure analysis and documentation, ISO9000 documentation, communication coaching, task-oriented manuals and guides, and editing for usability and translation.

FICTION—ACCEPTS: y/a or juvenile, short stories. **NONFICTION—ACCEPTS:** y/a or juvenile, articles/features, essays, memoirs, creative or narrative, biography/ autobiography, family history, self-help, how-to/instruction, technical, text, business, humor. **TYPICAL EVALUATION/REPORT:** 1–2 pages.

FEES/TERMS/CONTRACTS: $75/hour, W-2, short-term, temporary.

ACCOMPLISHMENTS: Northern California Technical Communication Competition awards.

EDUCATION: BA San Francisco State University, CA. **MEMBERSHIPS:** Society for

Technical Communication. Educational Society for Resource Management (APICS). AFCEA. Toastmasters.

CLIENTS WITHIN PRIOR YEAR: 1 large contract; typically no more than 25.

370	EDITOR	WRITER	CONSULTANT	F	NF

Morris, Taylor. New York, NY. P1/ 212-878-5931. P2/ 917-698-9785. taylordmorris@yahoo.com. Established: 1998.

SKILLS: freelance editor, independent book editor, book doctor, copyeditor or line editor, proofreader, ghostwriter. **MARKETS SERVED:** writers of young readers and young adults.

SPECIALTIES AND PREFERENCES: I work exclusively in the young adult and young reader market—books for kids ages eight to eighteen. This does not include books for children under the age of eight.

FICTION—ACCEPTS: y/a or juvenile, short stories, novels (genre, mainstream, literary, contemporary), poetry, scripts/screenplays, queries, synopses, treatments.

FEES/TERMS/CONTRACTS: editing $50/hour; copyediting and proofreading $35/hour; ghostwriting fee negotiable. No credit cards or PayPal. Uses contract.

ACCOMPLISHMENTS: I've always had a freakish knack for writing for and in the voice of teenagers. Former book editor, *Jump* magazine (for teen girls), freelance writer for *Girls' Life* magazine. Author of nonfiction book by Girl Press/Alloy Books on stage and screen stars.

EDUCATION: BFA Writing, Literature, and Publishing, cum laude, Emerson College, Boston, MA.

CLIENTS WITHIN PRIOR YEAR: 6–10.

371	EDITOR	WRITER	CONSULTANT	F	NF

Mosley, Shelley. 8619 N. 53rd Dr., Glendale, AZ 85302. P1/ 623-939-469. deborahshelley@mindspring.com. www.deborahshelley.com. Established: 1995.

SKILLS: freelance editor, researcher, reviewer, freelance writer. **MARKETS SERVED:** publishers, general public, cities, libraries, churches, schools, other writers.

SPECIALTIES AND PREFERENCES: experienced researcher; write on assignment.

FICTION—ACCEPTS: y/a or juvenile, short stories, novels (genre, contemporary), picture books, poetry, queries, synopses. **NONFICTION—ACCEPTS:** y/a or juvenile, articles/features, essays, memoirs, creative or narrative, biography/autobiography, family history, self-help, how-to/instruction, text or reference, humor, inspirational/religious, books proposals, queries. **TYPICAL EVALUATION/REPORT:** depends on the project.

FEES/TERMS/CONTRACTS: Terms and fees depend on project. No credit cards.

ACCOMPLISHMENTS: editor—two reference books; contributor—biannual reference;

dozens of reviews and articles in national magazines and journals; columns in two newspapers; four romantic comedies; one novella; 600+ limericks. RWA Veritas 1995, 2000. First Place, Golden Synopsis. Finalist, Holt Medallion. Finalist, Writer's Digest Inspirational Category. Finalist, Love and Laughter Contest. Finalist, IPPY.

EDUCATION: MLS Library Science, University of Arizona, Tucson. BS Education, Grand Canyon University, Phoenix. **MEMBERSHIPS:** Romance Writers of America—national; Valley of the Sun; Desert Rose; Society of Children's Book Writers and Illustrators.

CLIENTS WITHIN PRIOR YEAR: 5–10.

372	EDITOR	WRITER	CONSULTANT	F	NF

Murphy, Catherine. 209 Highland Ct., Santa Cruz, CA 95060. P1/ 831-460-0434. F1/ 831-460-0434. cathy@editrix.com. Established: 1999.

SKILLS: freelance editor. **MARKETS SERVED:** higher education textbooks in the life sciences, social sciences, and humanities.

SPECIALTIES AND PREFERENCES: I have twenty years of experience as an editor, handling both acquisitions of new titles and development of manuscripts. I work closely with authors and the editorial team to create books that will be market leaders and innovators. Primarily I work directly for publishers; occasionally I take on private clients.

NONFICTION—ACCEPTS: text or reference.

FEES/TERMS/CONTRACTS: Usually uses a contract or charges by the hour. No credit cards.

ACCOMPLISHMENTS: currently developing a book series with a well-known academic foundation. In addition, I am developing two major first-edition textbooks for college publishing clients. I have been a writer for *Syllabus Magazine* and have written and developed website material for many publishers.

EDUCATION: AB English, Occidental College, Los Angeles, CA. **MEMBERSHIPS:** Bay Area Editors' Forum.

CLIENTS WITHIN PRIOR YEAR: 6–10.

373	EDITOR	WRITER	CONSULTANT	F	NF

Nash, Leonard. Hollywood, FL. P1/ 954-925-4428. F1/ 954-925-4427. LDN@LeonardNash.com. www.LeonardNash.com. Established: 1993.

SKILLS: book doctor, proofreader, business writer or copywriter, literary consultant, writing coach, writing instructor, plagiarism consultant, forensic editor, document analyst, and expert witness. **MARKETS SERVED:** authors, universities, hospitals, lawyers, entrepreneurs.

SPECIALTIES AND PREFERENCES: works primarily on literary and popular novels, short story collections, memoirs. Considers all fiction, nonfiction, and business manuscripts, including ghostwriting projects. Prefers clients open to constructive criticism who welcome the opportunity to learn from a seasoned writer, editor, and university English instructor. Strives to promote and maintain healthy communication and teamwork.

FICTION—ACCEPTS: all. NONFICTION—ACCEPTS: all. TYPICAL EVALUATION/REPORT: 20–50 pages.

FEES/TERMS/CONTRACTS: editing, proofreading, coaching, and manuscript consulting—from $80/hour. Offers flat rate and per-page rates when feasible. Plagiarism consulting and expert witness testimony from $160/hour. Accepts credit cards via PayPal.

ACCOMPLISHMENTS: recent clients include *Lincoln Road Magazine, Las Olas Magazine, Fort Lauderdale Yachtsman, Vis-a-Vis Magazine, Jackson Health System*, and private authors. See website for curriculum vitae, links to publications, and additional information.

EDUCATION: MFA Creative Writing, Florida International University, Miami. BA English, Florida International University, Miami. AA, University of Florida, Gainesville.

CLIENTS WITHIN PRIOR YEAR: 11–20.

374	EDITOR	WRITER	CONSULTANT	F	NF

Nathan, Linda L. Logos Word Designs, Inc. PO Box 735, Maple Falls, WA 98266. P1/ 360-599-3429. F1/ 360-392-0216. editor@logosword.com. www.logosword.com. Established: 1992.

SKILLS: freelance editor, independent book editor, book doctor, copyeditor or line editor, proofreader, ghostwriter, business writer or copywriter, literary consultant, writing coach, publicist, author support services. MARKETS SERVED: academia; authors and writers; book publishers (nonfiction, textbook); businesses (marketing collateral); Christian ministries; Internet, newspapers/magazines.

SPECIALTIES AND PREFERENCES: academic/scholarly (undergraduate through post-doctoral), author support services, book proposals and queries, business, Christian apologetics and fiction, conservative political. Evaluates, edits, and provides writing assistance for fiction/nonfiction, interviews, journalism (features/press releases); publicity.

FICTION—ACCEPTS: y/a or juvenile, picture books, queries, synopses, treatments. NONFICTION—ACCEPTS: all. TYPICAL EVALUATION/REPORT: 10–15 pages.

FEES/TERMS/CONTRACTS: See website. PayPal. Terms. Typically uses agreement.

ACCOMPLISHMENTS: editor of four large publications. Author of one book, numerous published articles.

EDUCATION: BA Psychology, MA work, University of Oregon, Eugene.

MEMBERSHIPS: Editorial Freelancers Association. Northwest Independent Editors Guild. Writers' Information Network.

CLIENTS WITHIN PRIOR YEAR: 11–20 (including one who was offered a contract from a major New York publisher).

375	EDITOR	WRITER	CONSULTANT	F	NF

Neri, Kris. Granada Hills, CA. krisneri@earthlink.net. www.krisneri.com. Established: 1999.

SKILLS: independent book editor, writing coach, writing instructor. **MARKETS SERVED:** freelance writers.

SPECIALTIES AND PREFERENCES: prefers to work with experienced writers who need help making their novels publishable. Will ask to see sample/synopsis. Provides instruction along with critique as needed. Limited to the mystery-suspense genre; all sub-genres. Will consider cross-genre works if there's a crime component.

FICTION—ACCEPTS: short stories, novels (genre), humor, spiritual, queries. **TYPICAL EVALUATION/REPORT:** 3–15 pages.

FEES/TERMS/CONTRACTS: $1–$2/page, one half to begin, balance at completion. Accepts PayPal. No contract.

ACCOMPLISHMENTS: three novels published, one awaiting publication. More than fifty short stories published. Two-time winner of the Derringer Award for short fiction. Pushcart Prize nominee for short fiction. Novels nominated for Agatha, Anthony, and Macavity Awards. Novels won Samantha Award. **MEMBERSHIPS:** Sisters in Crime. Mystery Writers of America. The American Crime Writers' League.

CLIENTS WITHIN PRIOR YEAR: 1–5.

376	EDITOR	WRITER	CONSULTANT	F	NF

Netherton, Robin. St. Louis, Louis, MO. P1/ 314-439-1222. F1/ 314-439-1333. robin@netherton.net. Established: 1982.

SKILLS: freelance editor, independent book editor, book doctor, copyeditor or line editor, proofreader, substantive editor, web/online content editor, editorial consultant. **MARKETS SERVED:** magazines, newsletters, websites, nonprofits, professional associations, health organizations, government agencies, reference publishers.

SPECIALTIES AND PREFERENCES: expertise in translating specialist writing into accessible lay language. Includes magazine/newsletter articles, columns, websites, brochures, monographs, reports, reference materials, books.

NONFICTION—ACCEPTS: all.

FEES/TERMS/CONTRACTS: $35–$75/hour or project rate. No credit cards. PayPal if necessary. Typically uses contract or agreement.

ACCOMPLISHMENTS: over ten years as an editor with newspaper, magazine, and book publishers before turning freelance full-time. Have edited about a dozen books, hundreds of monographs and reports, and thousands of articles.

EDUCATION: BJ Journalism and BA English, University of Missouri, Columbia. Graduate work in Communications and Paleography, Cornell University, Ithaca, NY, and University of Iowa, Iowa City.

CLIENTS WITHIN PRIOR YEAR: 8–10.

377	EDITOR	WRITER	CONSULTANT	F	NF

Ninger, Laura. Rutherford, NJ. P1/ 201-635-5006. F1/ 201-635-9781. ljnedit@sprintmail.com. ljnedit@earthlink.net. Established: medical editor 1986; freelance editor/writer 1994.

SKILLS: freelance editor, copyeditor or line editor, technical writer, medical editor and writer. **MARKETS SERVED:** medical education companies, publishers, medical societies, US government, nonprofits, individual MD/PhDs, other independent contractors.

SPECIALTIES AND PREFERENCES: eighteen years of experience. Copyediting, substantive editing, abstracting, writing, fact checking, research, and project management for journal articles, books, newsletters, reports, slide presentations.

NONFICTION—ACCEPTS: articles/features, technical, text or reference.

FEES/TERMS/CONTRACTS: confidential.

ACCOMPLISHMENTS: certified as an Editor in the Life Sciences (ELS). Received editing/writing certificate from the American Medical Writers Association. Authored numerous articles and abstracts for medical publications. Graduated Phi Beta Kappa, *summa cum laude*.

EDUCATION: BA English, University of Pennsylvania, Philadelphia. Attended New York University Summer Publishing Institute. **MEMBERSHIPS:** American Medical Writers Association. Board of Editors in the Life Sciences. Council of Science Editors. Editorial Freelancers Association.

CLIENTS WITHIN PRIOR YEAR: 11–20.

378	EDITOR	WRITER	CONSULTANT	F	NF

Nordholm, Gayle. Daydream Publishing. PO Box 682, Woodinville, WA 98072. P1/ 425-488-7432. P2/ 360-668-1192. C1/ 206-234-7968. F1/ 425-488-7432. daydream.pub@verizon.net. Established: 2000.

SKILLS: freelance editor, independent book editor, copyeditor or line editor, proofreader, ghostwriter, business writer or copy writer. **MARKETS SERVED:** writers, publishers, nonprofits, and corporations.

SPECIALTIES AND PREFERENCES: provides research, creative development, writing, and editing.

FICTION—ACCEPTS: y/a or juvenile, picture books, short stories, and poetry. NONFICTION—ACCEPTS: y/a or juvenile, articles/features, essays, memoirs, self-help, how-to/instruction, business, humor, inspirational/religious. TYPICAL EVALUATION/REPORT: essays, short stories, articles rewritten using word processing. 2–10 page evaluation for larger projects.

FEES/TERMS/CONTRACTS: $25/hour. Accepts PayPal. No credit cards. Uses agreement.

ACCOMPLISHMENTS: one self-published children's picture book. Publishers Marketing Association 2003 Ben Franklin Award. Two articles published in national magazines.

EDUCATION: AA Business, American River College, Sacramento, CA. Two-year degree Theology, Pacific School of Theology, Burien, WA. Montessori teaching certificate from Edmonds Community College, WA. MEMBERSHIPS: Society of Children's Book Writing and Illustrating. Publisher's Marketing Association. Montessori Teachers Association.

CLIENTS WITHIN PRIOR YEAR: 6–10.

379	EDITOR	WRITER	CONSULTANT	F	NF

Nussbaum, Sue Carol. The Mightier Pen. 3960 Isla Ciudad Court, Naples, FL 34109. themightierpen@swfla.rr.com. Established: 1998.

SKILLS: freelance editor, book doctor, independent manuscript editor. MARKETS SERVED: national and international via Internet.

SPECIALTIES AND PREFERENCES: preference for fiction, but I will edit almost any novel, especially science fiction, or nonfiction book. Enjoy working with first-time writers.

FICTION—ACCEPTS: all. NONFICTION—ACCEPTS: all. TYPICAL EVALUATION/REPORT: approximately 3 pages.

FEES/TERMS/CONTRACTS: fee quoted by word count and writing sample. Full-length book approximately three-week turnaround. Contract by e-mail letter of intent.

ACCOMPLISHMENTS: practicing lawyer for twenty years. Retired. One regional and one international award for writing. Author of one published novel. Two published essays.

EDUCATION: JD Seton Hall University School of Law, Newark, NJ. MEMBERSHIPS: Writers' workshop of Creative Retirement Center.

CLIENTS WITHIN PRIOR YEAR: 11–20.

| 380 | EDITOR | WRITER | CONSULTANT | F | NF |

O'Brien, Dorrie. Arlington, TX. P1/ 817-652-3736. dorrie7908@sbcglobal.com. Established: 1985.

SKILLS: freelance editor, independent book editor, book doctor, copyeditor or line editor, proofreader, book typesetting/layout; critiques; mentor. **MARKETS SERVED:** authors.

SPECIALTIES AND PREFERENCES: unpublished fiction authors who recognize the need to have their manuscript edited before beginning the submittal process to agents and publishing houses, or as a first step in self-publishing.

FICTION—ACCEPTS: novels (genre, mainstream, literary, contemporary, historical), queries, synopses, treatments. **NONFICTION—ACCEPTS:** memoirs, creative or narrative, biography/autobiography, family history, book proposals, queries. **TYPICAL EVALUATION/REPORT:** 2–10 pages.

FEES/TERMS/CONTRACTS: sample online edit. 2–4 cents/word. Payment up front. Pre-pay over several months. References. Uses contract.

ACCOMPLISHMENTS: owned a fiction-only publishing house. Edited/published/ sold hundreds of titles both as a publisher and a freelance editor.

EDUCATION: BA English/American and British History, Columbia College, MO. **MEMBERSHIPS:** Editorial Freelancers Association. Copyeditor.com. Horror Writers of America. Romance Writers of America. Mystery Writers of America. Science Fiction/Fantasy Writers of America.

CLIENTS WITHIN PRIOR YEAR: 11–20.

| 381 | EDITOR | WRITER | CONSULTANT | F | NF |

O'Connell, Brian. Deadlines Ink, 79 Radcliff Dr, Doylestown, PA 18901. P1/ 267-880-3144. brian.oco@verizon.net. www.brianoc.com. Established: 1996.

SKILLS: freelance editor, independent book editor, book doctor, ghostwriter, business writer or copywriter. **MARKETS SERVED:** high-technology sectors.

SPECIALTIES AND PREFERENCES: personal finance, career management, health care, high-technology sectors—writing ghosted books, corporate collateral/website content, and speeches and ghosted articles.

NONFICTION—ACCEPTS: articles/features, memoirs, creative or narrative, biography/ autobiography, self-help, how-to/instruction, business, book proposals, queries.

FEES/TERMS/CONTRACTS: usually per-project or per-word basis. No credit cards or PayPal. Uses a contract.

ACCOMPLISHMENTS: ghostwriter and nonfiction book author with two Book of the Month Club selections. Bylines in *Wall Street Journal*, *USA Today*, CBS News Marketwatch, *Newsweek*, *Entrepreneur*, *Smart Business*, *Business 2.0*. Wall Street bond trader.

EDUCATION: MA Journalism, University of Massachusetts, Amherst. **MEMBERSHIPS:**

American Society of Journalists and Authors. Writers Room of Bucks County (writer in residence).
CLIENTS WITHIN PRIOR YEAR: 21–30.

382	EDITOR	WRITER	CONSULTANT	F	NF

O'Connell, Tracy. 103 Birch St., Rio Dell, CA 95562. P1/ 707-764-3768. C1/ 707-845-7686. tracyo@baldwin-telecom.net. Established: 1978.

SKILLS: freelance editor, copyeditor or line editor, proofreader, ghostwriter, business writer, coach. MARKETS SERVED: nonprofit organizations such as a women's business network, foundation, political candidate, hunter-safety organization, birdwatcher's group.

SPECIALTIES AND PREFERENCES: I write, edit, proofread, and/or manage promotional materials, public relations and marketing efforts, and other informative material for organizations. I take pride in treating clients with sensitivity and kindness. Even when bleeding all over their work, I find good points to discuss so that they aren't demoralized by criticism.

NONFICTION—ACCEPTS: articles/features, essays, memoirs, text or reference, business, book proposals, queries. TYPICAL EVALUATION/REPORT: 1 page.

FEES/TERMS/CONTRACTS: $25–$50/hour consulting/coaching, copywriting, editing, initial or final proofing. Larger projects, project fee. No credit cards. Uses agreement.

ACCOMPLISHMENTS: wrote a textbook, many brochures, catalogs, schedules, press releases, and other publicity. Awards for writing, ad campaigns, and publications. Managed public relations, marketing, and advertising in a Fortune 500 corporation.

EDUCATION: EdD Higher Education Administration, University of California, Los Angeles. MA Counseling with business emphasis, University of Wisconsin, Stout. BA Journalism, English, Sociology, University of Wisconsin, River Falls.

CLIENTS WITHIN PRIOR YEAR: 1–5.

383	EDITOR	WRITER	CONSULTANT	F	NF

O'Connor, Kathleen. Quality Editing. PO Box 344, Thurmont, MD 21788. poeteire@yahoo.com. Established: 1980.

SKILLS: book editor, copy or line editor, proofreader, ghostwriter, business writer, technical writer, writing coach. Other: TESOL editor, report writer, Web content editor, news writer, sermon/speechwriter, grant writer, abstract/references/index writer. MARKETS SERVED: individuals, corporations, government, and publishers.

SPECIALTIES AND PREFERENCES: fast, accurate, and reliable writing and editing services that meet style requirements, read well, and are interesting.

FICTION—ACCEPTS: all. NONFICTION—ACCEPTS: all. TYPICAL EVALUATION/REPORT: 2–10 pages.

FEES/TERMS/CONTRACTS: $35/hour corporate rate. May request retainer. No credit cards. Typically uses written agreement.

ACCOMPLISHMENTS: English editor Emmitsburg.net. Former editor for HUD publications. Former editor Homeland Security publications. Former writer/copyeditor agricultural publications. Published poems. Published news features/reports.

EDUCATION: MA work English, BA English teaching certificate, Michigan State University, East Lansing. Master Editor certificate, EEI Communications. MS Pro/PageMaker certificate. MEMBERSHIPS: Freelance Brunch Bunch, Alexandria, VA. The Writer's Center, Bethesda, MD.

CLIENTS WITHIN PRIOR YEAR: variable depending on workload.

384	EDITOR	WRITER	CONSULTANT	F	NF

O'Grady, Katy. D & O Creative Group. 4033 Hallman St., Fairfax, VA 22030. P1/ 703-385-7778. F1/ 703-991-8830. katyog@aol.com. wordforward@aol.com. Established: 2001.

SKILLS: freelance editor, ghostwriter, business writer or copywriter. MARKETS SERVED: professional and trade associations, public relations and marketing firms and their clients, federal government contractors, and small businesses.

SPECIALTIES AND PREFERENCES: I make business leaders look good on paper and online with ghostwriting and editing of articles, columns, and letters. By writing marketing copy, press releases, and news articles, I help companies and associations attract and retain customers, deliver compelling stories, and raise the profile of their organizations. I do not handle fiction projects or pure proofreading.

NONFICTION—ACCEPTS: articles/features, how-to/instruction, technical, business.

FEES/TERMS/CONTRACTS: first-time clients: one-third deposit on any project larger than $750, balance payable on completion. Accepts check, Visa, or MasterCard. Uses contract.

ACCOMPLISHMENTS: published in *NASW News* (National Association of Social Workers). Ghostwriting work has appeared in numerous magazines.

EDUCATION: BA Theater, College of Wooster, OH. MEMBERSHIPS: American Society of Association Executives. Central Fairfax Chamber of Commerce.

CLIENTS WITHIN PRIOR YEAR: 10–14.

385	EDITOR	WRITER	CONSULTANT	F	NF

O'Moore-Klopf, Katharine. KOK Edit. 15 Hare Lane, East Setauket, NY 11733-3606. P1/ 631-474-1170. F1/ 631-474-9849. editor@kokedit.com.

www.kokedit.com. Established: 1995.

Skills: freelance editor, copyeditor or line editor, developmental editor.
Markets served: publishers, packagers, authors.

Specialties and preferences: copyediting, substantive editing, developmental editing, and fact checking for book publishers, packagers, authors, and business websites. Biography, child care, environmentalism, psychology, mainstream health care, alternative health care, general fiction, education, reference works, business, clinical medicine, surgery, allied health, music therapy. For all manuscripts written in English by nonnative speakers, I offer skillful "translation" to standard English. As of 2004, I have twenty years of experience in publishing. I am considerate and straightforward with authors; I am on their side. I enjoy developing a good working relationship with my clients, many of whom are long term.

Fiction—accepts: novels (genre, mainstream, literary, contemporary, historical).
Nonfiction—accepts: all.

Fees/terms/contracts: For individuals and corporations new to me, I require a deposit. I invoice at least once during a job, and payment is due within 30 days. I accept corporate check, money order, or PayPal.

Education: BA Journalism, University of Houston, TX. **Memberships:** Editorial Freelancers Association.

Clients within prior year: 5–10.

386	EDITOR	WRITER	CONSULTANT	F	NF

O'Shea, Melody. Tampa, FL. P1/ 813-685-7402. moshea7@tampabay.rr.com. Established: 1987.

Skills: freelance editor, copyeditor and line editor, proofreader, ghostwriter, business writer or copywriter, literary consultant, writing instructor, publicist.
Markets served: *St. Petersburg Times*, *Florida Business Magazine*, *Florida Nursing News*, *Woman's World*, *The Rotarian*, and others.

Specialties and preferences: variety, in-depth interviews with corporate CEOs, legislators, small business owners, politicians, government officials, guys-in-the-street.

Fiction—accepts: short stories, novels (genre, mainstream, literary, contemporary, historical), query, synopsis. **Nonfiction—accepts:** articles/features, essays, memoirs, creative and narrative, biography, family history, self-help, how-to/instruction, business, inspirational/religious, spiritual, book proposals, queries.

Fees/terms/contracts: negotiated.

Accomplishments: award-winning fiction and nonfiction in newspapers and magazines. Research on First Amendment law as it relates to state and local government ordinances is a published resource for Florida government and businesses. Novel in progress.

EDUCATION: BA News Editorial, University of South Florida, Tampa. BA Spanish and Italian Language and Literature, Temple University, Philadelphia, PA.
MEMBERSHIPS: Society of Professional Journalists.
CLIENTS WITHIN PRIOR YEAR: 1–5.

387	EDITOR	WRITER	CONSULTANT	F	NF

Ober, Doris. 5959 State Rte. 1, Dogtown, CA 94924. P1/ 415-868-1299. F1/ 415-868-1500. ober@marincounty.net. Established: 1981.

SKILLS: independent book editor, ghostwriter, collaborator, literary consultant.
MARKETS SERVED: authors of full-length books.
SPECIALTIES AND PREFERENCES: full editorial service, from manuscript evaluations to book proposals, from simple improvements to full collaborations, ghost-written or with cover credit. Author's collaborator.
FICTION—ACCEPTS: novels (mainstream, literary, contemporary). **NONFICTION—ACCEPTS:** memoirs, creative or narrative, biography/autobiography, self-help, how-to/ instruction, book proposals. **TYPICAL EVALUATION/REPORT:** 2–8 pages.
FEES/TERMS/CONTRACTS: $90/hour. Clients should call for quotes. Contract or agreement if requested. No credit cards.
ACCOMPLISHMENTS: ten published novels, forty-plus published nonfiction titles, one self-published reference book. Listed in *Who's Who in America* 2004, 2005.
EDUCATION: courses in creative writing, Syracuse University, NY. Courses in English literature, Texas Western College, El Paso.
CLIENTS WITHIN PRIOR YEAR: 6–10.

388	EDITOR	WRITER	CONSULTANT	F	NF

Oberweger, Lorin. Free Expressions Seminars and Literary Services. 2420 W. Brandon Blvd., #198, Brandon, FL 33511. P1/ 813-684-7988. P2/ 866-497-4832. lorin@free-expressions.com. www.free-expressions.com/. Established: 1996.

SKILLS: freelance editor, independent book editor, book doctor, copyeditor or line editor, proofreader, ghostwriter, literary consultant, writing coach, writing instructor, promotional/marketing copy. **MARKETS SERVED:** primarily writers of literary and commercial fiction.
SPECIALTIES AND PREFERENCES: literary, mainstream, women's, speculative, suspense. Works with writers at all levels to help them reach beyond their current artistic capabilities, learn critical self-editing skills, and achieve publishing success.
FICTION—ACCEPTS: all. **NONFICTION—ACCEPTS:** all. **TYPICAL EVALUATION/REPORT:** 20–30 pages.
FEES/TERMS/CONTRACTS: complete manuscript evaluation and line editing: $1,675

for up to 400 pages. Partial manuscript evaluation: $600 for manuscripts up to 100 pages. Other projects: $7/per page or $40+/hour. Accepts MasterCard/Visa/Discover. Written contract upon request, prefers payment up front, will negotiate on fees/terms.

ACCOMPLISHMENTS: work has appeared in dozens of periodicals, including *French Quarter Fiction*, a literary anthology; *StoryQuarterly*; *Amelia*; *The Montserrat Review*; and others. Clients published by University of Texas Press, Three Continents Press, Warner Books, and others. See free-expressions.com for client comments.

EDUCATION: English Literature, Clark University, Worcester, MA.

CLIENTS WITHIN PRIOR YEAR: 25–30.

389	EDITOR	WRITER	CONSULTANT	F	NF

Older, Effin. MS MA. Older Unlimited. 1769 Broadway, #2, San Francisco, CA 94109. P1/ 415-775-3334. ewrite@att.net. www.allaboutenglish.com. Established: 1986.

SKILLS: freelance editor, independent book editor, book doctor, copyeditor or line editor, proofreader, ghostwriter, business writer or copywriter, literary consultant, writing coach, writing instructor; work with writers with English as a second language. **MARKETS SERVED:** speakers, writers, publishers, non-profits, corporations.

SPECIALTIES AND PREFERENCES: has written and edited for many markets, in many genres. Doesn't do poetry, religion, or technical writing.

FICTION—ACCEPTS: y/a or juvenile; picture books; short stories; novels (genre, mainstream, literary, contemporary, historical); scripts/screenplays; queries. **NONFICTION—ACCEPTS:** all. **TYPICAL EVALUATION/REPORT:** 2–6 pages.

FEES/TERMS/CONTRACTS: $75+/hour.

ACCOMPLISHMENTS: with brother, Jules Older, has written a few adult books and more than twenty for kids. Published hundreds of articles in everything from medical journals to ski magazines, newspapers to national and regional magazines.

EDUCATION: MA ESL, San Francisco University, CA. MS Education and Remedial Reading, City University of New York. BA, University of Vermont, Burlington. **MEMBERSHIPS:** PEN. League of Vermont Writers. Society of Children's Book Writers and Illustrators.

CLIENTS WITHIN PRIOR YEAR: 6–10.

390	EDITOR	WRITER	CONSULTANT	F	NF

Older, Jules. Older Unlimited. 1769 Broadway, #2, San Francisco, CA 94109. P1/ 415-775-3334. jules@julesolder.com. Established: 1986.

Skills: freelance editor, independent book editor, book doctor, copyeditor or line editor, proofreader, ghostwriter, business writer or copywriter, literary consultant, writing coach, writing instructor. **Markets served:** speakers, writers, publishers, nonprofits, corporations.

Specialties and preferences: has written and edited for many markets in many genres. Doesn't do poetry, religion, or technical writing.

Fiction—accepts: y/a or juvenile, short stories, novels (genre, mainstream, literary, contemporary, historical), picture books, scripts/screenplays, queries. **Nonfiction—accepts:** all. **Typical evaluation/report:** 2–6 pages.

Fees/terms/contracts: $75+/hour.

Accomplishments: has written a few adult books and more than twenty for kids. Published hundreds of articles in everything from medical journals to ski magazines, newspapers to national and regional magazines.

Education: PhD Clinical Psychology, New York University, NY. BA, University of Vermont, Burlington. **Memberships:** PEN. North American Snowsports Journalists Association. Travel Journalists Guild. League of Vermont Writers.

Clients within prior year: 6–10.

391	EDITOR	WRITER	CONSULTANT	F	NF

Oliver, Bob. Oliver & Company. 203 Kingsley Way, Woodstock, GA 30188. P1/ 770-360-7200. F1/ 770-360-7273. bob@oliverco.net. www.oliverco.net. www.AcademicEdits.com. Established: 1968.

Skills: freelance editor, independent book editor, book doctor, copyeditor or line editor, proofreader, ghostwriter, business writer, technical writer, literary consultant, mentor to several young writers. **Markets served:** corporate, nonprofit, first-time authors.

Specialties and preferences: specializing in speeches, white papers, case studies, marketing communications, marketing strategy, and program formulation/ execution. Edits and rewrites book-length manuscripts. Assists clients in locating publishers, negotiating book contracts.

Fiction—accepts: novels (genre), scripts/screenplays, synopses/treatments, queries. **Nonfiction—accepts:** articles/features, self-help, how-to, business, inspirational/religious, book proposals, queries.

Fees/terms/contracts: fee based on project, or $1,000/day. Uses agreement.

Accomplishments: first firm in Southeastern US dedicated to corporate presentations and communications. First ghostwriter for the late Earl Nightingale in Chicago 1963-1968. Syndicated radio broadcaster and founder Nightingale-Conant Corporation, the world's largest publisher of non-entertainment books and recordings. Our firm also names products and services. See website www.executivebranding.com.

Education: coursework, Emory University, Atlanta, GA.

CLIENTS WITHIN PRIOR YEAR: 6–10.

392	EDITOR	WRITER	CONSULTANT	F	NF

Opper, Susanna. Shawenon Communications. Alford, MA. P1/ 413-528-6494. Susanna@shawenon.com. www.shawenon.com. Established: 2003.

SKILLS: ghostwriter, technical writer, website copy, content. **MARKETS SERVED:** small business, corporations, entrepreneurs, consultants.

SPECIALTIES AND PREFERENCES: I specialize in translating technology and complex business processes into compelling, easy-to-understand messages. Because I have an extensive background in technology, I prefer writing for websites and web-based publications. But I also write white papers, articles, newsletters, and marketing communications.

NONFICTION—ACCEPTS: all.

FEES/TERMS/CONTRACTS: $80–$125/hour. No credit cards. Typically uses agreement.

ACCOMPLISHMENTS: one commercially published book. Four chapters in commercially published books. Dozens of articles in business publications. Two white papers.

EDUCATION: MBA Stern School of Business, New York University, NY. BA Philosophy with honors, magna cum laude, Phi Beta Kappa, Brown University, Providence, RI.

CLIENTS WITHIN PRIOR YEAR: 15–20.

393	EDITOR	WRITER	CONSULTANT	F	NF

Osa, Nancy. Writer in Residence. Portland, OR. P1/ 503-637-3497. Editorisin@aol.com. Established: 1993.

SKILLS: freelance editor, independent book editor, book doctor, copyeditor or line editor, proofreader, ghostwriter, business writer or copywriter, literary consultant, writing coach, writing instructor. **MARKETS SERVED:** authors, publishers, self-publishers, entrepreneurs, design agencies, institutions, new writers.

SPECIALTIES AND PREFERENCES: custom writing and editing services for authors, publishers, and scholars. Thoughtful evaluation and editing of works in progress or complete drafts. Comprehensive introduction to the publishing world for new writers. Clear, imaginative promotional and business writing from an award-winning author. My language expertise plus your project equal success!

FICTION—ACCEPTS: all. **NONFICTION—ACCEPTS:** all. **TYPICAL EVALUATION/REPORT:** customized.

FEES/TERMS/CONTRACTS: Please call or e-mail for payment terms.

ACCOMPLISHMENTS: award-winning young adult novel; short stories and articles in national publications; numerous speaking engagements, grants, fellowships, and artist's residencies.

EDUCATION: BA English Literature, Reed College, Portland, OR. MEMBERSHIPS: Society of Children's Book Writers and Illustrators (national and regional). ACME Writers.

CLIENTS WITHIN PRIOR YEAR: 25–50.

394	EDITOR	WRITER	CONSULTANT	F	NF

Osborn, Susan Titus. Christian Communicator. 3133 Puente St., Fullerto, CA 92835. P1/ 714-990-1532. P2/ 877-428-7992. F1/ 714-990-0310. Susanosb@aol.com. www.christiancommunicator.com. Established: 1978.

SKILLS: freelance editor, independent book editor, book doctor, copyeditor or line editor, proofreader, ghostwriter, freelance writer, business writer or copywriter, literary consultant, writing coach, writing instructor. MARKETS SERVED: Christian writers seeking to polish their skills.

SPECIALTIES AND PREFERENCES: book proposals containing cover letter, chapter synopsis, and three sample chapters; entire nonfiction book and novel manuscripts; children's picture books, early readers, and juvenile fiction.

FICTION—ACCEPTS: y/a or juvenile, short stories, novels (genre, mainstream, literary, contemporary, historical), poetry, scripts/screenplays, queries, synopses, treatments. NONFICTION—ACCEPTS: all. TYPICAL EVALUATION/REPORT: We do a line-by-line edit and a one-page overall evaluation.

FEES/TERMS/CONTRACTS: $115/book proposal; $25/hour for additional editing.

ACCOMPLISHMENTS: Our customers have won Christy Awards in the Christian market and Benjamin Franklin and Parenting Media Awards in the secular market.

EDUCATION: MA Communications, California State University, Fullerton. BA Religious Studies, California State University, Fullerton. MEMBERSHIPS: Christian Leaders and Speakers Services. Advanced Christian Writers and Speakers. American Christian Writers. Orange County Christian Writers Association.

CLIENTS WITHIN PRIOR YEAR: 60+.

395	EDITOR	WRITER	CONSULTANT	F	NF

Owens, Lisa. Owens Editorial Ink. Seattle, WA. lisa@owenseditorialink.com. lisa@llowens.com. www.llowens.com. Established: 1993.

SKILLS: freelance editor, copyeditor or line editor, proofreader, ghostwriter, copywriter, writing coach, writing instructor, children's book and curriculum writer, book reviewer, developmental editor, editorial consultant. MARKETS SERVED: children's book trade book and educational publishers. Magazines, newsletters, websites, nonprofit organizations, corporations, writers.

SPECIALTIES AND PREFERENCES: writes children's books, K–12 curriculum, web content, newsletter, reference articles, book reviews. Edits books, curriculum, scripts, and CD-ROMs for all age levels and in many genres. Teaches writing and editing classes.

FICTION—ACCEPTS: y/a or juvenile. NONFICTION—ACCEPTS: y/a or juvenile.

FEES/TERMS/CONTRACTS: editing $5–$10+/page, or $30–$100/hour. Writing 50 cents, $5+/word, or advance against royalties. Typically uses contract.

ACCOMPLISHMENTS: edited thousands of works for publication, including books, curriculum materials, ads, catalogs, public relations kits, scripts, articles. Written forty-plus books for children and young adults, hundreds of supplemental education materials, and dozens of book reviews and articles for regional and national publications.

EDUCATION: BS Journalism, University of Iowa, Iowa City. MEMBERSHIPS: The Authors Guild. Editorial Freelancers Association. Society of Children's Book Writers and Illustrators.

CLIENTS WITHIN PRIOR YEAR: 6–10.

396	EDITOR	WRITER	CONSULTANT	F	NF

Palmatier, Carol. Four Points Editing, LLP. Bokeelia, FL 33922. P1/ 239-283-5903. info@fourpointsediting.com. www.fourpointsediting.com. Established: 2003.

SKILLS: freelance editor, independent book editor, copyeditor or line editor, proofreader, business writer or copywriter, technical writer. MARKETS SERVED: businesses and nonprofits.

SPECIALTIES AND PREFERENCES: complete editorial services. Online content management, travel and destination content. Our experienced management team works with a global team of freelance writers and editors to provide high quality, flexible, and cost-effective content solutions.

NONFICTION—ACCEPTS: technical, text or reference, business, humor, queries.

FEES/TERMS/CONTRACTS: priced per job.

ACCOMPLISHMENTS: growing client list includes African-American Cultural Association; *Dining Out* magazine; Elizabeth Haydon, author of *Rhapsody* trilogy; Gargani + Company; Habitat for Humanity of Livingston County; Hometown Newspapers; Lee County Foundation; LMP Consulting & Artistic Management; Randall Funding & Development; Thomson Directories, UK.

EDUCATION: BA Public Education, College of Saint Rose, Albany, NY.

CLIENTS WITHIN PRIOR YEAR: 6–10.

397	EDITOR	WRITER	CONSULTANT	F	NF

Parkinson, Janet. JMP Editing. 11 Park St., Newport, RI 02840. P1/ 401-847-5040. jmp_edit@earthlink.net. Established: 1997.

SKILLS: freelance editor, copyeditor and line editor, proofreader. **MARKETS SERVED:** academic publishing, educational publishing, nonprofits.

SPECIALTIES AND PREFERENCES: precise, versatile editor. I specialize in academic and educational publishing, primarily the humanities and social sciences, as well as reports, newsletters, and marketing materials. Will edit on paper or electronically, depending on the client's preference.

NONFICTION—ACCEPTS: articles/features, text or reference, business.

FEES/TERMS/CONTRACTS: generally per-project rates. $25–$45/hour. Payment due within 30 days of invoice receipt. No credit cards.

EDUCATION: BA Medieval and Renaissance Studies (honors), Vassar College, Poughkeepsie, NY. **MEMBERSHIPS:** Editorial Freelancers Association. Jamestown (RI) Chamber of Commerce.

CLIENTS WITHIN PRIOR YEAR: 11–20.

398	EDITOR	WRITER	CONSULTANT	F	NF

Parks, Electa. Novel Ideal Publishing & Editorial Services Co. 2274 Salem Rd., PMB 173, Conyers, GA 30013. P1/ 770-620-9398. F1/ 770-787-7610. electaparks@yahoo.com. Established: 2003.

SKILLS: freelance editor, independent book editor, copyeditor or line editor, proofreader, literary consultant. **MARKETS SERVED:** self-published authors, independent authors, and aspiring writers.

SPECIALTIES AND PREFERENCES: I am a freelance editor and novelist. I specialize in content and copyediting of contemporary fiction, nonfiction, and romance novels/manuscripts.

FICTION—ACCEPTS: y/a or juvenile, novels (mainstream, contemporary), poetry, scripts/screenplays, queries, synopses, treatments. **NONFICTION—ACCEPTS:** self-help.

FEES/TERMS/CONTRACTS: requires 50 percent up front and the remaining 50 percent upon completion of the project. Accepts checks, money orders, and PayPal. Does not use a contract.

ACCOMPLISHMENTS: upon request, references will be provided. Self-published, well-reviewed writer of contemporary fiction.

EDUCATION: BBA Marketing, State University of West Georgia, Carrollton.

CLIENTS WITHIN PRIOR YEAR: 6–10.

399	EDITOR	WRITER	CONSULTANT	F	NF

Patterson, Jill. Inkwell Literary Services. PO Box 841, Ridgway, CO 81432.
P1/ 806-438-2385. F1/ 806-742-0989. inkwellliterary@mac.com.
www.homepage.mac.com/inkwellliterary. Established: 2001.

Skills: freelance editor, copyeditor or line editor, proofreader, literary consultant, writing coach, typesetter. **Markets served:** professional writers; student writers; small presses.

Specialties and preferences: prefers to work with students in university writing programs and regional writers who have a hard time getting noticed. Provides editorial feedback, offers suggestions for publication. Offers critique services for university presses and typesetting/proofreading for small publishers and literary journals. Hosts a summer conference.

Fiction—accepts: all. **Nonfiction—accepts:** essays, memoirs, creative or narrative, business, book proposals. **Typical evaluation/report:** 3 single-spaced pages.

Fees/terms/contracts: Critiques from $37 for short manuscripts to $225 for manuscripts up to 300 pages. Extensive proofreading/corrections, add 50 cents/page. Typesetting $1.50/manuscript typeset page. Proofreading $1.50/ manuscript page. $2/typeset page. See website for additional services and fees, including artwork. Accepts checks, money orders, or PayPal. Uses a contract.

Accomplishments: recipient of eight awards, author of over twenty publications and eight poems. College professor; fundraiser; director of summer writing workshops; typesetter.

Education: PhD Creative Writing, Oklahoma State University, Norman. **Memberships:** Associated Writing Programs. Texas Association of Creative Writing Teachers. Conference of College Teachers of English.

Clients within prior year: 11–20.

400	EDITOR	WRITER	CONSULTANT	F	NF

Patterson, William B. 6711 Country Swan, San Antonio, TX 78240.
P1/ 210-391-7991. P2/ 210-885-7991. scouterbillpatterson@hotmail.com.
Established: 2001.

Skills: freelance editor, proofreader. **Markets served:** school book publishers, technical writers, transcribers.

Specialties and preferences: I have many years of experience in editing and proofing newsletters and technical papers. I am sensitive to an author's feelings while making suggested improvements. I enjoy smoothing out awkward sentence structures, rewriting to eliminate redundancies, and maintaining continuity of voice and style.

Nonfiction—accepts: y/a or juvenile, articles/features, essays, memoirs, creative or narrative, biography/autobiography, family history, self-help, how-to/instruction, technical, text or reference, business, humor, inspirational/religious, spiritual, book proposals, queries.

Fees/terms/contracts: $20+/hour. Long works or repeat business, negotiable. Quote will be given before work begins.

Accomplishments: publications, awards, client successes. Editor, monthly newsletter of The Society of Photographers in Industry.

Education: BA Communications, Sam Houston University, Huntsville, Texas. Post-graduate coursework in English, San Antonio College, Texas. Academic requirements completed for Alternative Teacher Certification, San Antonio, Texas.

Clients within prior year: 1–5.

401	EDITOR	WRITER	CONSULTANT	F	NF

Payne, Lesley. 2203 E. Dinuba Ave., Fresno, CA 93725. P1/ 559-834-4295. lesleykp@direcway.com. Established: 1980.

Skills: freelance editor, book doctor, literary consultant, writing coach, writing instructor, line editor. **Markets served:** fiction writers aspiring and established.

Specialties and preferences: My greatest skill as an editor is supporting depth and effectiveness of characterization, particularly protagonists, and the essential relationship between characterization and plot. I like almost all kinds of fiction but have special enthusiasm for fiction with a feminist, metaphysical or spiritual element.

Fiction—accepts: y/a or juvenile, short stories, novels (genre, mainstream, literary, contemporary, historical), queries, synopses. **Typical evaluation/ report:** 15–25 pages.

Fees/terms/contracts: $50/hour; half estimated fee to begin work, balance upon completion. Accepts payment by check. No contract required.

Accomplishments: lead author, award-winning and notable listed clients in romance and spiritual thriller genres.

Education: BA English, summa cum laude and with College Honors, California State University, Fresno. Postgraduate work in education, English literature, and creative writing at Stanford and California State University, Fresno.

Clients within prior year: 20–25.

402	EDITOR	WRITER	CONSULTANT	F	NF

Perets, Abbi. DearAbbi.com. 12648 Martha St., Valley Village, CA 91607. P1/ 818-508-9505. abbi@perets.net. www.dearabbi.com. Established: 1999.

Skills: ghostwriter, business writer or copywriter, technical writer, freelance writer, writing coach, writing instructor. **Markets served:** corporate clients, national magazines, writing students.

SPECIALTIES AND PREFERENCES: I'm a freelance writer with a decade of professional experience and national credits. One of my greatest strengths is ghost-writing technical material, including nonfiction book proposals. I make even heavily technical content accessible—and appealing—to the masses. I teach "Successful Freelance Writing," and I love working one-on-one with my students as they venture out into the freelance world.

NONFICTION—ACCEPTS: articles/features, essays, memoirs, creative or narrative, biography/autobiography, self-help, how-to/instruction, technical, text or reference, business, book proposals, queries.

FEES/TERMS/CONTRACTS: 30–50 percent up front, depending on size of project.

ACCOMPLISHMENTS: two published books.

EDUCATION: course study in theater at Brandeis University, Waltham, MA.

CLIENTS WITHIN PRIOR YEAR: 11–15.

403	EDITOR	WRITER	CONSULTANT	F	NF

Perkins-Cooper, Barbie. Creative Communications. 641 Palmetto St., Mt. Pleasant, SC 29464. P1/ 843-884-7631. C1/ 843-437-2492. F1/ 843-881-6801. barbiepc@bellsouth.net. www.writergazette.com/barbiepc. Established: 1985.

SKILLS: freelance editor, proofreader, ghostwriter, business writer or copywriter, technical writer, writing instructor. **MARKETS SERVED:** construction, technical, trade, business, beauty, health.

SPECIALTIES AND PREFERENCES: public relations, magazine, newspaper, technical, business writing, screenwriting, technical scripts, public service announcements, business documents, brochures, proofread technical documents, resume writing.

FICTION—ACCEPTS: short stories, novels, poetry, scripts/screenplays, queries, synopses, treatments. **NONFICTION—ACCEPTS:** all.

FEES/TERMS/CONTRACTS: negotiable. Usually $25–$35/hour. No credit cards or PayPal.

ACCOMPLISHMENTS: professional writer since 1984, with experience in public relations, documentation (including DoD documents), magazine, newspaper, technical, business writing, and screenwriting. Author of numerous articles for regional construction publication; author of seven screenplays; three full-length plays.

EDUCATION: English major, Charleston Southern University, SC. Broadcasting and Film Production, Trident Technical College. **MEMBERSHIPS:** South Carolina Writers Workshop. South Carolina Scriptwriters Association. Southeastern Writers Association. Dramatists Guild. The National Writers Association.

CLIENTS WITHIN PRIOR YEAR: 6–10.

404	EDITOR	WRITER	CONSULTANT	F	NF

Petrillo, Alan. Excalibur Publications. PO Box 89667, Tucson, AZ 85752-9667. P1/ 520-575-9057. excalibureditor@earthlink.net. Established: 1982.

SKILLS: freelance editor, independent book editor, line editor, ghostwriter, freelance writer, business writer or copy writer. **MARKETS SERVED:** authors.

SPECIALTIES AND PREFERENCES: I offer writers help in getting manuscripts ready to submit to publishers, editors, and agents. I show writers how to say what they mean—clearly, precisely, and directly—while retaining their voice and tone. I do both content editing that focuses on the big picture issues in a work and specialized line editing where necessary.

FICTION—ACCEPTS: y/a or juvenile, short stories, novels, scripts/screenplays, queries, synopses, treatments. **NONFICTION—ACCEPTS:** y/a or juvenile, articles/features, essays, memoirs, biography, self-help, humor, book proposals, queries. **TYPICAL EVALUATION/REPORT:** 2–4 pages. Content and line editing with written evaluation; read-through with evaluation.

FEES/TERMS/CONTRACTS: $5/double-spaced, typed page. Retainer; final payment after acceptance of work. Uses contract.

ACCOMPLISHMENTS: traditionally published mystery novel. Published hundreds of articles in national, regional, and local magazines. Edited magazines and newspapers; wire service reporter.

EDUCATION: BA English, Siena College, Loudonville, NY. **MEMBERSHIPS:** Director at large, Society of Southwestern Authors. Director, Wrangling With Writing Conference, Tucson.

CLIENTS WITHIN PRIOR YEAR: 60+.

405	EDITOR	WRITER	CONSULTANT	F	NF

Petroff, Natasha. Editorial Services. 15924 88th St. SE, Snohomish, WA 98290. P1/ 360-563-0123. F1/ 425-876-4481. npetroff@nwlink.com. Established: 2000.

SKILLS: freelance editor, copyeditor or line editor, proofreader, business writer or copywriter, technical writer. **MARKETS SERVED:** high tech, social services, health care, education, and other industries.

SPECIALTIES AND PREFERENCES: I write and edit marketing and general content for print and digital media. Content is non-technical and light technical in nature. Reduced rates for nonprofits related to social, educational, and environmental causes.

NONFICTION—ACCEPTS: articles/features, autobiography, how-to/instruction, technical, text or reference, business, humor.

FEES/TERMS/CONTRACTS: charges within the (mid) market range. Invoices twice monthly, requiring payment within 15 days. No credit cards or PayPal. Uses a contract.

ACCOMPLISHMENTS: I have worked on diverse projects, for a wide range of companies and organizations—Microsoft, InfoSpace, the American Cancer Society, Central Washington University, others. I offer unmatched versatility and high standards, creativity, innovation, and an adventurous approach to work and life. MEMBERSHIPS: Northwest Independent Editors Guild. Freelance Seattle.

EDUCATION: BA Literature and Writing, Minor in Cultural Anthropology, University of California, San Diego.

CLIENTS WITHIN PRIOR YEAR: 5–10.

406	EDITOR	WRITER	CONSULTANT	F	NF

Piazza, Nancy. Writeperson, Ltd. PO Box 293, Novelty, OH 44072. P1/ 440-338-8687. editor@writeperson.com. www.writeperson.com. Established: 1999.

SKILLS: freelance editor, independent book editor, copyeditor or line editor, proofreader, writers' conference coordinator. MARKETS SERVED: writers, authors, publishers, nonprofits, and corporations.

SPECIALTIES AND PREFERENCES: Writeperson, Ltd., edits both aspiring and published writers and business clients. I offer free initial consultations and sample edits of writers' work. I edit grammar, punctuation, and offer suggestions and improvements in ink. I respect writers' manuscripts and do high-quality editing at reasonable rates.

FICTION—ACCEPTS: short stories, novels, picture books, poetry, queries, and synopses. NONFICTION—ACCEPTS: all.

FEES/TERMS/CONTRACTS: $27/hour. No credit cards. Uses agreement.

ACCOMPLISHMENTS: Western Reserve Writers' Conference Coordinator since 2001, voted among top 100 writers' conferences in US. Won first place national and regional awards for editing, 1997. Inducted into American Federation Editors' Hall of Fame, 1999. Editor since 1989. Numerous published pieces.

EDUCATION: AAB Computer Programming, Lakeland College, Kirtland, OH. MEMBERSHIPS: Writers of the Western Reserve. Poets' and Writers' League of Greater Cleveland.

CLIENTS WITHIN PRIOR YEAR: 6–10.

407	EDITOR	WRITER	CONSULTANT	F	NF

Pierce, Marian. Portland, OR. P1/ 503-284-0259. marian.pierce@juno.com. Established: 1999.

SKILLS: freelance editor, independent book editor, book doctor, copyeditor or line editor, proofreader, writing coach, writing instructor. MARKETS SERVED: scientists and physicians, graduate students, academics, fiction and nonfiction writers.

SPECIALTIES AND PREFERENCES: edits scientific, medical papers for publication. Edits academic papers, theses, reports, dissertations. Experienced in editing for foreigners writing in English. Comprehensive critiques for fiction. Assists applicants in preparing portfolio for MFA applications.

FICTION—ACCEPTS: short stories, novels (genre, mainstream, literary, contemporary, historical). **NONFICTION—ACCEPTS:** essays, memoirs, creative or narrative, biography /autobiography, family history, self-help, how-to/instruction, technical, text or reference. **TYPICAL EVALUATION/REPORT:** 3–10 pages.

FEES/TERMS/CONTRACTS: fiction $40/hour; editing science/academic papers $25–$45/hour.

ACCOMPLISHMENTS: seven published short stories, major fellowship, first place in fiction contest, excellence in teaching award, *Who's Who in American Women.*

EDUCATION: MFA Fiction, University of Iowa, Iowa City. Fiction, Iowa Writers' Workshop. BA English Literature, University of Iowa, Iowa City. **MEMBERSHIPS:** Willamette Writers.

CLIENTS WITHIN PRIOR YEAR: 31–40.

408	EDITOR	**WRITER**	CONSULTANT	F	**NF**

Piggins, Kathleen Bowen. 762 Wilderness Dr., Saugatuck, MI 49453. P1/ 269-857-3038. jkpiggys3@aol.com. www.kpiggins.com. Established: 1991.

SKILLS: business writer or copywriter. **MARKETS SERVED:** health and dental businesses, nonprofit organizations, regional publications, newspapers.

SPECIALTIES AND PREFERENCES: I specialize in article creation and placement for several organizations. I have a column on parenting teens/preteens and another on general issues related to parenting. I am lead correspondent for a local newspaper and a frequent contributor to regional/national publications.

NONFICTION—ACCEPTS: articles/features, essays, memoirs, creative or narrative, family history, business, humor, queries.

FEES/TERMS/CONTRACTS: The hourly rate varies depending on the size and scope of the project from $60–$155/hour. On a project-by-project basis; charges hourly rates for retainer clients and per-project fee for others. Uses a contract.

ACCOMPLISHMENTS: published in *Women's Lifestyle Magazine, The Local Observer, Our Children, Splash, Metro Parent, The Grand Rapids Press, Lifetime Magazine,* many more. Recipient of the American Legion's Heart of Michigan Award, 2003. Ad sales for TV stations, newspapers; communications director; marketing and development director.

EDUCATION: ongoing writing training in various seminars and classes. BA Communications/Journalism, Michigan State University, East Lansing.

CLIENTS WITHIN PRIOR YEAR: 6–10.

409	EDITOR	WRITER	CONSULTANT	F	NF

Pinckard, Mara. Canyon View Indexing. PO Box 1107, Seligman, AZ 86337. P1/ 928-699-9087. F1/ 928-223-0063. canyonviewindexing@starband.net. Established: 2000.

SKILLS: proofreader, indexer. MARKETS SERVED: publishers, editors.

SPECIALTIES AND PREFERENCES: I proofread and write thorough and appropriate indexes for books and journals, based on *The Chicago Manual of Style* standards and variations requested. I specialize in scholarly subjects— library science/info tech, sciences, and medicine.

NONFICTION—ACCEPTS: self-help, text or reference.

FEES/TERMS/CONTRACTS: per-page rate. Invoices/30 days for payment. Uses contract.

ACCOMPLISHMENTS: science reference librarian for twenty-five years; an administrator in an academic special library. Knowledge and terminology in all the sciences, engineering, nursing and medicine, library and information science. Competence in PC environment, including dedicated indexing software.

EDUCATION: Master of Library Science, University of Arizona, Tucson. Courses in indexing, abstracting. Graduate courses, Microbiology, University of Hawaii, Honolulu. BS Microbiology, University of New Hampshire, Durham. MEMBERSHIPS: American Society of Indexers. Arizona Chapter of American Society of Indexers.

CLIENTS WITHIN PRIOR YEAR: 1–5.

410	EDITOR	WRITER	CONSULTANT	F	NF

Plantier, Paula. EditAmerica. 115 Jacobs Creek Rd., Ewing, NJ 08628. P1/ 609-882-5852. editamerica@usa.com. www.editamerica.com. Established: 1979.

SKILLS: freelance editor, independent book editor, copyeditor or line editor, proofreader, business writer or copywriter, writing instructor. Also read, write, edit in French and Spanish. MARKETS SERVED: business consultants, advertising, communications, engineering, Fortune 500, graphics, pharmaceuticals, nonprofits, publishers, start-ups, universities, writers.

SPECIALTIES AND PREFERENCES: current clients are large firms that use my editorial services to publish corporate communications, public relations pieces, company newsletters, annual reports, press releases. Other clients are small graphics houses producing material for large companies.

FICTION—ACCEPTS: y/a or juvenile, picture books, short stories, novels (genre, mainstream, literary, contemporary, historical), poetry, scripts/screenplays, queries, synopses, treatments. NONFICTION—ACCEPTS: all.

FEES/TERMS/CONTRACTS: client dictates whether hourly, per page, or contract. Fees vary.

ACCOMPLISHMENTS: expertly edited and proofed more than 250,000 pages of copy.

EDUCATION: BA French/Spanish, Queens College of the City University of New York, Flushing.

CLIENTS WITHIN PRIOR YEAR: 11–20.

411	EDITOR	WRITER	CONSULTANT	F	NF

Pohle, Linda. The Marketing Department. Denver, CO. P1/ 303-755-5249. F1/ 303-745-6266. lpwords@aol.com. Established: 1987.

SKILLS: freelance editor, copyeditor or line editor, proofreader, business writer or copywriter, technical writer. MARKETS SERVED: financial, telecommunications, environmental, nonprofits.

SPECIALTIES AND PREFERENCES: taking complex, difficult business, company, outdoor/environmental information and turning it into readable stories that engage readers and prospects in brochures, websites, and articles. Easy to work with, efficient, budget-minded. Excellent interviewer. Seeking only a few quality-minded new clients.

NONFICTION—ACCEPTS: articles/features, creative or narrative, how-to/instruction, technical, text or reference, business.

FEES/TERMS/CONTRACTS: $100/hour. Up front fee negotiable with new clients. Payments net 30 days. No credit cards or PayPal.

ACCOMPLISHMENTS: hundreds of brochures; dozens of articles in regional and national consumer/trade magazines. Commendations from clients for work quality. Denver Woman's Press Club writing awards. Projects have moved sales to millions of dollars.

EDUCATION: MA English Literature, University of Denver, CO. BA English Literature, Knox College, Galesburg, IL. MEMBERSHIPS: Denver Woman's Press Club. Volunteer Naturalist, Castlewood Canyon State Park.

CLIENTS WITHIN PRIOR YEAR: 6–10.

412	EDITOR	WRITER	CONSULTANT	F	NF

Powers, Hilary. Editorial Services. Oakland, CA. P1/ 510-834-1066. hilary@powersedit.com. Established: 1994.

SKILLS: freelance editor, independent book editor, copyeditor or line editor. MARKETS SERVED: publishers, nonprofit organizations, writers.

SPECIALTIES AND PREFERENCES: My motto: "The edit you want—when you want it done, online, on time, and on target." Services range from light copyediting through developmental work, always based on what the client requests. Especially enjoy sci-fi and fantasy, but may edit other genres. New to electronic editing? Let me show you how easy it can be for publisher or author!

FICTION—ACCEPTS: novels (genre). **NONFICTION—ACCEPTS:** articles/features, creative or narrative, self-help, how-to/instruction, technical, business, humor.

FEES/TERMS/CONTRACTS: fees/250-word page, negotiated. PayPal available. Uses agreement.

ACCOMPLISHMENTS: more than 350 successful editing projects completed. Search www.editorsforum.org for my name to see my approach to editing.

EDUCATION: BA Journalism, Stanford University, Palo Alto, CA. **MEMBERSHIPS:** Editorial Freelancers Association. Bay Area Editors' Forum. Editors Guild (SF Bay Area). Bookbuilders West (publishers and supporting trades from western US).

CLIENTS WITHIN PRIOR YEAR: 6–10.

413	EDITOR	WRITER	CONSULTANT	F	NF

Priestman, Sarah. 3417A S. Stafford St., Arlington, VA 22206. P1/ 703-933-3804. spriestman@aol.com. Established: 1995.

SKILLS: freelance editor, independent book editor, ghostwriter, business writer or copywriter, literary consultant, writing coach, writing instructor, research, book proposals. Marketing direct mail, creative copy, branding. Publications production and project management. **MARKETS SERVED:** health, business, social services, personal growth, education.

SPECIALTIES AND PREFERENCES: I bring extensive experience in holistic health and can easily convey the messages of healing and personal growth in a way that anyone will understand. I can also turn dry research in any subject into an interesting story.

FICTION—ACCEPTS: all. **NONFICTION—ACCEPTS:** all.

FEES/TERMS/CONTRACTS: depends on project.

ACCOMPLISHMENTS: literary publications, residencies and awards. Nominated for the Pushcart Prize. Writer-in-residence awards from Cummington Colony for the Arts, MA, and The Virginia Center for Creative Arts, Sweet Briar. DC Commission on the Arts/National Endowment on the Arts Award for Literary Excellence.

EDUCATION: MFA Creative Writing, American University, Washington, DC.

CLIENTS WITHIN PRIOR YEAR: 10–15.

414	EDITOR	WRITER	CONSULTANT	F	NF

Prow, Cameron. Type-Rite II. Bend, OR. P1/ 541-388-4495. typerit2@uci.net. Established: 1981.

SKILLS: freelance editor, copyeditor or line editor, business writer, technical writer, communications consultant, writing workshop leader. **MARKETS SERVED:** writers, publishers, nonprofits, corporations, governmental agencies, general public.

SPECIALTIES AND PREFERENCES: technical writer of minutes, résumés, correspondence, reports, newsletters, membership directories, employee manuals, business plans. Strengths—conceptual understanding of client needs, interviewing, problem solving.

FICTION—ACCEPTS: y/a or juvenile, picture books, short stories, novels (genre, mainstream, literary, contemporary, historical), poetry, scripts/screenplays, queries, synopses, treatments. **NONFICTION—ACCEPTS:** all. **TYPICAL EVALUATION/ REPORT:** 1–5 pages.

FEES/TERMS/CONTRACTS: manuscript editing/writing $35–$40/hour. Technical writing $45/hour. 50 percent deposit required. Cash or check only. No credit cards. Uses agreement.

ACCOMPLISHMENTS: twenty-four poems and three short stories published in anthologies. Thirteen editorials published in daily newspaper and newsletters. Thirty years of writing for clients with college degrees.

EDUCATION: twenty workshops in creative and technical writing. College—one term creative writing, two terms technical writing. **MEMBERSHIPS:** Farewell Bend Writers Roundtable. Oregon State Poetry Association. PoetsWest. Friends of the Bend Library.

CLIENTS WITHIN PRIOR YEAR: 1–5.

415	EDITOR	WRITER	CONSULTANT	F	NF

Ptacek, Kathryn. PO Box 97, Newton, NJ 07860. P1/ 973-579-1537. gilaqueen@att.net. katptacek@yahoo.com. Established: 2000, but editor/ writer for over twenty years.

SKILLS: freelance editor, independent book editor, book doctor, copyeditor or line editor, proofreader, literary consultant, writing coach. **MARKETS SERVED:** typically individual writers new to their field, although I've worked on multiple books of one novelist.

SPECIALTIES AND PREFERENCES: all kinds of books (nonfiction and fiction) or short stories/articles and all different genres within fiction, but my specialties are horror, science fiction, fantasy, romance, and mystery/suspense.

FICTION—ACCEPTS: all. **NONFICTION—ACCEPTS:** all. **TYPICAL EVALUATION/REPORT:** 8–11 pages.

FEES/TERMS/CONTRACTS: sliding scale based on the number of pages in a manuscript; the fee also depends on the level of editing the client seeks. Accepts PayPal. Uses e-mail confirmation for contract. **ACCOMPLISHMENTS:** eighteen novels published with major houses in New York; three anthologies I've edited (major houses); close to 200 articles/short stories/essays, reviews, columns, etc., for magazines and newsletters. I also edit the monthly newsletter for the Horror Writers Association, and for the past fifteen years, I have edited a market newsletter for writers and artists, *The Gila Queen's Guide to Markets* (www.gilaqueen.us/).

EDUCATION: BA Journalism, University of New Mexico, Albuquerque. **MEMBERSHIPS:** Horror Writers Association.

CLIENTS WITHIN PRIOR YEAR: not available.

416	EDITOR	WRITER	CONSULTANT	F	NF

Raham, R. Biostration. PO Box 399, Wellington, CO 80549-0399. P1/ 970-568-3557. GRahamBios@aol.com. www.biostration.com. Established: full-time since 1997; part-time since 1975.

SKILLS: freelance editor, independent book editor, book doctor, copyeditor or line editor, proofreader, ghostwriter, business writer or copywriter, technical writer, literary consultant, writing coach, writing instructor, writer, illustrator, graphic designer. **MARKETS SERVED:** children's books and magazines, adult science fiction magazines and newspapers, educational publishing, textbook illustration, and graphic design.

SPECIALTIES AND PREFERENCES: writes and illustrates science books and articles for students and teachers. Designs book interiors and covers. Available for author/illustrator visits and teacher workshops in nature journaling and Earth science.

FICTION—ACCEPTS: all. **NONFICTION—ACCEPTS:** all.

FEES/TERMS/CONTRACTS: $60/hour. Check within 30 days. May require deposit.

ACCOMPLISHMENTS: written and illustrated five books, numerous articles for national magazines, and many nature columns and articles for a regional newspaper. Won awards for nonfiction articles, books, video scripts, and short stories.

EDUCATION: MS, BS Biology, University of Michigan, Ann Arbor. Postgraduate work at Colorado State University. **MEMBERSHIPS:** Society of Children's Book Writers and Illustrators. Science Fiction Writers of America. Guild of Natural Science Illustrators. National Science Teachers Association. Colorado Author's League.

CLIENTS WITHIN PRIOR YEAR: 11–20.

417	EDITOR	WRITER	CONSULTANT	F	NF

Raintree, Elizabeth. Raintree Lee & Associates (State Certified). Portland, OR. P1/ 503-224-9479. eraintree@raintreelee.com. Established: 1999.

SKILLS: freelance editor, independent book editor, copyeditor or line editor, technical editor, literary consultant, substantive editor. **MARKETS SERVED:** government agencies, nonprofits, academic, English-as-a-second-language, and first-time writers.

Specialties and preferences: editing. Informational writing for government, nonprofits. Keen interests in women's issues, civil rights, alternative medicine, drama, audio drama, film.

Fiction—accepts: scripts/screenplays, queries, synopses, treatments. **Non-fiction—accepts:** articles/features, essays, memoirs, creative or narrative, biography/autobiography, family history, self-help, how-to/instruction, text or reference, spiritual, book proposals, queries. **Typical evaluation/report:** if requested. Length varies.

Fees/terms/contracts: $35–$50/hour. No credit cards. Typically uses agreement.

Accomplishments: former college/university professor in US and UK. Award-winning academic, creative publications. Advocacy journalism, government testimony. Editorial consulting for academic, business, governmental, journalistic writing, fiction, screenwriting. Founded Raintree Lee & Associates Consortium.

Education: PhD English, University of Pennsylvania, Philadelphia. MA Creative Writing, Antioch University International, London, UK. **Memberships:** Northwest Independent Editors Guild. National Writers Union. **Clients within prior year:** 1–5 (including two large contracts).

418	EDITOR	WRITER	CONSULTANT	F	NF

Ralston, Carolyn. Write Away. 2418 7th Ave., Sacramento, CA 95818. P1/ 916-456-8575. CarolynR@macnexus.org. Established: 1991.

Skills: freelance editor, copyeditor or line editor, proofreader, ghostwriter, business writer or copywriter, writing coach, publicist. **Markets served:** government, nonprofits, individuals.

Specialties and preferences: developmental and line editing of governmental reports, academic projects, and business writing. I specialize in developmental editing, in which I consider emphasis, clarity, coherence, organization, diction, tone, and audience. I also write original documents and do line editing.

Nonfiction—accepts: articles/features, essays, memoirs, creative or narrative, biography/autobiography, family history, self-help, how-to/instruction, technical, text or reference, business, inspirational/religious, spiritual.

Fees/terms/contracts: $45/hour or negotiated job fee.

Accomplishments: editing—numerous governmental reports published. Writing—artist profiles, journal article, book chapter, and op-ed published. I started by working freelance for a small public relations firm that moved from this area five years ago. I did other small jobs for schools, individuals, and nonprofits. Five years ago, the California Bureau of State Audits hired me as a contract editor.

EDUCATION: MA English, Tulane University, New Orleans, LA. BA English, Midwestern University, Wichita Falls, TX.
CLIENTS WITHIN PRIOR YEAR: 1–5.

419	EDITOR	WRITER	CONSULTANT	F	NF

Reece, Deborah. Vallejo, CA. P1/ 707-645-8572. djreece@mail.com. Established: 1996.

SKILLS: freelance editor, independent book editor, copyeditor or line editor, proofreader, ghostwriter, business writer or copywriter, writing coach, book designer. MARKETS SERVED: scholarly and trade publishers, authors, businesses, political candidates and organizations, nonprofits, churches, news media.

SPECIALTIES AND PREFERENCES: editing scholarly books (economics and public policy); working with authors for whom English is second language.

FICTION—ACCEPTS: all. NONFICTION—ACCEPTS: all. TYPICAL EVALUATION/REPORT: 2–5 pages.

FEES/TERMS/CONTRACTS: fees—flat fee or hourly rate. Coaching authors $45/hour, copyediting $28/hour, proofreading $20/hour, writing $60+/hour, design $60+/hour. Terms—with publishers, bills upon completion; with author or other organization, one-third up front, one-third at completion of rough draft or initial evaluation, and one-third upon completion. Can accept credit cards through PayPal. Uses agreement.

ACCOMPLISHMENTS: Highest Academic Achievement in Journalism and Outstanding News-Editorial Graduate at Liberty University (1992). National Merit Finalist (1988). Articles published in international, national, and local publications. Edited and produced dozens of scholarly and trade books, executive summaries, and newsletters.

EDUCATION: BS Journalism, AA Religion, Liberty University, Lynchburg, VA.
CLIENTS WITHIN PRIOR YEAR: 6–10.

420	EDITOR	WRITER	CONSULTANT	F	NF

Relles, Helaine R. PO Box 231463, Ansonia Station, New York, NY 10023. P1/ 212-715-1950. P2/ 908-352-5984. hrrelles@aol.com. Established: 1990.

SKILLS: freelance editor, ghostwriter, freelance—legal, medical, pharmaceutical, scientific, psychology, general academic and political commentary, research. MARKETS SERVED: authors of medical, pharmaceutical, psychological, and other scientific topics, academics, attorneys, political individuals and organizations.

SPECIALTIES AND PREFERENCES: If you want it researched, digested, clarified, and the subject matter is legal, medical, scientific, political, or academic, you've come to the right source. Besides editing the social sciences, literary, and financial/business papers, I render abstruse and often complex content more readable. Improved substantively on first drafts for various academic and journal publications.

NONFICTION—ACCEPTS: all.

FEES/TERMS/CONTRACTS: depends if it is a repeat customer and how many referrals or contacts I potentially will have as a result of the work. Money orders or certified checks. No credit cards. No contract.

ACCOMPLISHMENTS: published book on vocal technique. Published opinion-editorial newspaper pieces.

EDUCATION: PhD candidate Clinical Psychology, New York University, NY. BA Psychology, Kean University, Union, NJ. BM Manhattan School of Music, NY.

CLIENTS WITHIN PRIOR YEAR: 6–10.

421	EDITOR	WRITER	CONSULTANT	F	NF

Reynolds, Marjorie. Writers' Doctor. 6706 127th Pl. SE, Bellevue, WA 98006. P1/ 425-603-9787. ezwrtr@earthlink.net. Established: 2002, but writing for publication for twenty years.

SKILLS: independent book editor, book doctor, copyeditor or line editor, proofreader, business writer or copywriter, literary consultant, writing coach, writing instructor, story consultant. **MARKETS SERVED:** individual writers.

SPECIALTIES AND PREFERENCES: story consulting, editing, and teaching.

FICTION—ACCEPTS: y/a or juvenile, short stories, novels (genre, mainstream, literary, contemporary), queries, synopses. **NONFICTION—ACCEPTS:** y/a or juvenile, articles/features, memoirs, creative or narrative, biography/ autobiography, family history, book proposals, queries. **TYPICAL EVALUATION/ REPORT:** 10–15 pages, up to five hours of phone consultation, and continued assistance with manuscript.

FEES/TERMS/CONTRACTS: $5 per 1,000 words or as negotiated; written agreement; payment by check (half in advance, half upon delivery of manuscript to author).

ACCOMPLISHMENTS: author of *The Civil Wars of Jonah Moran* and *The Starlite Drive-in*, a recipient of a Barnes & Noble Discover Great New Writers Award and one of the American Library Association's Top Ten Best Books of 1998 for Young Adults, sold to seven foreign countries. Workshop on the craft of fiction now available on DVD.

EDUCATION: BA Journalism, Indiana University, Bloomington. **MEMBERSHIPS:** Pacific Northwest Writers Association. Oregon Writers Colony.

CLIENTS WITHIN PRIOR YEAR: 10–15.

422	EDITOR	WRITER	CONSULTANT	F	NF

Reynolds, Mary. 905 E. Second St., Austin, TX 78702-4212. P1/ 512-477-2175. mareynolds@ev1.net. Established: 2002.

SKILLS: independent book editor, copyeditor or line editor, proofreader, technical writer. MARKETS SERVED: telecommunications, software and computer companies, small and large companies, individuals.

SPECIALTIES AND PREFERENCES: specialty in technical writing and editing. Also offers freelance writing and editing of nontechnical books and written material, such as flyers, brochures, and websites.

NONFICTION—ACCEPTS: articles/features, memoirs, creative or narrative, technical.

FEES/TERMS/CONTRACTS: vary. May do a sample of the work, invoice, check with client, then complete work and invoice. No credit cards. Verbal contracts okay.

ACCOMPLISHMENTS: edited manuals for Dell Computer, Vignette Corporation, Nortel Networks, and others. Also edited a self-published memoir. Former copyeditor at a daily newspaper in Oklahoma. Technical writer/editor since 1997, former copyeditor at a daily; graphic artist, proofreader, librarian.

EDUCATION: Technical Writing Certificate, Richland College, Dallas, TX. MS Urban Planning, University of Texas, Austin. BA Social Work, University of Oklahoma, Norman. MEMBERSHIPS: Freelance Austin.

CLIENTS WITHIN PRIOR YEAR: 6–10.

423	EDITOR	WRITER	CONSULTANT	F	NF

Richerson, Sheri. ExoticGardening.com. P1/ 765-664-6916. F1/ 765-664-6916. SheriAnnRicherson@exoticgardening.com. www.exoticgardening.com. Established: 1981.

SKILLS: freelance editor, proofreader, photographer, speaker, and freelance writer. MARKETS SERVED: individuals, businesses, magazine and book publishers, web-based e-zines.

SPECIALTIES AND PREFERENCES: writing and editing for periodicals. Sheri Richerson has over twenty years of experience in newspaper, magazine, and creative writing, including an eclectic mix of articles on current events, herbs, aromatherapy, tropical and exotic plants, as well as various pieces on Harley-Davidson motorcycles.

NONFICTION—ACCEPTS: articles/features, technical, text or reference, business.

FEES/TERMS/CONTRACTS: Fees vary with specific job; I'm flexible due to client locations, publication times, etc. Accepts PayPal, check, money order, or cash. No contracts.

ACCOMPLISHMENTS: published freelancer and editor in over thirty magazines, newspapers, and e-zines. Subjects include gardening, herbs, pets, health, consumer interest, product reviews, and lifestyles. Sheri has a well-deserved reputation for delivering quality work, on time and on budget. She is a hard-working, bright, very motivated self-starter, but she also works comfortably in team environments. She is also a Master Gardener.

EDUCATION: writing workshops, Ball State University, Muncie, IN. **MEMBERSHIPS:** many horticulture associations, clubs, and societies. Association of America Investigative Reporters and Editors. Garden Writers Association.

CLIENTS WITHIN PRIOR YEAR: 11–20.

424	EDITOR	WRITER	CONSULTANT	F	NF

Rigler, Laurie. Pasadena, CA. P1/ 626-799-7230. F1/ 626-799-7564. laviera@earthlink.net. www.publishersmarketplace.com/members/ LaurieViera. www.laurievierarigler.com. Established: 1989.

SKILLS: book doctor, freelance editor, copyeditor or line editor, ghostwriter, literary consultant, writing coach, writing instructor, business writer or copywriter. **MARKETS SERVED:** authors, design studios, manufacturing industry, nonprofit organizations.

SPECIALTIES AND PREFERENCES: in-depth analysis. Masterful editing. Confidence building. Dedicated attention to substance, style, and structure. Coaching that inspires. Translating complexities into accessible language. Techniques that touch and transform your readers. Proposals that persuade. Writing that sings. Sharp, innovative copywriting.

FICTION—ACCEPTS: short stories, novels (mainstream, literary, contemporary, historical), synopses. **NONFICTION—ACCEPTS:** all. **TYPICAL EVALUATION/REPORT:** Fiction, 20–50 pages; nonfiction 5–9 pages.

FEES/TERMS/CONTRACTS: editing $4+/page or $50/hour, depending on assignment. Crash-course Critique $125 up front. Writing by project varies, by hour $50–$75, consulting/coaching $50/hour. Half up front, half on delivery, or incremental billing.

ACCOMPLISHMENTS: two published nonfiction books; one novel in progress. Many clients' nonfiction books sold to major houses. Screenwriter; producer of films shown at Cannes, aired on *Showtime*. Contributed to *The Big Book of Life's Instructions*, and a reference book.

EDUCATION: BA Classical Civilization, *summa cum laude*, State University of New York, Buffalo. **MEMBERSHIPS:** Editorial Freelancers Association. Authors Guild.

CLIENTS WITHIN PRIOR YEAR: 31–40.

425	EDITOR	WRITER	CONSULTANT	F	NF

Rigney, Melanie. Editor for You. 4201 Wilson Blvd., #110328, Arlington, VA 22203-1859. P1/ 571-235-1743. info@editorforyou.com. www.editorforyou.com. www.melanierigney.com. Established: 2004.

SKILLS: freelance editor, independent book editor, book doctor, copyeditor or line editor, literary consultant, writing coach, writing instructor. MARKETS SERVED: writers, publishers, nonfiction book authors (biography, self-help, how-to) with a special emphasis on those planning to self-publish.

SPECIALTIES AND PREFERENCES: content through copyediting. Nonfiction, especially how-to, self-help, and memoir. Evaluation of fiction and nonfiction. I help writers maintain their unique voice while helping their work sing.

FICTION—ACCEPTS: all. NONFICTION—ACCEPTS: biography/autobiography, how-to/instruction, business. TYPICAL EVALUATION/REPORT: 3–5 pages.

FEES/TERMS/CONTRACTS: copyediting 1 cent/word; evaluation/content editing varies by project but always set in advance. 50 percent up front with contract, 50 percent upon completion. Contract, checks, PayPal.

ACCOMPLISHMENTS: more than twenty-five years of publishing experience, including five years as editor of *Writer's Digest* magazine and acquisition experience at WD, Macmillan Computer Publishing, and Thomson Financial Publishing. Clients include Tufts University, AMG International, and Xulon Press.

EDUCATION: BA, majors in journalism, French, and political science, South Dakota State University, Brookings.

CLIENTS WITHIN PRIOR YEAR: 20–25.

426	EDITOR	WRITER	CONSULTANT	F	NF

Rimel, Linda. Eugene, OR. P1/ 541-431-1196. F1/ 541-431-1196. rhymeswithprimal@juno.com. www.webspawner.com/users/collateral/. www.webspawner.com/users/qualityediting/. www.webspawner.com/users/rimel/. Established: 1979.

SKILLS: freelance editor, independent book editor, copyeditor or line editor, writing coach, book publicity writer. MARKETS SERVED: book publishers, authors.

SPECIALTIES AND PREFERENCES: I know the correct formats for scripts, legal writing, how-to materials, newspapers, magazines, and books. I have experience writing such collateral materials as press releases, fact sheets, author profiles, and cover letters. I tutor writing and English as a Second Language (ESL), train employees, and edit business writing, legal briefs, creative writing, and technical writing.

FICTION—ACCEPTS: y/a or juvenile, poetry, scripts/screenplays, queries, synopses, treatments. NONFICTION—ACCEPTS: all.

FEES/TERMS/CONTRACTS: Flat rate. Requires payment in advance by check or money order, in full or incrementally. No credit cards. Does not use a contract.

ACCOMPLISHMENTS: Listed in *Who's Who in America*. I have taught writing to university students and professionals. I have written a quilting book, theatrical program notes, features, reviews, humor, and book and lyrics for musical theater.

Education: Studied law, Willamette University, Salem, OR. BA General Humanities, University of Oregon, Eugene.

Clients within prior year: 6–10.

427	EDITOR	WRITER	CONSULTANT	F	NF

Roberson, France. Frances L Roberson MA—Communications Consultant. Fair Oaks, CA. P1/ 916-965-0314. F1/ 916-965-0314. flroberson3@hotmail.com. flroberson1@sbcglobal.net. www.flroberson.com. Established: 2000.

Skills: freelance editor, copyeditor and line editor, proofreader, business writer or copywriter, technical writer, literary consultant, writing coach, writing instructor, publicity. **Markets served:** university foundations, nonprofits, educational organizations.

Specialties and preferences: prefers writing educational materials, newsletters, grants, brochures, features; editing, and coaching adult groups.

Fiction—accepts: y/a or juvenile, picture books, short stories, novels (genre, mainstream, literary, contemporary, historical), poetry. **Nonfiction—accepts:** y/a or juvenile, articles/features, essays, memoirs, creative or narrative, biography/autobiography, family history, self-help, how-to/instruction, technical, text or reference, business, humor, inspirational/religious, spiritual.

Fees/terms/contracts: $50–$90/hour. PayPal. Typically uses contract.

Accomplishments: short story award. National feature article award. Ten GED workbooks. Two teacher's manuals. Published feature article. Newsletter development, writing, editing. Brochures. Edited all thirty-nine workbooks in GED series.

Education: MA Education, Career Development Certification, California State University, Sacramento. BA Journalism/English, New Mexico Highlands University, Las Vegas.

Clients within prior year: 1–5.

428	EDITOR	WRITER	CONSULTANT	F	NF

Roberts, Hilary. 962 Euclid Ave., Berkeley, CA 94708-1436. P1/ 510-525-7673. worddoc101@earthlink.net. hilroberts@earthlink.net. Established: 1974.

Skills: freelance editor; book, article, and script doctor/writer; ghostwriter, business writer; website and speech editor/writer; literary consultant; writing coach; dissertation, thesis, and essay tutor. **Markets served:** individual writers, businesspeople, students, publishers. Agents and producers refer clients to me.

Specialties and preferences: I help all writers say what they mean and do it well. I've studied screenplay structure, narrative theory, and literary style. I have a strong specialty in college admissions essays.

FICTION—ACCEPTS: poetry, scripts/screenplays, queries, synopses, treatments. **NONFICTION—ACCEPTS:** all. **TYPICAL EVALUATION/REPORT:** 2–10 pages, plus plenty of marginalia, consultation as requested.

FEES/TERMS/CONTRACTS: $48/hour and up. Terms by verbal agreement.

ACCOMPLISHMENTS: I have thirty years of experience, long-term clients, versatility—you write it; I improve it. I work fast.

EDUCATION: PhD English and Linguistics, BA English, University of California, Berkeley. MA English Language and Literature, University of Michigan, Ann Arbor. **MEMBERSHIPS:** Phi Beta Kappa.

CLIENTS WITHIN PRIOR YEAR: 15–20.

429	EDITOR	WRITER	CONSULTANT	F	NF

Roberts, Sherry. The Roberts Group. 1530 Thomas Lake Pointe Rd., #119, Eagan, MN 55122. P1/ 651-330-1457, F1/ 651-330-0892. sherry@editorialservice.com. www.editorialservice.com. Established: 1990.

SKILLS: freelance editor, independent book editor, copyeditor or line editor, proofreader, business writer or copywriter, literary consultant, writing instructor, book designer, newsletter designer, brochure designer. **MARKETS SERVED:** publishers, writers, businesses, nonprofits.

SPECIALTIES AND PREFERENCES: We are a one-stop resource for publishers and self-publishers, providing professional book production services since 1990. Our services include writing, editing, proofreading, interior book design, typesetting and layout, cover design, and indexing. We also provide web design and development.

FICTION—ACCEPTS: y/a or juvenile. **NONFICTION—ACCEPTS:** y/a or juvenile, articles/features, essays, memoirs, narrative nonfiction, biography/ autobiography, family history, self-help, how-to/instruction, technical, text or reference, business, humor, inspirational/religious, spiritual, book proposals, queries.

FEES/TERMS/CONTRACTS: accepts credit cards and online payments. Uses agreement letter.

ACCOMPLISHMENTS: one novel, numerous short stories, articles, and essays published in national media, successful websites developed.

EDUCATION: BJ Journalism, University of Missouri Journalism School, Columbia. **MEMBERSHIPS:** Publishers Marketing Association. Small Publishers Association of North America. Twin Cities Professional Editors Network.

CLIENTS WITHIN PRIOR YEAR: 20–30.

430	EDITOR	WRITER	CONSULTANT	F	NF

Robinson, Arlene. Winder, GA. P1/ 678-425-2456. C1/ 404-395-2389. BettyBoopWrites@aol.com. Established: 1996.

SKILLS: freelance editor, copyeditor or line editor, proofreader, ghostwriter, business writer or copywriter, literary consultant, developmental, web pages, book jacket text. **MARKETS SERVED:** writers, publishers, businesses, nonprofits, educators.

SPECIALTIES AND PREFERENCES: offers full range of services to both new and multiply published writers. Enjoys helping journalistic, business, academic, and ESL writers transform their writings for mainstream readers. Informal critique with all editing projects, plus marked and "clean" copies. Works from tapes/hard copy (for additional fee). Free sample edit on accepted manuscripts.

FICTION—ACCEPTS: y/a or juvenile, novels (genre, mainstream, contemporary), queries, synopses, treatments. **NONFICTION—ACCEPTS:** all. **TYPICAL EVALUATION/REPORT:** 2–5 pages.

FEES/TERMS/CONTRACTS: editing averages 2–4 cents/word. All others—per project flat fee, or minimum $300 retainer. Accepts PayPal, credit cards, money orders, checks. Uses agreement.

ACCOMPLISHMENTS: one nonfiction self-published book, several articles.

EDUCATION: some college. **MEMBERSHIPS:** Georgia Freelance Writer's Association. Professional editing network (www.book-editing.com).

CLIENTS WITHIN PRIOR YEAR: 50–55.

431	EDITOR	WRITER	CONSULTANT	F	NF

Roddick, Hawley. PO Box 3794, Santa Barbara, CA 93130. P1/ 805-682-6366. HRoddick@writeassets.com. www.writeassets.com. Established: 1984.

SKILLS: freelance editor, independent book editor, book doctor, copyeditor or line editor, ghostwriter, business writer or copy writer, literary consultant, writing coach. **MARKETS SERVED:** individuals and businesses.

SPECIALTIES AND PREFERENCES: I edit nonfiction books; provide development and editing of book proposals. Many distinguished corporate clients have learned from my workshops how to think clearly and write effectively in business. I offer coaching in this field. Three of my books were initiated by publishers. I welcome publishers with ideas for books.

NONFICTION—ACCEPTS: articles/features, how-to/instruction, business, book proposals. **TYPICAL EVALUATION/REPORT:** 3 pages.

FEES/TERMS/CONTRACTS: small projects $55–$80/hour. Large project fees vary according to scope. Evaluation of nonfiction $2/page. Editing $20/page. Small writing projects $50–$80/page. One-third total up front, one-third halfway, one-third at end. No credit cards. Uses letter of agreement.

Accomplishments: See website for client list. Author of seven books. Articles or columns have been published in *Top7Business* and *PR Fuel* (online), *Stanford Magazine Centennial Issue, Sunburst Communications, Cosmopolitan,* and many others. **Education:** BA English Literature, Wellesley College, MA. **Memberships:** Authors Guild.
Clients within prior year: 1–5.

432	EDITOR	WRITER	CONSULTANT	F	NF

Rojany-Buccieri, Lisa. Editorial Services of Los Angeles. 1543 Sycamore Canyon Dr., Westlake Village, CA 91361. P1/ 818-707-1042. C1/ 310-488-1248. F1/ 818-707-1042. esola@adelphia.net. www.absolutewrite.com/novels/lisa_rojany. htm. www.publishersmarketplace.com/members/lbuccieri/. Established: 1988

Skills: freelance editor, independent book editor, book doctor, copyeditor or line editor, proofreader, ghostwriter, business writer or copywriter, technical writer, literary consultant, writing coach, writing instructor. **Markets served:** writers, publishers, corporations.
Specialties and preferences: I have helped hundreds of writers get published by making their work the best it can be—a job I really enjoy.
Fiction—accepts: y/a or juvenile, picture books, short stories, novels (mainstream, literary, historical), queries, synopses. **Nonfiction—accepts:** all. **Typical evaluation/report:** 2–10 pages, depending on length, plus comments on hard copy.
Fees/terms/contracts: $150/hour, discounts to SCBWI and Author's Guild members, need-based clients. After estimate approved, up front payment. Two-week turnaround.
Accomplishments: experienced editor and author of over 35 children's books, y/a novels, a *New York Times* Business Bestseller, 100+ ghosted titles. Many awards won.
Education: MA English and American Literature, Brown University, Providence, RI. BA Communication Studies, UCLA, CA. **Memberships:** Society of Children's Book Writers and Illustrators.
Clients within prior year: 50–55.

433	EDITOR	WRITER	CONSULTANT	F	NF

Romanchik, Dan. 1325 Orkney Dr., Ann Arbor, MI 48103.
dan@danromanchik.com. www.danromanchik.com. Established: 1992.

Skills: freelance editor, ghostwriter, business writer or copywriter, technical writer, writing coach, writing instructor, website copy. **Markets served:** high-tech companies, ghostwriting articles for trade magazines, and working with professionals.

SPECIALTIES AND PREFERENCES: I specialize in writing about technology, including electronics, software, the Internet, and automotive topics. I also have an interesting talent of turning literally translated documents into readable English.

NONFICTION—ACCEPTS: articles/features, essays, memoirs, creative or narrative, biography/autobiography, family history, self-help, how-to/instruction, technical, text or reference, business.

FEES/TERMS/CONTRACTS: fees quoted on a per-project basis. Invoices on completion of project.

ACCOMPLISHMENTS: contributing editor for several different engineering trade magazines. Ghostwriter for several high-tech companies.

EDUCATION: BS Electrical Engineering, University of Detroit, MI. MEMBERSHIPS: Institute of Electrical and Electronic Engineers. Society of Automotive Engineers. Automotive Press Association.

CLIENTS WITHIN PRIOR YEAR: 6–10.

434	EDITOR	WRITER	CONSULTANT	F	NF

Rose, Sarah. New York, NY. P1/ 212-472-2475. F1/ 212-472-2475. sarahmrose@earthlink.net. Established: not available.

SKILLS: freelance editor, independent book editor, book doctor, copyeditor or line editor, proofreader, ghostwriter, technical writer, writing coach. MARKETS SERVED: politics, radio, magazines, newspaper, speechmakers, academia.

SPECIALTIES AND PREFERENCES: For the past two years, I have been focused on writing my first commercial nonfiction book for Random House. I am eager to get back to editing.

NONFICTION—ACCEPTS: articles/features, essays, memoirs, creative or narrative, biography/autobiography, text or reference, business, book proposals, queries.

FEES/TERMS/CONTRACTS: uses rates listed by the Editorial Freelancers Association.

ACCOMPLISHMENTS: John T. Lupton "New Voices in Literature" Award, Finalist Nonfiction, 2003. New York Foundation for the Arts, Arts Recovery Fund Grant Recipient, 2001. Many published articles in newspapers and magazines. Former political ghostwriter for radio, newspapers, and speeches. Worked as an editor at Time Inc. Asia, as an assistant to the *Boston Globe*, *The Sunday Telegraph*, and as a correspondent for *Outlook Magazine*. Former journalist with Reuters; editor/producer of NYC political staff. Nonfiction book forthcoming with Random House.

EDUCATION: MA Humanities, Philosophy, University of Chicago, IL. BA English Literature, Harvard University, Cambridge. MEMBERSHIPS: Authors Guild.

CLIENTS WITHIN PRIOR YEAR: 1–5.

435	EDITOR	WRITER	CONSULTANT	F	NF

Rosen, Diana. Los Angeles, CA. P1/ 323-857-0183. coachforwriters@aol.com. www.dianarosen.com. www.dianarosen.com. Established: 1989.

SKILLS: freelance editor, book doctor, ghostwriter, business writer or copywriter, literary consultant, writing coach, writing instructor. **MARKETS SERVED:** people who want to improve their business writing; students who want to develop essay writing skills, and people who want to add depth to short fiction or poetry.

SPECIALTIES AND PREFERENCES: interested in motivated, diligent clients eager to challenge themselves and the idea of what it means to be a writer. I critique with specificity, offer compassion and humor, but I'm not your mommy, so be prepared to work.

FICTION—ACCEPTS: short stories, poetry. **NONFICTION—ACCEPTS:** articles/features, essays, memoirs, creative or narrative, family history, self-help, how-to/ instruction, business, humor, book proposals, queries. **TYPICAL EVALUATION/ REPORT:** 10–20 pages.

FEES/TERMS/CONTRACTS: hourly or project rates, to be negotiated. Uses agreement.

ACCOMPLISHMENTS: I have been either a staff writer or a published freelance writer for magazines, newspapers, and advertising my entire life, and have written thirteen nonfiction books. Since 1993, I have worked as a workshop facilitator and now as a writing coach helping a primarily business-centered audience prepare books and articles for publication to use as promotional tools.

EDUCATION: BS Journalism, Arizona State University, Tempe. **MEMBERSHIPS:** Authors Guild.

CLIENTS WITHIN PRIOR YEAR: 5–8.

436	EDITOR	WRITER	CONSULTANT	F	NF

Ruff, Miriam. Bumbershoot, Inc. PO Box 12252, Silver Spring, MD 20908. P1/ 301-871-4860. F1/ 240-363-0052. msruff@juno.com. bbshoot1@netzero.com. Established: 2000.

SKILLS: freelance editor, independent book editor, book doctor, copyeditor or line editor, proofreader, ghostwriter, business writer or copywriter, technical writer, literary consultant, writing coach, writing instructor, test set developer; educational curriculum developer. **MARKETS SERVED:** educational agencies; companies looking for writing/editing of technical/informational documents; agencies requiring newsletters; independently offer screenplay writing/review and poetry.

SPECIALTIES AND PREFERENCES: a full-service writing and editing company. Specializes in educational/informational/technical writing and editing, particularly in biological sciences. Handles testing materials, PR materials, general articles, screenplays, poetry.

FICTION—ACCEPTS: all. NONFICTION—ACCEPTS: all.

FEES/TERMS/CONTRACTS: $30–$50/hour, per complexity and deadline, or work per contract.

ACCOMPLISHMENTS: author of many instructional/educational books and software. Awarded second place, 1984 Honeywell Futurist Awards Competition. International *Who's Who of Professional Management*. Poetry in journals, anthologies, on websites.

EDUCATION: BS Zoology with High Honors, University of Maryland, College Park. Some graduate school (cell biology), Columbia University, NY. MEMBERSHIPS: inactive memberships—Washington Independent Writers. Wisconsin Screenwriter's Forum.

CLIENTS WITHIN PRIOR YEAR: 1–5.

437	EDITOR	WRITER	CONSULTANT	F	NF

Ruhl, Jordis. Yellow Springs, OH. P1/ 937-767-8775. C1/ 937-684-7748. jordisruhl@att.net. Established: 1999, writing and editing since 1988.

SKILLS: freelance editor, copyeditor or line editor, proofreader, ghostwriter, business writer. MARKETS SERVED: health care, education, foundations, and other nonprofits. For-profits.

SPECIALTIES AND PREFERENCES: communications of all types, including brochures, annual reports, feature articles, ads, direct mail, web content, speeches, scripts, ghostwriting. One-person shop; will only take clients that are bright and interesting.

NONFICTION—ACCEPTS: articles/features, business.

FEES/TERMS/CONTRACTS: nonprofit $70/hour. For-profit $80/hour. Will also work on a per-project basis. Half up front. No contract.

ACCOMPLISHMENTS: twenty years of public relations and communications experience. Multiple first-place awards for advertising campaign, annual reports, magazines, newsletters. Silver Anvil, Public Relations Society of America, highest national award. My clients couldn't be happier.

EDUCATION: no degree. Some college, majoring in biology and math. Apprenticed to an owner of a public relations agency, and learned the communications business through experience.

CLIENTS WITHIN PRIOR YEAR: 6–10.

438	EDITOR	WRITER	CONSULTANT	F	NF

Rusch, Elizabeth. 2757 NW Raleigh St., Portland, OR 97210. P1/ 503-827-4817. lrusch@usa.net; author@generationfix.com. www.generationfix.com. Established: 1996.

SKILLS: freelance editor, ghostwriter, literary consultant, writing coach, writing instructor, communications consultant. MARKETS SERVED: individual writers;

book, magazine, newspaper, newsletter, and website publishers; nonprofits, foundations, policy makers.

SPECIALTIES AND PREFERENCES: capturing a writer's, speaker's, or subject's true voice.

FICTION—ACCEPTS: all. NONFICTION—ACCEPTS: all. TYPICAL EVALUATION/REPORT: 3–10 pages.

FEES/TERMS/CONTRACTS: editing $40–$80/hour or negotiated per project; ghost-writing $1–$3/word, $40–$80/hour, or negotiated per project. Pay by check only. Contract available.

ACCOMPLISHMENTS: over a 100 articles published in, among others, *Harper's*, *Mother Jones*, *Child*, *Parents*, *Beliefnet.com*, *The Oregonian*, *Denver Post*. Awards from Literary Arts, International Reading Association, Education Writers Association, and others. Authored *Generation Fix*, a Smithsonian magazine Best Book of the Year. As a US Senate Fellow, I ghostwrote speeches and press materials for Senator Edward M. Kennedy. Editor-in-Chief of Pointsbeyond.com, Managing Editor of *Teacher Magazine*, Contributing Editor to *Child* magazine and *Fit Pregnancy*.

EDUCATION: Master's in Public Policy, University of California at Berkeley. BA Economics, Duke University, Durham, North Carolina. MEMBERSHIPS: Willamette Writers. Society of Children's Book Writers and Illustrators.

CLIENTS WITHIN PRIOR YEAR: 1–4.

439	EDITOR	WRITER	CONSULTANT	F	NF

Ryan, Ben. Gamble Bay Publishing Services. PO Box 245, Port Gamble, WA 98364-0245. P1/ 360-297-8071. F1/ 360-297-8071. gamblebay@fastmail.us. Established: 2003.

SKILLS: freelance editor, project management (multiple-author works, corporate assignments); market research; desktop publishing/composition; website content; CD-ROM compilation and preflight; software documentation; indexing. MARKETS SERVED: publishers and corporations, often in the high-tech industry; schools; individuals.

SPECIALTIES AND PREFERENCES: technology-to-English translations. Others listed above.

FICTION—ACCEPTS: y/a or juvenile. NONFICTION—ACCEPTS: y/a or juvenile, articles/features, essays, memoirs, creative or narrative, how-to/instruction, technical, text or reference, business, book proposals. TYPICAL EVALUATION/REPORT: 5–10 pages for nonfiction; longer for fiction.

FEES/TERMS/CONTRACTS: Fee varies—hourly basis, per page basis, or on a project basis. Invoices established businesses. No credit cards. For individuals, negotiates payments or payments in kind. Uses a contract.

ACCOMPLISHMENTS: more than eight years of experience in acquisitions (over

200 books) for major publishers. Former positions as publisher's sales rep., bookstore buyer, others.

EDUCATION: BA American Studies, Lake Forest College, IL. Graduate work in Public Affairs, University of Oregon, Eugene. Archaeology, Hebrew Union College, Jerusalem. **MEMBERSHIPS:** NW Independent Editors Guild. Society for Technical Communication.

CLIENTS WITHIN PRIOR YEAR: 6–10.

440	EDITOR	WRITER	CONSULTANT	F	NF

Salat, Cristina. Kulana, The Affordable Artist Sanctuary. PO Box 190, Volcano, HI 96785. P1/ 808-985-9055. sharkdolphintunes@yahoo.com (checked sporadically). www.panpolynesia.net/kulana. Established: 1980s. Please note: due to Internet idiosyncrasies in Hawaii, best way to reach me is via regular mail/phone.

SKILLS: freelance editor, independent book editor, developmental editor, ghost-writer, literary consultant; manuscript/publishing/contract consultant. **MARKETS SERVED:** book publishers, magazines, newspapers, small presses, organizations, and emerging and established authors nationwide.

SPECIALTIES AND PREFERENCES: editor-of-color. Enjoys multicultural (African American/Asian American/Latino/Native American or other indigenous cultures/Hawaiian/etc.) and socially impactful (spiritual, ethical, sexual-affectional preferenced) themes. Works with all genres, fiction and nonfiction, schedule permitting.

FICTION—ACCEPTS: all. **NONFICTION—ACCEPTS:** all.

FEES/TERMS/CONTRACTS: developmental editing, 1–10 double-spaced pages $150 + $100 for an overall assessment and industry update report as it pertains to the work. 20 percent "second pass" discount for projects already reviewed. Consultations $100/hr. No credit cards.

ACCOMPLISHMENTS: Publishers I've worked with include Bantam, HarperCollins, Prentice Hall, Children's Television Workshop, etc., along with smaller presses like Two Bears Press, Sidewalk Revolution Press, Eighth Mountain Press, etc.

EDUCATION: BA Writing; editorial skills learned on the job for publishers East and West.

CLIENTS WITHIN PRIOR YEAR: Some years many manuscripts cross my desk from publishers and individuals; other years I'm making independent films or writing my own books.

441	EDITOR	WRITER	CONSULTANT	F	NF

Sargent, Carole. A Word in Time. Washington, DC. P1/ 703-683-1800. F1/ 703-548-3620. carole@awordintime.com. www.awordintime.com. Established: 1998.

SKILLS: freelance editor, independent book editor, ghostwriter, literary consultant, writing coach, book proposals, media consultant. MARKETS SERVED: top law partners, national journalists, politicians, senior academics.

SPECIALTIES AND PREFERENCES: highly selective. Works with previously published writers who have superb backgrounds and professional seniority or the equivalent in academic achievement.

FICTION—ACCEPTS: short stories, novels (literary, contemporary, historical). NONFICTION—ACCEPTS: essays, memoirs, creative or narrative, biography/autobiography. TYPICAL EVALUATION/REPORT: 2–5 pages.

FEES/TERMS/CONTRACTS: $150/hour plus percentage on sale. Uses agreement.

ACCOMPLISHMENTS: two nonfiction books, three works of fiction, numerous features, and national media coverage. Georgetown University professor, media commentator.

EDUCATION: PhD, MA English Literature, University of Virginia, Charlottesville. MEMBERSHIPS: National Press Club. Authors Guild. Bibliographical Society of the University of Virginia. American Society for Eighteenth Century Studies. CLIENTS WITHIN PRIOR YEAR: 25–30.

442	EDITOR	WRITER	CONSULTANT	F	NF

Sawyer, Carol. 260 Louisiana Ave., Vernonia, OR 97064. P1/ 503-429-4748. csawyer@easystreet.com. Established: 2001.

SKILLS: freelance editor, copyeditor or line editor, book doctor, proofreader, ghostwriter, writing instructor, translator of English, Spanish, French—any direction. MARKETS SERVED: writers, academic and nonprofit organizations.

SPECIALTIES AND PREFERENCES: years of academic writing. World traveled, multicultural, multilingual translator. Expertise in psychology/self-help, spirituality/world religions, symbol systems. Movieola translation for synch.

FICTION—ACCEPTS: poetry. NONFICTION—ACCEPTS: articles/features, essays, memoirs, creative or narrative, biography/autobiography, family history, self-help, how-to/instruction, inspirational/religious, spiritual.

FEES/TERMS/CONTRACTS: long documents 25 cents/word. Short $20/page. Terms/contract to be negotiated.

ACCOMPLISHMENTS: poetry regularly published. Honorable Mention Maui Writers' Poetry.

EDUCATION: PhD candidate Consciousness and Transformation, California Institute of Integral Studies, San Francisco. BA Psychology, New College,

San Francisco. **MEMBERSHIPS:** Teachers and Writers Collaborative. Willamette Writers. World Future Society. National Writers Union. **CLIENTS WITHIN PRIOR YEAR:** 1-5.

443	EDITOR	WRITER	CONSULTANT	F	NF

Scholfield, Diane. 3533 Sea Ridge Rd., Oceanside, CA 92054. P1/ 760-433-3225. C1/ 760-415-9099. F1/ 760-433-1123. diane@websitemaid.com. www.websitemaid.com. Established: 1985.

SKILLS: freelance editor, independent book editor, book doctor, proofreader, ghostwriter, business writer or copywriter, website editor and designer. **MARKETS SERVED:** book publishers, authors, newspapers, magazines, and websites.

SPECIALTIES AND PREFERENCES: editing, writing, proofreading. Travel, tourism, sports.

NONFICTION—ACCEPTS: y/a or juvenile, articles/features, biography/autobiography, self-help, how-to/instruction, business. **TYPICAL EVALUATION/REPORT:** 2–10 pages.

FEES/TERMS/CONTRACTS: proofing $2/page. Editing $5–$7/page. Rewriting and fact checking $7–$10/page. Typically uses written agreement.

ACCOMPLISHMENTS: lead editor and fact checker of travel guide for seven years. Editor of two large websites. More than 300 articles published in newspapers and magazines. Have been editing and writing for more than twenty years.

EDUCATION: BA Print Journalism, University of Southern California, Los Angeles.

CLIENTS WITHIN PRIOR YEAR: 4–5.

444	EDITOR	WRITER	CONSULTANT	F	NF

Schoolfield, Stacy. Innerstace Productions, Inc. 4102 Rosedale Ave., Austin, TX 78756. P1/ 512-302-4430. F1/ 512-302-4430. stacys@innerstace.com. www.innerstace.com. Established: 1998.

SKILLS: freelance editor, book editor, copyeditor or line editor, business writing or copywriting. **MARKETS SERVED:** textbook or trade publishers, magazines/ publications, small businesses, nonprofits.

SPECIALTIES AND PREFERENCES: provides services for book, screen, or web, including writing, editing, and production. Specializes in concise, engaging text and ability to meet deadlines.

FICTION—ACCEPTS: scripts/screenplays. **NONFICTION—ACCEPTS:** articles/features, creative or narrative, self-help, how-to/instruction, technical, text or reference, business, book proposals. **TYPICAL EVALUATION/REPORT:** client specified.

FEES/TERMS/CONTRACTS: $35–$75/hour depending on project.

Accomplishments: creates educational materials, writes and edits copy. Edits text for Web, books, and screen. Experienced in publishing, education, technical and software industries.
Education: BA English, North Texas State University, Denton, TX. Courses in Literature, University College of Swansea, Swansea, Wales, UK. Courses in photography, digital video, computer programming, at various locations.
Clients within prior year: 1–5.

445	EDITOR	WRITER	CONSULTANT	F	NF

Schreiber, Brad. Storytech Literary Consulting. 11362 Homedale St., Los Angeles, CA 90049. P1/ 310-471-3280. brashcyber@pcmagic.net. www.thewritersjourney.com. Established: 2000.

Skills: freelance editor, book doctor, ghostwriter, literary consultant, writing coach, writing instructor, screenwriter, author, journalist. **Markets served:** publishers, producers, writers.
Specialties and preferences: specializes in projects utilizing mythic and archetypal influences.
Fiction—accepts: all. **Nonfiction—accepts:** all. **Typical evaluation/report:** one-hour minimum on phone, audiotaped by us, allowing for two-way brainstorming, plus notes written directly on manuscript.
Fees/terms/contracts: $600/screenplay under 125 pages. $600 per manuscript up to 200 pages, $100 per additional 100 pages or portion thereof. No credit cards.
Accomplishments: four books. Fifteen years of journalism, national and California newspapers and magazines. Taught at American Film Institute, UCLA Extension, writers' conferences in U.S. and Europe. Edward Albee Foundation award.
Education: English/Creative Writing, San Francisco State University, CA. **Memberships:** National Writers Union. PEN Center USA West (twice judge for Drama awards).
Clients within prior year: 11–20.

446	EDITOR	WRITER	CONSULTANT	F	NF

Schultz, Sherri. 1508 10th Ave. East, #302, Seattle, WA 98102. P1/ 206-325-3523. sherrischultz@earthlink.net. www.wordswithgrace.com. Established: 1992.

Skills: freelance editor, copyeditor or line editor, proofreader. **Markets served:** Clients include book publishers, designers, nonprofit organizations, and periodicals.
Specialties and preferences: more than fifteen years of experience. Familiar

with Chicago and AP style. Specialties include arts, creative/narrative nonfiction, environment, Northwest, politics, travel, women's issues.

NONFICTION—ACCEPTS: articles/features, essays, memoirs, creative or narrative, self-help, how-to/instruction, text or reference, business.

FEES/TERMS/CONTRACTS: $25–$40/hour copyediting/proofreading, depending on complexity; $60/hour developmental/substantive editing. One to two months' notice recommended. Prepares estimate from sample of project. No credit cards. Uses a contract.

EDUCATION: BA Political Science, *magna cum laude*, Honors College, University of Oregon, Eugene. Phi Beta Kappa.

CLIENTS WITHIN PRIOR YEAR: 21–30.

447	EDITOR	WRITER	CONSULTANT	F	NF

Schwartz, Susan. Manhattan, NY. P1/ 212-877-3211. sas22@ix.netcom.com. www.susanschwartzeditor.com. Established: 1998.

SKILLS: freelance editor, independent book editor, book doctor, copyeditor or line editor, proofreader, ghostwriter, business writer or copywriter, ghostwriter of nonfiction book proposals. **MARKETS SERVED:** writers, literary agents, publishers, corporations, nonprofits.

SPECIALTIES AND PREFERENCES: ghostwriting nonfiction business and health books. Edits general nonfiction, adult fiction—women's interest, thrillers, and general categories. Corporate and business are limited to manuscripts for mainstream trade. On staff twenty-eight years at Doubleday, Random House, and Facts On File. Ghostwrote four books; working on three more.

FICTION—ACCEPTS: novels (genre, mainstream, contemporary, historical). **NONFICTION—ACCEPTS:** articles/features, memoirs, narrative, biography/autobiography, family history, self-help, how-to/instruction, reference, business, book proposals, queries. **TYPICAL EVALUATION/REPORT:** 2–25 pages.

FEES/TERMS/CONTRACTS: negotiable. No credit cards. Typically uses contract.

ACCOMPLISHMENTS: four published ghostwritten books. Known as an "editor who turns promising material into published books."

EDUCATION: BA English Literature, Chatham College, Pittsburgh, PA. **MEMBERSHIPS:** wordsintoprint.org. Women's Media Group. Women's National Book Association.

CLIENTS WITHIN PRIOR YEAR: 20–25.

448	EDITOR	WRITER	CONSULTANT	F	NF

Scraper, Katherine. Winfield, KS. P1/ 620-221-6534. F1/ 620-221-1549. dscraper@hit.net. Established: 1999.

SKILLS: business writer or copywriter, educational materials development and review. **MARKETS SERVED:** educational publishing companies.

SPECIALTIES AND PREFERENCES: preschool, elementary, and middle school language-arts materials; teacher resource books; leveled fiction and nonfiction readers with teacher guides; product reviews.

FICTION—ACCEPTS: y/a or juvenile, picture books, poetry, scripts. **NONFICTION—ACCEPTS:** y/a or juvenile, articles/features, creative or narrative, biography, self-help, how-to/instruction, text or reference, humor, inspirational/religious. **FEES/TERMS/CONTRACTS:** agreed-upon fee by hour, page, or project. Payment by check. Typically uses contracts.

ACCOMPLISHMENTS: published three stories, ten articles, one research project, thirteen resource guides, seventeen teacher resource books, six juvenile nonfiction books, twenty-two juvenile fiction books. Wal-Mart Teacher of the Year.

EDUCATION: Master's Education, *summa cum laude*, Southwestern College, Winfield, KS. BA Elementary Education, Wichita State University, KS. Reading Recovery®. **MEMBERSHIPS:** International Reading Association. Delta Kappa Gamma.

CLIENTS WITHIN PRIOR YEAR: 5–10.

449	EDITOR	WRITER	CONSULTANT	F	NF

Shabazz, Tia. Pentouch Communications. PO Box 2341, Cedar Hill, TX 75106-2341. P1/ 972-291-8919. P2/ 877-778-5481. help@pentouch.com. www.pentouch.com. Established: 2001; freelancing since 1995.

SKILLS: freelance editor, independent book editor, copyeditor, proofreader, business writer, technical writer, indexing, typesetting, manuscript preparation, desktop publishing. **MARKETS SERVED:** authors (esp. of African-American literature), publishers, website developers, nonprofits, attorneys, corporations, and businesses.

SPECIALTIES AND PREFERENCES: Pentouch specializes in African-American literature and is dedicated to improving clients' writing beyond their current projects.

FICTION—ACCEPTS: y/a or juvenile, novels (genre, mainstream, literary, contemporary, historical), queries, synopses. **NONFICTION—ACCEPTS:** all. **TYPICAL EVALUATION/REPORT:** from a few paragraphs to several pages.

FEES/TERMS/CONTRACTS: service agreement. Payment plans are available. Payments may be divided over the duration of the work. One-third to one-half of the estimated total required up front. Credit cards accepted.

EDUCATION: Certificate in Editorial Practices. Associate of Arts degree. Certificate in *Chicago Manual of Style*.

CLIENTS WITHIN PRIOR YEAR: 21–30.

450	EDITOR	**WRITER**	CONSULTANT	F	**NF**

Shafer, Kelly. Shafer Communications. Fort Worth, TX. P1/ 817-236-6075.
F1/ 817-236-6075. kelly@kellyshafer.com. www.shafercommunications.com.
Established: 1997.

SKILLS: business writer or copywriter. MARKETS SERVED: consumer and business (including technology, telecommunications, family, and travel)

SPECIALTIES AND PREFERENCES: I specialize in taking complicated information and transforming it into marketing materials that sell.

NONFICTION—ACCEPTS: articles/features, technical, business.

FEES/TERMS/CONTRACTS: per project basis.

ACCOMPLISHMENTS: fifteen years of marketing and writing experience. As director of marketing for a consulting firm, I helped take the company public in 1999 and managed/wrote everything from annual reports to print collateral, website copy, and press releases. Recent client list includes the popular VocationVacations company.

EDUCATION: BBA, Marketing, *summa cum laude*, Ohio University, Athens.

MEMBERSHIPS: National Association of Women Writers. Stepfamily Association of America.

CLIENTS WITHIN PRIOR YEAR: 8–12.

451	**EDITOR**	**WRITER**	**CONSULTANT**	**F**	**NF**

Shafer, Mary A. The Word Forge. P.O. Box 97, Ferndale, PA 18921.
P1/ 610-847-2456. C1/ 215-872-1443. F1/ 610-847-8220. info@thewordforge.com.
www.thewordforge.com. Established: 1985.

SKILLS: freelance editor, proofreader, ghostwriter, business writer or copywriter, technical writer, literary consultant, writing instructor, publicist, book designer/producer. MARKETS SERVED: business, individual, industry/trade.

SPECIALTIES AND PREFERENCES: nonfiction—building and liquid-waste industry, history, weather, painting, women soldiers, nature, corporate ghostwriting, newsletters, websites.

FICTION—ACCEPTS: y/a or juvenile, picture books, novels (genre, mainstream, literary, contemporary, historical), queries, synopses. NONFICTION—ACCEPTS: all. TYPICAL EVALUATION/REPORT: nonfiction.

FEES/TERMS/CONTRACTS: $85–$125/hour, in thirds. Credit cards through PayPal. Uses contract.

ACCOMPLISHMENTS: two hardcover histories. Contributed to regional anthology. Honorable Mention for essay. Many articles and features.

EDUCATION: BS Commercial Art, Milwaukee Area Technical College, WI. Two semesters of creative writing/history at University of Wisconsin-Stout and Milwaukee.

MEMBERSHIPS: National Writers Union. Writers Room of Bucks County.

CLIENTS WITHIN PRIOR YEAR: 11–20.

452	EDITOR	WRITER	CONSULTANT	F	NF

Shannon, Lizzy J. Pacific NW Literary Associates. PO Box 5141, Portland, OR 97208. P1/ 503-201-3195. lizzyshannon@yahoo.com. www.lizzyshannon.com. Established: 1996.

SKILLS: freelance editor, independent book editor, copyeditor or line editor, proofreader, business writer or copywriter, literary consultant, writing coach, writing instructor. MARKETS SERVED: writers, publishers, corporations.

SPECIALTIES AND PREFERENCES: As long as I believe the project has merit, I will provide a wide range of services to all writers of varying experience. As an ex-agent with the Ricia Mainhardt Agency, NYC, and the Pacific NW Literary Agency, I have an inside track on what agents seek and how to bypass the slush pile. Everybody's different; everybody has his or her own style. It's not my job to change that, but to groom and encourage it.

FICTION—ACCEPTS: short stories, novels (genre, mainstream, literary, contemporary, historical), scripts/screenplays, queries, synopses, treatments. NONFICTION—ACCEPTS: articles/features, self-help, how-to/instruction, business, humor, inspirational/religious, spiritual, book proposals, queries. TYPICAL EVALUATION/REPORT: 3–6 pages.

FEES/TERMS/CONTRACTS: $1–$10/page. Checks or PayPal accepted. No credit cards. Typically uses contracts.

ACCOMPLISHMENTS: science fiction published novel. Nominated for the Endeavor Award.

EDUCATION: BA Arts and Literature, London Theatre School, UK. MEMBERSHIPS: Willamette Writers (Board Member).

CLIENTS WITHIN PRIOR YEAR: 5–10.

453	EDITOR	WRITER	CONSULTANT	F	NF

Shapiro, David. Accurate & Intriguing Writing & Editing. Washington, DC. P1/ 301-699-8833. writer@davidelishapiro.com. www.davidelishapiro.com/writer. Established: mid-1980s.

SKILLS: freelance editor, independent book editor, copyeditor or line editor, proofreader, ghostwriter, business writer or copywriter, technical writer. MARKETS SERVED: publishers, business newsletters, educators.

SPECIALTIES AND PREFERENCES: Nonfiction writing is teaching. I correct and fine-tune language for easy access, and even enjoyment, by the intended audience. I take even more pain, though, to prevent misreading. In technical matters, accurate understanding can be essential. Misunderstandings can prove annoying—or deadly.

NONFICTION—ACCEPTS: all. TYPICAL EVALUATION/REPORT: My offerings are fully customized to clients' needs.

FEES/TERMS/CONTRACTS: $60–$70+/hour. Money discussed up front. Write for a per-word fee. No open indemnification clauses. Travel charged. No credit cards.

ACCOMPLISHMENTS: two nonfiction books, scores of feature articles, a twenty-one-year newsletter, years of magazine columns, more than a dozen meeting reports, fiction, poetry, reviews.

EDUCATION: MS Psychology, Lehigh University, Bethlehem, PA. BS Psychology, State University of New York at Buffalo. MEMBERSHIPS: National Writers Union. DC Science Writers Association. Washington Independent Writers. International Association of Electrical Inspectors. Mensa.

CLIENTS WITHIN PRIOR YEAR: 1–5.

454	EDITOR	WRITER	CONSULTANT	F	NF

Shaw, Barbara. Barbara Shaw Editing Services. 61 W. 34th, Eugene, OR 97405. barbshaw@efn.org. Established: 1988.

SKILLS: freelance editor, ghostwriter, business writer or copywriter. MARKETS SERVED: writers of business, how-to, popularized science, health and fitness, academic, general nonfiction. Anyone who doesn't have the skill or time to polish their work for submission.

SPECIALTIES AND PREFERENCES: transform hasty rough drafts into professional finished manuscripts. Have great ideas, but not really a writer? You need my input.

NONFICTION—ACCEPTS: articles/features, creative or narrative, self-help, how-to/instruction, text or reference, business. TYPICAL EVALUATION/REPORT: work returned to you transformed, for your input before my final polishing.

FEES/TERMS/CONTRACTS: $30/hour. Average 1 hour/1,000 words. Uses a contract.

ACCOMPLISHMENTS: five years as newspaper columnist on science and conservation topics, taught writing at community college. Sold dozens of magazine articles; stories appeared in two collections. Edited books and CDs for academic and business professionals; wrote and edited three newsletters. Developed PR plan for college.

EDUCATION: MA Journalism, University of Oregon, Eugene. MS Physiology, Georgetown University, Washington, DC. BA Biology, UCLA, Los Angeles.

CLIENTS WITHIN PRIOR YEAR: typically 2–5 large projects per year. Three this year— a database CD, dissertation, and business how-to book. All published.

455	EDITOR	WRITER	CONSULTANT	F	NF

Shé, Elizabeth. Wordsmith. Olympia, WA. P1/ 360-570-2236. elizabethshe@hotmail.com. suzylespeed@yahoo.com. Established: 1999.

SKILLS: freelance editor, independent book editor, copyeditor or line editor, ghostwriter, business writer or copywriter, writing coach, writing instructor. **MARKETS SERVED:** writers, small businesses, nonprofit organizations.

SPECIALTIES AND PREFERENCES: funny feminist fiction, the arts, environment, educational materials.

FICTION—ACCEPTS: all. **NONFICTION—ACCEPTS:** all. **TYPICAL EVALUATION/REPORT:** 2–10 pages.

FEES/TERMS/CONTRACTS: negotiable; no credit cards; typically uses contract or agreement.

ACCOMPLISHMENTS: known to float poetry boats, hang poetry clotheslines, and post poetry mailboxes. Literary work can be found in *Wild Child: Girlhoods in the Counterculture, Evergreen Magazine*, both *Northwest Edge* anthologies, *Vox Populi, Co-op News*, and www.poetsagainstthewar.org. Starred in *Howling V: The Rebirth*, as well as other films and theater projects.

EDUCATION: BA Literature and Writing, The Evergreen State College, Olympia, WA. Studied Interdisciplinary Art at Cornish College of the Arts, Seattle, WA. Attended American Conservatory Theatre Summer Training Congress, San Francisco, CA. **MEMBERSHIPS:** Northwest Independent Editors Guild.

CLIENTS WITHIN PRIOR YEAR: 1–5.

456	EDITOR	WRITER	CONSULTANT	F	NF

Sherman, Suzanne. Grants Pass, OR. P1/ 541-471-3087. P2/ 707-478-3819. onlines@sonic.net. www.thewritingmentor.net. Established: 1985.

SKILLS: independent book editor, book doctor, copyeditor, proofreader, ghost-writer, business writer or copywriter, literary consultant, writing coach, writing instructor. **MARKETS SERVED:** established and new writers, publishers, nonprofit organizations, corporations, graduate students.

SPECIALTIES AND PREFERENCES: I give clients 110 percent, from conception through publication prep, working as a team to reach their goals. E-mail coaching and individualized online courses help writers maintain self-created schedules. My intelligent, detailed, thoughtful critique is never judgmental; I offer an educated perspective and provide useful guideposts for writers to advance themselves.

FICTION—ACCEPTS: y/a or juvenile, short stories, novels (literary, historical), picture books, poetry, scripts/screenplays, queries, synopses, treatments. **NONFICTION—ACCEPTS:** y/a or juvenile, essays, memoirs, creative or narrative, biography, family history, self-help, how-to/instruction, inspirational, spiritual, articles/features, book proposals, queries. **TYPICAL EVALUATION/REPORT:** 2-10 pages.

FEES/TERMS/CONTRACTS: $75/hour editing; $90/hour writing. Retainers on larger projects. No credit cards. Uses agreement.

ACCOMPLISHMENTS: nonfiction book. Several published articles, creative nonfiction, poetry in national magazines and literary magazines.

EDUCATION: MA candidate Creative Writing, San Francisco State University, CA. BA Creative Writing, University of California, Santa Cruz. Fiction and screenwriting studies at UCLA Extension, Squaw Valley Community of Writers, Iowa Summer Writer's Workshop. **MEMBERSHIPS:** Author's Guild. **CLIENTS WITHIN PRIOR YEAR:** 21–30.

457	EDITOR	WRITER	CONSULTANT	F	NF

Sikchi, Sonali. Seattle, WA. sonali_sikchi@hotmail.com. Established: 2002.

SKILLS: freelance editor, book doctor, copyeditor or line editor, proofreader, ghostwriter, business writer or copywriter, developmental and substantive editor, nonfiction writer, book reviewer, research assistant, project manager, typist. **MARKETS SERVED:** individual authors, nonprofits, magazines, book publishers.

SPECIALTIES AND PREFERENCES: historical, literary, mainstream, romance fiction. Memoirs, creative, narrative, historical nonfiction. Short stories, magazine feature articles, book proposals, synopses, outlines, queries. No experience with science fiction, fantasy, religious, gay and lesbian, erotica, and pornography literature, poetry, highly technical work, plays, screenplays.

FICTION—ACCEPTS: all. **NONFICTION—ACCEPTS:** all. **TYPICAL EVALUATION/REPORT:** full-length 25–30 pages, follow-up 3–10 pages.

FEES/TERMS/CONTRACTS: manuscripts up to 400 pages, comprehensive first edit/critique $750, second/follow-up critique $250. Longer manuscripts first edit $900, second edit $400. Developmental editing, telephone, e-mail consultations, smaller editing projects, copywriting $50/hour. Proofreading & research assistance $25/hour. Typing $20/hour.

ACCOMPLISHMENTS: dozens of articles published in national and regional magazines. **MEMBERSHIPS:** Northwest Independent Editors' Guild. Seattle Free Lances. **CLIENTS WITHIN PRIOR YEAR:** 8–12.

458	EDITOR	WRITER	CONSULTANT	F	NF

Silverstein, Patrice. Portland, OR. P1/ 503-244-4147. F1/ 503-244-4147. PatriceHS@comcast.net. Established: 1994.

SKILLS: freelance editor, independent book editor, book doctor, copyeditor or line editor, proofreader, manuscript and book developer, project manager, for-hire writer or rewriter. **MARKETS SERVED:** publishers, writers.

SPECIALTIES AND PREFERENCES: highly skilled nonfiction developer, line editor, rewriter, and copyeditor, working with trade authors and publishers from draft to final manuscript, and academic writers writing for trade audience. Highly experienced with genre/mass market fiction.

FICTION—ACCEPTS: y/a or juvenile, short stories, novels (genre, mainstream, literary, contemporary, historical). **NONFICTION—ACCEPTS:** y/a or juvenile, articles/features, essays.

FEES/TERMS/CONTRACTS: negotiable industry rates per project and project evaluation; half on signing, proportional payments as goals reached. No credit cards. Uses contract.

ACCOMPLISHMENTS: editorial for Oliver Sacks, Tim Cahill, Tom Miller, William Kittredge, Jan Morris, Stephen Jay Gould, Jamaica Kincaid, and publishers National Geographic Books, Smithsonian National Museum of Natural History, HarperCollins, Knopf, MacGillivray-Freeman Films. Published writer-for-hire children's book.

EDUCATION: BA Psychology, Stony Brook University, NY, and UCLA. Masters work in Art History, Hunter College, NY. Urban Planning, Columbia University, NY.

CLIENTS WITHIN PRIOR YEAR: 6–10.

459	EDITOR	WRITER	CONSULTANT	F	NF

Simon, Elliot. Simon & Associates. Santa Rosa, CA. P1/ 707-527-7099. esimon@corecomm.net. Established: 1970.

SKILLS: freelance editor, copyeditor or line editor, proofreader. **MARKETS SERVED:** publishers, independent book producers.

SPECIALTIES AND PREFERENCES: functional—copyediting, technical editing, proofreading, online editing; content—academic/scholarly, engineering, mathematics, and/or science content. Works online or on hard copy.

NONFICTION—ACCEPTS: y/a or juvenile, articles/features, essays, creative or narrative, self-help, how-to/instruction, technical, text or reference.

FEES/TERMS/CONTRACTS: $25–$50/hour depending on difficulty level; $2.50–$5.00/page; or variable per-job fee. Client pays shipping. No credit cards.

ACCOMPLISHMENTS: over thirty years in book production handling math, physical and social sciences, engineering, programming, nursing/medicine, business/finance, humanities, music, art.

EDUCATION: MA Human Development, University of Chicago, IL. BS Psychology, College of the City of New York. **MEMBERSHIPS:** Bay Area Editors Forum. Society for Technical Communication.

CLIENTS WITHIN PRIOR YEAR: 1–5.

460	EDITOR	WRITER	CONSULTANT	F	NF

Sitzes, Jason. Writers Retreat Workshop (WRW) Editorial Services. 5721 Magazine St., #161, New Orleans, LA 70115. P1/ 800-642-2494. wrw04@netscape.net. www.writersretreatworkshop.com. Established: 1987.

SKILLS: freelance editor, independent book editor, ghostwriter, literary consultant, writing coach. **MARKETS SERVED:** writers of novels, novellas, or narrative nonfiction.

SPECIALTIES AND PREFERENCES: offers a detailed manuscript evaluation of your completed or partial manuscript and a copy of Gary Provost's at-home study course—the Audio Novel Workshop. Other editorial and ghostwriting projects are accepted after consultation only.

FICTION—ACCEPTS: y/a or juvenile, short stories, novels (genre), scripts/screenplays, queries, synopses, treatments. **NONFICTION—ACCEPTS:** memoirs, creative or narrative, self-help, how-to/instruction, technical, humor, inspirational/religious, spiritual, queries. **TYPICAL EVALUATION/REPORT:** 25–30 single-spaced pages.

FEES/TERMS/CONTRACTS: $1,400 full manuscript evaluation; $650 for partial. Ghostwriting varies. Half up front payment. Accepts most credit cards. Sometimes uses a contract.

ACCOMPLISHMENTS: 2001 Tennessee Mountain Writers Short Story Award. 2000 Gary Provost Memorial Scholarship. 1999 Whispering Pines Quarterly Fiction Award. Also offers services to other editorial companies, including Free Expressions. Former editorial/proposal/publishing coordinator for Fortune 500 companies.

EDUCATION: BA Creative Writing with specialty in Technical Writing, Editing, Literature, University of Tennessee, Knoxville.

CLIENTS WITHIN PRIOR YEAR: 10–15.

461	EDITOR	WRITER	CONSULTANT	F	NF

Six, Jan. Your Friendly Copyeditor. 1840 Burton Dr., #111, Austin, TX 78741-4271. P1/ 512-912-0983. FriendlyCopyEd@aol.com. Established: 1999.

SKILLS: freelance editor, copyeditor or line editor, ghostwriter, technical writer, language consultant. **MARKETS SERVED:** small press publishers, typesetters, aspiring authors.

SPECIALTIES AND PREFERENCES: copyediting ranging from journal articles to book length in many fields—sociology, art history, criminology, psychology, education; particular expertise in biology, linguistics. Language consulting to fiction writers and "worldbuilders" on design and/or analysis of constructed (fictitious) languages.

FICTION—ACCEPTS: novels (genre). **NONFICTION—ACCEPTS:** y/a or juvenile, articles/features, memoirs, creative or narrative, text or reference.

FEES/TERMS/CONTRACTS: editing $3–$5/page or $18–$25/hour, depending on job. Language consulting negotiable. Accepts checks. No credit cards.

ACCOMPLISHMENTS: copyediting for many journals and book publishers. Editing for my fellow neurological researchers led to paid work. I am, however, hoping over time to break into editing fiction, where the breadth of my interests and experience would be more of an asset. I am an aspiring author of genre fiction.

EDUCATION: PhD Biomedical Sciences, *summa cum laude*, University of Antwerp, Belgium (my native country). Most of my formal training has been in neurology. I am fluent in Dutch, French, German, Finnish, Latin, plus. **MEMBERSHIPS:** Austin SlugTribe.

CLIENTS WITHIN PRIOR YEAR: 1–5.

462	EDITOR	WRITER	CONSULTANT	F	NF

Skarnulis, Leanna. Austin, TX. P1/ 512-249-0829. leanna@skarnulis.com www.skarnulis.com. www.skarnulis.com. Established: 1995.

SKILLS: ghostwriter, business writer or copywriter, speeches. **MARKETS SERVED:** publishers of magazines and subscription newsletters. Ad agencies. Corporations.

SPECIALTIES AND PREFERENCES: I'm a freelance writer of ads, press releases, newsletters, brochures (corporate, sales, fundraising), feature articles, speeches, and web content. My clients have included ad agencies, construction companies, hospitals, high-tech companies, colleges, publisher of subscription newsletters for banking and manufacturing, and more.

NONFICTION—ACCEPTS: articles/features, self-help, how-to/instruction, text or reference, business.

FEES/TERMS/CONTRACTS: $75/hour. PayPal accepted.

ACCOMPLISHMENTS: hundreds of articles published in national general interest and consumer health magazines and in subscription newsletters for manufacturing and banking.

EDUCATION: MA Speech Communication, University of Nebraska at Omaha. BA English, Omaha University, NE. **MEMBERSHIPS:** Association for Women in Communications. Freelance Austin. Freelance Success.

CLIENTS WITHIN PRIOR YEAR: 11–20.

463	EDITOR	WRITER	CONSULTANT	F	NF

Smith, Cheryl. 496 Gasman Rd., Port Angeles, WA 98362. P1/ 360-457-1458. winsmith@olypen.com. www.writedog.com. Established: 1983.

SKILLS: freelance editor, independent book editor, book doctor, copyeditor or line editor, proofreader, ghostwriter, business writer or copywriter, technical writer, literary consultant, writing coach, writing instructor, freelance writer of magazine articles and books. **MARKETS SERVED:** editing—texts on the sciences, the humanities, almost any general subject. Writing—pets and pet care, human health, science.

SPECIALTIES AND PREFERENCES: For editing, I see a lot of hard science because I understand it. For writing, I have written mainly about dogs but am moving into general science (health, medicine, behavior).

FICTION—ACCEPTS: all. NONFICTION—ACCEPTS: all.

FEES/TERMS/CONTRACTS: editing—charge by page or per hour; writing—charge by word or article, or by advance and royalties for book.

ACCOMPLISHMENTS: ten published books, four ghostwritten books, hundreds of articles. Maxwell Medallion winner 2002, Eukanuba Canine Health Award 2002, and many other awards. Former production editor for Prentice Hall.

EDUCATION: some college and lots of self-study. MEMBERSHIPS: National Association of Science Writers. Dog Writers Association of America. Association of Pet Dog Trainers. Garden Writers Association.

CLIENTS WITHIN PRIOR YEAR: 11–20.

464	EDITOR	WRITER	CONSULTANT	F	NF

Smith, Robin. Robin Smith Ink. 218 Morgan Cove Rd., Candler, NC 28715. P1/ 828-667-4390. F1/ 828-670-9160. robinsmithink@charter.net. www.robinsmithink.com. Established: 1986.

SKILLS: freelance editor, independent book editor, book doctor, copyeditor or line editor, developmental editor. MARKETS SERVED: writers, publishers.

SPECIALTIES AND PREFERENCES: I help sharpen and focus work so that it can be strong and compelling. Enjoy editing literary, women's, mystery, suspense, horror, sci-fi/speculative fiction.

FICTION—ACCEPTS: y/a or juvenile, novels (genre, mainstream, literary, contemporary, historical), queries, synopses. NONFICTION—ACCEPTS: all.

TYPICAL EVALUATION/REPORT: 3–7 pages.

FEES/TERMS/CONTRACTS: free sample edit. $2.25–$3.50/page. Shorter than 100 pages, $45/hourly. 50 percent up front, balance on return. Checks and PayPal.

ACCOMPLISHMENTS: twenty-one years in New York publishing companies.

EDUCATION: BA English, Hiram College, OH.

CLIENTS WITHIN PRIOR YEAR: 40–45.

465	EDITOR	WRITER	CONSULTANT	F	NF

Smith, Stephanie. 433 County Rd. 1006, Wolfe City, TX 75496. P1/ 903-496-9147. lambdakennels1@juno.com. Established: 1990.

SKILLS: business writer or copywriter, technical writer, literary consultant, writing coach, writing instructor, publicist, grant writer, freelance and scientific author. MARKETS SERVED: nonprofits, nonfiction magazines, researchers.

SPECIALTIES AND PREFERENCES: history, dog issues, gardening, psychology, nonprofit grant applications, scientific articles.

NONFICTION—ACCEPTS: y/a or juvenile, articles/features, essays, memoirs, creative or narrative, biography/autobiography, family history, self-help,

how-to/instruction, technical, text or reference, business, queries.
FEES/TERMS/CONTRACTS: grants, 10 percent grant awarded. Articles—vary by market, payment on acceptance. Grants—payment on award disbursement. Check or money order only. Uses contract.
ACCOMPLISHMENTS: ten magazine articles, monthly column for three and a half years, hundreds of technical reports, five grants, three scientific publications.
EDUCATION: PhD Psychology, Texas A&M University, College Station. MS Psychology, Texas A&M University, College Station. BS Psychology, Texas Christian University, Ft. Worth. **MEMBERSHIPS:** Sigma Xi. Dog Writers Association of America.
CLIENTS WITHIN PRIOR YEAR: variable due to workload.

466	EDITOR	WRITER	CONSULTANT	F	NF

Solow, Harrison. 3835-R E. Thousand Oaks Blvd., Ste. 228, Westlake Village, CA 91362. P1/ 310-457-9848. harrisonsolow@solowtwo.com. Established: 1984.

SKILLS: independent book editor, ghostwriter, literary consultant, writing instructor, strategic creative writer/consultant on corporate, literary, academic, government, entertainment, religious (Catholic and Jewish only), nonprofit material. **MARKETS SERVED:** as above. Paramount Pictures, Sci Fi channel, NASA, publishers, universities, institutes.
SPECIALTIES AND PREFERENCES: high-end trade nonfiction, sci-fi, educational, and religious material. Policy and position papers/briefs/scripts/campaigns. Celebrity speeches.
FICTION—ACCEPTS: novels (genre, mainstream, literary, contemporary, historical); scripts/screenplays. **NONFICTION—ACCEPTS:** articles/features essays, memoirs, creative or narrative, biography/autobiography, religious, spiritual.
FEES/TERMS/CONTRACTS: negotiable. 50 percent up front. No single or aggregate projects under $5,000. Letter agreement up to $10,000. Contract for projects over $10,000.
ACCOMPLISHMENTS: published by major commercial publishers and university press. Rare and versatile experience. Highly confidential material and clients. Over 400 publications.
EDUCATION: Ph.D. pending, Literature and Theology, University of Wales, Lampeter, U.K. MFA English Literature and Writing, Mills College, Oakland, CA. BA, English Literature, St. Mary's University. Halifax, Canada. **MEMBERSHIPS:** Women's Faculty Club, UCB. Modern Humanities Research Association. Modern Language Association. Various think-tanks. PEN.
CLIENTS WITHIN PRIOR YEAR: 6–10.

467	EDITOR	WRITER	CONSULTANT	F	NF

Spear, Robert K. Sharp Spear Enterprises. 16313 Springdale Rd., Leavenworth, KS 66048. P1/ 913-772-8253. sharpspear@kc.rr.com. www.sharpspear.com. Established: 1997.

SKILLS: freelance editor, independent book editor, book doctor, copyeditor or line editor, ghostwriter, business writer or copywriter, self-publishing consultant. **MARKETS SERVED:** authors, independent publishers, direct mail marketers, corporate.

SPECIALTIES AND PREFERENCES: We review books in seventeen genres and post them in our Internet-based bimonthly newsletter. I provide copy, line, and content editing services, as well as rewriting services. I lay out book interiors using PageMaker and InDesign.

FICTION—ACCEPTS: y/a or juvenile, picture books. **NONFICTION—ACCEPTS:** y/a or juvenile, queries.

FEES/TERMS/CONTRACTS: copy/line edit $6/1,000 words, proof $4/1,000 words, both in advance by check. Consult $50/hour, charged monthly. Edit/proof— no contract. Write/consult—contract.

ACCOMPLISHMENTS: 10 nonfiction books published, 500+ reviews, 50+ edited books, 15 interior designs.

EDUCATION: MS Business Management, University of Northern Colorado, Greeley. BS Orchestral Management, Indiana University, Bloomington. **MEMBERSHIPS:** American Booksellers Association. Upper Midwest Booksellers Association.

CLIENTS WITHIN PRIOR YEAR: 20–25.

468	EDITOR	WRITER	CONSULTANT	F	NF

Spiegel, Phyllis. Phyllis Spiegel Associates. Plainsboro, NJ. P1/ 609-799-9636. PRPhyllis@Juno.com. Established: 1984.

SKILLS: ghostwriter, business writer or copywriter, literary consultant, writing coach, publicist. **MARKETS SERVED:** professionals, business firms, nonprofits, health care industry.

SPECIALTIES AND PREFERENCES: features, press releases, position papers, trade magazine articles, interviews, ghost-written pieces. I've written about everything from costume jewelry to funeral insurance. Highly experienced in real estate, senior living, weight management. Reviews, travel.

NONFICTION—ACCEPTS: articles/features, essays, memoirs, creative or narrative, biography/autobiography, family history, self-help, how-to/instruction, business.

FEES/TERMS/CONTRACTS: public relations—monthly retainers or project fees. Writing—fees based on time involved and complexity.

ACCOMPLISHMENTS: commended by the governor of New Jersey for campaign for UMDNJ's Bicycle Race for Health PR campaign. Listed in *Who's Who in*

American Women. Commended by New Jersey Pharmaceutical Association for program for their industry members. Editor college newspaper.

EDUCATION: BA English, New York University, New York. Minor in Psychology. Additional courses through the years at The New School, Princeton University, and other institutions. **MEMBERSHIPS:** Professional Writers Alliance of Mercer County, NJ.

CLIENTS WITHIN PRIOR YEAR: 6–10.

469	EDITOR	WRITER	CONSULTANT	F	NF

Stackler, Ed. Stackler Editorial Agency. 555 Lincoln Ave, Alameda, CA 94501. P1/ 510-814-9694. stackler@aol.com. www.fictioneditor.com. Established: 1996.

SKILLS: freelance editor, independent book editor, book doctor. **MARKETS SERVED:** writers, authors.

SPECIALTIES AND PREFERENCES: mystery, thriller, suspense, and crime fiction. I read a few chapters, gratis, to determine whether the book interests me sufficiently; plays to my strengths as an editor and market knowledge; is publishable; will benefit significantly from my editing. The emphasis of my editing tends to be structural, addressing matters of character, plot, pace, and commerciality. Line editing, if necessary, comes in a subsequent draft. When an author and I have gotten the manuscript ready for market, I advise them in their hunt for an agent and publisher.

FICTION—ACCEPTS: novels. **NONFICTION—ACCEPTS:** memoirs, creative or narrative, biography/autobiography, self-help, how-to/instruction. **TYPICAL EVALUATION/ REPORT:** 5–25 pages.

FEES/TERMS/CONTRACTS: $100/hour. Retainer. No credit cards. Uses agreement.

ACCOMPLISHMENTS: previously acquisitions editor with two New York publishers; editor of two *New York Times* bestselling novelists. Semifinalist in Nicholls Fellowship Award for screenwriting, 2003.

EDUCATION: BA English, Stanford University, CA.

CLIENTS WITHIN PRIOR YEAR: 11–20.

470	EDITOR	WRITER	CONSULTANT	F	NF

Stanbrough, Harvey E. Pittsboro, IN. hmpeditor@hotmail.com. harveystan@yahoo.com. www.StoneThread.com. Established: 1996.

SKILLS: freelance editor, independent book editor, book doctor, copyeditor or line editor, proofreader, writing instructor. **MARKETS SERVED:** writers, publishers.

SPECIALTIES AND PREFERENCES: prefer MS Word (.doc or .rtf) attachments. Low fees because I only accept manuscripts that interest me. Quick turnaround time, providing line and content editing as well as instruction via embedded comments. I'm a writer and editor, so I concentrate on preserving your voice. A well-edited manuscript should not look like it's been edited.

FICTION—ACCEPTS: short stories, novels (genre, mainstream, literary, contemporary, historical), treatments. **NONFICTION—ACCEPTS:** articles/features, essays, memoirs, creative or narrative, self-help, how-to/instruction, humor, spiritual.

FEES/TERMS/CONTRACTS: fees seldom more than 1½ cents/word, usually lower. Prefers one-third down. Negotiates terms on case-by-case basis. Free ten-page sample edit.

ACCOMPLISHMENTS: publication of two how-to writing books on punctuation and dialogue, and five poetry collections. Nominee Pulitzer Prize, Frankfurt E-Book Award.

EDUCATION: BA English/Writing, Eastern New Mexico University, Portales.

CLIENTS WITHIN PRIOR YEAR: 10–15.

471	EDITOR	WRITER	CONSULTANT	F	NF

Stanford, Eric. Stanford Creative Services. 7645 N. Union Blvd., #235, Colorado Springs, CO 80920. P1/ 719-599-7808. eric@stanfordcreative.com. www.stanfordcreative.com. Established: 1998.

SKILLS: freelance editor, independent book editor, book doctor, copyeditor or line editor, ghostwriter, business writer or copywriter, writing coach, project management. **MARKETS SERVED:** publishers, packagers, nonprofits, businesses, writers.

SPECIALTIES AND PREFERENCES: With the help of a network of publishing professionals, I have made outsourcing work for organizations that publish as either their primary or a secondary enterprise. My company offers writing and editing services in a way that is flexible, effective, and fun!

NONFICTION—ACCEPTS: y/a or juvenile, articles/features, essays, memoirs, creative or narrative, biography/autobiography, self-help, how-to/instruction, text or reference, business, inspirational/religious, spiritual.

FEES/TERMS/CONTRACTS: copyediting $20+/hour. Content editing $30+/hour. Writing, coaching, negotiable. No credit cards. Typically uses contract.

ACCOMPLISHMENTS: over 100 books written or edited.

EDUCATION: MA Theology, Gordon-Conwell Theological Seminary, South Hamilton, MA. BA English, Judson College, Elgin, IL. **MEMBERSHIPS:** Academy of Christian Editors.

CLIENTS WITHIN PRIOR YEAR: 11–20.

472	EDITOR	WRITER	CONSULTANT	F	NF

Starkey, Mariann S. Starkey Editorial Services. Denver, CO. P1/ 303-238-9638. P2/ 303-238-9638. F1/ 303-238-0197. starkeyms@aol.com. Established: 1998.

Skills: freelance editor, independent book editor, book doctor, copyeditor or line editor, proofreader, business writer or copywriter, technical writer, indexer, features, travel, presentations, desktop publisher. **Markets served:** writers, publishers, professors, newspapers, magazines, nonprofits, corporations.

Specialties and preferences: academic and corporate proofreading, nonfiction editing, feature writing (art, movies, recreation), environmental writing, newsletter publishing.

Fiction—accepts: y/a or juvenile, short stories, novels (genre, mainstream, literary, contemporary, historical) scripts/screenplays. **Nonfiction—accepts:** y/a or juvenile, articles/features, essays, memoirs, creative or narrative, biography/autobiography, self-help, how-to/instruction, technical, text or reference, business, humor, inspirational/religious, spiritual, book proposals. **Typical evaluation/report:** 2–10 pages.

Fees/terms/contracts: indexing $2+/page. Editing, proofreading $17+/hour. Writing 50+ cents/word. Credit cards. Typically uses agreement.

Accomplishments: dozens of articles published.

Education: MA Journalism, Colorado University, Boulder. BS Business Administration, Finance, Regis University, Denver, CO. **Memberships:** Rocky Mountain Association of Publishing Professionals.

Clients within prior year: 6–10.

473	EDITOR	WRITER	CONSULTANT	F	NF

Starr, Sarah. Sarah Starr Editing. 1765 Pilgrim St. SE, Salem, OR 97302. P1/ 503-585-4088. starrediting@hotmail.com. www.starrediting.com. Established: 1989.

Skills: freelance editor, independent book editor, book doctor, copyeditor or line editor, proofreader, ghostwriter, business writer or copywriter, technical writer, literary consultant, writing coach, writing instructor. **Markets served:** authors, service businesses, publishers.

Specialties and preferences: I fix manuscripts and teach authors the reasons behind the rules; I also ghostwrite if clients prefer. Fiction specialties include children's books and Regencies. I'm especially good at making trade information accessible to laypeople.

Fiction—accepts: y/a or juvenile, short stories, novels (genre, mainstream, literary, contemporary, historical), queries, synopses. **Nonfiction—accepts:** all. **Typical evaluation/report:** 6 pages. Send four pages for a free sample edit!

Fees/terms/contracts: substantive editing and copyediting $3/page, $20 min. Word processing, ghostwriting, desktop publishing $20+/hour. No credit cards. Uses contract.

Accomplishments: published novel. I have sold more than 350 articles since 1995. I write for and currently am the associate editor of a trade magazine.

I also wrote book reviews for two years, a bi-weekly general consumer column for almost three years, and business and grammar articles for international newsletters.

EDUCATION: coursework in English, Western Oregon State College, Monmouth. **MEMBERSHIPS:** Romance Writers of America. The Beau Monde. **CLIENTS WITHIN PRIOR YEAR:** 1–5.

474	EDITOR	WRITER	CONSULTANT	F	NF

Starrett-Bigg, Carla. Portland, OR. P1/ 503-244-1335. C1/ 503-502-1978. cstarbi@yahoo.com. Established: 1999.

SKILLS: freelance editor, business writer or copywriter, technical writer, grant writer, fiction writer. **MARKETS SERVED:** corporations, publishers, academic press, nonprofits, individuals.

SPECIALTIES AND PREFERENCES: edits history, business, technical, and academic work, for clarity and ease of reading, as well as grammar and structure. Edits fiction for scene, pace, general flow. Coaches song-lyric writing.

FICTION—ACCEPTS: y/a or juvenile, short stories, novels (genre, mainstream, literary, contemporary, historical), queries, synopses. **NONFICTION—ACCEPTS:** all. **TYPICAL EVALUATION/REPORT:** 2–25 pages.

FEES/TERMS/CONTRACTS: rates by hour, page, or project. PayPal. Typically uses contract.

ACCOMPLISHMENTS: former journalist and feature writer for a major daily newspaper, written freelance articles for a number of magazines. Copyeditor for a book publisher in England. Background in theater, which I use to coach novelists in creating dramatic tension. Have edited translated texts, extensive copy and line editing experience. Twenty years of grant writing experience, extensive experience coaching, and judging song lyrics.

EDUCATION: BS Communications, Lewis and Clark College, Portland, OR. **CLIENTS WITHIN PRIOR YEAR:** 11–20.

475	EDITOR	WRITER	CONSULTANT	F	NF

Stein, Sol. The Stein Software Corporation. 277E S. Broadway, Tarrytown, NY 10591. F1/ 914-366-4264. solstein@aol.com. www.solstein.com. Established: 1989.

SKILLS: freelance editor, literary consultant, writing coach, writing instructor. **MARKETS SERVED:** professional writers.

SPECIALTIES AND PREFERENCES: works only with established professional writers of standing, fiction and nonfiction.

FICTION—ACCEPTS: novels (literary). **NONFICTION—ACCEPTS:** essays, memoirs, creative or narrative, biography/autobiography. **TYPICAL EVALUATION/REPORT:** 2–10 pages.

Fees/terms/contracts: $300/hour. Retainer required. No credit cards.

Accomplishments: nine novels including one million-copy seller; five nonfiction books; two plays in Broadway theaters, one prize-winning as best full-length play of year; anthologized poetry; award-winning computer programs used by over 100,000 writers in thirty-eight countries. Distinguished Instructor Award, University of California.

Education: postgraduate doctoral studies, MA English and Comparative Literature, Columbia University, New York. BSS, City College of New York. **Memberships:** Authors Guild.

Clients within prior year: one client #1 *New York Times* Fiction Bestseller List, 2003, 2004. Another current client received $1 million advance for first novel.

476	EDITOR	WRITER	CONSULTANT	F	NF

Stein, Toby. Stein Seminars. 45 Church St., Montclair, NJ 07042. P1/ 973-744-0475. tobyfstein@aol.com. tobystein@comcast.net. Established: 1984.

Skills: freelance editor, independent book editor, book doctor, copyeditor or line editor, business writer or copywriter, literary consultant, writing coach, writing instructor, writes business brochures and ads. **Markets served:** writers, publishers, nonprofits, corporations.

Specialties and preferences: business and professionals new to publishing, experienced/first-time novelists. Detailed critiques serve as revision guide. Nonfiction—nontechnical business, management, how-to, Christian and Jewish spiritual. Fiction—mainstream novels. Trained actress. Replicates author's voice for seamless rewriting.

Fiction—accepts: y/a or juvenile, novels (genre, mainstream, literary, contemporary, historical). **Nonfiction—accepts:** all. **Typical evaluation/report:** 15–20 pages.

Fees/terms/contracts: critiques $1,430 up to 400-page manuscript. Entire critique fee sent with manuscript. Editing/rewriting $165/hour; payment schedule negotiated. No credit cards.

Accomplishments: three published novels, two published nonfiction books. Numerous articles in national magazines.

Education: MA History, Columbia University, New York. BA British Civilization, Barnard College, New York. Studied Christianity and Judaism, various venues including Union Theological Seminary, New York.

Clients within prior year: 5–10.

477	EDITOR	WRITER	CONSULTANT	F	NF

Steinberg, Rafael. Tarrytown, NY. P1/ 914-332-0003. F1/ 914-332-0003. rafesteinberg@post.harvard.edu. Established: 1970.

Skills: freelance editor, independent book editor, copyeditor or line editor, ghostwriter. **Markets served:** aspiring and professional writers.

Specialties and preferences: My specialty is editing/rewriting prose; increasing the effectiveness of sentences and paragraphs. I can handle any subject except extremely technical matters. Regarding subject matter, I also specialize in international affairs, particularly East Asia and World War II, writing about news and politics.

Fiction—accepts: short stories; novels. **Nonfiction—accepts:** articles/features, essays, memoirs, creative or narrative, biography/autobiography.

Fees/terms/contracts: reading fee of $35 to look over about 50 pages and provide a sample edit of three or four pages; substantive editing $3–$7/page Some payment in advance, large chunks along the way, final payment on completion. No credit cards. Usually uses a contract.

Accomplishments: author of eight published books; foreign correspondent; war correspondent; business proprietor (entrepreneur); teacher

Education: BA American History and Literature, Harvard College, Cambridge, MA. **Memberships:** Editorial Freelancers Association.

Clients within prior year: 1–5.

478	EDITOR	WRITER	CONSULTANT	F	NF

Stephens, Lori. Verbatim Publishing Services. 4755 SW Caldew, Ste. B, Portland, OR 97219. P1/ 503-977-3693. VerbPub@aol.com. www.lori-stephens.com. Established: 1999.

Skills: freelance editor, independent book editor, book doctor, copyeditor or line editor, proofreader, ghostwriter, business writer or copywriter, technical writer, literary consultant, writing coach, writing instructor, developmental editor. **Markets served:** therapists and trainers in psychology, hypnosis, Neurolinguistics, Enneagram, behavioral science, education, self-help, and health.

Specialties and preferences: My experience as a developmental editor spans sixteen years and has shaped over fifty published titles. I offer specialized expertise for cognitive therapists and trainers in the fields listed above. My extensive know-how and personable working style help authors to clarify their goals and develop their narrative style.

Nonfiction—accepts: memoirs, self-help.

Fees/terms/contracts: $50–$75/hour. No Credit cards. After a review of the material, I compose a Statement of Services. Statement of Services becomes a working contract.

Accomplishments: two books published.

Education: BA English, University of Oregon, Eugene. **Memberships:** Willamette Writers. Northwest Independent Editors Guild.

Clients within prior year: 1–5.

479	EDITOR	WRITER	CONSULTANT	F	NF

Stephens, Stephanie. StephensInk. Laguna Niguel, CA. P1/ 949-388 8439. C1/ 949-246 0075. stephaniestephens@cox.net. Established: 1990.

Skills: Writer ghost, business or copy. Consultant coach. Other media relations consultant. **Markets served:** corporate and nonprofit clients.

Specialties and preferences: shorts and feature articles comprise my consumer, trade and custom magazine activity. I write news releases, speeches, ads, scripts (audio and video), brochures, and more.

Nonfiction—accepts: creative or narrative, business, queries.

Fees/terms/contracts: vary per assignment/project. Usually by the hour or project. Paid by check, amount agreed in advance.

Accomplishments: award-winning corporate communications professional and journalist, with experience in radio and television. Work has appeared in forty publications—consumer, trade, and custom. Freelance pieces on pets, wildlife, veterinary, health, celebrities, retail, service/how-to. Profiles, travel (consumer and destination), lifestyle, entertainment. Most subjects except law, finance, high-tech.

Education: MA New York University. BA Wake Forest University, Winston-Salem, NC. City University, London, England. **Memberships:** American Society of Journalists Association. American Horse Publications. National Writers Union. Editorial Freelancers Association.

Clients within prior year: 21–30.

480	EDITOR	WRITER	CONSULTANT	F	NF

Stern, Rochelle. 35 Highmont Dr., Princeton Jct., NJ 08550. P1/ 609-275-5019. P2/ 609-275-4816. RStern5019@aol.com. www.diabetesinthefamily.com. Established: 1986.

Skills: freelance editor, independent book editor, book doctor, copyeditor or line editor, proofreader, business writer or copywriter, writing coach. **Markets served:** corporations and publishers.

Specialties and preferences: editing of corporate reports, medical text, and documentation, technical/mathematical text and documentation, reference material.

Nonfiction—accepts: articles/features, essays, creative or narrative, technical, text or reference, business, inspirational/religious, spiritual, book proposals, queries. **Typical evaluation/report:** 2–10 pages.

Fees/terms/contracts: hard copy and on-screen editing—$35/hour. Proofreading and read-throughs—$25/hour. Writing coach—$20/hour.

Accomplishments: one self-published children's book. Dozens of general newsletter articles.

Education: MLIS candidate Library Information Science, BA Print Journalism, Douglass College, Rutgers University, New Brunswick, NJ. **Memberships:** Princeton Writers' Alliance. L-Soft International. Sisterhood vice president of Beth El Synagogue, East Windsor, NJ.

Clients within prior year: 1–5.

481	EDITOR	WRITER	CONSULTANT	F	NF

Stewart, Anna. Mother Hands Services. Boulder, CO. P1/ 303-499-7681. write@motherhands.com. www.motherhands.com. Established: 1995.

Skills: freelance editor, book doctor, business or copy, literary consultant, writing instructor, book proposal consultant. **Markets served:** writers, businesses, nonprofits.

Specialties and preferences: I offer current, careful, creative writing and editing services for individuals and businesses. Expertise in parenting, disabilities issues, travel, and children's books. I produce newsletters, copywriting, and book proposal editing and consulting. Experienced working with new writers to help them develop their work for publication.

Fiction—accepts: picture books. **Nonfiction—accepts:** all. **Typical evaluation/ report:** 2–10 pages.

Fees/terms/contracts: $30–$50/hour. PayPal or check. No credit cards.

Accomplishments: essays in three books. Under contract for nonfiction book. 80+ book reviews. 250+ columns, articles, and essays. Columnist for five publications.

Education: BA Integrative Health Studies, San Francisco State University, CA. Certificates in massage therapy, hypnotherapy, and childbirth assistance. **Memberships:** Boulder Media Women. Society of Children's Book Writers and Illustrators.

Clients within prior year: 21–30.

482	EDITOR	WRITER	CONSULTANT	F	NF

Stewart, Melissa. Honeybee Productions. Acton, MA. P1/ 978-263-7279. hbeeprod@msn.com. www.melissa.stewat.com. Established: 1990.

Skills: freelance editor, independent book editor, book doctor, copyeditor or line editor, proofreader, ghostwriter, business writer or copywriter, writing coach, writing instructor. **Markets served:** writers, publishers, nonprofits, corporations.

Specialties and preferences: writes/edits science books and articles for children/adults. Critiques manuscripts. Writes articles, brochures, newsletters, and web content for organizations and corporations.

FICTION—ACCEPTS: y/a or juvenile, picture books, short stories, novels, queries, synopses. **NONFICTION—ACCEPTS:** all. **TYPICAL EVALUATION/REPORT:** varies.

FEES/TERMS/CONTRACTS: $40–$80/hour. May use contract.

ACCOMPLISHMENTS: written 50+ children's science books. Edited 200+ children's books. Written 30+ articles for children/adults. Contributed to adult trade books and textbooks. Awards—National Science Teachers Association's Recommended Title, New York Public Library's Books for the Teen Age, Science Books & Films Best Book of the Year.

EDUCATION: MA Science Journalism, New York University, New York. BS Biology, Union College, Schenectady, NY. **MEMBERSHIPS:** American Association for the Advancement of Science. Society of Children's Book Writers and Illustrators.

CLIENTS WITHIN PRIOR YEAR: 11–20.

483	EDITOR	WRITER	CONSULTANT	F	NF

Stockwell, Gail. Writers Retreat Workshop. South Lancaster, MA. P1/ 800-642-2494. wrwwisi@cox.net. www.writersretreatworkshop.com. Established: 1987.

SKILLS: book doctor, writing coach. **MARKETS SERVED:** serious intermediate writers of fiction and nonfiction, especially novels and full-length books.

SPECIALTIES AND PREFERENCES: I'm interested in writers who feel passionate about improving a work-in-progress, and ready to develop their "story sense."

FICTION—ACCEPTS: y/a or juvenile, novels (genre, mainstream, literary, contemporary, historical), synopses, treatments. **NONFICTION—ACCEPTS:** memoirs, creative and narrative. **TYPICAL EVALUATION/REPORT:** 25–30 pages, including written evaluation/report, read-through and evaluation (no page editing), instructional material, books on craft or marketing, rewriting.

FEES/TERMS/CONTRACTS: $1,250 for detailed report and related materials, which include Gary Provost's Audio Novel Workshop. Credit cards through Writers Retreat Workshop manuscript evaluation services.

ACCOMPLISHMENTS: cofounder and creative director of Writers Retreat Workshop, 1987–2003.

EDUCATION: BS Art Education, University of Bridgeport, CT. Thirteen years assisting Gary Provost. **MEMBERSHIPS:** Author's Guild.

CLIENTS WITHIN PRIOR YEAR: limited, 1–5.

484	EDITOR	WRITER	CONSULTANT	F	NF

Storey, Meg. 4908 SE Taylor St., Portland, OR 97215. P1/ 503-233-9308. marlenemeg@yahoo.com. Established: 2003.

SKILLS: freelance editor, independent book editor, book doctor, copyeditor or line editor, proofreader, literary consultant, fact checker. **MARKETS SERVED:** academic journals, small presses, writers, arts publications.

SPECIALTIES AND PREFERENCES: humanities- and arts-related academic and nonfiction articles and books, novels, and short stories. I work one-on-one with author, developing concepts, theses, story lines, and text. I provide extensive feedback on overall text, detailed copy and line editing, and fact checking.

FICTION—ACCEPTS: short stories, novels (genre, mainstream, literary, contemporary, historical), picture books, scripts/screenplays, queries, synopses, treatments. **NONFICTION—ACCEPTS:** articles/features, essays, memoirs, creative or narrative, biography/autobiography, family history, self-help, how-to/instruction, text or reference, business, humor, inspirational/religious, spiritual, book proposals, queries.

FEES/TERMS/CONTRACTS: $20–$25/hour. Payment schedule negotiable. No credit cards.

EDUCATION: BA Literature/Costume Design, Bennington College, VT. **MEMBERSHIPS:** Northwest Independent Editors Guild.

CLIENTS WITHIN PRIOR YEAR: 5–10.

| 485 | EDITOR | WRITER | CONSULTANT | F | NF |

Strauss, Ron. Editcetera. Middletown, CA. P1/ 707-928-4170. P2/ 530-245-9016. healself@jps.net. Established: 1980.

SKILLS: indexer. **MARKETS SERVED:** publishers, authors, book packagers.

SPECIALTIES AND PREFERENCES: fully cross-referenced, highly sophisticated, back-of-the-book indexes for all subjects, including highly technical scientific and medical texts. Indexes for information technology books are one of my specialties. I do not work on legal texts and materials. Technically accurate, and sufficiently detailed and cross-referenced indexes that provide the reader with easy access to the content of the book.

FICTION—ACCEPTS: all. **NONFICTION—ACCEPTS:** all.

FEES/TERMS/CONTRACTS: $3–$6/page depending on the complexity of the material. No PayPal or credit cards. Editcetera will provide contract.

ACCOMPLISHMENTS: hundreds of titles indexed for major publishers—many in the information technology and scientific fields. Resume available.

EDUCATION: BA English, University of Miami, FL. Specialized training in indexing at UC Berkeley, CA, as well as specialized training in Sky Indexing Software.

CLIENTS WITHIN PRIOR YEAR: 25–30.

486	EDITOR	WRITER	CONSULTANT	F	NF

Stuckey, Maggie. 6744 NE Hancock St., Portland, OR 97213. P1/ 503-253-1999. maggiest@juno.com. Established: 1985.

Skills: freelance editor, independent book editor, book doctor, ghostwriter, freelance writer, nonfiction collaborator. **Markets served:** literary agents, acquiring editors at trade publishing houses. Business leaders who are, or aspire to be, authors.

Specialties and preferences: demonstrated success as a collaborator on best-selling business books for the general reader; emphasis on general management, marketing, human resources, finance, investing, sales management. Personal interests, publishing experience—environmental issues, outdoor recreation, gardening, food reference.

Nonfiction—accepts: creative or narrative, technical, text or reference, business, book proposals.

Fees/terms/contracts: consultation $100/hour. Collaboration contracts between author and myself specify a percentage split of advance and future earnings, with a guaranteed minimum.

Accomplishments: publications, awards, client successes. Author (under own name) of eleven books of general nonfiction, from major publishing houses. Collaborator for book on *New York Times* bestseller list for twenty-seven weeks.

Education: BA, double major History and English, *magna cum laude*. Meredith College, Raleigh NC.

Clients within prior year: 1–5.

487	EDITOR	WRITER	CONSULTANT	F	NF

Sullivan, Barbara. Writer-to-Writer. Eugene, OR. P1/ 541-687-1422. barbara@pacinfo.com. Established: 1995.

Skills: freelance editor, independent book editor, book doctor, literary consultant, writing coach, writing instructor. **Markets served:** writers.

Specialties and preferences: My editing is like midwifery, with prenatal care; favorite "babies" give voice to the silenced and have strong hearts and bones. I'm literary, but hanker for happy endings, or at least meaningful ones. I take on very few full editing projects; every book I've edited has been published when submitted.

Fiction—accepts: short stories, novels (mainstream, literary, contemporary, historical). **Nonfiction—accepts:** memoirs, creative or narrative, biography/autobiography, family history, self-help, how-to/instruction, humor, spiritual. **Typical evaluation/report:** diagnostic 15–30+ pages. Full edit 50+ pages and multiple drafts, sometimes with more pencil in the margins than ink on the page.

Fees/terms/contracts: book diagnostic $1,500, or $50/hour. Full edit about $3,000–$5,000.

Accomplishments: Heekin Award for best novel-in-progress. Grants/awards from UCC, Centrum, Lannan Foundation, Breadloaf, University of Oregon. Published and anthologized short stories, essays, and poems.

Education: MFA Fiction, University of Oregon, Eugene. BA Fine Art, Antioch College, Yellow Springs, OH. **Memberships:** Willamette Writers. Oregon Writers Colony.

Clients within prior year: 1–5.

488	EDITOR	WRITER	CONSULTANT	F	NF

Sunshine, Catherine. Washington, DC. csunshine@igc.org. Established: 1988.

Skills: freelance editor, independent book editor, book doctor, copyeditor or line editor, technical writer, translator—French/Spanish to English. **Markets served:** nonprofits, academic publishers, authors.

Specialties and preferences: international development, public health, education, immigration, ethnic diversity, labor issues, civil rights, human rights. Chicano, Puerto Rican, African, Caribbean, and Latin American studies.

Nonfiction—accepts: articles/features, essays, memoirs, creative or narrative, biography/autobiography, family history, text or reference.

Fees/terms/contracts: Each project is negotiated individually. The fee depends on the services requested, the material, the deadline, and other factors.

Accomplishments: high rate of repeat business. Most clients send several projects per year. Most new clients come as referrals from existing clients.

Education: BA Government, Oberlin College, OH. **Memberships:** Editorial Freelancers Association. National Capital Area Chapter of the American Translators Association.

Clients within prior year: 11–20.

489	EDITOR	WRITER	CONSULTANT	F	NF

Sunshower, Suzanne. Sun Editing. Box 261, Scotland, SD 57059. P1/ 605-583-2896. sun_editing@yahoo.com. editor@sunshowerdesigns.net. Established: 1983.

Skills: freelance editor, copyeditor or line editor, proofreader, ghostwriter, literary consultant, writing coach, publicist. **Markets served:** nonprofit organizations, writers, rock bands.

Specialties and preferences: copyediting for beginning or unpublished writers; public relations for-profits, and bands.

FICTION—ACCEPTS: short stories, novels (mainstream, literary, contemporary), poetry, queries, synopses. NONFICTION—ACCEPTS: articles/features, essays, memoirs, creative or narrative, biography/autobiography, family history, self-help, how-to/instruction, technical, text or reference, business, humor, inspirational/religious, spiritual, book proposals, queries. TYPICAL EVALUATION/ REPORT: 1–10 pages.

FEES/TERMS/CONTRACTS: $45/hour. One-half-hour minimum retainer. PayPal. Uses contract.

ACCOMPLISHMENTS: dozens of published press articles, feminist essays, and poems.

EDUCATION: BA Psychology, BA Political Science, Wayne State University, Detroit, MI. MEMBERSHIPS: International Women's Writing Guild. National Writers Union. Academy of American Poets. American Psychological Association.

CLIENTS WITHIN PRIOR YEAR: 1–5.

490	EDITOR	WRITER	CONSULTANT	F	NF

Sussman, Soll. 6117 Mountain Villa Cove, Austin, TX 78731. P1/ 512-917-9463. write_soll@hotmail.com. Established: 2001.

SKILLS: freelance editor, copyeditor or line editor, ghostwriter, business writer or copywriter, media training. MARKETS SERVED: publishers, nonprofits, small businesses.

SPECIALTIES AND PREFERENCES: news releases, writing for annual reports and other special projects, culture writing, business publications, feature writing, NONFICTION—ACCEPTS: all.

FEES/TERMS/CONTRACTS: generally $50/hour for news releases and special projects. Negotiable on an individual basis for feature writing.

ACCOMPLISHMENTS: fifteen years of experience in journalism, including positions as correspondent, news editor, and bureau chief for The Associated Press. Now working freelance from base in Austin, published by a variety of Texas and other publications, including Internet sites. Experience in media training.

EDUCATION: MA Latin American Studies, specializing in history and journalism, Institute of Latin American Studies, University of Texas at Austin. BA Romance Languages, Johns Hopkins University, Baltimore, MD. MEMBERSHIPS: Writers League of Texas.

CLIENTS WITHIN PRIOR YEAR: 6–10.

491	EDITOR	WRITER	CONSULTANT	F	NF

Swain, Liz. PO Box 19185, San Diego, CA 92159. P1/ 619-465-6029. F1/ 619-461- 5110. lizsfiles@aol.com. Established: 1990.

SKILLS: copyeditor or line editor, proofreader, business writer or copywriter, freelance writer, writing coach, writing instructor. MARKETS SERVED: magazines, websites. Research, write entries for science and social science encyclopedias. Travel writer, media relations, adult education writing instructor.

SPECIALTIES AND PREFERENCES: business and education features, research. Markets, writes articles for publications, websites. Writes business, feature, travel articles. Researches, writes encyclopedia entries. Develops publicity for organizations. Writes and distributes news releases, serves as media liaison. Produces brochures, fliers. Copyedits articles, manuscripts.

FICTION—ACCEPTS: all. NONFICTION—ACCEPTS: all.

FEES/TERMS/CONTRACTS: depends on assignment.

ACCOMPLISHMENTS: writing awards—North San Diego Press Club, First Place, column writing and spot news for fire coverage. Blade-Citizen: First Place award for spot news coverage of arrest of policeman charged with series of rapes. San Diego Press Club: Third Place, column writing. Catholic Press Association: National Third Place for feature about people over fifty. Judge San Diego Book Awards, 1999–present.

EDUCATION: BA Journalism, San Diego State University, California. Adult teaching credential. MEMBERSHIPS: National Writers Union. Sisters in Crime.

CLIENTS WITHIN PRIOR YEAR: 1–5.

492	EDITOR	WRITER	CONSULTANT	F	NF

Swanson, Winfield. Winfield Swanson Editorial Services. 2853 Ontario Rd. NW, #402, Washington, DC 20009. P1/ 202-265-2762. winfields@earthlink.net. Established: 1979.

SKILLS: freelance editor, independent book editor, book doctor, copyeditor or line editor, proofreader, ghostwriter, business writer or copywriter, technical writer, compile indexes. MARKETS SERVED: federal agencies, university presses, associations, museums.

SPECIALTIES AND PREFERENCES: writing and research, editing and indexing for science, medicine, technical.

NONFICTION—ACCEPTS: articles/features, essays, memoirs, creative or narrative, biography/autobiography, family history, self-help, how-to/instruction, technical, text or reference, business, humor, book proposals, queries.

FEES/TERMS/CONTRACTS: $40–$60/hour depending on assignment. Indexing $3.50+/page, depending on depth.

ACCOMPLISHMENTS: former managing editor for National Geographic Society, *Research & Exploration* magazine. Credits of dozens of published articles and reviews on subjects such as indexing, science, health, economics, and other topics. Researcher for several books.

EDUCATION: BA Biology, Adelphi University, MD. Graduate study, anthropology and microbiology. MEMBERSHIPS: Washington Book Publishers. American Medical Writers Association. DC Science Writers.

CLIENTS WITHIN PRIOR YEAR: 6–10.

493	EDITOR	WRITER	CONSULTANT	F	NF

Talbot, Alice "Amy." New York, NY. P1/ 212-534-5214. F1/ 212-534-5214. txynk1219@aol.com. Established: 2003.

SKILLS: freelance editor, copyeditor or line editor, proofreader, business writer or copywriter. MARKETS SERVED: educational, children's, women's magazines, legal.

SPECIALTIES AND PREFERENCES: My specialty is educational and children's markets. I also write for women's magazines. I proofread any kind of document. I also write test questions/passages, and edit legal documents.

NONFICTION—ACCEPTS: articles/features.

FEES/TERMS/CONTRACTS: variable. No credit cards. Uses a contract.

ACCOMPLISHMENTS: After I quit my full-time teaching job, I tried to get a full-time job in publishing and was not successful. I turned toward becoming a freelancer, whereas before writing was just a hobby. I've had one article published in the January issue of *Instructor* magazine. I won a pie from *Country* magazine for an article I wrote—does that count? EDUCATION: MS Reading. BA English. MEMBERSHIPS: Society of Children's Book Writers and Illustrators.

CLIENTS WITHIN PRIOR YEAR: 1–5.

494	EDITOR	WRITER	CONSULTANT	F	NF

Tempesta, Michele. 102 W. 75th St., New York, NY 10023. P1/ 212-873-5992. mstempesta@aol.com. Established: 1980.

SKILLS: freelance editor, independent book editor, book doctor, line editor, proofreader, literary consultant. MARKETS SERVED: writers, agents, publishers.

SPECIALTIES AND PREFERENCES: I'll only work with a writer if I think I can make a difference; I obviously can't guarantee publication, but I do extensive line editing and work very hard to improve the manuscript without interfering with the author's voice.

FICTION—ACCEPTS: y/a or juvenile, short stories, novels (genre, mainstream, literary, contemporary, historical), scripts/screenplays. NONFICTION—ACCEPTS: all. TYPICAL EVALUATION/REPORT: extensive line editing and a detailed evaluation, 5–30 pages.

FEES/TERMS/CONTRACTS: $10–$12/page, certainly negotiable; no credit cards, checks only; usually half the money up front; contracts only on large projects with major subrights commitments, which have been initiated by publishing houses.

ACCOMPLISHMENTS: many, many client successes—some on best-seller lists.

Twenty-two years as a senior editor and publisher of the mystery imprint at Doubleday, as well as other fiction and nonfiction.

EDUCATION: BA English Literature, Wells College, Aurora, NY.

CLIENTS WITHIN PRIOR YEAR: variable, depending on workload: usually 15–20.

495	EDITOR	WRITER	CONSULTANT	F	NF

Terzian, Mary. Hacienda Heights, CA. P1/ 626-333-1610. Nayri@aol.com. www.maryterzian.com. Established: 1994.

SKILLS: business writer or copywriter, witty nonfiction articles. **MARKETS SERVED:** nonprofit organizations.

SPECIALTIES AND PREFERENCES: essays, travel, lifestyle, humor, reflections on life, interviews, profiles. Business press releases, financial and management reports.

NONFICTION—ACCEPTS: articles/features, essays, memoirs, creative or narrative, biography/autobiography, family history, self-help, how-to/instruction, business humor.

FEES/TERMS/CONTRACTS: by negotiation and written agreement.

ACCOMPLISHMENTS: 2001 PEN Scholarship. Numerous contest awards, newsletter editor awards, humorous speech and writing awards by reputable organizations and writing clubs.

EDUCATION: BA Business Administration/Management, California State University, Los Angeles. Studied nonfiction writing in various schools. **MEMBERSHIPS:** California Writers' Club, San Fernando Valley Branch. Writers' Club of Whittier, CA.

CLIENTS WITHIN PRIOR YEAR: 1–5.

496	EDITOR	WRITER	CONSULTANT	F	NF

Tevlin, Michael. Tevlin Strategic Communication. Lake Oswego, OR 97034. P1/ 503-697-4434. F1/ 503-697-4434. mtevlin@comcast.net. Established: 1996.

SKILLS: business writer or copywriter; editor. **MARKETS SERVED:** government agencies, nongovernmental agencies, and companies working in renewable energy, health care, environmental and land-use planning; advertising, marketing, public relations agencies and media that serve them.

SPECIALTIES AND PREFERENCES: I help progressive businesses and executives build reputations and relationships. More than twenty years as a writer helping clients develop effective communications to reach more customers, build those relationships, and create the reputations they deserve.

NONFICTION—ACCEPTS: articles/features, creative or narrative, business brochures, newsletters, news releases, ads, web copy.

FEES/TERMS/CONTRACTS: market-driven fee based on estimate. Net 30 days. 1.5

percent finance charge over 30 days unless otherwise noted. No credit cards. Sometimes uses contract.

ACCOMPLISHMENTS: articles published in *Alaska Airlines* magazine, *Hooked on the Outdoors* magazine, *Business Journal of Portland*, and others. Left public relations job in 1996 to form own writing and communications practice. Former National Park Service ranger.

EDUCATION: MA Journalism, University of Oregon, Eugene. BA General Studies, State University of New York, Oneonta. **MEMBERSHIPS:** Self-Employed Creative Professionals. Portland Advertising Federation.

CLIENTS WITHIN PRIOR YEAR: 21–30.

497	EDITOR	WRITER	CONSULTANT	F	NF

Thayer, Paul. Thayer Literary Services. 2619 Terry Lane, Sarasota, FL 34231. P1/ 941-926-7968. pteditor@earthlink.net. pteditor@comcast.net. www.pro-editor.com. Established: 1997.

SKILLS: freelance editor, independent book editor, book doctor, copyeditor or line editor, writing coach, writing instructor, rewrite fiction and nonfiction. **MARKETS SERVED:** published, unpublished authors.

SPECIALTIES AND PREFERENCES: genre, historical, and literary fiction. No children's books or poetry.

FICTION—ACCEPTS: y/a or juvenile, short stories, novels (genre, mainstream, literary, contemporary, historical), queries, synopses. **NONFICTION—ACCEPTS:** all. **TYPICAL EVALUATION/REPORT:** 40–50 pages.

FEES/TERMS/CONTRACTS: fees determined by word count. Reading or copyediting, fifteen pages/hour. Line editing 7–10 pages/hour.

ACCOMPLISHMENTS: published thousands of newspaper and magazine pieces, *Atlantic City* magazine. Awards from the Florida Magazine Association (feature article), the Florida Newspaper Association. Edited books for Harvey Diamond (*Fit for Life* author) and Dr. Carl Hammerschlag.

EDUCATION: BA English, Florida Atlantic University, Boca Raton. Graduate school, English Education, University of South Florida, Tampa.

CLIENTS WITHIN PRIOR YEAR: 11–20.

498	EDITOR	WRITER	CONSULTANT	F	NF

Theobald, Lisa. Eugene, OR. P1/ 541-345-8658. ltheo842@aol.com. Established: 2000, writing since 1987.

SKILLS: freelance editor, independent book editor, copyeditor or line editor, proofreader, ghostwriter, developmental editor, coauthor. **MARKETS SERVED:** independent contractor who offers editing, writing, and publishing assistance for individual authors, publishers, and corporations, particularly in the nonfiction market. I have more than twenty-five years of experience in publishing—most of it as an editor.

SPECIALTIES AND PREFERENCES: books/articles on natural and earth science, botany, ecology, arboriculture, soil, horticulture, gardening, some technical and computer.

NONFICTION—ACCEPTS: all.

FEES/TERMS/CONTRACTS: hourly or per page.

ACCOMPLISHMENTS: Master Gardener.

EDUCATION: BA Journalism/Environmental Studies, Iowa State University, Ames. **MEMBERSHIPS:** International Society of Arboriculture. Board of Trustees, Eugene Tree Foundation.

CLIENTS WITHIN PRIOR YEAR: 1–5.

499	EDITOR	WRITER	CONSULTANT	F	NF

Thole, Marsha L. PO Box 91057, Albuquerque, NM 87199-1057. P1/ 505-856-2080. F1/ 505-856-3352. mthole@earthlink.net. Established: 1980.

SKILLS: freelance editor, independent book editor, copyeditor or line editor, proofreader, business writer or copywriter, technical writer, writing coach, scrapbooker-for-hire. **MARKETS SERVED:** businesses, defense contractors, individuals, academia, legal community.

SPECIALTIES AND PREFERENCES: I critique and edit websites (have been a programmer). Contracting documentation, marketing plans, training courses, staffing packages, interviewing plans, policies and procedures, inspection checklists, military and defense publications, retirement briefings, legal documents. I work on career management and HR/personnel (guides, downsizing plans, interviewing, customer service, discipline).

NONFICTION—ACCEPTS: all.

FEES/TERMS/CONTRACTS: sample editing for fee. Hourly or by project. No credit cards or PayPal. Uses contract.

ACCOMPLISHMENTS: twenty-plus years of writing, editing, and producing a wide variety of written communications. Taught college courses in English, Business Writing, Technical Writing, Job Communication Skills. Designed and taught writing workshops.

EDUCATION: MS Education, MA Management (Liberal Studies, Communications), BS Education, BS Computer Information Systems, BS Paralegal Studies. **MEMBERSHIPS:** SouthWest Writers. Military Officers Association of America. Reserve Officers Association.

CLIENTS WITHIN PRIOR YEAR: 15–20.

500	EDITOR	WRITER	CONSULTANT	F	NF

Thomas, Milt. 686 Glenview Terrace, Vero Beach, FL 32962; P1/ 772-567-2897. F1/ 772-567-2897. miltthomas@aol.com. Established: 1993.

Skills: proofreader, ghostwriter, business writer or copywriter. **Markets served:** individuals, families, small and large businesses.

Specialties and preferences: works for hire—personal, family, and corporate histories; ghostwriting; biographies; on-site travel features; retail business management.

Fiction—accepts: short stories. **Nonfiction—accepts:** articles/features, essays, memoirs, creative or narrative, biography/autobiography, family history, self-help, how-to/instruction, text or reference, business.

Fees/terms/contracts: Charges are based on an estimate of hours involved, skill level of activities associated with the project. Terms of contract are flexible, but typically involve one-third down, one-third upon completion of rough draft, one-third upon delivery of finished project. Accepts PayPal. Uses a contract.

Accomplishments: Addy Award for brochure copy. Former editor/chief writer of *Treasure Coast Business Journal, Fifty Plus Lifestyles*. Many other publications as correspondent and feature writer. Writer of business book (Jain Publishing), biography (Arkham House). Three published short stories. Vice president for CBS division—music.

Education: BA Psychology, Florida State University, Tallahassee. **Memberships:** Florida Freelance Writer's Association. Space Coast Writer's Guild.

Clients within prior year: 6–10.

501	EDITOR	WRITER	CONSULTANT	F	NF

Thompson, Jennifer. JMT Editorial Services. 9526 Rockport Rd., Vienna, VA 22180. P1/ 703-242-8899. F1/ 703-242-8899. jmt_edit@yahoo.com. jmt.edit@starpower.net. Established: 1996.

Skills: freelance editor, copyeditor or line editor, proofreader, desktop publisher, word processor, brochure or newsletter designer, indexer. **Markets served:** trade associations, book publishers, newspapers, nonprofits, educational and medical groups, corporations.

Specialties and preferences: medicine and health, family, parenting, and women's issues, education, home, real estate, entertainment. Fiction and how-to books.

Fiction—accepts: y/a or juvenile, short stories, novels (mainstream, contemporary). **Nonfiction—accepts:** all.

Fees/terms/contracts: proofreading $25/hour. Copyediting, indexing, design/desktop publishing $30/hour. Provides estimate beforehand; bills for work after completion. No credit cards. Accepts PayPal. Uses agreement.

Accomplishments: wrote and sold a self-published nonfiction book. Published dozens of articles in daily newspapers, including a regular parenting column. Won a first-place national award for a weekly real estate section (*Washington Times*). Received accolades from the Gannett Co. for editing and layout work at The Journal Newspapers.

EDUCATION: MS News-Editorial Journalism, University of Illinois, Urbana-Champaign. BA English, University of Illinois, Urbana-Champaign. **MEMBERSHIPS:** Freelance Bunch Brunch. Publications Professionals. Online editorial networking and professional list-serves.

CLIENTS WITHIN PRIOR YEAR: 11–20.

502	EDITOR	WRITER	CONSULTANT	F	NF

Thompson, Lynn Maria. Thompson Writing & Editing. 228 Davis St., Neptune Beach, FL 32266. P1/ 904-242-0054. F1/ 904-242-0730 (call first). lynn@thompsonwriting.com. www.thompsonwriting.com. Established: 2003.

SKILLS: freelance editor, independent book editor, copyeditor or line editor, proofreader, ghostwriter, business writer or copywriter, technical writer. **MARKETS SERVED:** writers, publishers, private companies, government, nonprofits, individuals.

SPECIALTIES AND PREFERENCES: writes documents of all types. Specializes in books, magazines, newsletters. Three levels of editing to meet all needs.

FICTION—ACCEPTS: y/a or juvenile, short stories, novels. **NONFICTION—ACCEPTS:** y/a or juvenile, articles/features, essays, memoirs, creative or narrative, biography/autobiography, family history, self-help, how-to/instruction, technical, text or reference, business, humor, inspirational/religious. **TYPICAL EVALUATION/REPORT:** editing notes provided as notes or footnotes on document itself.

FEES/TERMS/CONTRACTS: full list of services and current prices on website.

ACCOMPLISHMENTS: coauthor of nonfiction book—see website. Editor of *The Florida Palm* magazine for Florida Writers' Association. Editor of *Gator Breeze* newsletter writer for *Home & Garden Improvement Guide*, *Jax HealthSource*, *North Florida Doctor*, *Jax Islander*.

EDUCATION: BS Business Administration, University of Florida, Gainesville. **MEMBERSHIPS:** Florida Writers' Association. Jacksonville Chamber of Commerce.

CLIENTS WITHIN PRIOR YEAR: 15–20.

503	EDITOR	WRITER	CONSULTANT	F	NF

Thorsen-Snipes, Nanette. P.O. Box 1596, Buford, GA 30515. P1/ 770-945-3093. C1/ 770-312-4461. F1/ 770-945-3093. nsnipes212@bellsouth.net. www.nanettesnipes.com. Established: 1981.

SKILLS: freelance editor, independent book editor, book doctor, copyeditor or line editor, proofreader, ghostwriter, business writer or copywriter, work-for-hire projects with publishers. **MARKETS SERVED:** writers, nonprofits, corporations.

SPECIALTIES AND PREFERENCES: specializes in Christian field.

FICTION—ACCEPTS: y/a or juvenile fiction, short stories. **NONFICTION—ACCEPTS:** y/a or juvenile, articles/features, creative and narrative, business, humor, inspirational/religious.

FEES/TERMS/CONTRACTS: editing/proofreading $35/hour, writing negotiable. No credit cards. Typically uses contracts.

ACCOMPLISHMENTS: over forty articles/reprints in national/regional print magazines. Stories in thirty compilation books including *Chicken Soup* and Christian books. Work-for-hire six publishers, columnist, freelance editor. Proofreader for writers.

EDUCATION: attended more than ten writing conferences from 1985 through 2001. **MEMBERSHIPS:** Christian Writers Fellowship International. Writers Information Network. The Writers View. Fellowship of Christian Writers. Christian Writers Group.

CLIENTS WITHIN PRIOR YEAR: 5–10.

504	EDITOR	WRITER	CONSULTANT	F	NF

Thryft, Ann. 15520 Big Basin Way, Boulder Creek, CA 95006. P1/ 831-338-8228. athryft@earthlink.net. Established: 1988.

SKILLS: freelance editor, independent book editor, copyeditor or line editor, proofreader, ghostwriter, business writer or copywriter, technical writer, writing coach, publicist. **MARKETS SERVED:** technical and small business; also technical, business, or academic individuals.

SPECIALTIES AND PREFERENCES: ghostwrites, edits (line and substantive), and proofreads business and technical contributed articles, website copy, white papers, brochures and newsletters, and academic books and articles.

NONFICTION—ACCEPTS: articles/features, essays, how-to/instruction, technical, text or reference, business, queries.

FEES/TERMS/CONTRACTS: uses project fees. Hourly equivalent $50–$85, depending on service, subject, turnaround, document type. Accepts PayPal.

ACCOMPLISHMENTS: hundreds of articles published in national/international trade publications. Excellence in Editorial Award for Best Technology Feature, 1985 and 1986, CMP Media.

EDUCATION: BA Cultural Anthropology, Stanford University, CA. **MEMBERSHIPS:** National Writers Union. Bay Area Editors' Forum. Society of Professional Journalists.

CLIENTS WITHIN PRIOR YEAR: 11–20.

505	EDITOR	WRITER	CONSULTANT	F	NF

Thunder, Michael. Thunder for Writers. 906 Chelsey Lane, Durango, CO 81301-3408. thunder@thunderforwriters.com. Established: 1997.

SKILLS: freelance editor, independent book editor, book doctor, copyeditor or line editor, proofreader, literary consultant, writing coach, writing instructor, publicist. MARKETS SERVED: script and novel writers. Some nonfiction.

SPECIALTIES AND PREFERENCES: coaching from concept to market, and script development.

FICTION—ACCEPTS: y/a or juvenile, picture books, short stories, novels (genre, mainstream, literary, contemporary, historical), poetry, scripts/screenplays, queries, synopses, treatments. NONFICTION—ACCEPTS: all. TYPICAL EVALUATION/ REPORT: project development, whatever that includes. Everything from plotting to hand holding.

FEES/TERMS/CONTRACTS: $75/hour and fees for script analysis.

ACCOMPLISHMENTS: several scripts in various stages of production. Published by Scribner and Bantam in US and Victor Gollancz in England.

EDUCATION: MFA University of Iowa Writer's Workshop, Iowa City.

CLIENTS WITHIN PRIOR YEAR: 12–15.

506	EDITOR	WRITER	CONSULTANT	F	NF

Tibbetts, Peggy. PO Box 129, Silt, CO 81652. P1/ 970-876-2196. peggyt@siltnet.net. www.peggytibbetts.net. Established: 1986.

SKILLS: freelance editor, ghostwriter, business writer or copywriter, writing instructor. MARKETS SERVED: writers.

SPECIALTIES AND PREFERENCES: children's books, including picture books. Services include analysis of content and line-by-line editing, plus marketing consultation. Clients may submit up to two revisions.

FICTION—ACCEPTS: y/a or juvenile, short stories, novels (genre, mainstream, literary, contemporary, historical), poetry, queries, synopses. NONFICTION— ACCEPTS: y/a or juvenile, articles/features, essays, memoirs, creative or narrative, business. TYPICAL EVALUATION/REPORT: 3–6 pages.

FEES/TERMS/CONTRACTS: $150/under 5,000 words. $300/5,000+ words. PayPal. No credit cards.

ACCOMPLISHMENTS: two published middle-grade novels. One self-published adult novel. One nonfiction e-book. Managing editor e-mail newsletter. Editor of Children's Writing Resource website. Associate editor children's magazine. Assistant editor academic journal. Production editor educational film company. Dozens of articles, stories, and columns published in print and online. MEMBERSHIPS: Society of Children's Book Writers & Illustrators.

CLIENTS WITHIN PRIOR YEAR: 1–5.

507	EDITOR	WRITER	CONSULTANT	F	NF

Uslander, Arlene. Writeway Editing. 1920 Chestnut Ave Apt. 105, Glenview, IL 60025. P1/ 847-729-7757. auslander@theramp.net. www.uslander.net. Established: 1983.

SKILLS: freelance editor, independent book editor, book doctor, copyeditor or line editor, proofreader. **MARKETS SERVED:** writers, publishers.

SPECIALTIES AND PREFERENCES: nonfiction. I am interested in any and all manuscripts that I feel have publishing potential.

FICTION—ACCEPTS: y/a or juvenile, short stories, novels (genre, mainstream, literary, contemporary, historical), picture books, queries, synopses, treatments. **NONFICTION—ACCEPTS:** all. **TYPICAL EVALUATION/REPORT:** 4–6 pages.

FEES/TERMS/CONTRACTS: $2–$5/page. No contract.

ACCOMPLISHMENTS: author of fourteen nonfiction books and over 400 articles. Recipient of six media awards for excellence in journalism. Honored twice by Illinois Library Association for Contributions to Literature. Featured in *Writer's Digest Handbook 2004*.

EDUCATION: BS Education, Northwestern University, Evanston, IL.

CLIENTS WITHIN PRIOR YEAR: 25–30.

508	EDITOR	WRITER	CONSULTANT	F	NF

Valenzi, Kathleen. Red Hill Communications. Charlottesville, VA. P1/ 434-977-0882. C1/ 434-760-4229. kathleen@redhill.net. Established: 1991.

SKILLS: freelance editor, independent book editor, book doctor, copyeditor or line editor, proofreader, ghostwriter, business writer or copywriter, technical writer, publicist. **MARKETS SERVED:** writers, publishers, nonprofits, higher education.

SPECIALTIES AND PREFERENCES: humanities, medicine, higher education, and technology. Publicity/press releases, sales/marketing copy, and newsletters.

NONFICTION—ACCEPTS: articles/features, essays, memoirs, creative or narrative, biography/autobiography, family history, self-help, how-to/instruction, technical, text or reference, business.

FEES/TERMS/CONTRACTS: $75/hour. One-fourth in advance. No credit cards. Typically uses contracts.

ACCOMPLISHMENTS: writer of numerous articles for higher education and regional magazines. Editor of numerous books and magazine articles.

EDUCATION: BA English, University of Virginia, Charlottesville.

CLIENTS WITHIN PRIOR YEAR: 1–5.

509	EDITOR	WRITER	CONSULTANT	F	NF

Vallar, Cindy. PO Box 425, Keller, TX 76244-0425. cindy@cindyvallar.com. bonniebookaneer@hotmail.com. www.cindyvallar.com/. Established: 2001.

SKILLS: freelance editor, copyeditor or line editor. MARKETS SERVED: writers, publishers.

SPECIALTIES AND PREFERENCES: identify logic errors, passive sentences, point-of-view shifts. Free edit of first chapter. Does not accept horror, science fiction, erotica.

FICTION—ACCEPTS: y/a or juvenile, short stories, novels (genre, mainstream, contemporary, historical), queries, synopses. NONFICTION—ACCEPTS: y/a or juvenile, creative or narrative, biography/autobiography, book proposals, queries. TYPICAL EVALUATION/REPORT: 2–10 pages.

FEES/TERMS/CONTRACTS: $6/1,000 words. Check or money order in advance.

ACCOMPLISHMENTS: one published novel. Monthly column. One published short story. Eight nonfiction articles. Dozens of book reviews in national and international journals.

EDUCATION: MLS Library Science, University of Maryland, College Park. BA Education, Towson University, MD. MEMBERSHIPS: Historical Novel Society. Texas Coalition of Authors. Electronically Published Internet Connection. Laffite Society.

CLIENTS WITHIN PRIOR YEAR: 6–10.

510	EDITOR	WRITER	CONSULTANT	F	NF

Valls, Maria. Portland, OR. P1/ 503-227-4104. C1/ 503-703-9280. mvalls@comcast.net. Established: 2002.

SKILLS: freelance editor, copyeditor or line editor, proofreader. MARKETS SERVED: writers, publishers, corporations, nonprofit organizations.

SPECIALTIES AND PREFERENCES: novels (murder mystery) are my fiction specialty. Nonfiction specialties include websites, travel, adventure/mountaineering, biography, business, history, and true crime.

FICTION—ACCEPTS: novels (genre, mainstream, contemporary, historical), scripts/screenplays, queries, synopses. NONFICTION—ACCEPTS: all. TYPICAL EVALUATION/REPORT: 2–10 pages.

FEES/TERMS/CONTRACTS: $3–$5/page depending on type of work. 50 percent deposit at start, final payment at report delivery. Cash, check, or PayPal accepted.

ACCOMPLISHMENTS: performed final edit of fiction manuscript for first-time published author, May 2003; book published January 2004. Edited early drafts of yet-to-be published murder mystery author 2001-2002.

EDUCATION: Master's Certificate, Project Management, George Washington University, DC. BA English Literature and Art History, Purdue University, West Lafayette, IN.

CLIENTS WITHIN PRIOR YEAR: 1–5.

511	EDITOR	WRITER	CONSULTANT	F	NF

VanScoy, Holly. Syzzyggy, Inc. 500 S. lst St., Pflugerville, TX 78660. P1/ 512-252-0985. F1/ 512-857-0330. academres@aol.com. Established: 1994.

SKILLS: business editor or copyeditor, ghostwriter, business writer or copywriter, technical writer, writing coach. MARKETS SERVED: individuals and businesses, for-profit and nonprofit organizations.

SPECIALTIES AND PREFERENCES: all writing and editorial support on all types of nonfiction, including synopses or treatments, grant proposals, and speeches, with a specialty in legal public relations and medical/scientific topics.

NONFICTION—ACCEPTS: y/a or juvenile, articles/features, essays, memoirs, creative or narrative, biography/autobiography, family history, self-help, how-to/instruction, technical, text or reference, business, book proposals, queries. TYPICAL EVALUATION/REPORT: varies.

FEES/TERMS/CONTRACTS: proposal development services $75–$85/hour; public relations and other business writing $85/hour, with a two-hour minimum; speechwriting $1/word. Other writing $75–$100/hour. Can do rush assignments. Willing to accept credit cards. Uses a contract.

ACCOMPLISHMENTS: fifteen years of journalism, magazine writing; college professor; high school English teacher; curriculum development specialist.

EDUCATION: PhD Social Research, University of Texas, Austin. Master's of Social Work (MSW), University of Louisville, KY. BA English, Baylor University, Waco, TX.

CLIENTS WITHIN PRIOR YEAR: 11–20.

512	EDITOR	WRITER	CONSULTANT	F	NF

Voldseth, Steve. PO Box 1363, Campbell, CA 95009-1363. P1/ 408-370-2554. F1/ 408-378-4321. Steve@ScriptSpecialist.com. www.ScriptSpecialist.com. Established: 1990.

SKILLS: ghostwriter, writing coach, comedy writer, screenwriting coach, screenwriter (original works and adaptations). MARKETS SERVED: comedians, corporate speakers, MCs, cartoonists, animation production companies, screenwriters.

SPECIALTIES AND PREFERENCES: original material, collaboration, and punch-up. I serve TV producers—monologue jokes, bits, sketch comedy—and Internet animation producers (scripts). I provide corporate speeches and presentations.

FICTION—ACCEPTS: scripts/screenplays, synopses, treatments. NONFICTION—ACCEPTS: articles/features, humor.

FEES/TERMS/CONTRACTS: $75–$105/hour. Day rate and longer project rates negotiable. New clients, 50 percent up front, 50 percent on delivery. Cash or check only. No credit cards. Uses contract upon client request.

ACCOMPLISHMENTS: clients have included Dennis the Menace (King Features Syndicate); Jay Leno (*The Tonight Show with Jay Leno*); *Exposed* (film 2003), Mistico Productions; *Saturday Night Live*; *The Late, Late Show with Craig Kilborn*.

EDUCATION: BA Psychology; Graduate, UCLA Professional Screenwriting Program. Professional Screenwriting Program. **MEMBERSHIPS:** National Cartoonists Society.

CLIENTS WITHIN PRIOR YEAR: 6–10.

513	EDITOR	WRITER	CONSULTANT	F	NF

Walkowicz, Chris. Walkoway. 1396 265th St., Sherrard, IL 61281. P1/ 309-754-8723. walkoway.dogbooks@mchsi.com. Established: 1980.

SKILLS: freelance editor, copyeditor or line editor, proofreader, literary consultant, writing instructor. **MARKETS SERVED:** publishers.

SPECIALTIES AND PREFERENCES: pets.

FICTION—ACCEPTS: y/a or juvenile, short stories, novels (genre, mainstream, literary, contemporary, historical), queries, synopses. **NONFICTION—ACCEPTS:** y/a or juvenile, articles/features, essays, memoirs, creative or narrative, biography/autobiography, family history, self-help, how-to/instruction, humor, inspirational/religious, spiritual, book proposals, queries. **TYPICAL EVALUATION/REPORT:** 2–4.

FEES/TERMS/CONTRACTS: $50/hour. Contract.

ACCOMPLISHMENTS: eight books, 900+ articles/columns, Book of the Year. **MEMBERSHIPS:** President, Dog Writers Association of America. AKC dog-show judge.

CLIENTS WITHIN PRIOR YEAR: 1–5.

514	EDITOR	WRITER	CONSULTANT	F	NF

Wathen, Cindy. 1542 E. Alluvial, #239, Fresno, CA 93720. P1/ 559-298-1507. C1/ 559-647-1397. F1/ 559-298-1507. cindy@cindywathen.com. www.cindywathen.com. Established: 1997.

SKILLS: freelance editor, copyeditor or line editor, proofreader, ghostwriter, business writer or copywriter, technical writer, literary consultant, writing conference speaker, art researcher, photographer. **MARKETS SERVED:** writers, publishers, agents, nonprofit organizations, corporations.

SPECIALTIES AND PREFERENCES: freelance writer/editor of fiction and nonfiction. Employers—McGraw-Hill, The University of California Press, and Quill Driver Books.

FICTION—ACCEPTS: short stories, novels (genre, mainstream, literary, contemporary, historical), poetry, queries, synopses, treatments. NONFICTION—ACCEPTS: articles/features, essays, memoirs, creative or narrative, biography/autobiography, self-help, how-to/instruction, technical, text or reference, business, humor, inspirational/religious, spiritual, book proposals, queries. TYPICAL EVALUATION/REPORT: 1–10 pages.

FEES/TERMS/CONTRACTS: variable fees. No credit cards. Uses contract.

ACCOMPLISHMENTS: author of first book endorsed by the Cesar E. Chavez Foundation and winner of the Valley Independent Publishers' first gold medal in the history category.

EDUCATION: JD San Joaquin College of Law, Clovis, CA. BS Psychology, BA Business, California State University, Fresno. Many editing, writing, and design courses. MEMBERSHIPS: National Writers Union. Bay Area Editors Forum. California Writers Club.

CLIENTS WITHIN PRIOR YEAR: 20–25.

515	EDITOR	WRITER	CONSULTANT	F	NF

Wayman, Anne. 4026 Iowa St., San Diego, CA 92104. P1/ 619-280-2192. anne@annewayman.com. www.annewayman.com.
Established: 30+ years ago.

SKILLS: freelance editor, independent book editor, book doctor, ghost writer, business writer or copywriter, technical writer, writing coach, writing instructor, web content, back of jacket copy, marketing materials. MARKETS SERVED: individuals, speakers, radio talk-show hosts, writers, publishers.

SPECIALTIES AND PREFERENCES: If you want your voice duplicated by a ghostwriter, plus a real understanding of the publishing process, including marketing, give me a call. If you need help defining your project and setting workable milestones, you will benefit from my coaching services.

NONFICTION—ACCEPTS: all. TYPICAL EVALUATION/REPORT: simple to comprehensive.

FEES/TERMS/CONTRACTS: $100/hour or flat fee. Sometimes accepts percentage as partial payment. Packages available for coaching.

ACCOMPLISHMENTS: ghosted for two bestselling, self-help authors. Authored allegory that is in negotiation with a major publisher. Awards for articles. Knows the ins and outs of self-publishing and e-books. I am an accomplished nonfiction writer, self-help ghost, and coach.

EDUCATION: privately educated. MEMBERSHIPS: National Writers Union.

CLIENTS WITHIN PRIOR YEAR: 5–10.

| 516 | EDITOR | WRITER | CONSULTANT | F | NF |

Weeks, Janet (Jan). Weeks Literary Service. PO Box 2704, Grand Junction, CO 81502. P1/ 970-255-6679. renegade@acsol.net. www.weekslit.com. Established: 2000.

SKILLS: freelance editor, manuscript editor, copyeditor or line editor, proofreader, writing instructor, writer of fiction, nonfiction, screenplays. Seminar and workshop presenter. **MARKETS SERVED:** novice or experienced writers, schools, businesses.

SPECIALTIES AND PREFERENCES: I work with beginning and experienced writers who have a story to tell or a point to make. I'll work in any media, but prefer not to edit/critique business and technical writing.

FICTION—ACCEPTS: all. **NONFICTION—ACCEPTS:** y/a or juvenile, articles/features, essays, memoirs, creative or narrative, biography/autobiography, family history, self-help, how-to/instruction, humor, inspirational/religious, spiritual. **TYPICAL EVALUATION/REPORT:** 4–20 pages, depending on length, complexity, and subject.

FEES/TERMS/CONTRACTS: See website or contact.

ACCOMPLISHMENTS: quarter-finalist in Chesterfield Screenwriting competition, honorable mention (script) *Writer's Digest* annual contest, two published novels. Complete publication history available at www.weekslit.com.

EDUCATION: BA English and Speech, University of Northern Colorado, Greeley. **MEMBERSHIPS:** National Writers' Association. Western Colorado Writers' Workshop.

CLIENTS WITHIN PRIOR YEAR: 1–5.

| 517 | EDITOR | WRITER | CONSULTANT | F | NF |

Weishaar, Marilyn. The Weis Revise. 1511 S. 6th St., Aberdeen, SD 57401. P1/ 605-725-1021. weisrevise@nvc.net. www.theweisrevise.com. Established: 2001.

SKILLS: freelance editor, independent book editor, book doctor, copyeditor or line editor, proofreader, ghostwriter, rewriting. **MARKETS SERVED:** writers.

SPECIALTIES AND PREFERENCES: My skills are based on a long career in the daily newspaper business. While I edit all work, with the exception of the very technical and dissertations or theses, I prefer fiction. I have an ongoing dialogue with my clients throughout the editing process.

FICTION—ACCEPTS: y/a or juvenile, short stories, novels (genre, mainstream, literary, contemporary, historical), queries, synopses. **NONFICTION—ACCEPTS:** y/a or juvenile, articles/features, essays, memoirs, creative or narrative, biography/ autobiography, family history, self-help, how-to/instruction, business, humor, inspirational/religious, spiritual, book proposals, queries. **TYPICAL EVALUATION/REPORT:** differs with projects/requests. No more than 2 pages.

FEES/TERMS/CONTRACTS: editing $20/page. Rewriting $25/page. Ghostwriting $30/page. Proofing $20/page.

ACCOMPLISHMENTS: thousands of articles published in/edited for daily newspaper.

EDUCATION: BS Journalism, South Dakota State University, Brookings. MEMBERSHIPS: South Dakota Press Women. National Press Women.

CLIENTS WITHIN PRIOR YEAR: 6–12.

518	EDITOR	WRITER	CONSULTANT	F	NF

Wetherold, Rosemary. 4507 Cliffstone Cove, Austin, TX 78735. P1/ 512-892-1606. rosemaryw@rosemaryw.net. www.rosemaryw.net. Established: 1985.

SKILLS: freelance editor, independent book editor, book doctor, copyeditor or line editor, proofreader, caption and jacket copywriter; indexing. MARKETS SERVED: academic and mainstream publishers; corporations and other businesses; nonprofits; individual writers.

SPECIALTIES AND PREFERENCES: wide-ranging experience, from academic textbooks and scholarly books to corporate advertising materials and nonprofit newsletters. Prefers corporate projects and average-length books from clients with publishing experience.

FICTION—ACCEPTS: all. NONFICTION—ACCEPTS: all.

FEES/TERMS/CONTRACTS: base fees are $4.50/standard manuscript page; $40/hour, or per-project estimates; the fee type and amount depends on the nature and complexity of the project. Prefers written contract. PayPal and checks accepted; no credit cards.

ACCOMPLISHMENTS: I have worked in publishing industry since 1978, with favorable testimonials from book publishers and authors, as well as from other clients; often mentioned by book authors in their acknowledgments. Clients have included university presses, textbook publishers, Smithsonian Institution Press, *Texas Monthly*.

EDUCATION: BA Biology with highest honors, University of Texas, Austin. Graphic design courses, Austin Community College. Undergraduate studies in art and Spanish, Southwest Texas State University, San Marcos. Massage school training, Austin.

CLIENTS WITHIN PRIOR YEAR: 6–10.

519	EDITOR	WRITER	CONSULTANT	F	NF

Williams, Helen. Walden Press, Inc. PO Box 1177, Walden, CO 80480. P1/ 970-723-8639. hmwden@hotmail.com. www.helenwilliams.net. Established: 2003.

SKILLS: freelance editor copyeditor or line editor, proofreader, ghostwriter, business writer or copywriter, literary consultant, writing coach, writing instructor. MARKETS SERVED: writers.

SPECIALTIES AND PREFERENCES: fiction and memoir editing and marketing.

FICTION—ACCEPTS: y/a or juvenile, short stories, novels (genre, mainstream, literary, contemporary, historical), queries, synopses. NONFICTION—ACCEPTS: y/a or juvenile, articles/features, essays, memoirs, creative or narrative, biography/ autobiography, family history, business, humor, spiritual, book proposals, queries. TYPICAL EVALUATION/REPORT: 2–10 pages.

FEES/TERMS/CONTRACTS: $30/hour. No credit cards.

ACCOMPLISHMENTS: one self-published biography/memoir. Numerous published articles/newspaper columns. 2004 Evvy Award winner, Colorado Independent Publishers Association. One year teaching English at Mexican orphanage.

EDUCATION: BA Broadcast Journalism, *magna cum laude*, Metropolitan State College, Denver, CO. MEMBERSHIPS: Colorado Independent Publishers Association.

CLIENTS WITHIN PRIOR YEAR: 1–5.

520	EDITOR	WRITER	CONSULTANT	F	NF

Williams, Michelle. 12632 SE Flavel St., Portland, OR 97236. P1/ 503-762-2524. graycat@spiritone.com. Established: 1997.

SKILLS: freelance editor, independent book editor, book doctor, copyeditor or line editor, proofreader ghostwriter, business writer or copywriter. MARKETS SERVED: book publishing.

SPECIALTIES AND PREFERENCES: writing, research, copyediting, proofreading, project management for books; especially interested in nonfiction— art/architecture, yoga, Eastern spirituality, travel, culture, gardening, hiking, history.

FICTION—ACCEPTS: scripts/screenplays. NONFICTION—ACCEPTS: adult, y/a or juvenile, articles/features, essays, memoirs, creative or narrative, biography/ autobiography, how-to/instruction, technical, text or reference, business.

FEES/TERMS/CONTRACTS: negotiable. No credit cards. Uses a contract.

ACCOMPLISHMENTS: eight years on the editorial staffs of various high-tech magazines at a publishing company in San Francisco. Staff editor at a high-tech public relations firm for two and a half years. Ran her own freelance writing and editing business for four years. Edited two book-length projects. Lifelong creative writing endeavors.

EDUCATION: BA Journalism, BA French, University of Missouri, Columbia.

CLIENTS WITHIN PRIOR YEAR: 6–10.

521	EDITOR	WRITER	CONSULTANT	F	NF

Williamson, Miryam Ehrlich. 162 Old Winchester Rd., Warwick, MA 01378. P1/ 978-544-7010. miryam@mwilliamson.com. www.mwilliamson.com. Established: 1983.

SKILLS: copyeditor or line editor, proofreader, ghostwriter, book collaborator. **MARKETS SERVED:** book publishers, individual physicians, and scientists.

SPECIALTIES AND PREFERENCES: medical/health writing for lay audience; medical/ health editing; medical/general copyediting. Book proposals a specialty.

NONFICTION—ACCEPTS: articles/features, essays, memoirs, creative or narrative, biography/autobiography, family history, self-help, how-to/instruction, reference, book proposals, queries.

FEES/TERMS/CONTRACTS: $50–$125/hour. No credit cards. Letter of agreement.

ACCOMPLISHMENTS: six published books. 200+ articles on advanced computer technologies. Various stories and poems in literary journals. Winner of American Medical Writers Association award for excellence in medical communication. Honors in English and Life Sciences.

EDUCATION: MA Education, University of Pennsylvania, Philadelphia. BA English/Life Sciences, University of Pennsylvania, Philadelphia. **MEMBERSHIPS:** Authors Guild. American Society of Journalists and Authors. Association of Health Care Journalists. National Writers Union.

CLIENTS WITHIN PRIOR YEAR: 1–5.

522	EDITOR	WRITER	CONSULTANT	F	NF

Witchey, Eric. Cyberscribe, Inc. PO Box 3640, Salem, OR 97302-0640. P1/ 503-581-0458. Established: 1991.

SKILLS: freelance editor, proofreader, writer, technical writer, writing coach and instructor. **MARKETS SERVED:** creative writers, conferences, editors, agents, high-tech, medical.

SPECIALTIES AND PREFERENCES: consulting, fiction, teaching, tutoring, custom courses.

FICTION—ACCEPTS: all. **NONFICTION—ACCEPTS:** how-to/instruction, technical, text or reference. **TYPICAL EVALUATION/REPORT:** 10–20 pages.

FEES/TERMS/CONTRACTS: 1099 contract work @ $50–$150/hour, depending on the nature of the project. Tutoring and custom courses on per project basis.

ACCOMPLISHMENTS: fifteen years freelance; university and conference teaching experience; attended Clarion West; recognition for fiction from New Century Writers, Writers of the Future, *Writer's Digest*, and other organizations; fiction sales in seven genres; writing article sales to *Writers Digest*, *Writers Northwest*, and *Northwest Ink*.

EDUCATION: MA CD (Literature, Theoretical Linguistics, Computer Science,

InstructingWriting);BAEnglish;ColoradoStateUniversity,Pueblo.Miscellaneous course work in philosophy, religion, biological sciences. **MEMBERSHIPS:** Sci-Fi and Fantasy Writers of America. Wordos Writer's Workshop. Clarion West. Pacific Northwest Writers Association. Society for Technical Communication. Oregon Writers' Colony (board member 1993–1997). Willamette Writers. **CLIENTS WITHIN PRIOR YEAR:** 20–25.

523	EDITOR	WRITER	CONSULTANT	F	NF

Wolf, Michele. 606B Main St., Gaithersburg, MD 20878-6424. P1/ 301-718-9408. C1/ 240-876-4638. F1/ 301-718-9408. MicheleWolf@juno.com. Established: 1987.

SKILLS: freelance editor, independent book editor, book doctor, copyeditor or line editor, proofreader, ghostwriter, business writer or copywriter, literary consultant, writing coach, writing instructor, publicist, poet, feature writer. **MARKETS SERVED:** book publishers, magazines, companies, nonprofits, associations, government agencies, and individual writers.

SPECIALTIES AND PREFERENCES: writing, content editing, copyediting, and literary/editorial consulting for book publishers, magazines, corporations, nonprofits, government agencies, and individual writers. I edit fiction, nonfiction, and poetry, write nonfiction and poetry, and teach poetry and editing workshops at The Writer's Center in Bethesda, Maryland.

FICTION—ACCEPTS: all. **NONFICTION—ACCEPTS:** all.

FEES/TERMS/CONTRACTS: editing $75/hour. Copyediting $50/hour. No credit cards. Uses agreement.

ACCOMPLISHMENTS: two poetry books. Editor for Scribner, Simon & Schuster, Kirkus Reviews. Scores of magazine features. National Magazine Award. Anhinga Prize, poetry.

EDUCATION: MS Columbia University, New York. BS Boston University, MA. **MEMBERSHIPS:** PEN. Associated Writing Programs. American Society of Journalists & Authors.

CLIENTS WITHIN PRIOR YEAR: 21–30.

524	EDITOR	WRITER	CONSULTANT	F	NF

Wright, Fred, Jr. Words, Images & Co. PO Box 86158, St. Petersburg, Petersburg, FL 33738-6158. P1/ 727-595-5004. P2/ 1-800-8-WRITER. TravelWord@aol.com. www.fredwright.net. Established: 1975.

SKILLS: freelance editor, independent book editor, book doctor, copyeditor or line editor, proofreader, ghostwriter, business writer or copywriter, technical writer, literary consultant, writing coach, writing instructor. **MARKETS SERVED:** United States, especially Florida and Southeast, but also North America and Europe.

SPECIALTIES AND PREFERENCES: I have credits with all aspects of the written word—nonfiction, fiction, poetry, film. Any genre. I also teach writing on the college level.

FICTION—ACCEPTS: all. NONFICTION—ACCEPTS: all. TYPICAL EVALUATION/REPORT: I respond with a detailed written analysis of any work critiqued. No less than two typewritten pages.

FEES/TERMS/CONTRACTS: fees based on number of words in work. Contact me for schedule.

ACCOMPLISHMENTS: publications, awards, client successes. More than 3,500 articles published plus dozens of poems, books, screenplays. Too many to list.

EDUCATION: MA English Literature, University of South Florida, Tampa. BA English Literature, Eckerd College, St. Petersburg, FL. MEMBERSHIPS: Society of American Travel Writers. Mensa.

CLIENTS WITHIN PRIOR YEAR: 30–40.

525	EDITOR	WRITER	CONSULTANT	F	NF

Yehling, Bob. Word Journeys, Inc. 77 Fifth Ave., Ste. 16C, New York, NY 10003. P1/ 917-826-7880. bob@wordjourneys.com. www.wordjourneys.com. Established: 1996.

SKILLS: copyeditor and content book editor, book doctor, proofreader, ghostwriter, writing coach, website editor. MARKETS SERVED: fiction and nonfiction.

SPECIALTIES AND PREFERENCES: all types of business, fiction, nonfiction, with ultimate care given to author's voice. Ghostwrites business, autobiographies, memoirs, how-to.

FICTION—ACCEPTS: adult, novels (genre, mainstream, literary, contemporary, historical), poetry, synopses, treatments. NONFICTION—ACCEPTS: adult, articles/features, business, essays, memoirs, biography/autobiography, self-help, how-to/self-help, spiritual, book proposals. TYPICAL EVALUATION/REPORT: 3–5 pages.

FEES/TERMS/CONTRACTS: $4/double-spaced page. 25 percent down, 25 percent upon completion of first half, and 50 percent net 10 days of delivery of full manuscript. Accepts credit cards online. No contract.

ACCOMPLISHMENTS: worked as magazine editor and writer for twenty years; began editing books in 1998. Edited business publications for ten years. Ghostwrote for champion golfer Payne Stewart, Apollo 12 astronaut Pete Conrad and musician Marty Balin. Teach writing/editing workshops nationally and online. Author of *Make Me An Eagle* and *The Voice* (publishing in 2005); three others in progress: *Finish!*, *Writes of Life*, and *Blockbusting*, with Lucasfilm Ltd. National award winner.

EDUCATION: BA English/minor Psychology, U.S. International University, San Diego.

CLIENTS WITHIN PRIOR YEAR: 20+.

526	EDITOR	WRITER	CONSULTANT	F	NF

Zack, Elizabeth. BookCrafters LLC. Box C, Convent Station, NJ 07961. P1/ 973-984-7880. ezack@bookcraftersllc.com. www.bookcraftersllc.com. Established: 2003.

SKILLS: freelance editor, independent book editor, book doctor, copyeditor or line editor, proofreader, ghostwriter, business writer or copywriter, literary consultant, writing coach, coauthor. **MARKETS SERVED:** writers, publishers.

SPECIALTIES AND PREFERENCES: I help writers and authors to craft salable book proposals or manuscripts. Nonfiction, specifically self-help, health, parenting, spirituality, reference, and biography, is my specialty. I provide line editing and developmental editing on manuscripts, ghostwriting, and/or assistance in creating commercially viable book proposals.

FICTION—ACCEPTS: short stories, novels (genre, mainstream, literary, contemporary, historical), queries, synopses. **NONFICTION—ACCEPTS:** articles/features, essays, memoirs, creative or narrative, biography/autobiography, family history, self-help, how-to/instruction, reference, humor, inspirational/religious, spiritual, book proposals, queries.

FEES/TERMS/CONTRACTS: hourly rates. Retainer. Final payment. No credit cards. Uses agreement.

ACCOMPLISHMENTS: one published nonfiction title. Two articles in reference books for writers.

EDUCATION: BA English and Psychology, Colgate University, Hamilton, NY.

CLIENTS WITHIN PRIOR YEAR: 21–30.

527	EDITOR	WRITER	CONSULTANT	F	NF

Zackheim, Victoria. San Francisco, CA. vdzack@aol.com. www.theboneweaver.com. Established: 1982.

SKILLS: freelance editor, independent book editor, book doctor, copyeditor or line editor, proofreader, writing coach, speechwriter, speech coach. **MARKETS SERVED:** fiction and nonfiction writers; high-tech and financial institutions.

SPECIALTIES AND PREFERENCES: fiction, nonfiction, children's.

FICTION—ACCEPTS: (literary), y/a or juvenile. **NONFICTION—ACCEPTS:** articles/features, creative or narrative, self-help, how-to/instruction, technical, business. **TYPICAL EVALUATION/REPORT:** 1–3 pages.

FEES/TERMS/CONTRACTS: literary editing $45–$60/hour. Marketing communications $80–$125/hour. Proofreading $35/hour. 50 percent up front, 50 percent upon completion. No credit cards.

ACCOMPLISHMENTS: one novel, one play, regular contributor to *San Francisco Chronicle* as a book reviewer; advertising copywriting awards.

EDUCATION: MA Speech Pathology/Audiology, California State University, San

Francisco. BA Speech/English, UCLA. First-level diploma, L'Alliance Française, Paris. **MEMBERSHIPS:** PEN West. National Association of Women Writers. **CLIENTS WITHIN PRIOR YEAR:** 6–10.

528	EDITOR	WRITER	CONSULTANT	F	NF

Zuckerman, Linda. The Friday Group. 15418 SW Ashley Dr., Tigard, OR 97224. P1/ 503-590-6947. lindaz@teleport.com. Established: 1999.

SKILLS: freelance editor, independent book editor, book doctor, copyeditor or line editor. **MARKETS SERVED:** writers, illustrators, publishers.

SPECIALTIES AND PREFERENCES: children's literature, all genres, including picture books, poetry, easy readers, chapter books, middle grade, y/a. Guidance provided for illustrators on picture book sketches, dummies, finished art. Sympathetic and knowledgeable support and feedback. Line edit and/or letter discussing problems and suggesting direction for revision.

FICTION—ACCEPTS: y/a or juvenile, short stories, novels (genre, mainstream, literary, contemporary, historical), picture books, poetry. **NONFICTION— ACCEPTS:** y/a or juvenile.

FEES/TERMS/CONTRACTS: $125/hour with a one-hour minimum. If I need more time, I'll contact you before going ahead. Turnaround 8–10 weeks. No credit cards. E-mail for queries only; no manuscripts, please.

ACCOMPLISHMENTS: editor of two Caldecott Award-winning books and two Newbery Honors. Many other notable and award-winning titles. Director of annual Pacific Northwest Children's Book Conference. Frequent conference speaker.

EDUCATION: BA English Literature, Brooklyn College, NY. **MEMBERSHIPS:** Society of Children's Book Writers and Illustrators.

CLIENTS WITHIN PRIOR YEAR: 41–50.

529	EDITOR	WRITER	CONSULTANT	F	NF

Zukowski, Gregg. Apollo Editorial. 750 Washington Ave., Ste. 2LR, Brooklyn, NY 11238. P1/ 917-658-9467. gregg.zukowski@apolloeditorial.com. Established: 1998.

SKILLS: freelance editor, copyeditor or line editor, proofreader, production editor, newsletter creator. **MARKETS SERVED:** financial and financial services; general services.

SPECIALTIES AND PREFERENCES: complete editorial and production solution provider for financial and financial services industries and for other industries on a case-by-case basis. Services include copyediting, proofreading, researching, and desktop production using Quark, Excel, Photoshop, Illustrator, trafficking, and copy creation. Specializes in newsletters, magazines, and corporate communication. Provides sample editing—no fee.

NONFICTION—ACCEPTS: business.

FEES/TERMS/CONTRACTS: Apollo Editorial issues project fee proposals on a case-by-case basis. Invoices with the expectation of payment within fifteen business days. No credit cards.

ACCOMPLISHMENTS: emerging markets research publications, including daily, weekly, monthly, quarterly, annual, and stand-alone reports.

EDUCATION: BA Politics, Occidental College, Los Angeles. Additional coursework, American Press Institute, The New School, and New York University.

MEMBERSHIPS: Editorial Freelancers Association.

CLIENTS WITHIN PRIOR YEAR: 1–5.

530	EDITOR	WRITER	CONSULTANT	F	NF

Zylius, Patricia. 114 Pennsylvania Ave., Santa Cruz, CA 95062-2428. P1/ 831-429-1184. paz@cruzio.com. Established: 2002.

SKILLS: freelance editor, independent book editor, copyeditor or line editor, proofreader. **MARKETS SERVED:** publishers, corporations.

SPECIALTIES AND PREFERENCES: specializes in software documentation, including print documentation and help systems. Experienced editing offshore writers. Interested in other material, including general interest books, articles, and essays, nature, the environment, spirituality, music, gardening.

NONFICTION—ACCEPTS: y/a or juvenile, articles/features, essays, memoirs, creative or narrative, self-help, how-to/instruction, technical, spiritual. **TYPICAL EVALUATION/REPORT:** 1–2 pages.

FEES/TERMS/CONTRACTS: $25–$30/hour general trade, $45–$50/hour software documentation. No credit cards. Typically uses contract provided by publisher/corporation.

ACCOMPLISHMENTS: four poems published in yearly reviews. General college honors.

EDUCATION: BA English Literature, University of California, Santa Cruz.

MEMBERSHIPS: Society for Technical Communication. Bay Area Editors' Forum.

CLIENTS WITHIN PRIOR YEAR: 1–5.

Company Index

NOTE: Numbers correspond to contributor identification numbers, not to page numbers.

Genre Index

NOTE: Numbers correspond to contributor identification numbers, not to page numbers.

Fiction—accepts:

Marketing (Fiction and Nonfiction):

Nonfiction—Accepts:

Specialties Index

NOTE: Numbers correspond to contributor identification numbers, not to page numbers.

Geographic Index

NOTE: Numbers correspond to contributor identification numbers, not to page numbers.

Foreign Countries

About the Author

ELIZABETH LYON is a veteran book editor and author of many acclaimed books for writers, including *A Writer's Guide to Fiction*, *A Writer's Guide to Nonfiction*, *The Sell Your Novel Tool Kit*, and *Nonfiction Book Proposals Anybody Can Write*. Her articles and essays have appeared in *The Writer's Handbook*, *The Complete Handbook of Novel Writing*, *The Writer* magazine, *Writer's Digest*, the Bedford/St. Martin's *Language Awareness*, and many print and online newsletters. Each year she travels throughout the United States and to British Columbia as a speaker and workshop teacher. Elizabeth lives in Eugene, Oregon, with her animal family, Riley, Harley, and Hunter. She may be reached through her e-mail, elyon123@comcast.net, or through her websites, www.4-edit.com, www.elizabethlyon.com.